I0004772

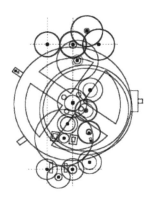

BUSINESS DATABASE TRIAGE

An introduction for both Business Managers and Information Technology Practitioners to classifying the symptoms and ills of business databases and how to take the first steps toward treating them.

- Why and how business databases came to be poorly designed and illogically constructed.

- How poor database design inflates system development and maintenance costs, limits the flexibility and extensibility of business software, and generally leads to System Constipation.

Although replete with detailed examples and strategies, this is not primarily a book about database design, nor is it intended to be particularly technical. Rather, this book is an introduction to the fundamental logical principles behind the organization of data, since an unfamiliarity with these principles is one of the primary causes of poor database design.

Frank Oberle

With contributions by Aristotle, Lewis Carroll, Ludwig van Beethoven, Bill Clinton, and other world-renowned data management experts.

Business Database Triage

Publication Information:

Antikythera Publications
e-Mail: antikythera@rcn.com

Copyright © 2013 by Frank Oberle
All Rights Reserved.

No part of this publication may be reproduced in any form or by any means, including electronic reproduction or reproduction via the Internet without the prior written consent of the author.

ISBN-10: 0615916937
ISBN-13: 978-0615916934
iii.

Business Database Triage

Aristotle
384 bce – 322 bce

Charles L. Dodgson
27 Jan 1832 – 14 Jan 1898

Bertrand Russell
18 May 1872 – 2 Feb 1970

– Famous but Neglected Data Management Experts of the Past –

TABLE OF CONTENTS

Business Database Triage

"Enough Already!"

Opposite Page – "Beethon"
1986 Concrete Sculpture of Beethoven
by Klaus Akmmericks
Located on the grounds of the Beethovenhalle in Bonn, Germany
Photographed by the Author

Preface

The musical quotation below is from:
Symphony No 9 in D minor, Opus 125
4ᵗʰ Movement: Introduction to Choral Portion
Text and Music by Ludwig van Beethoven (1770 – 1827)
First performed in May 1824.

Although Ludwig van Beethoven's Ninth Symphony is considered one of the most monumental works produced by any composer, it still reflected what he himself had done earlier, and more importantly, what had been accomplished by his musical predecessors. Beethoven has been called by some a musical revolutionary, but this is merely hyperbole – like any true genius, he built on his study, knowledge and understanding of the past: the works of J.S. Bach and Handel, for instance, were well known to him. Beethoven's Ninth Symphony then, although informed by his imaginative genius, would likely not have resulted without his assimilation, consolidation and expansion of earlier knowledge.

But while Beethoven had already opened up new possibilities and opportunities in the art of Music, he still felt constrained and unfulfilled. Thus, in his new work's fourth movement, after thrashing through several themes from earlier sections, Beethoven brought the orchestra to a complete halt – dead silence ! – then had a lone baritone break in quite forcibly to give vent to this frustration: *"O Freunde, nicht diese Töne! Sondern laßt uns angenehmere anstimmen, und freunden-vollere."*[1] Beethoven then followed this with his famous setting of Friedrich

---

1   Beethoven's introductory text to Schiller's ode is typically translated as *"Oh Friends, not these songs! Let us begin with more pleasant sounds, and be more joyful."* Colloquially, "Enough already!"

Schiller's "*Freude, schöner Götterfunken*" (in English known colloquially, if not quite accurately, as the "Ode to Joy") – a quite deceptively simple melody that eventually brought his final published symphony to a rousing and glorious close.

In spite of his reputation as often being unkempt, crude, intolerant, sarcastic, and curmudgeonly, Beethoven was known to have a terrific (if somewhat coarse) sense of humor and was incredibly erudite – a Renaissance man of sorts – known to be well-read and familiar with history's great authors – both the Ancients as well as his contemporaries. He took an active interest in the new technical discoveries of his age – writing music specifically for novel mechanical instruments[2], and even poking musical fun at the inventions of his good friend Johann Mälzel[3]. Were Beethoven around today, it is not inconceivable that he might have taken an interest (as many smart people with musical bents do) in the softer aspects of what is pretentiously referred to as Computer "Science."

If so, he likely would have been both amazed and appalled at what he found. We can only salivate at what he might have done with Finale, MuseScore, or a modern Synthesizer, but such speculation would be rather off topic for this book.

Had he been acquainted with Aristotle's writings[4], though, Beethoven would have probably been quite aghast that the current state of business data management seems to ignore so much of what had been known by the Ancients about intelligent and logical organization and categorization of information. My good friend Ludwig knew intuitively that one should not attempt to reinvent the wheel without knowing at least something about the past history of wheels.

Beethoven, sadly, isn't the young firebrand he used to be, and certainly hasn't shown much interest in calling out today's database designers on their failure to learn from their ancient predecessors. He is, after all, well over two hundred

---

2   This was the beginning of the industrial revolution, so there were quite a few of these.

3   The most famous of these jibes was a three-voice canon satirizing the dry tick-tock of the metronome Mälzel had invented; the theme of this canon later became the basis for the Allegretto (second movement) of Beethoven's eighth symphony.

4   He was known to be familiar with similar works, although Beethoven's biographers don't specifically mention finding any of Aristotle's writings among his effects.

forty years old[5], and still insists on using his old laptop with its pitiful seven bytes of memory. So, being possibly more curmudgeonly than Beethoven (and retired, so I don't much care whom I offend), and having resigned myself to the idea that Beethoven isn't going to step into this fray any time soon, I've taken it upon myself with this book to say "enough already!" to the status quo represented by the typical business database.

It's tempting to begin by singing "Oh Colleagues, not these Database Designs and Architectures! Let us begin more logically and permit our businesses and programmers to function more happily and efficiently," but my singing voice leaves much to be desired, and Ludwig has always been rather snippy about anything that might be regarded as plagiarism. Therefore, you'll have to be content with the following more traditional opening.

Intended Audience:

This book is intended for the following groups:

► **Business Database Developers**, particularly those who believe (mistakenly in many, if not most, cases) that they are using a relational database to store the facts that their businesses rely on. The information in this book will hopefully be technical enough to be actionable, and not merely a mildly amusing expression of my odd "religious" beliefs.

► **Business Application Developers**, particularly those who need to deal with Business Database Developers, or who have found it necessary or more expedient do such development themselves.

Business Application Developers comprise a particularly important target audience, since many seem to have been deceived into a misguided belief that the purpose of a database is to provide "persistence" for their applications' data – admittedly, this is occasionally the case but, in a business database, acting as if that is the objective is usually quite a counterproductive approach leading, more often than not, to many unpleasant consequences, and

---

5   Yes, I've heard the rumors that he is dead, but as far as I know, they are unsubstantiated.

resulting in more busy work over the long term. For this group, I also hope this book will be technical enough to be actionable, but not excessively so.

► **System Architects**, particularly those who often suspect there is something amiss with their corporate data architectures, but can't quite identify what. This book may help you see the forest in spite of all the distracting trees.

► **Canned Application Vendors**, whose embedded database designs should be expected to be flexible and adaptable enough to easily integrate with those of any typical business, but whose designs often seem instead to resist business needs – particularly even what should be relatively straightforward integration with existing data stores.

And finally, we have perhaps the most important group:

► **Business Managers**, particularly those who have become disillusioned by (and quite justifiably suspicious of) much of what they are told by their development groups.

▼ Business Managers are often skeptical when developers explain why the company's operational data needs to be "cleansed" before being consolidated for analysis, often at a significant cost. They become understandably apprehensive when forced to contemplate what "uncleanliness" may be lurking in the operational data used to run the day-to-day transactions of their business.

▼ Additionally, these Business Managers don't quite understand why their corporation's data is so redundant and fragmented in the first place. This incomprehension is exacerbated when they are told that they need to "invest" additional time, money, and effort into getting an overall picture of their business data.

▼ Many, although certainly not all, Business Managers, are able to walk through the warehouses where their parts, finished products, and so forth are stored, and quickly get at least a general sense of how competently their physical inventories are being managed. Unfortunately, the manager who can achieve a similar gut-level sense of how the company's data assets are managed is a rarity – there is a certain mystique associated with the supposedly highly technical world behind the closed doors of the computer centers that is apparently infectious. Hopefully, this book will instill a little confidence in their ability to apply common sense to such evaluations and ignore the techno-babble.

▼ Many Business Managers who would like to expand their sales into foreign countries are often frustrated by the seemingly endless list of impediments presented by their technology departments when confronted with this idea.

The progress made in the application of technology to the support of business has progressed sufficiently over the past sixty years that the situation described above, although somewhat understandable given the history of I/T, is no longer justifiable. The information in this book will hopefully strike an adequate balance between technical and non-technical discussions to be useful and actionable by business managers[6].

Triage

So what is Triage? And how does it apply to the Business Database?

The word Triage is most often encountered in hospital emergency rooms, at disaster scenes, or in combat operations, where it is defined by the United States Department of Defense as "... the evaluation and classification of casualties for purposes of treatment and evacuation. It consists of the immediate sorting of patients according to type and seriousness of injury, and likelihood of survival, and the establishment of priority for treatment and evacuation to assure medical care of the greatest benefit to the largest number."

In this case, the various database designs I use as examples in this book are the "casualties" in need of treatment, and one purpose of this book is to provide the background necessary to evaluate the analogous criteria for seriousness and likelihood of survival, and hopefully to select the most suitable candidates for treatment.

We obviously can't treat or cure all the ills that afflict our business databases at once, so there needs to be a selection as well as an evaluation process. Since the word triage is also used for similar non-medical evaluations such as grading coffee beans – certainly a staple of I/T departments everywhere – I see no problem using the word in the context of these discussions.

6　It is often said that "a little knowledge is a dangerous thing," but it can also be said that, now and then, a little knowledge whets the appetite for more. There will be further discussion of business management perspectives in Chapter 1.

Approach and Scope

In order to lay a logical foundation for discussing what is a significant but hidden issue in many enterprises, I'll begin by defining in the very first chapter what I mean by "business," discuss the history of our profession (how we came to have our current bad habits and biases), outline what business should expect from its technical providers, and provide a mostly general (although occasionally quite specific and detailed) approach to heading in a better direction.

Along the way, there will be very informal introductions to Set Theory and Predicate Logic (the foundation of the Relational Model, by the way), but these will be incidental and, hopefully, not at all threatening. Suggestions for further exploration of these subjects will, of course, be included.

A few chapters will be offered to provide real-world examples of typical, but quite disturbing, database designs and how they impede the smooth conduct of business. I will discuss precisely *why* they are poor designs and, to some extent, will show how to correct them. Although it isn't my intention to provide a technical manual for database design, it will be necessary to get very specific on occasion to avoid the accusation that this book is simply a theoretical rant about some unrealistic and unattainable goal. Hopefully, it will be possible to strike an appropriate balance between philosophy and technology to suit all the intended audiences without too much oversimplification of any one group's needs.

Unlike many books of this type, this one is most useful if it is read from beginning to end, at least initially, since many of the arguments and examples are presented piecemeal and build upon what has been presented earlier.

Objectives

It is the intent of this book to support, as informally as practical and by relatively simple (although hopefully not simplistic) examples rather than through theoretical discussions, the following assertions.

► Validation, organization, categorization, and maintenance of computerized information, sometimes referred to as data management, are key components of any business. This is also one of the very few practice areas in I/T for which there is a solid logical and mathematical foundation – a foundation with a very long history – and a foundation which also forms the underpinning for virtually all the "hard sciences." Inexplicably, the I/T profession largely ignores this foundation and gives way too little attention to data management and good database design. This results in far more difficulties and expense than is generally recognized, both for the business and, ironically, for IT departments, particularly application developers, as well.

► The current poor state of database design is one reason that companies are not achieving the "Return On Investment" they have a right to expect and could be achieving from their investments in information technology.

► The current poor state of database design is a significant, but largely unrecognized reason for the lengthy and protracted efforts needed to modify existing applications to handle new or changing business requirements, even when the changes seem relatively trivial from a business perspective.

► The current poor state of database design is one reason that the continuing procession of new programming languages and paradigms, new products, and new methodologies haven't been as successful as they first promised. To the extent that these have not addressed business needs, the significant time spent learning them and the money and time spent acquiring and implementing them have been wasted.

► The current poor state of database design is a significant, but largely unrecognized reason for poor object hierarchies, convoluted and inflexible application designs, limited reuse opportunities, and the high costs of application and database maintenance, inter-connectivity and data consolidation.

► The current poor state of database design, and the resulting prevalence of many inflexible application designs, is in far too many cases due to faulty logic: the use of logically invalid or incomplete corollaries to user requirements as the basis for design will be illustrated in some examples.

► The current poor state of database design is one indirect reason that programmers must spend substantially more time on application maintenance and support than on the development of new business functionality.

► The current poor state of data management in business is, in some cases, the result of misinformation in the trade press or misconceptions about the relational model among developers, but more often from a lack of information about the need for logical database design (rather than simple assembly of tables and columns) and the need for database design training. Unfortunately, "ad hoc" database design appears to be an easier and more economical path for many organizations and their database administrators and software developers to take. In the long run, it isn't!

► There is a common practice of treating database design as something intended to "support" business applications, and we often hear references to "the application's data." This might be justified in a very few cases, but such an attitude – mostly a holdover from the early days of computers – is fairly reprehensible given the current state of technology and needs to be rethought and, if need be, unlearned.

► The use of a Relational Database is the only logically defensible solution for adequately handling business databases. Unfortunately, many companies believe that they have been using relational databases for some time, but also (incorrectly) believe that the relational model has not really fulfilled its promise. A significant percentage of these organizations are **not** using relational databases (they only think they are because they are using a Relational Database Management System) and have never been given a chance to see that promise in action, much less fulfilled.

► Most businesses should be using, or actively moving to the use of, a single database for their day-to-day operations – this is not (yet) a mainstream viewpoint, and must be tempered by the definition of what constitutes "day-to-day operations" and even "business." The first chapter will address these terms as I intend them.

► Most businesses should be sharing a core data model as the basis for their databases; the reasoning for and merits of this will be addressed later.

By inference, although indirectly, the following assertions are also suggested:

► Even before design begins on many projects, the absence of good data analysis and management practices often leads to poor requirements management (after all, a set of requirements is nothing more than a collection of data!), often rendering the results of requirements gathering exercises useless enough to developers that such efforts often appear to be fundamentally wasteful and unnecessarily intrusive.

  Further, Requirements Gathering as a practice needs to be based on a much greater awareness of the fundamental difference between DATA RULES and BUSINESS RULES, since the proper approach to implementing each often differs significantly and, if these two are confused, results in development delays and continuing systemic problems.

► Project management, based on a collection of data, is also adversely affected by poor data management practices. During development, project management efforts are fraught with frustration and their results are often misleading. There is a connection!

Recognizing the effects of poor data architecture and database design as well as ineffective data management is the first step in addressing these issues. Attempting to think "outside the box" when we don't know where the box is in the first place is futile since, as Beethoven knew, imagination and innovation are generally useful only when based on strong foundations.

It would be naive, of course, to suggest that either Businesses or I/T Departments are very interested in Logic or Good Design on their own merits: Businesses exist to make a profit, and I/T departments are simply along for the ride. A final and underlying objective of this book, therefore, is to provide enough examples of how a lack of Logic in Database Design **wastes money** and, by implication, how the use of Logic results in better Database Designs and ultimately **saves money** and decreases the maintenance workload of I/T Departments. It really is that simple.

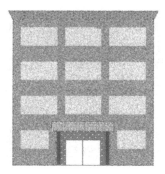

Further clarify the scope and applicability of this book.
Preview of the Party Concept.
Expectations of Business for Information Technology Departments.
Responsibilities of Information Technology Departments.
Deficiencies in Information Management in many Companies.

1 - DEFINITION OF "BUSINESS"

While many of the concepts discussed in this book are applicable to other types of databases, our focus, as stated in the preface, will be on the classic operational business database – a database that supports the day-to-day activity of a business. We begin, therefore, by defining exactly what we mean by "business," and outline how we distinguish a business database from other types of databases.

Business, as I am using the term, includes any interactions between two or more PARTIES, and is based on some form of implied or explicit contract. This definition of Business also includes all activities conducted by any of the individual Parties to further or support these mutual interactions, such as payroll, inventory management, marketing, promotional mailings, sales, billing, and so forth.

Business, as I am using the term, specifically does not include (although doesn't necessarily exclude) the collection of performance data, such as that recorded by sensors, nor does it include the use of non-transactional data, such as that contained in data warehouses[7]. While these often contain data about business transactions, they are not themselves transactional. To reiterate the first sentence of this chapter, some techniques and approaches described in this book might occasionally be useful for such databases, but these databases are not their focus.

---

7   See Common Aliases for "Business Database" on page 4 for a more explicit description.

An I/T Department Must Have Parties

A PARTY, as the term is introduced above, can be any of the various entities such as a PERSON, CORPORATION, PARTNERSHIP, GOVERNMENT, or similar "Thing," that takes part in or accepts certain responsibilities, whether explicit or implicit, related to any of the contractual agreements referred to above.

The implied or explicit Contracts that define and govern business can include anything from one-time informal agreements during a single transaction – such as an unidentified consumer's purchase of a single candy bar from a gas station in return for the posted price – or much more formal, explicit and complex contracts – such as a three year agreement for a refinery to supply gasoline on a recurring basis to a gas station. Either of these extremes is easily identifiable as a transaction or series of transactions between two or more Parties.

Party Guest List

Examples of common interactions between Parties that constitute "Business" as I am using the term include:

Party providing Services or Products	Party consuming Services or Products
Seller → Buyer	
Vendor → Customer	
Vendor → Manufacturer	
Manufacturer → Retailer	
Employee → Employer	
Contractor → Employer	
Doctor → Patient	
Government → Taxpayer	
et cetera → et cetera	

None of these roles need be mutually exclusive. An Employee, for example, might also be a Customer of his own Employer, and a Hospital employee might also be a patient of the same Hospital. Note that some of these Party roles are relatively synonymous (e.g. Seller and Vendor, Buyer and Customer), differing only by the names traditionally used in specific industries.

Without one or more Parties, or the expectation that another Party will soon be available with which to "do business," no transactional data will ever be generated and no business database will be needed. The primary Entity in a business database, therefore, would reasonably seem to be the PARTY. It would also seem reasonable that all other data would be organized around the Party. Although there are exceptions, most business databases do indeed have the concept of at least a few specific subclasses of PARTY (e.g. CUSTOMER, EMPLOYEE, etc.) in their structures, but very few acknowledge that these are subsets of some larger entity set. This oversight, as we shall demonstrate in later chapters, leads to many inefficiencies in business data management, to rampant data redundancy, and can significantly impede future development efforts.

Party Seating Chart

If we were to create a very simple diagram showing each type of Party as a separate grouping within the larger overall rubric of Party, it might look something like the illustration below:

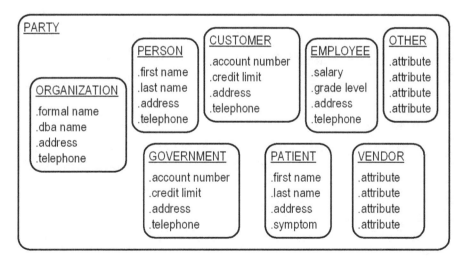

For those who aren't familiar with this sort of diagram[8], each rounded box represents a Class or Set. Patient, for example, one subset of Party discussed above, can be distinguished as a specific sub-class of Party because it has the unique attribute **Symptom** that isn't shared with any of the other Party classes. In this diagram, Party is known as a super-class because it contains other identifiable Classes within it. Super-class and sub-class, however, are relative terms.

Remember, of course, that it is often possible that some of these Classes may overlap, as we discussed in the section "Party Guest List" above, but no such overlaps are illustrated in this simple diagram. We will refer back to this particular drawing in chapter 4 (A Corporate Merger – Part 1) to see how exactly we can make use of these sorts of illustrations in the analysis and design of "real" database structures, and how doing so can provide us with a wide variety of both business and technical advantages.

Common Aliases for "Business Database"

In much published material, a business database as I am defining it is sometimes called by many other names, most often "operational" database – as opposed to "analytical" database – the "analytical" database typically being one that has a collection of data from many sources collected into a form that is useful for corporate projections, historical analysis and similar purposes.

The following (very general) descriptions will help distinguish one type of database from the other:

▶ An operational business database as I am using the term typically has a relatively high volume of smaller sized transactions, whereas an analytic database has a relatively low number of very high volume transactions. Because of this characteristic, the term Transactional Database[9] is also used, although I don't prefer that term for a variety of reasons.

---

8   Similar to those used in Barker [1]. This is not a Venn diagram, Carroll diagram or Set diagram, but a more primitive form closer to what Euler used.

9   For such a database to fall into the subject matter of this book, however, the database must be a "*Business* Transactional Database," as opposed to other types.

▶ An operational business database as I am using the term tends to have a high level of volatility – data is being added, read, and modified continuously during the course of everyday business activities. Analytical databases, on the other hand are only updated on a regular schedule (however frequently that might occur), and by automated (and presumably trusted) processes rather than user interactions.

▶ An operational business database as I am using the term tends to require protection by more rules – very specific and granular Constraints that are intended to guarantee that no invalid data is permitted into the database[10]. An analytical database, aside from the periodic updates referred to above, is used only for analysis and output. These "read-only" data stores can therefore dispense with many of the rules needed to protect against the entry of undesirable data and may also utilize redundancy for greater speed.

It also needs to be stated that, although many businesses collect large amounts of non-transactional data, such as web logs, data from monitoring systems, and so forth, the methods described in this book are not represented as being typically applicable to the handling of those data stores.

The Avowed Mission of I/T Departments

Business expectations of I/T departments vary, as do the mission statements for these departments, but generally revolve around the idea that the company's information (or at least that information which can be represented as data) is to be organized and managed to benefit the company, protected from contamination or loss, and secured from unauthorized access while still made easily accessible to those who need it, etc. In addition, I/T practitioners are tasked with building (or evaluating and purchasing) applications to create, manipulate and make use of this information for various purposes.

---

10 The sorely misunderstood subject of Constraints is treated in its own chapter beginning on page 169.

The Two Primary Functions of a Business I/T Department

A business runs on its information and processes. The automation brought about by electronic computers was intended:

► ...at first, to automate and standardize the processes (application programs) that interact with the organization's data, and then

► ...once reasonable amounts of non-volatile random access electronic storage[11] became available, to refine how businesses organize and categorize their data (data management).

Certainly the provision of physical computing and networking infrastructures are also key responsibilities of I/T but, for the purposes of this discussion, have little relevance, and will not be addressed. Compared to the issues encountered in data management and application development, I/T infrastructure management is far more mature, stable and reliable.[12]

It is enlightening to note that, in most of the titles given to the profession (consider the acronyms DP, EDP, MIS, IS, I/T[13], etc), the words "data" or "information" figure prominently. Although the department may occasionally be called "Programming," it seems that, at least in the naming of the profession, the management of data has always been given priority over process.

Relative Importance of an I/T Department's Two Primary Functions

While the implicit suggestion given by the naming of the department is that programming is done to support the collection, analysis, protection and presentation of data, I/T personnel generally tend to view data collection and management as being a poor cousin to application development. We'll discuss examples of this in "Science and Current Data Management Practices" on page 8.

---

11   As opposed to paper tape, punched cards, magnetic tape and the like – see chapter 6 (Recent History of Data Management).

12   What this means, in effect, is that it is much more obvious when something goes wrong.

13   Oh alright; Data Processing, Electronic Data Processing, Management Information Systems, Information Systems, Information Technology. Talk to other old people.

Such a view, however, is contrary to the needs and expectations of Business and, in fact, quite often has the effect of making further development and enhancements of these same applications quite problematic. Some ideas we need to keep in mind when evaluating the relative importance of the programming and database management responsibilities of I/T Departments are:

► There are fundamental differences between data and process.

  ▼ Data elements, representing discrete facts, tend to have a constant definition.

  ▼ Processes, by their nature, tend to be arbitrary and changeable, whether by choice, circumstance, legal decree, change in business objectives, or for other reasons.

  The storage and management of data tends to be viewed – wrongly, as it turns out – as a much more straightforward effort than the definition of the often complex and volatile processes that create and manipulate the data.

► As a Benchmark, consider the following contrasting disaster scenarios:

  ▼ Scenario A: The company's computer center is destroyed, and only the data backups have survived, or

  ▼ Scenario B: The company's computer center is destroyed, and only the application backups have survived.

While attempting to continue operations under Scenario A would hardly be pleasant, much less guaranteed to be successful, the availability of the company's data would certainly make it *possible*. Continuation of operations under Scenario B, however, *would seldom ever be possible*. Furthermore, process, being a series of repetitive actions (such as how the company handles rebates on sale items), tends to survive in the corporate memory, while individual data elements (such as the names and addresses of our most profitable customers) do not.

Today, most people would greatly expand the mission of Information Technology departments to include terms like flexibility, adaptability, connectivity and the like, but these are matters of degree and do not substantively change the fundamental mission. Ironically, as we shall see, data organization and management is surprisingly inept in most I/T operations.

The Inevitable Conclusions

For most businesses, utilizing multiple databases – with each database designed specifically to meet the needs of a particular application[14] – is at best a questionable approach to I/T and, in my view, professionally irresponsible – a view that, hopefully, will be supported by the examples provided in later chapters.

Science and Current Data Management Practices

Several decades ago, someone decided that I/T qualified as "Computer *Science*," certainly a worthwhile desire[15]. One could argue though, and I suppose I am, that using the term "Computer Science" for our current application and database management practices has given Science in general a bad name. Aside from hardware design, there is only one area of information technology – data organization – for which there is a solid theoretical foundation, and that foundation is virtually ignored by most developers and vendors.

Organization and categorization of information and data, as stated earlier, are among the most fundamental responsibilities of I/T. Organization and categorization of information and data are essential to Science as well[16]; no scientific effort can succeed without first properly organizing the data to be studied or acted upon. Logical principles for organizing and categorizing information and data were first formalized thousands of years ago, formed the basis for subsequent Scientific progress, and have been refined and proven continuously in scientific

---

14 As mentioned in the preface, it is common for I/T personnel to refer to "the application's data," but you seldom ever hear about "the data's application." Neither is appropriate (I just have a slight urge to be confrontational), because we are discussing two separate and distinct responsibilities that, of necessity, happen to overlap.

15 Indeed, as we shall see in "Recent History of Data Management," the earliest practitioners were, in fact, Scientists.

16 ...and, according to most historians, are the foundation of Scientific investigation.

endeavors throughout history.[17] This history will be outlined briefly in "Early History of Data Management" beginning on page 15.

Given our profession's use of the word *Science*, an outsider might be forgiven for assuming that historically proven logical principles for the organization and categorization of data were in common use in I/T, but it is easy to demonstrate that this is not at all the case. In far too many organizations, including those of the vendors and consultants who regularly show up with some new product that will solve all the business world's I/T failings, data management issues are not seriously addressed at all. If this seems to be a brash statement, consider that:

► Database considerations are usually associated with a new application or system – and hardly ever treated as ends unto themselves. Data management is viewed, in effect, as a sideline to application development. This directly results in the data silos most businesses would be delighted to eliminate, as well as a host of other application maintenance headaches.

► Data analysis and initial design is typically done by business analysts, application developers, or database administrators. While there are certainly examples of knowledgeable and skilled database designers (as well as tennis players, pianists, swimmers, and sculptors in about the same proportions) within these ranks, there is little evidence to assume that logic, data analysis or database design are actually in their skill repertoires.

► Physical database design and implementation are usually accomplished by database administrators, although sometimes by specialists called "development DBAs" who also write stored procedures and application interfaces. Database Administrators are certainly critical to any I/T organization, but their skill sets are quite often fairly product-centric. It is curious, given that organization and categorization of data are fundamental needs, database design is not even a recognized specialty. Consider the following posting:

---

17   It is tempting to refer to such proven, logical principles as "best practices" for information and data management, but that term has been rendered meaningless by I/T product and service peddlers who are often promoting their own products and methodologies.

Data Administrator / Business Analyst

"We currently have a full time employment opportunity as a Data Administrator/ Business Analyst. Qualified candidates must have 5 plus years as a Data Administrator or 5 plus years experience as a Business Analyst. Qualified candidates must also be proficient in SQL or PL/SQL programming, and 5+ years of data modeling experience. This position requires strong analytical skills and techniques. If you are a Database Administrator, you are over qualified for this position. Qualified candidates will be working closely with the Data Administration team."

The sentence: "If you are a Database Administrator, you are over qualified for this position." provides a clear case of mixed domains, since a DBA could just as easily be unqualified as overqualified for the position described. This is somewhat akin to advertising for a pastry chef and stating that "if you are a linebacker, you are overqualified."

► Consulting firms who offer "Full Lifecycle" support seldom mention data architecture or database design. A typical description looks something like this (taken from an actual promotional brochure):

"ABC is a global consulting company focused on providing technology solutions to the xyz industry. We provide complete software lifecycle services, from program management, business analysis, technology planning, architecture, application development, package implementation and customization, maintenance, and support."

Note that data architecture, strategy or design is never mentioned even though, as we have seen, organization and categorization of information and data are among Information Technology's most *fundamental* responsibilities. So much for "*complete* life cycle."

► Browse the computer science section of your local book store or on-line source. Observe that...

▼ ... a clear majority of the non-academic[18] books on database design and technology is product-based – there are *very* few available that concentrate on the fundamental logical principles behind good database design;

---

18 "non-academic" books being those likely to be of interest to "working" database designers.

▼ ... while a reasonable number of the product-centric books devote a chapter or two to database design, these often contain minimally useful or very misleading information[19];

▼ ... virtually every book on application development is product based – these also may devote a chapter or two to database design, but also contain minimally useful or very misleading information and typically imply that the database should be built to support the needs of the application.

Business and Current Data Management Practices

We've seen what the computer industry thinks it should be, at least as reflected by the various names it's adopted over the years. Although this leaves unanswered the question as to why its focus seems to be centered elsewhere, such a discussion would only be speculative, so we'll now turn to what business wants from I/T.

The first thing to recognize is that business has always viewed technology (information or otherwise) and its related expenditures as a means to an end.

As for data management technology specifically, businesses have historically struggled with the idea that key information was scattered across numerous desks and filing cabinets and, later, across buildings and even cities. Lost or incomplete data, duplication of effort and failure to share information across departments, conflicting records, and an inability to locate information quickly were (and, to a large extent, still are) all common concerns for any business that employed more than one person – and these concerns seemed to increase exponentially with each increase in the number of employees, departments, or geographic locations. Computer-based storage initially seemed like a perfect long-term solution, even though the early benefits were minimal due to the understandable limits of technology. As machines grew more powerful, and memory increased in size and decreased in cost simultaneously, this initial confidence grew, albeit with a slight impatience at the rate of growth. When inter-connec-

---

19 The subject of such material is generally database administration – a title that should actually be DBMS administration. There are a few egregious examples given in later chapters (usually titled "Freedom of the Press") to illustrate and justify the assertion that many of these publications provide "misleading information."

tivity and networking began to become more prevalent and mature, business management had every reason to continue being optimistic about the future contributions of information technology. Fortunately for our profession, the expectations of business were never very concrete or specific, so it isn't (yet) all that obvious that much of their investment has not provided the benefits it should have.

In the very simplest terms (and certainly without any consideration of the current state of technology), business would prefer to have all its relevant data in a single, internally consistent, easily accessible (with proper access controls at a very granular level, of course), secure and reliable database!

But, of course, any information technology professional will usually dismiss that idea as impractical if not impossible – and will cite numerous technical reasons for such an opinion. Although there are also numerous non-

The term "single, internally consistent" is actually redundant. If there are multiple databases, there is no technical way for them to be consistent across instances even when using the unnecessarily expensive and performance hogging Rube Goldberg cross-database synchronization contraptions that continue to be offered by some vendors. Even then, the "consistency" is the result of many often arbitrary decisions that often sacrifice accuracy for the sake of appearance.

technical reasons[20] why the use of a single large database could be impractical, the fact that *technical* reasons are most often cited should serve as a significant caution! But more on that in the next-to-last chapter "The Single Operational Database".

Before presenting our first "real-world" example, we'll digress for a bit and discuss the virtually unknown (or at least unacknowledged) early history of data management and then comment on some published nonsense in the first of several "Freedom of the Press" chapters.

---

20   And it is these non-technical reasons that should be of particular interest to any Business
      Managers who have made it this far.

LESSONS FOR CHAPTER 1
DEFINITION OF "BUSINESS"

► Business as we are using the term consists of transactions between (and among) various Parties, such as Persons, Corporations and the like.

► Information Technology departments have some very clear responsibilities to the Businesses they support, but these are often given short shrift.

► The primary function of Information Technology groups is managing data. All their other responsibilities, including application programming, provision of computers and networks, and so forth, while critically important, are secondary to data management.

► Without very compelling reasons to do otherwise, a Business should have a single database for all its day-to-day operations. The idea that a single business has multiple operational databases that need to be consolidated to obtain a realistic overview of the company, or that redundant data may be stored throughout an enterprise, is simply no longer justified by any reasonable technical criteria.

"No one is so eager to gain new experience as he who doesn't know how to make use of the old ones."
— Baroness Marie von Ebner-Eschenbach (1830-1916)

"Those who cannot remember the past are condemned to repeat it"
(see text below) — George Santayana.

Illustration: Ἀριστοτέλης (Aristotle) (384-322 BCE);
The Father of Formal Data Organization

2 - EARLY HISTORY OF DATA MANAGEMENT

Having mentioned the long and distinguished history of science and logic, it is only fair to provide a brief summary and a few pertinent references for further exploration. Although a comprehensive listing of key figures and synopses of their works is far beyond the scope of this book, we'll at least briefly explore the early and recent history behind our profession. This chapter will present a rather informal overview of the early philosophy, mathematics and science underpinning data management; a later chapter will discuss the past century – when we really got going, although, sadly, not all in the same direction.

Santayana's famous quotation (see above) is most often interpreted to mean that those who don't study and learn from past mistakes will only continue to repeat them. But, an equally valid and far more general interpretation would be that if we don't study and learn from past successes, we will be unable to fully capital-ize on those successes. This is why the history of data organization and catego-rization which, in effect, has been key to the growth of science, is important to database design – hopefully, future chapters will buttress this assertion. If this particular chapter seems somewhat tongue-in-cheek, it's likely the fault of your own warped pedestrian perceptions, and I see no need to apologize.

Data Management Time Line (445 bce to 1910)

This period saw an introduction of formal Taxonomies, Sets, and Classes as a means of logical organization of information.

Cynicism

▶ 445 bce

Ἀντισθένης (Antisthenes), who lived between about 445 bce and 365 bce, was a pupil of Σωκράτης (Socrates). Antisthenes was the first professionally-certified Cynic.

For some time, Cynicism was thought to be simply an odd Philosophy or a personality flaw, but we now know it's just another word for life-experience (and possibly business experience), particularly in I/T groups.

The Birth of Logic, Categorization, Taxonomy, and Science:

▶ 350 bce

The Greek philosopher Ἀριστοτέλης (Aristotle, who lived from 384bce to 322 bce)[21], in the course of pondering the world, its meaning, and how we can make sense of it, began the process of formalizing logic, categorization, and the rational organization of data relating to THINGS and their ATTRIBUTES. Aristotle's conclusions became the foundation of Science as an independent, formal process. Aristotle himself made major contributions to the physical sciences using these approaches, but his major contributions to database design in general are:

▼ the concept that Things of interest can be categorized as either Primary or Secondary substances (see the chapter titled "Grammar, Sets, and (Predicate) Logic – Part 1" beginning on page 67 for details),

---

21 Like his famous pupil Alexander III, Aristotle was actually Macedonian. However, once young Alex had conquered Greece and most of the known world to form the "Greek Empire" (thereby becoming "Alexander the Great"), it wasn't considered good politics to bring this up. Aristotle did find it expedient to "retire" back to Macedonia after Alexander's final journey to the Elysian Fields though.

▼ an orderly means for distinguishing between Essential and Accidental attributes (discussed in the same chapter), and

Aristotle's *Organon* (Logic)[22], particularly the Introduction and Categories section, is a valuable guide to approaching the design of a database.

► Circa 300 bce

Εὐκλείδης (Euclid, fl c300 bce) is the first to use Aristotle's principles (other than Aristotle himself, of course) in his *Elements* to organize and provide the theoretical structure behind the scattered pieces of information related to what we now call Plane Geometry.

An Aside – The Egyptian Rule

Note that Euclid is not credited with *inventing* or *discovering* Geometry. There is clear evidence that the Egyptians, for instance, utilized principles of Geometry, as well as Trigonometry, Astronomy, and other branches of science and mathematics. There is no evidence, however, that the Egyptians viewed this knowledge as anything other than a pragmatic set of skills; they seemed to have little if any interest in the theoretical or general implications of this knowledge. Additionally, there is much evidence to suggest that Euclid even incorporated ideas from earlier Greeks, such as Eudoxus. Euclid's contribution was collecting and logically organizing all known information, and then using that organization to expose (and, in Euclid's case, to fill and rigorously refine) the theoretical gaps thus exposed, and to present that to the world in an orderly method. That is why he is so important, and why he gets historical credit as the "father of geometry."

The idea that one could take a rope or chain with twelve equally sized segments and create a perfect (90°) right angle by placing them in a 3-4-5[23] arrangement was very well known, and regularly used to reestablish property boundaries after the annual Nile floods. But, although it seems likely that

---

22   See Aristotle [1] in the bibliography on page 380.

23   The Pythagorean Theorem. Pythagorus of Samos (Πυθαγόρας) lived from 570 to 490 bce.

someone must have known the mathematics behind this, the average Egyptian farmer probably didn't know and didn't care.

As Carver Mead puts it: "To understand reality, you have to understand how things work. If you do that, you can start to do engineering with it, build things. And if you can't, whatever you're doing probably isn't good science. To me, engineering and science aren't separate endeavors."[24]

The Continuing 2,100 year Maturation Process (300 bce – 1910)

Aristotle's approach to organization and categorization proves itself over time. Mathematics, Logic, and the various hard Sciences continue to mature over thousands of years, but the fundamentals remain valid and stable. Some relevant highlights include:

► circa 225 bce

Ἀρχιμήδης (Archimedes) of Syracuse (287-212 bce), the famous early streaker of "Eureka" and "overflowing bathtub" fame, is credited with defining the foundation of theoretical mechanics, and was one of the first to use Logical principles to ensure the integrity of his employer's assets, although in that instance it was the integrity of King Hiero II's supposedly golden crown, not the King's royal database, that was in question.

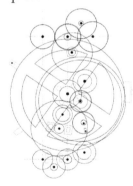

Archimedes is now considered to be the creative mind behind (if not the actual builder of) the Μηχανισμός Αντικυθήρων (the Antikythera Mechanism) – a very early analog computer used to track and predict moon phases, planetary motion, solar and lunar eclipses, and other astronomical phenomena. The engineering and mathematical sophistication of this device, (e.g. use of floating pins in the circular gears to simulate several of the elliptical orbits it tracked) is breathtaking.[25]

---

24   Mead [1].

25   See videos of this device at http://www.youtube.com/watch?v=UpLcnAIpVRA and http://www.youtube.com/watch?v=4Rdi1Cr3y1c&list=PL5882B15115E435A0.

The data required for these calculations was stored as a series of gears with specific numbers (many of them prime numbers) of teeth.

▶ 1604

Robert Cawdrey (1538-after 1604) publishes *A Table Alphabeticall*, the first attempt at an English Language Dictionary. This was an even more significant contribution to data management than it appears on the surface since, in order to make the book useful, Mr. Cawdrey need to "invent" alphabetical[26] order, thus paving the way for the many sorting algorithms that followed in the twentieth century. In what later turned out to be an embarrassment, the English, showing a callous disregard for Cawdrey's accomplishments, eventually changed the spelling of Alphabeticall to Alphabetical – possibly the first primitive example of data compression.

▶ 1671-1673

Gottfried Wilhelm von Leibniz (1646-1716) invented the first workable MECHANICAL COMPUTER to extract square roots[27]. An early pioneer in the development of mathematical logic, Leibniz opines that a Thing is the sum of all its Attributes. Although Aristotle had already suggested something like this two thousand years earlier, Leibniz' opinions apparently started people thinking about categorization of data once again.

Leibniz and Newton (see next entry) are noted as independent developers of the Calculus.

---

26 Obviously earlier librarians going back as far as the third century bce had organized their materials in some sort of order, but these were very inconsistent. By publishing a dictionary, Cawdrey was able to establish one of the first de facto standards of the I/T world.

27 Leibnitz's "Stepped Reckoner" was the first mechanical contraption capable of performing all four basic arithmetic functions (addition, subtraction, multiplication, and division). Although there is no evidence that he coined the term "four-banger," he did say that he created the device because "... it is beneath the dignity of excellent men to waste their time in calculation when any peasant could do the work just as accurately with the aid of a machine." Because of his patronizing disdain for those peasant users, he has been granted "Honorary I/T Practitioner" status – not as prestigious as a knighthood, perhaps, but close.

► 5 July 1687

Sir Isaac Newton (1642-1727), most famous for *Philosophiæ Naturalis Principia Mathematica* (Mathematical Principles of Natural Philosophy, usually called simply: *Principia*) and his contributions to physics, optics and mechanics, developed the Theory of Equations, which first hints at RELATIONAL THEORY. He was knighted, indicating that he was at least as important in English history as Sir Elton John or Sir Paul McCartney are today.

► Circa 1770

Carl Linnaeus (1707-1778) was called the "Father of Taxonomy" by those who didn't know or had forgotten Aristotle's work. Linnaeus did refine Aristotle's methods significantly, however, by introducing a consistent form of naming that could be used to define relationships across any taxonomy. His form of identifying a particular Class with a genus.species (or Class.Subclass) nomenclature is still used today. In programming this is also quite familiar as "dot notation."

► circa 1800

Joseph Louis Lagrange (1736-1813), most known for analytic mechanics, made major contributions to the theory behind weights and measures – another fairly mature science that is largely ignored by database designers and DBMS vendors at a significant cost to Business. We'll begin to explore the proper (i.e. logically defensible) handling of weights and measures in the eponymous chapter "Weights & Measures – Part 1" that begins on page 201.

► 1801 - Introduction of the punched card:

Joseph Marie Jacquard (1752-1834) developed a programmable automated loom that used punched cards to set the desired weave patterns, revolutionizing the weaving industry. Charles Babbage (1792-1871) specified Jacquard's method as a means of programming the instructions to be followed by his Analytical Engine, although the machine was never built in Babbage's lifetime.

► 1854

George Boole's (1815-1864) primary work of interest to modern database design is *"An Investigation of the Laws of Thought on which are founded the Mathematical Theories of Logic and Probabilities,"* published in 1854. The title alone probably ensures that most I/T folks will never read this. Bertrand Russell[28], however, said "Pure mathematics was discovered by Boole, in a work which he called 'The Laws of Thought' ". This is the first instance of pure hyperbole related (albeit peripherally) to I/T, logic, and database design, but Boole certainly seems to have impressed Russell. Boole's name survives mostly in the term "Boolean."

► 1878

Herman Hollerith (1860-1929) used Jacquard's idea of punched cards to store statistical data, so that it could be sorted and summarized through mechanical means. Hollerith's machine and its punched cards were used to record, collate and analyze the data collected during the 1880 and 1890 United States censuses. Interestingly, most of the 1890 data was destroyed by fire; the need for backups had, unfortunately, not yet been recognized by our nascent industry. Hollerith founded the Tabulating Machine Company in 1896, which later became IBM.

► 1879

Georg Cantor (1845-1918) publishes the *Theory of Sets* in a series of six papers in *Mathematische Annalen*, a basic introduction to and elaboration of his earlier 1874 article. Although intended as pure mathematics (at the time, he was working on the Theory of Transfinite Numbers), this provided a formal foundation for many aspects of CLASSIFICATION, ORGANIZATION and CATEGORIZATION that Aristotle had first introduced over two millennia earlier.

---

28   If you aren't familiar with Bertrand Russell, he was the first to prove that 1+1=2. Really! See the 1910 entry about him below. (the last entry in this chapter)

► 1896

The Reverend Charles L. Dodgson (1832-1898), best known by
his pseudonym Lewis Carroll and as the creator of *Alice in Wonder-land*, writes a very clear explanation of THINGS, LOGIC, PREDICATES
and NORMALIZATION, while taking jabs at some of his competitors, including a
very unfair, but quite humorous, jab at Mr. Venn (of Venn-diagram fame).
Aside from demonstrating the importance of good (and formal) grammar in
effectively organizing and categorizing THINGS, Carroll doesn't contribute
anything particularly new. He is primarily mentioned because his book, *Sym-bolic Logic*, particularly Books (chapters) I and II, is a "must-read" for any In-formation Technology professional[29]. Although the description of Wonder-land in his more famous works could easily apply to many I/T shops, Alice
and her friends don't provide nearly as much guidance to database designers.

► 1903

Gottlob Frege publishes *Concept-Script: A Concept Language of Pure
Thought on the Pattern of Arithmetic*, an elaborate system of logic
now known simply as PREDICATE LOGIC.

► 1910-1913

Bertrand Russell (1872-1970) and his co-author Alfred North
Whitehead publish their *Principia Mathematica*, a work that pro-vided the first (yes – the first) formal proof that 1+1=2, a huge
gap in mathematics and science that had annoyed mathematicians for cen-turies. *Principia Mathematica* outlined the proofs that mathematics itself can
be stated in terms of logical concepts such as CLASS and MEMBERSHIP IN A
CLASS. From the time of this publication, there has been no question that
Logic and Mathematics are different reflections of the same concepts.

Of all the contributors to the Sciences that gave us the foundations we need
to successfully build logical database structures, Bertrand Russell is, I believe,
the earliest of our profession's forebears who can be viewed on YouTube[30].

---

29 A very low cost version is Carroll [1] (see page 381 for information). Read it!

30 A search for "YouTube Bertrand Russell" should get you started.

And some final notes:

"The great arrogance of the present is to forget the intelligence of the past"[31]

"The farther back you can look, the farther forward you are likely to see."[32]

---

31   Ken Burns, documentary filmmaker.

32   Winston Churchill, polymath.

LESSONS FOR CHAPTER 2
EARLY HISTORY OF DATA MANAGEMENT

► We store data, not information. Information is derived or inferred from logically well-organized data. If the data is not logically organized (or is internally inconsistent, or *[insert your favorite failing here]*), it follows that what is derived or inferred from that data can better be described as **mis-information**.

► Disorganized data, therefore, gives only the appearance of Information.

► The techniques for organization and categorization of data have been known for centuries and form the basis of our scientific knowledge.

Many persons are either ignorant of or, worse, willfully ignore that history, but I've yet to see any evidence suggesting that this has resulted in better database design.

► All existing evidence suggests that there are clear ties among the fields of logic, mathematics, and database design.

We will continue with the "Recent History of Data Management" in a later chapter (see page 97), but before doing so we need to digress with our first "Freedom of the Press" discussion and our first "real-world" database design example, after which we'll delve into a few of the lessons bequeathed to us by our not so distant data management forebears.

What is a Database?
What is a Database Management System?
How should the Design of a Database be approached?

3

"Science is what we understand well enough to explain to a computer.
Art is everything else we do."
- Donald Knuth (see bibliography)

3 - FREEDOM OF THE PRESS: WHAT IS A DATABASE?

Freedom of the Press is, of course, one of the fundamental underpinnings of a free society. In any intellectual endeavor, and particularly in information technology (which is still in its adolescence), it would be foolish and unpatriotic to attempt any restrictions on what is written. Of course, any "right" we claim carries with it some implied concomitant obligation – acceptance of Freedom of the Press implies that we must take on the responsibility to distinguish between good and bad sources, between accurate and mistaken sources, and between impartial sources and those with some agenda in mind. With those thoughts as guidelines, here are some of this book's first examples of Freedom of Press in action within the I/T industry – those dealing with the very fundamental question of what exactly a database is in the first place.

What is a Database? – Dangerous Literature

As we know from history, there have been collections of data for several millenia that could without many qualms be called databases. In the modern era, however, we consider that, to be a database, the data must be stored on some form of media from which it can be easily accessed, and we have invented sometimes quite elaborate software – which we call database management systems (DBMSs) – to assist us in handling such electronically stored data.

For some reason that seems difficult to comprehend, however, there are many books and articles (as well as numerous advertising examples) that make no distinction between databases and database management systems. This is so fundamental a distinction, though, that any literature confusing the two is not likely to have been written by anyone whose advice should be trusted. Such advice, if taken, should at least be viewed critically or with skepticism. This may seem on the surface to be what is colloquially called "picky" but, since much of the material available for learning and using the two is really applicable to only one or the other, the lack of distinction can be confusing or quite misleading and results in practices which are not at all in the best interests of the developers[33] or the businesses that employ them.

Before providing some examples, let's acknowledge that, pickiness aside, there can be several legitimate definitions for Data, Database, Database Management System, and Relational Database Management System, although the following will suffice for now:

> ***Data***: Known or assumed facts or figures at an **appropriate level of granularity** for their intended use. We'll discuss what this means later in "More Normal Form Confusion" on page 33.

> ***Database***: A logically categorized collection of data stored in an organized and accessible fashion, usually, but not necessarily, in a computer system. There don't actually seem to be many business databases that fully comply with even this simple definition.

> ***Database Management System***: (DBMS) Computer **software** intended to automate the processes that allow a user or programmer to build database systems that create, store, read, update, and delete data that is held in a computer system.[34]

---

33 There will be sufficient examples in subsequent chapters to support this assertion.

34 In the section of his e-book describing MySQL, Moeller [1] says "Put simply, a database is any system designed to create, store, retrieve, and manage a large amount of digital information." - a nice enough definition of a **database management system**, but definitely not a good or useful description of a **database**.

Relational Database Management System: (RDBMS) A spe-cialized database management system (but still a DBMS, and therefore still **software**) specifically designed to implement and manipulate databases designed in accordance with the Relational Model. Beyond the basic create, read, update, and delete func-tionality[35], the term RDBMS implies declarative (non-pro-cedural) support for such things as referential integrity, provision of one or more formal query languages, etc. Additionally, these RDBMS products usually permit a good deal of flexibility (e.g. selection and sorting criteria) when retrieving data.

For more information on what precisely constitutes a Relational Database Management System, see the two-part 1985 *Computer-World* article[36] that discusses how to determine whether and to what extent a particular DBMS software product can be consid-ered Relational.

While all the required overhead makes it extremely difficult and impractical to build and manage a relational database without utilizing a relational database management system, **it is quite easy to build a non-relational database using a relational database management system.**

Building non-relational databases using RDBMS products is actually quite common[37], and the widespread proliferation of such non-relational databases provides much of the rationale for those who disparage or simply fail to grasp the benefits of the relational model.

---

35   Generally referred to by the acronym "CRUD" (create, read, update and delete).

36   Codd [2] On page 381. "Codd's 12 Rules" (Rule 0 was added later to make 13) is one of the classic texts in the field.

37   This is partially because RDBMS products provide benefits beyond those derived from im-plementing the relational model. It should not go without saying, though, that the return on RDBMS investments (ROI) can never be fully realized when Relational Database Manage-ment Systems are used to build non-relational databases in a typical business. See the chap-ter titled "Recent History of Data Management" for more details.

Particularly Egregious Literature

In the popular book *Microsoft SQL Server 2000 for Dummies*[38], chapter 3 is devoted to the design of databases, a topic somewhat out of place in a book that is primarily devoted to product-specific aspects of the SQL Server RDBMS that are of interest to the intended audience of Database Administrators (DBAs).[39]

The first section of chapter 3, *Understanding the Relational Model*, begins on page 43 with the following two sentences: "Microsoft SQL Server is a relational database. A *relational database* is one that's organized in a series of two-dimensional tables." (Italics are the author's own!)

This is not an auspicious beginning, since **both these statements are completely false**! It should therefore be immediately apparent that information presented in this chapter is suspect. SQL Server may qualify as much as its competitors as a relational database management system (RDBMS), i.e. a program (*an application!*) with which one can build a relational database, but it is decidedly not a relational database itself. Having countless would-be database designers attempting to learn something from a book that glosses over such a fundamental distinction does not bode well for the businesses that rely on them.

As for the second sentence – while data in a relational database must *appear to the user* as a set of rows and columns, it is completely incorrect to suggest that any database "organized in a series of two-dimensional tables" is therefore relational (in Logic, this is known as an INVALID COROLLARY).

---

38 Mann [1]. The categorization "popular" is my own, and is based solely on the facts that the book has been reprinted for several successive versions of the product (albeit with different authors), and has also been a continuing presence in major on-line and retail bookstores.

39 I say "somewhat out-of-place" only because discussion of a skill like throwing a curve ball would be more out-of-place, and although there is admittedly the need for coordination between DBAs and database designers at some point, there is no innate reason why these skills would or should be covered in the same document. This is not to suggest, of course, that any particular DBA is incapable of possessing database design knowledge and skills (I know quite a few who do). A Catcher needs to understand how a Pitcher's skills at throwing a curve ball relate to his own catching skills and vice-versa, but training on how to throw a curve ball, although interesting, is out-of-place in a Catcher's core training regimen and should be a separate course of instruction.

In the second section, *Schema Objects*, the author notes (correctly) that "an improper data design can severely affect performance of your database", but neglects to mention that an improper design also inevitably impacts opportunities for reuse, extensibility, flexibility across a company's application portfolio, the ability to easily consolidate and exchange data, and other capabilities that should be close to a business database designer's heart. In contrast to performance[40] issues with the database, we are actually dealing with programmer productivity issues and business productivity issues as well!

Under *Primary Keys* on page 45, the author states that "A primary key refers to one or more columns in a table that uniquely identify how rows of data are stored in that table." This is another completely false and misleading statement. If several words were dropped this could be corrected – for instance "A primary key refers to one or more columns in a table that uniquely identify a row of data stored in that table" might be acceptable, although it doesn't fully define the meaning of Primary Key. A fundamental tenet of the relational model is removal of the need to know or care "how rows are stored" and statements like this are less than useful.

In the *What is a Relational Model* section, the author writes on page 50 that "Breaking this table into parts so that data is not repeated is called *normalization*." While not completely incorrect, this leaves the reader with the false impression that normalization can be adequately or properly accomplished by breaking the table into parts, and specifically doing this by following the three normalization

---

40 The author is using the "Vroom, vroom" definition of performance – like a young immature male driver measures performance (both his own and the vehicle's) by the speed that can be attained when pressing the accelerator pedal. A large contingent of Information Technology practitioners seem to feel likewise. If Information Technology is to become mature, we need to grow to a state where equal (if not greater) emphasis is placed on cornering, braking ability, reliability, serviceability, safety features, etc. Up to a point, speed is certainly a part of performance, but Business is not usually a drag race – it's a cross-country marathon. Performance, in any case, should be considered in the context of the Enterprise and total cost to the Business (both initially and over the life of the system), not simply for a single application or project. Performance must be considered in the context of the overall architecture, application portfolio, ability for extensibility, adaptability, etc.

"rules" (the author's incorrect word) that follow. This is misleading at best. As discussed in the next section, the "normal form" tests are really a set of quality control checks that assist with identifying common design problems; they do not even uncover all instances of non-normalized structures (this is certainly evident when looking at Figure 3.9 on page 57 of the author's book).

After describing the meaning of first, second, and third normal forms, the author notes on page 50 that "As you might expect, 2NF is somewhere in the middle between 1NF and 3NF" as if there is some sort of continuum along which one might choose to locate a design. There isn't. This chapter of the book is definitely "for dummies", and will help them remain that way.

In the *Warning* on page 51, the author correctly points out that "every time you split your data model from one table to two tables, a query will take longer to execute." The implication (and I believe this is the author's implication, not simply my inference) is that the term "longer" has some sinister or even meaningful significance. If one is using a reasonably adequate RDBMS that is reasonably installed with a reasonable data model, and the join query is competently written to run against reasonably well-indexed tables, this difference, even in a multi-table join, is quite minimal and usually negligible, particularly in light of, and when contrasted against, the many advantages of a well designed database.

Some other books go further, however, suggesting that any reduction in the number of tables is somehow desirable, which it isn't. The number of independent entities that a Business deals with **is what it is**, and attempting to arbitrarily reduce that number for "developer convenience" is usually misguided and results in severe penalties and long-term costs to the business[41].

There is a troubling *Note* on page 57 that implies (at least to me) some fundamental misconceptions of the "user's" role in database design. A database should not be designed based on "data flow" considerations or other user

---

41   See the reference to Emperor Joseph II in Weights & Measures – Part 1 on page 219.

"wishes"[42] as the author suggests, nor should it be designed to reflect business processes, which are essentially arbitrary and often short-lived.

> *"A database should be designed to reflect the reality of the facts it is storing and the relationships among these things, regardless of how they are to be used."* [43]

To be sure, the design should be trimmed, tuned, and massaged as needed, but should never be made logically incorrect during any of these processes.

And, as mentioned earlier, figure 3-9 of his book demonstrates that any normalization lessons the author was attempting to illustrate have not been applied. The corrected "Customers" table as he shows it is not even in first normal form! Furthermore, as can easily be shown, this design (minimal as it is) has already enforced several unintended "business rules"[44] that will reduce the flexibility or extensibility of any application built to use or maintain it.

Particularly Egregious Beliefs: Normal Forms

Far too many books and other material perpetuate the myth that the design process for a relational database consists of something like the following steps:

▼ Gather up all the data elements you need,

▼ Put them into Tables, then

▼ Normalize the Tables using "Normal Form Rules."

This is more or less akin to designing a house by doing the following:

▼ Gather up all your building materials,

▼ Attach them together to form a house, then

---

42 This is similar in some respects to adjusting accounting records to match the CFO's "wishes" which, as we have seen too often, is called fraud, even though it provides some short term benefits for a few that the many pay for unfairly in the long run. Of course, there is no law against database design fraud, but there probably should be.

43 Kimball [1]. As emphasized by data warehouse experts Ralph Kimball and Margie Ross, the corollary stricture that data marts should be built around physical measurement processes or events rather than on the needs of a particular department or report is equally as valid.

44 We shall demonstrate on page 44 in "Data Structures as Unintentional Business Rules" how this occurs in some typical database designs, and what the impacts can be.

▼ Call in the Building Inspector for a review and then change whatever is necessary to resolve any identified discrepancies.

To use an analogy, let's assume that we build a wall using 2"x4" studs spaced 19 inches apart[45], and that we then drill 3" holes through each of these studs for a drain pipe[46], and that we then run our electrical wires through those same holes[47]. Then we call in the building inspector to see if the construction is in "normal form."

Although these are both bone-headed, expensive, and time-consuming approaches that create much additional work, the former tactic, described in many I/T tomes, is defended by suggesting that this use of normal forms as a design technique somehow originates with "Codd and Date" or is somehow implied by the relational model. While it is certainly true that the identification and definition of the normal forms as used in database design originated with Dr. Codd, and that Date recommended that "the database designer should aim for relvars in the 'ultimate' normal form (5NF)[48]," the clear sense of both their writings is that, like a building inspection, classification of a design by its normal form is meant to be an evaluation technique — a quality control measure, if you will — and **not** a design technique.

Actual statements from Chris Date's book referenced above, and considered by many as "the bible" of relational database theory, include:

▼ "Normalization is a useful aid in the [database design] process, but it is not a panacea; thus, anyone designing a database is certainly advised to be familiar with normalization principles, but we do not mean to suggest that the design should necessarily be based on those principles alone."

---

45 I almost didn't include these next footnotes and then realized that, by not doing so, I would be acting on my assumption that the average database designer knows more about home design than database design — something I believe, but find psychologically unsettling. So, to be clear, the standard spacing for studs is usually 16 inches; this is in order to ensure that the edges of a standard piece of 4'x8' wallboard will always be supported.

46 The strength of the wall depends on the 4" stud width, which we've just reduced to 1".

47 ...and, as you can guess, nothing good can come from increasing the odds that electricity and liquid (even the sweat on the pipes) can inadvertently come in contact.

48 Date [1], Chapter 11.1. Remember, if you're skeptical, you can always read this yourself.

▼ "...we do not mean to suggest that database design is actually done by applying that procedure [i.e. normalization] in practice; in fact, it probably is not"

▼ [after a design has been completed...] "the ideas of normalization can then be used to verify that the resulting design does not unintentionally violate any of the normalization principles. Nevertheless, the normalization procedure does provide a convenient framework in which to describe those principles. For the purposes of this chapter, therefore, we adopt the useful fiction that we are indeed carrying out the design process by applying that procedure."

Many designers seem to overlook these last two sentences in particular! Normalization is **not** a design technique (although it can help), and Date's use of normalization to illustrate a design process is what he himself calls a "useful fiction."

More Normal Form Confusion

After mentioning that "you may be called upon to design a relational database", one book that implicitly accepts the use of Normal Form evaluation as a design technique begins its explanation of Normal Forms as follows:

> *"First Normal Form (FNF) – This rule states that a column cannot contain multiple values. For example, a person's name must be broken down into last name, middle name, and first name to follow FNF."* [49]

Well, not exactly, and not always. To take an analogous situation, would we need to take what is typically called Address_Line_1 or something similar (containing for example "123 South Main Boulevard") and break it apart into number, direction, name, type, and so forth? The answer is, of course, maybe! It depends largely on the level of granularity required by the business as a whole. For most businesses, names should indeed be stored in a granular fashion [50] in order to be

---

49 Waymire [1]; "1NF" is the more usual and sensible abbreviation, by the way. Assuming "FNF" means 1st normal form, it isn't clear how the author planned to abbreviate 4th normal form and 5th normal form, since he never gets that far. In any case, the author's definition of first normal form isn't very accurate. Even worse, normal forms are not "rules" to begin with. A database designer is much better served by reading Date [1].

50 ...although the three components listed by the author may often be inadequate, particularly

useful to the business, and for most businesses, separation of address lines into components would more likely be a significant annoyance[51] serving no purpose.

If, however, your particular business is one that utilizes a door-to-door sales force, it might make perfect sense.[52] The lesson, clearly, is that what constitutes a particular Normal Form may actually vary with the granularity required (or desired) by your business. Granularity requirements are often overlooked.

Even More Normal Form Confusion

Looking at the table to the right, it is easy to see that Home_Phone and Work_Phone are REPEATING ELEMENTS, and that the similar Home_Address | Home_City pair[53] and the Work_Address | Work_City pair are REPEATING GROUPS.

PERSON		Sample Data
ID	pk	987654321
First_Name	c15	John
Last_Name	c25	Smith
Home_Phone	c10	123-456-7890
Work_Phone	c10	345-678-9012
Home_Address	c25	123 Main Street
Home_City	c25	Anytown
Work_Address	c25	456 Side Street
Work_City	c25	Anotherville

Examining the Home_Phone and Work_Phone elements, we see that they are formed as combinations of Thing (Phone) and Type-of-Thing ("Home" or "Work"). The fact that they form a repeating element is, of course, a **symptom** – and their presence in this table is a first normal form violation. The actual **problem** is that each is an entity in its own right. The two phone numbers have no inherent relation to one another, their only tenuous connection being that they happen to be currently assigned to John Smith. Most importantly, *their existence doesn't depend at all on his existence*. At the risk of being repetitive, remember that even having a single phone number in this table presents the same problem – and looking for

---

in database structures intended to support multinational or multicultural businesses.

51   The chapter "Contact Mechanisms" demonstrates why this may be far more annoying than it appears on the surface.

52   It might seem that emergency response services might also benefit from such granularity, but these by and large are better served by using GPS coordinates.

53   Other typical address elements, such as "state" have been eliminated for clarity.

normal form violations won't be much help in that case. The phone numbers should therefore be placed in a **Phone_Number** (or similarly named) table, and some sort of relationship established between that table and the **Person** in question[54]. Of course, it isn't always that simple in practice[55], but for the moment this will do.

Although the presence of the repeating **Address** groups also "violates" first normal form, and the problems described for the phone numbers above also exist with Addresses, repeating groups present an additional difficulty in that each of the repeating groups has several attributes of its own. For Addresses specifically, these typically include elements such as **Street**, **City**, and **State**. Whether or not we consider Normal Forms, the presence of any collection of "sub-attributes" in a table is a clear indication that the design is flawed.

Earlier, in "More Normal Form Confusion" on page 33, we discussed the issue of granularity within **First_Name** and **Last_Name** columns, but it is worthwhile revisiting these. When the pairs of attributes for "John Smith" (**First_Name** and **Last_Name**) and (**Home_Phone** and **Work_Phone**) are placed side by side, it might seem that, since both appear to be (Type-of-Thing and Thing) constructs, some parallels can be drawn between how the two are handled, but this is quite misleading. It is important, therefore, to develop the ability to recognize the fundamental differences, since these are seldom addressed in most literature.

RED FLAG

If, in the course of reviewing your proposed table structures, you discover any "normal form violations," experience suggests that there are most assuredly other logical flaws lurking in the design.

A valid corollary to this is that the fact that no normal form violations may have been found cannot be construed to mean that the design is necessarily correct. If the building inspector* finds no flaws, that is certainly an encouraging sign, but not much more.

* see "Particularly Egregious Beliefs: Normal Forms" earlier in this chapter.

---

54 But not, as we shall demonstrate later, between the Phone_Number and Person tables.
55 Logical handling of phone numbers, addresses, and other forms of contact mechanism will be discussed in future chapters.

Type of something	*Component* of something
"Home" and "Work" are Types of Phone, and in no way can they be considered Component parts of Phone. "Home Phone" and "Work Phone" are therefore independent entities and, although "related" to John Smith, have no connection to each other. Additionally, neither of them describe, define, or specify John Smith.	While "First" and "Last" are referred to in some literature as "types" of Name – they are not; "First" and "Last" are actually descriptions of component parts of the attribute **Name**. These component parts are not simply "related" to John Smith – they actually define or specify John Smith.

Any **Phone** entity may, of course, have component parts, such as area-code, prefix and suffix[56], but whether these would be considered to be separate attributes depends largely on the desired level of granularity that would be appropriate for a particular business.

Mildly Offensive Beliefs

In chapter one of "Data Modeling Essentials,"[57] section "1.4 Design, Choice, and Creativity," author Graham Simsion says the following:

> *"First, our objective is to classify data into tables and columns, and there is usually more than one way of doing this. In our insurance model, we might, for example, have specified separate tables for personal customers and corporate customers, or for accident insurance policies and life insurance policies."*

I don't agree. At all. Our first objective is to collect the information, and then define and categorize it appropriately; classification into tables and columns is several steps beyond that. The idea that "there is usually more than one way of doing this" is a bit disingenuous, however and, since it is presented with the implication that this is generally true, certainly cannot be considered good advice. The example that follows in the second sentence is certainly "one way of doing

---

56   Again, be careful, as this breakdown is only valid in North America. Better approaches to handling telephone numbers in a more universal fashion, while maintaining an increased level of data integrity, will be given in the chapter devoted to "Contact Mechanisms."

57   Simsion [1]

this" for example, but in fact, it is logically incorrect. In the chapter "Freedom of the Press: The Customer," we'll show why this is so, and how to prove it.

Particularly Egregious Post-Logical Product Tag Line

When the product Caché was introduced, it was advertised as a "post-relational database." Although possibly an attempt to stress their company's differences in approach from those of the existing relational database management system vendors, they seem to have confused the actual meaning of the word "relational" with its prevailing misinterpretation. The tag line is more or less akin to offering a new pocket calculator that is "post-mathematical." And, of course, Caché isn't a database at all, but yet another (albeit a supposedly "object-relational") database management system[58].

The Cynics Corner

What Ἀντισθένης (Antisthenes), might have thought:

Caché's marketing literature suggests that "If your backend database isn't a good match for your front-end development, you need a new database." Although this is likely true, most businesses could redesign their **database** using the database management product they already own – and that their developers were already somewhat familiar with – so it isn't at all clear how simply purchasing a different **database management system** will address any fundamental design deficiencies.

Always consider the Design before the Product; it's usually more cost-effective.

Particularly Egregious Product Name

A few generations ago, the Oracle Corporation decided to give their flagship product a cooler name, and began calling it "The Oracle Database." Although they were pioneers in the introduction of commercial products intended to support the relational model, Oracle has been steadily expanding their product's scope so, to some extent, the renaming might be be viewed as a marketing ploy to distance themselves from the "Relational" aspects of their RDBMS product. Unfortunately, they also seem to be distancing themselves from precision and logic. When a third party book such as the one described earlier blurs the distinctions between software and data, it is unfortunate; when a major DBMS

---

58 This commentary isn't to be interpreted as an evaluation of the Caché product, simply of its somewhat misleading marketing. As we'll discuss in chapter 9, the "object-relational" impedance mismatch is more of a technical obfuscation than an actual problem.

vendor blurs the distinction, it is a cause for concern since, as stated earlier, what is true or appropriate for one is often not true or appropriate for the other.

In a somewhat related commentary on the distinction between database design and database management, it should be noted that the Oracle Academy, although purportedly offering some lessons on "database design," uses that term to mean "data modeling" – which is not at all the same thing[59], being more closely related to construction than design. As far as I can determine, Oracle doesn't actually offer courses on database design.

Dangerous Comparisons: Databases and Spreadsheets

Under "Relational Database Concepts" on page 170 of their book[60], Welling and Thomson have this to say:

"You don't need to understand relational theory to use a relational database (which is a good thing), but you do need to understand some basic database concepts" and *"If you've used an electronic spreadsheet, you've already used a relational table."*

The authors clearly have no understanding of the relational model whatsoever, although this is but one of many published references that imply some similarity between relational database tables and spreadsheets. Relational tables and spreadsheet pages are not at all similar.

In a spreadsheet, cells, rows and columns are quite independent of each other, whether we wish to assign some meaning to them as groups or not. In a relational table (assuming you actually have such a thing), a row is the primary element. Columns contain attributes that describe and identify the Row, and Columns have no meaning whatever without reference to a specific Row. Columns in a relational table are constrained[61]. In a spreadsheet, a column might

---

59 This isn't in any way intended to single out Oracle (at least they make a wide variety of useful resources available), but simply to suggest that lessons in the use of such products are primarily aimed at developing mechanical skills. These are necessary, but insufficient.

60 Welling [1]; see page 385.

61 The chapter "Handling Constraints" discusses the wide variety of these. If there are no constraints present in a particular table, you are not likely dealing with a relational table.

easily be sorted without any consideration for the spreadsheet's other columns, whereas in a relational table, such a concept isn't meaningful. Should you encounter any material suggesting that lessons learned from working with spreadsheet tables are applicable to relational database tables, do the responsible thing and recycle that material.[62]

In subsequent "Freedom of the Press" chapters as well as in occasional sidebars, we'll discuss other issues, such as the definition of a Customer, use of a single database, misidentification of the Customer, and so forth.

Chainsaws and Relational Databases

A guy walks into a hardware store and says, "I want a chain saw that will cut down ten trees in an hour." So the clerk sells him one.

The next day, the customer comes in, upset. "This chain saw cut down only one little tree in an hour!" The clerk says, "Let me take a look."

He pulls the starter rope, the saw roars to life, and the customer screams, "What's that noise!?"[63]

Given the cost of chainsaws, the above anecdote can be viewed as humorous; given the cost of most RDBMS products, the parallel situation with "relational databases"[64] should raise the ire of most business management personnel.

Many examples of the misuse of RDBMS technology will be presented throughout this book; indeed, an entire chapter is devoted to the silliness of the mythical object-relational impedance mismatch, so continue reading.

---

62 I tend to get tongue-tied when confronted with absurd and illogical nonsense, so you might be advised to read Joe Celko's more reasoned discussion of the differences between spreadsheets and relational tables that appears on page 13 of Celko [1]. And notice how early in his book that appears!

63 This unattributed anecdote appeared in "Laughter, the Best Medicine" on page 24 of the November 2012 issue of the Reader's Digest.

64 A term commonly and mistakenly used by many I/T personnel for non-relational databases built with Relational Database Management Systems.

LESSONS FOR CHAPTER 3

FREEDOM OF THE PRESS: WHAT IS A DATABASE?

► Freedom of the Press is desirable, but results in us having to accept an increased responsibility for validating the information available.

► The terms DATABASE and DATABASE MANAGEMENT SYSTEM are often used interchangeably, but they are not at all the same things, and nothing good will come from conflating the two or confusing their definitions.

► Literature regarding DBMS products, even when provided by the DBMS vendor, is not often the best source for information on database **design**.

► The proposition "Implementing a relational database requires use of a relational database management system," while true, does not equate to "A database implemented using a relational database management system is a relational database."

► A database should be designed to reflect the reality of the facts it is storing and the relationships among these things, regardless of how this data is to be used by any given application or report.

► Identification of Normal Forms is a method of evaluation, not a design technique. Although identifying a table as being in some normal form can be useful, good design requires a more fundamental approach.

   ▼ It helps to understand why having two instances of Phone (e.g. "home phone" and work phone") in a table is a violation of first normal form, while two instances of Name (e.g. "first name" and "last name") is not.

First (and relatively simple) Real-World Example.

How to look critically at existing database structures.
How We Enforce Unintended Business Rules.
How Vague or Inappropriate Naming Causes Harm.

4

4 - A CORPORATE MERGER – PART 1

This chapter will present the first example of how poor database designs directly and negatively affect businesses and their applications. This example will peripherally address a few of the previous assertions about the poor state of database design in a rather gentle, non-threatening manner. While grossly simplified, this first example is based on an actual business[65] or, more correctly, on two actual businesses that eventually merged.

The first of the two companies in this example, which we'll call Wonderful Widgets Corporation (who did business under the acronym WWC), began in a garage by manufacturing and selling its widgets in unit quantities through mail order. Its customers were, for the most part, individual consumers.

Occasionally another business would make a bulk purchase from WWC and, although their customer table (shown on page 42) didn't cleanly accommodate such customers, their employees were able to handle these orders manually and with no particular difficulty. But, the CEO of Wonderful Widgets Corporation was ready to expand, and our team was engaged to assist in the technical aspect of their due diligence and, eventually, in the consolidation of the businesses.

---

65 As the cliche goes: "the names have been changed to protect the guilty" or at least to avoid any embarrassment to them. This is true for all the examples in this book.

On the CEO's behalf, WWC's Chief Financial Officer had just completed negotiations to purchase Corporate Widget Experts (CWX), a much older but complementary business and, in fact, a sometime customer of WWC's that sold similar widgets – primarily in various pack sizes to mid-sized corporate clients.

Knowing that both businesses tracked their respective customers with relational database technology, even using the same RDBMS (Oracle) – and knowing that both used the same programming language (Visual Basic), the expectation of WWC's management was that integration of the two information systems and consolidation of their inventories shouldn't be very difficult or time consuming.

Sample Database Tables from WWC and CWX

Four representative tables from each company are shown below. Common column names have been used to illustrate fundamentally similar attributes, but the table names used by each company are original. The data types, where indicated, are shown as generic character (c) and numeric (n) types for convenience.

Two of WWC's Database Tables

CUSTOMER	
Customer_ID	pk
First_Name	c15
Last_Name	c25
Home_Phone	c10
Work_Phone	c10
Address	c25
City	c25
State	c2
Zip_Code	nc5
Credit_Limit	curr
Income	curr

EMPLOYEE	
Employee_ID	pk
First_Name	c15
Last_Name	c25
Phone_Extension	n3
Home_Address	c25
Home_City	c25
Home_State	c2
Home_Zip_Code	nc5
Home_Phone	n10
Salary	curr
Age	n2
Hire_Date	date

Two of CWX's Database Tables

CUSTOMER	
Customer_ID	pk
Company_Name	c30
Contact_Name	c50
Phone	nc10
Fax	nc10
Billing_Address	c30
Billing_City	c30
Billing_State	c2
Billing_Zip_Code	c9
Shipping_Address	c30
Shipping_City	c30
Shipping_State	c2
Shipping_Zip_Code	c9

VENDOR	
Vendor_ID	pk
Vendor_Name	c35
Phone	nc10
Fax	nc10
Remittance_Address	
Remittance_City	c30
Remittance_State	c2
Remittance_Zip_Code	
Contact_Name	c40
Contact_Phone	nc10

More of WWC's Database Tables

ORDER	
Order_Number	pk
Customer_ID	fk
Order_Date	date
Salesperson	fk
Shipping_Address	c25
Shipping_City	c25
Shipping_State	c2
Shipping_Zip_Code	c5

LINE_ITEM	
Order_Number	pk,fk
Line_Item_Number	pk
Quantity	n3
Part_Number	fk
Unit_Price	curr
Extended_Price	curr

More of CWX's Database Tables

ORDER	
Order_Number	pk
Customer_ID	fk
Order_Date	nc8
Shipping_Address	c30
Shipping_City	c30
Shipping_State	c2
Shipping_Zip_Code	c9

LINE_ITEM	
Order_Number	pk, fk
Line_Item_Number	pk
Quantity	n3
Part_Number	fk
Unit_of_Issue	c4
Unit_Price	curr
Extended_Price	curr

The boards of both corporations were looking forward to strong growth from increased sales opportunities, increased profits, reduced expenses (based on reduced RDBMS and other software licensing costs), and lower inventory management expenses. The I/T groups weren't so sure.

Looking at the disparity in just the few non-relational structures[66] shown here, and knowing that there are many more tables and countless lines of proprietary code within each company's applications, should give pause to anyone having experienced similar integration efforts, whether across departments or enterprises. It is easy for experienced I/T personnel to harbor suspicions that the CEO's expectations of a quick consolidation might have been just a bit naive!

Certainly, there were the typical mismatches that are tedious to reconcile, but usually don't present insurmountable difficulties that can't be addressed with a bit of unpaid overtime. Some of these, in case you hadn't noticed, are:

► WWC used Date data types, while CWX still used a holdover eight-digit numeric format of "yyyymmdd"[67] to store dates.

---

66 If there is the slightest doubt that neither of these companies was using a relational database, you've been snookered. Only three of the eight tables shown are relational, and two of those are incompletely so. By the time you get much further into this book, you'll be able to recognize immediately – often from just looking at a single table – that a database or at least a specific table is not relational.

67 Well, I said they were a much older company, but at least they were Y2K compliant.

► WWC's maximum lengths for its **Address** and **City** elements were generally smaller than those used by CWX.

► For their **Zip_Code** data, WWC specified five numeric characters, while CWX had the respective columns specified more freely as nine alphanumeric characters. CWX had earlier made a change to accommodate six-character Canadian postal codes (which use a combination of alphabetical and numeric characters), and decided that increasing the length to nine characters would also permit them to add nine digit Zip Codes where those were known.

It should be mentioned that neither of the relatively common means of handling addresses used by these companies was very useful from a business standpoint, but that's grist for a specific discussion to come much later.[68]

So precisely why might we suspect that the CEO's expectations might be unrealistic? And how exactly do the data table designs themselves impede the integration process? How would a logical definition and organization of the data (e.g. actual relational database structures) have made this whole process easier? After all, the data structures *seemed* to be serving each companies' existing needs quite adequately!

The first reason is that each of the companies' database designs were enforcing quite a number of unintended BUSINESS RULES that, in some cases, conflicted with the other company's unintentional BUSINESS RULES.

Data Structures as Unintentional Business Rules

This section of the discussion will focus on how Invalid Corollaries result in the **unintentional enforcement of unwanted business restrictions.** *Although reading what looks like a long list of trivial complaints may seem unnecessarily tedious, it is important to at least consider each point, even if you still remain unconvinced there is a better solution to data organization.*

In the trade press, there are occasionally discussions about the wisdom of enforcing business rules in the database, most of which are pointless and annoying, since the critical distinction between BUSINESS (PROCESS) RULES and DATA RULES

---

68 In the chapter titled "Contact Mechanisms" that begins on page 311.

doesn't seem to occur to those making the arguments.[69] In spite of these discussions, common wisdom, even among a lot of I/T people who should know better, is that it is quite difficult to implement and enforce business process rules through data structures alone.

While it is seldom desirable to do so, it is not only possible, but actually easy. It is, in fact, done surprisingly often, albeit unintentionally, by many database designers. The following observations about each example table's elements will illustrate how this happens:

Unintended Business Rules enforced by WWC's CUSTOMER *Table*

We'll start with the most significant business rule being enforced in WWC's database:

☑ "1. Prevent another organization from ever doing business with our company."

CUSTOMER	
Customer_ID	pk
First_Name	c15
Last_Name	c25
Home_Phone	c10
Work_Phone	c10
Address	c25
City	c25
State	c2
Zip_Code	nc5
Credit_Limit	curr
Income	curr

Or, since it has already been noted that such business did, in fact, take place on occasion, the rule might better be stated as:

"1. Make it very difficult, and even require manual intervention[70], to accommodate another organization that wishes to purchase items from our company."

The columns **First_Name**, **Last_Name**, and **Home_Phone** effectively limit the design to handling persons. At the very least, the structure suggests to a casual observer that a potential customer of WWC's must obviously be a person – i.e. Corporations need not apply.

This is a good example of how an INVALID COROLLARY has slipped into the design. The original business requirements, assuming these were ever formally created,

---

69   One such example is discussed in ' "Business Rules" Revisited ' beginning on page 63.

70   … which seems to negate the whole purpose of process automation, and certainly presents scalability issues.

likely stated something along the lines of "we will need to keep information on our customers, including their first and last names," or something similar.

Vague requirements[71] such as this are often fulfilled by implementing contrary rules. "Prevent our company from ever doing business with an organization" is certainly one effective method of implementing what was probably an implied but unstated business requirement:

Requirement: "We are only interested in doing business with individual consumers."

or even:

Requirement: "We have no interest in doing business with any organizations,"

but it is not a sensible or logical method of implementing either one.[72]

In the context of a single application, this may not *appear* to be a serious flaw, but as soon as the business needs to expand, its weakness is revealed. In any larger context, it is simply an unacceptable design.

Remember: these are BUSINESS RULES that have nothing whatever to do with data definitions.

---

71 Interestingly, it has been my observation that the more fundamental the requirement (and recording data about customers would seem to be fundamental), the less likely it is to be satisfactorily stated. The reason for this seems to be an assumption that "everyone knows this" and it would be pointless, a waste of time, or even insulting to clarify the definition.

72 One is tempted to observe that implementing a rule like "Prevent our company from ever doing business with an organization" almost sounds like something a spiteful four year old database designer might do in a pique when confronted by such a requirement: "if I can't eat that cookie, I won't eat anything." I rather suspect that temper tantrums have little if anything to do with most such design decisions, but this common practice does serve to suggest (at least with tongue in cheek) that there is still a bit of immaturity in I/T practices.

☑ "2. Do not permit more than two telephone numbers to be recorded for a Customer, and ensure that the use of these numbers is not flexible."

In this case, one of the numbers was forced to be treated (or at least recorded) as a home phone number and the other as a work phone number.

This is another example of an *INVALID COROLLARY* creeping into the design.

"Don't permit anything but home and work phone numbers" is not a valid or logical corollary to a Requirement stating: "We need to handle both home and work phone numbers."

RED FLAG

The "repeating element" of telephone number (not, as it is sometimes referred to, a "repeating group" - see the comments in rule 4 of the CWX Customer table on page 42) is the type of construct usually presented as an example of a first normal form violation (which it certainly is), but Normal Form Violations are symptoms, and using them as a means of correcting poor database design seldom exposes any but the most egregious errors.

The relatively limited benefits of using Normal Forms to drive design decisions are discussed in "Particularly Egregious Beliefs: Normal Forms" on page 31.

Although no column definitions are given for these example tables (to keep our example simple), it is obvious that one of the following rules exists:

☑ "3. Only permit North American telephone numbers (U.S., Canada, and Mexico and their territories) to be handled.", or

"3. Minimize the restrictions placed on telephone number data (thus encouraging entry of questionable data)."

☑ "4. Do not permit more than one address for a Customer." You probably get the point by now!

Based on the structure of the Address lines, an additional and more interesting rule is being enforced:

☑ "5. Make it difficult, if not impossible, to accept business from customers outside of the United States." This also is an invalid corollary but, if this is like most companies, it is likely that there was no explicit requirement that "we only need to deal with customers in the U.S." – simply an unwarranted (and, again, most likely unrecognized) assumption from which an invalid corollary was illogically derived and then unintentionally enforced.[73]

The need to use multiple columns (we could call them sub-attributes I suppose except that, logically, no such thing exists) for what is essentially a single attribute (Address) clearly indicates that Address should be implemented as a separate table, but that is a separate discussion for a later chapter. See the comments under Rule 5 above.

Certainly Rule 5 is further enforced by the Credit Limit and Income columns, both of which seem to assume U.S. currency (or at least a single common currency across all Customers).

Unintended Business Rules enforced by WWC's EMPLOYEE Table

☑ "6. Make it difficult to upgrade the company's telephone service."

EMPLOYEE	
Employee_ID	pk
First_Name	c15
Last_Name	c25
Phone_Extension	n3
Home_Address	c25
Home_City	c25
Home_State	c2
Home_Zip_Code	nc5
Home_Phone	n10
Salary	curr
Age	n2
Hire_Date	date

Based on the solitary "Phone Extension" column, there is an implication that all employees have the same unspecified base telephone number at work, thus establishing a business rule that will be difficult to overcome should the company shift to a DID[74] telephone system, a circumstance quite likely if the anticipated growth from the CEO's contemplated acquisition occurs. Depending on the particular environment, permitting four or five digit extensions in the future might be difficult with a construct such as this. Proper handling of telephone numbers and other contact mechanisms is discussed in a later chapter.

☑ "7. Do not permit more than one address for an Employee." This, of course, is yet another invalid corollary!

---

73   … and we have the cheek to call this Computer "*Science?*"

74   Direct Inward Dialing, where each person has an individual "outside number" that can be dialed to reach them directly.

A more subtle rule directly affecting the I/T department and the business as a whole is uncovered when we realize that there are Address structures in both the Customer and Employee table: This problem is not generally recognized as a normal form violation since the redundancy occurs over two tables, but it is, in fact, the same logical design flaw even if they are identical.

☑ "8. Ensure that database stored procedures and application code for handling Addresses exist in multiple locations across the company's application portfolio."

The **Address** structures of both the **Company** and **Employee** tables happen to be virtually identical, so it is conceivable that application code can be copied, or even shared under some circumstances, but keep in mind that the number of tables in this example has been severely restricted. And on the off-chance that the company wishes to "go international", this code redundancy as well as lack of reuse could prove extremely costly. It could be therefore argued that this type of design borders on professional irresponsibility! So much for using Normal Form violations as a design technique. Handling of Addresses is discussed in a later chapter.

☑ "9. Maximize the opportunities for maintaining redundant and unsynchronized data throughout the model."

That such a rule exists is evident as soon as we consider the possibility that a Person could be a Customer as well as an Employee.

☑ "10. Do not permit more than one outside telephone number for an Employee. Restrict this to Home Phone. Don't allow a cell-phone number to be stored without modifying the application(s)." Bad!

☑ "11. Ensure that code for handling Telephone numbers is duplicated many times across the company's application portfolio."

Based on the previous rule, and the corresponding Customer rule, this should be easy to spot.

☑ "12. Maximize the potential for invalid data."

An "Age" column is almost always illogical, and certainly impractical, since it requires periodic maintenance in order to remain current. In this case, the Human Resources department insisted that maintaining "age" as a data element was required by law so that potential age discrimination issues could be tracked. I have also encountered use of an "Age" data element in a (at the time) major market research organization. Unlike the broken clock that is right twice a day, data in an Age column begins to decay rather quickly, and is, by definition, obsolete in no more than a year.

Although slightly out of scope here, it should be mentioned that in some countries, age is considered to be an ordinal rather than cardinal number. In other words, you are in your first year at the time of birth (i.e. your age is 1) rather than only being considered age 1 after having reached the first anniversary of your birth as is traditional in the United States.

☑ "13. Make it difficult or confusing to hire anyone who has previously been an employee."

The use of "Hire Date" as a column is not necessarily wrong, but in this case provides incomplete information.

Unintended Business Rules enforced by WWC's ORDER Table

☑ "14. Make it difficult for a non-employee to be tracked as a Salesperson."

☑ "15. Only one Salesperson may be given credit for each Order."

☑ "16. Prevent a single order from being shipped to multiple locations without significant manual intervention." Alternatively, this rule could be stated as:

ORDER	
Order_Number	pk
Customer_ID	fk
Order_Date	date
Salesperson	fk
Shipping_Address	c25
Shipping_City	c25
Shipping_State	c2
Shipping_Zip_Code	c5

"16. Ensure that all line items in each order are shipped to the same address." This rule must, of course, be considered in conjunction with the structure of the Line_Item table below.

Unintended Business Rules enforced by WWC's LINE ITEM Table

☑ "17. Make it difficult for a Customer to order anything but unit quantities of our product. Assume that all units are 'each'."

LINE_ITEM	
Order_Number	pk,fk
Line_Item_Number	pk
Quantity	n3
Part_Number	fk
Unit_Price	curr
Extended_Price	curr

Reinforce the previously established rule "5. Make it difficult, if not impossible, to accept business from customers outside of the United States." by assuming that all unit prices must be in a single currency.

Reinforce the previously established rule "16. Ensure that all line items in each order are shipped to the same address."

As always, whether these rules have any impact on a specific business varies according to the business itself, but the importance of recognizing such occurrences cannot be overstated.

None of these seventeen implicitly existing Business Rules, it should be noted, were clearly recognized when the merger was being considered. As happens in many companies, the programmers had already written code to overcome several of these unintended business rules. Writing code to compensate for illogical, non-relational structures, while unfortunately necessary far more often than it should be, leads very often to increased complexity – not an ideal situation to deal with when a system needs to be updated for any reason.

A common objection to associating shipping addresses with an Order's Line Items rather than the Order itself is that this will usually result in significant data redundancy, but this depends entirely on how the system functions.

First, consider that adding shipping address data to Line Items doesn't necessarily imply that it must be removed from the Order.

Secondly, if the Line Item shipping address information is permitted to be NULL, it can be viewed as an "override" to the Order's address value, rather than a necessary attribute.

How this might be done is beyond the scope of this discussion, but shouldn't present many difficulties to experienced developers.

See the discussion on page 330 for one method of accomplishing this.

Before considering the real significance of these rules, however, let's look at the tables used by the newly acquired CWX operation.

Unintended Business Rules enforced by CWX's Customer Table

For the newly acquired company, the most significant business rule is:

CUSTOMER	
Customer_ID	pk
Company_Name	c30
Contact_Name	c50
Phone	nc10
Fax	nc10
Billing_Address	c30
Billing_City	c30
Billing_State	c2
Billing_Zip_Code	c9
Shipping_Address	c30
Shipping_City	c30
Shipping_State	c2
Shipping_Zip_Code	c9

☑ "1. Prevent (or make it difficult for) an individual person from ever doing business with our company." The single Company Name column implies that this design is meant to handle only organizations.

The parallels between this rule and WWC's rule 1 are not surprising, given that this sort of layout is almost an "industry standard" or (shudder) "best practice."

☑ "2. Do not permit any more than one Contact to be established for each Customer."

☑ "3. Do not permit more than two telephone numbers to be recorded for a Customer, and ensure that their use is not flexible." In this case, one is a generic phone number and the other a fax number.

☑ "4. Do not permit any more than two addresses to be recorded for a Customer, and ensure that their use is not flexible." Another invalid corollary — have you been keeping count?

The two groups of columns dedicated to **Billing_Address** and **Shipping_Address**, by the way, constitute an actual repeating group, unlike the repeating element shown in Rule 2 of WWC's **Customer** table on page 45. Recognition that this constitutes a FIRST NORMAL FORM violation does, in this case, assist us in determining that there is a problem with our design, unlike the parallel situation referred to in Rule 5 of WWC's **Customer** table.

Based on the structure of the Address lines, a further rule being enforced is:

☑ "5. Make it difficult, if not impossible, to accept business from customers outside of the United States."

Unintended Business Rules enforced by CWX's VENDOR Table

☑ "6. Help ensure that code for handling Telephone numbers is duplicated many times across the company's application portfolio."

☑ "7. Help ensure that code for handling Addresses is duplicated many times across the company's application portfolio."

We shall see later (in "Contact Mechanisms") that any contact information, such as telephone numbers and addresses belong to a higher level in the Class structures of most database designs.

VENDOR	
Vendor_ID	pk
Vendor_Name	c35
Phone	nc10
Fax	nc10
Remittance_Address	
Remittance_City	c30
Remittance_State	c2
Remittance_Zip_Code	
Contact_Name	c40
Contact_Phone	nc10

Unintended Business Rules enforced by CWX's ORDER Table

☑ "8. Ensure that all Customer orders can only go to one address." (or make it difficult to do otherwise)

☑ "9. Ensure that hard-copy invoices, statements and other notifications can only be sent to the customer's Billing Address or Shipping Address and standardize this rule across all customers."

ORDER	
Order_Number	pk
Customer_ID	fk
Order_Date	nc8
Shipping_Address	c30
Shipping_City	c30
Shipping_State	c2
Shipping_Zip_Code	c9

Unintended Business Rules enforced by CWX's LINE_ITEM Table

☑ Reinforce rule #5 "Make it difficult, if not impossible, to accept business from customers outside of the United States" by assuming a single, unspecified currency for both unit and extended price columns.

LINE_ITEM	
Order_Number	pk, fk
Line_Item_Number	pk
Quantity	n3
Part_Number	fk
Unit_of_Issue	c4
Unit_Price	curr
Extended_Price	curr

Unwanted and Unintended Business Rules – Conclusions

Implementing non-relational[75] database designs similar to those above needlessly limits the flexibility required by any typical business. I've heard it argued that the impact of such unintentional rules is trivial. Tell that to the business manager who has spent several times the projected cost for a system, and who is then told that it will take two weeks or more to update the database and modify all the affected applications and reports in order to simply add a second contact to the customer information. It is troubling that this type of "business rule" exists at all. It is more troubling to observe that many I/T practitioners seem unaware not only that such rules exist, but that they can have far-reaching and cumulative effects.[76]

But it isn't only invalid and/or unintended business rules that interfere with extensibility and flexibility. A very obvious difficulty with consolidating the models of the existing and acquired companies in this example is that their respective definitions of *Customer*, at least as implemented, were quite different. As we shall see, each was thought (or more likely just assumed) to be correct in its own myopic view, but neither of them was correct in the real world.

Accidents often occur at Intersections

Drivers, passengers, and pedestrians are known to be at great risk when traversing intersections. Database designs are also at risk when they cross intersections, particularly when no one recognizes them. As with pedestrians on the street, it is often the innocent bystanders: business operations, information architecture, ap-

---

75   We shall see in a subsequent section precisely what makes these structures non-relational, and illustrate that use of a relational database design would have prevented many of these "unintended business rules" from ever being implemented in the first place.

76   Some "unintentional rules" originate with analysts who fail to recognize the difference between requirements and thinly disguised implementation instructions. Invalid corollaries can and do originate just as often in the user community as they do in the I/T community. But this isn't a treatise on requirements, so pursuing this observation to its logical conclusion would be out of scope. Consider such a pursuit to be an optional homework exercise.

plication development, etc. that are most seriously harmed by negligence. Before proceeding, let's review what an INTERSECTION is in logical terms.

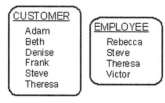

First, consider some possible entries in WWC's Customer and Employee tables (obviously greatly abbreviated): WWC has four employees (Rebecca, Steve, Theresa and Victor) who handle the orders from their six customers (Adam, Beth, Denise, Frank, Steve, and Theresa). Although this diagram is simply a reflection of the existing design, the company is apparently storing at least some redundant data (at the very least, the names) about their customers Steve and Theresa, who both also happen to be their employees.

Because Steve and Theresa are members of both sets[77], we say that the Customer and Employee sets intersect, as shown graphically on the right. Obviously, there is some overlap between these two Classes, and if this isn't properly reflected in the database design, we aren't taking advantage of all the relational model (as well as the particular RDBMS product we invested in) has to offer.

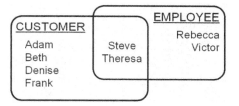

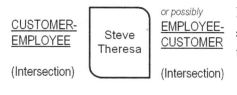

In an actual database, an INTERSECTION such as the one shown above can either be a transient *result set*, e.g. based on the SQL:

```
SELECT c.name
    FROM customer c, employee e
WHERE c.name = e.name),
```

---

77   In *Set* notation, this could be represented as: "C ={a, b, d, f, s, t}" and "E = {r, s, t, v}" where, by convention, capital letters represent *Sets* and small letters represent *Members* of the set. In the synopsis, it was mentioned that this document is not intended to be a tutorial on database design. Neither is it intended to be a tutorial on set theory (or much else for that matter). Examples such as this are provided merely to illustrate the effects of poor analysis and how these effects can neutralize many of the promised benefits of RDBMS products, programming methodologies, etc.

---

or it can be physically implemented as a table (not appropriate in this example), in which case it is usually given a meaningful name of its own, like **Customer-Employee** or **Employee-Customer**, as shown in the illustration[78].

Determining whether an INTERSECTION should be physically implemented is largely based on whether the intersection itself has (*or could have*) unique attributes. In this example, however, the **Employee-Customer** intersection has no unique attributes (**Employee_Discount** might be a possibility, particularly if the percentage varied across employees). Although it seems trivial, it is apparent that, if either Steve or Theresa have a name change, the change must be made in at least two places in order for the company's data to remain internally consistent. The larger impact of this type of design becomes painfully apparent when companies begin to integrate data within their organization, exchange data with other companies, or embark on CRM, ERP, EAI, or similar efforts. Where one such example of the potential for data redundancy (and therefore unnecessary costs) exists, it is likely that many do.

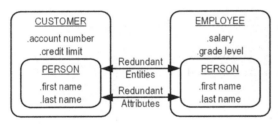

In this graphic representation of WWC's **Customer** and **Employee** tables, it should be apparent that each of these entities are really intersections that have been physically (and mistakenly) implemented as separate tables.

WWC's **Customer** table should actually have been an INTERSECTION that is really a collection of data about "Persons who are Customers" or "Customers who are Persons", not simply "Customers." In similar fashion, their **Employee** table should have been an INTERSECTION representing "Employees who are Persons" or "Persons who are Employees."

---

78 The choice often leads to vicious religious conflict in some organizations, so it is helpful early in the design stages to settle on some mutually acceptable rules for prioritization. In most cases, one requirement should always be that a cogent argument can be made for the choice. Logically, it really makes no difference, but some consistency should be evident. See the discussion of Naming in "A Corporate Merger – Part 2."

Note that, in each case, the name given by Wonderful Widgets Corporation to the combination of the two entities is the same as the name of only one component of the INTERSECTION entity. The potential for redundant data about any Persons who happen to be both Customers as well as some other type of Person (e.g. contact, employee, and so forth) should also be apparent.

Interestingly enough, however, although the name given to WWC's **Customer** table is obviously wrong (it is really an INTERSECTION and logically should be called **Customer-Person** or **Person-Customer**), applying the name **Employee-Person** or **Person-Employee** to the table currently called **Employee** doesn't seem to (and indeed would not) be correct. The intuitive reason for this is that it would be redundant to specify that an Employee is a Person (what else could an employee be, after all?). There is another reason, but we'll get to that later on.

To understand the difference between the two situations, and why intuition is correct in this example, consider the following pairs of Propositions[79]:

Customers and Persons	Employees and Persons
T "A Customer may be a Person" is **TRUE**.	? "An Employee may be a Person" is **INCOMPLETE**.
T "A Person may be a Customer" is **TRUE**.	T "A Person may be an Employee" is **TRUE**.
F "A Customer must be a Person" is **FALSE**.	T "An Employee must be a Person" is **TRUE**.
F "A Person must be a Customer" is **FALSE**.	F "A Person must be an Employee" is **FALSE**.
F "Any Customer is a Person" is **FALSE**.	T "Any Employee is a Person" is **TRUE**.
F "Any Person is a Customer" is **FALSE**	F "Any Person is an Employee" is **FALSE**
F "All Customers are Persons" is **FALSE**.	T "All Employees are Persons" is **TRUE**.
F "All Persons are Customers" is **FALSE**.	F "All Persons are Employees" is **FALSE**.

For Customers and Persons, the paired statements are either **both true** or **both false**, but for Employees and Persons, only one of each pair is true. When the

---

79 I will reiterate that this book is not intended primarily as a tutorial on database design, but merely an effort to demonstrate *why* better database designs are needed. Nonetheless, analysis of statements (normalized propositions) like this that are derived from an existing database schema can be very useful in determining whether the design reflects reality. "May be a Person" and similar constructs are Predicates, by the way. Since one premise of this book is that Logic is an immensely useful tool in achieving useful and non-obstructive database designs, we will begin exploring that subject in a little more detail in the next chapter.

truth or falsehood of both the statements and their reversals are identical (as with Customers and Persons), the subjects intersect, but have no dependency on one another. Further, there is no superset-subset relationship between them.

On the other hand, when one proposition of each pair is true and the proposition with the subjects reversed is false (as with Employees and Persons), the subject for which the statements are true is a subset of the subject for which the statements are false (Employee, being the subject of the true statements, is a subset of Person). These facts appear more clearly and intuitively when shown in graphic form: Customer and Person overlap, forming an INTERSECTION. Note however that there are areas of Customer that do not fall within the Person boundary and areas of Person that do not fall within the Customer boundary.

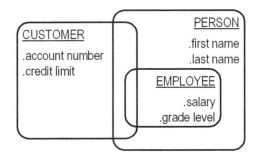

The case with the Employee set is quite different, since there are no areas within the Employee boundary that are not also within the Person boundary and, in fact, there cannot be any. Employee is therefore said to be a PROPER SUBSET of Person. For the remainder of this discussion, I will follow the convention of using the term INTERSECTION to refer only to any such crossovers between sets regardless of whether they have a Superset-Subset relationship to one another.

Note the enterprise/global/architectural perspective of showing Person as a single entity (i.e. both examples share the Person set rather than repeating it for each pair). Using this perspective ensures that our design remains congruent with reality.

> *Propositions such as those in the chart above can easily be derived from existing database designs for testing and validation, by the way.*

Graphic representations, such as that above, can further clarify the model. Any part of a database schema, while it may not completely represent reality (perhaps because, as in our example, the company doesn't currently care about customers who are not employees), must never *conflict* with reality.

Models that conflict with reality or that represent data about "Things the company is interested in" in a way that suits only a specific application or department will inevitably impede any attempts at application (and therefore business) extension, flexibility, etc.[80]

Unlike any approach that renders the sets of "Things the company is interested in" in a way that suits only a specific application or department, the reality-based approach will always work. Further, although this approach will not guarantee extensibility on its own, it will permit and encourage it, and will certainly expose more opportunities for code reuse. More importantly, the longer term benefits to the business far outweigh the effort involved. More surprisingly, the longer term benefits to I/T personnel, particularly application programmers, will also outweigh the effort. This makes sense when one considers that simplification is really a process of eliminating the unnecessary, not distorting it as poor database designs usually do.

Integration of the two Companies

Chris Date emphasizes the applicability of predicate logic to the internals of an individual RelVar (as he calls the structure to distinguish it from its contents, which form the actual relation). It is clear from the earlier foundations of the relational model that predicate logic can and should be applied to the database as a whole, and that ignoring this is one of the factors leading to the appearance of what has been termed an object-relational impedance mismatch. The previous section actually broached the use of very basic predicate logic, and this section will add a trivial example of how integrating the example tables based on a natural taxonomy can help considerably.

Each of the companies in the example had based its implementation of **Customer** on the needs of a specific application or on its current business model. Nei-

---

80 There are those who claim that a downside to reality-based models is that the applications incur performance hits. In the few examples where this is noticeable, there are usually other factors in play, but these will be addressed in a later section. It is nonetheless disconcerting to listen to arguments from "computer-*scientists*" advocating designs that do not reflect reality or logic, but merely their own convenience.

ther of these is a good or even sensible idea. Data should represent facts in their natural taxonomies[81], without regard to processes or practices.

Collapsed Hierarchies

The term "collapsed hierarchies" simply refers to the situations where designers have inappropriately included one class within another. An example of this is the inclusion of person attributes within an employee entity set, as described above. Consider the diagram below, which illustrates portions of the structures that need to be consolidated to merge WWC with CWX.

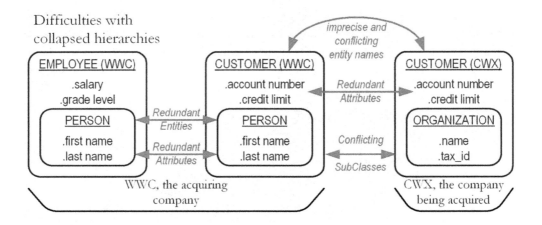

If we compare CWX's **Customer** table to WWC's **Customer** and **Employee** tables in the diagrams presented earlier, it becomes very clear that the improper naming (and perhaps lack of recognition) of intersections will require reworking the application code for each company if the integration is not going to result in even more unworkable (and further limiting) compromises in the design. On the other hand, if the tables were, respectively, **Person**, **Employee**, **Customer**, **Customer-Person** and **Customer-Organization**, the integration would have been relatively painless.

---

81   Or, at the very least, as we will repeat ad nauseum, the data structures should not *conflict* with any natural taxonomies.

The logically correct integration of these sets is shown to the right with the sample attributes assigned to the correct sets.

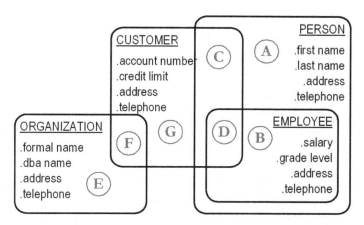

The letters A through G represent members of the various classes and will not be discussed until we revisit these diagrams in the chapter dealing with implementation. The most important thing we can learn from this diagram (actually, it's the thought that counts, but the diagram helps to illustrate the point) is that *there are redundant attributes listed*. These attributes, which are common to **all** the Classes, include Address and Telephone Number, and tell us logically that each of these four entities **must be a subset of some more generic set**, which we'll illustrate in the figure below.

Deja Vu

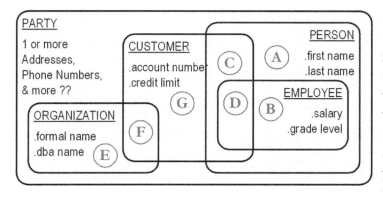

Comparing this to the similar diagram in "Party Seating Chart" on page 3, we discover that we've stumbled on a super-class through our bottom-up analysis that seems to be the same thing as the Party entity set we postulated in the earlier top-down analysis. In technical terms, this is called a "Good Sign" and tends to validate our earlier conclusion.

It should be reasonably easy to see that neither WWC nor CWX had a reality based model, and this contributed to the difficulties encountered when integrating the two data models and their associated application portfolios. Once both were fit into a reality based logical model, however (essentially as shown in the figure below, although this is incomplete and glosses over some obvious complexities), the integration was fairly straightforward. Nonetheless, due to the original myopic designs, the level of application rework for table name changes, column sizes, and the like was still significant.

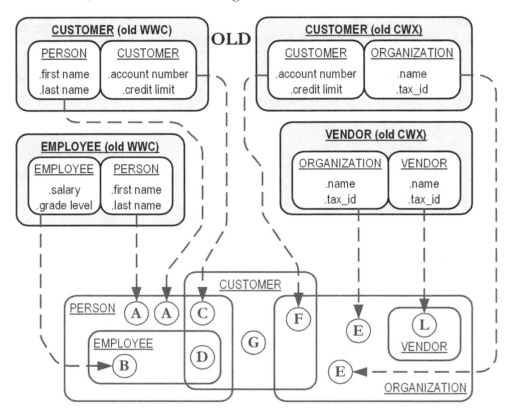

The overall mapping of information from the four sample tables in the example to the new model is shown above. Since the previously existing models did not actually *conflict* with reality in terms of their customer taxonomies (i.e. they were simply incomplete, ill-named, and tended to impede extension), the mapping of the data presented few serious challenges.

The original intersections of WWC and CWX are shaded in the diagram for clarity. Not shown is that all the entities in the diagram were implemented as subsets of Party – the supertype that "has" Addresses, Communications Mechanisms (e.g. telephone numbers, e-mail addresses, etc.).[82]

Consider that, at this point, the diagram of the integrated company's data model looks way more like a hierarchical object model than the more commonly used ERD (Entity-Relationship Diagram). This is not at all coincidental, and will be discussed in greater detail in the chapter "Freedom of the Press - Impedance Mismatches" which begins on page 145.

"Business Rules" Revisited

In "What Not How,"[83] Chris Date says "Frankly, it's hard to draw a sharp dividing line between database rules and application rules." He further says "Foreign Keys are an important special case of business rules in general," and uses the following (which I've paraphrased) to illustrate his point.

A **Customer** can have 0, 1, or many **Order**s.	An **Order** is only from 1 **Customer**.
An **Order** can have 1 or more **Line Item**s.	A **Line Item** belongs to only 1 **Order**.
A **Part** can be associated with many **Line Item**s.	A **Line Item** involves just 1 **Part**.

It's not that I draw the dividing line between business rules and application rules in a different location than he does; in my definition, none of these propositions are either type of "rule," but rather simply reflections of reality. I therefore fully support the use of foreign keys to enforce these facts. It may be possible that some company exists for which these rules do not reflect the reality, but I believe any such example would qualify as an exception deserving special handling.

---

82 Another reminder – this is not a tutorial on database design. For a very good description of why and how Party is used, see page 22 of Silverston [1].

83 Date [3], Chapter 4; page 25; see page 382 for details.

To clarify: these propositions are all taxonomically correct – an order must be placed by some Party; by definition the Party placing the order is or represents a Customer. These are therefore statements of fact – not specific to any business. These statements reflect reality, not some corporate policy. These statements will always be true; unlike corporate policies and processes, they will not change.

Of course if Date simply means that a business must conform to reality – that is it must not create database designs that are not in conformance with reality – then I agree completely.

Conclusion

The physical redesign and integration of the WWC and CWX systems obviously needed to address the issues of redundancy, code duplication, inconsistency across tables and applications and so forth. The redesign will be covered in "A Corporate Merger – Part 2" beginning on page 127. Before doing that, though, we will first visit the subjects of "Grammar, Sets, and (Predicate) Logic – Part 1" and the "Recent History of Data Management".

LESSONS FOR CHAPTER 4
A CORPORATE MERGER - PART I

► This Chapter provides examples of how

▼ Poor (actually logically incorrect) naming of entities or data elements can cause a variety of difficulties that are felt, but not always recognized.

▼ Poor database designs can and do enforce unintended and often undesirable "business rules."

▼ These unintended rules are often unrecognized until the business attempts some change or expansion. Programmers often "code around" these restrictions as a matter of course without ever realizing they are compensating for poor and/or illogical database design.

► Lack of recognition of the fundamental difference between subclasses and intersections causes difficulties, and these are felt throughout the company's application portfolio.

► Good relational models of fundamental business entities often bear a surprising[84] (to some folks) resemblance to good object models.

► Data *structures* should never be used to enforce Business Rules, only to enforce Data Rules.[85]

---

84   ...surprising only to amateurs or those taken in by a belief in the mythical "object-relational impedance mismatch." See the chapter "Freedom of the Press - Impedance Mismatches".

85   In example 4 of chapter 15 in Date [2], the structures Chris Date discusses present a perfect opportunity to consider the effects of such a rule in a common situation. Note his arbitrary assumption that a Programmer is an Employee, which is really a business rule, not a data rule. See the discussions on pages 245 and 249 for a logically correct solution.

'Ἐπεὶ δ' ἀδύνατον ἄλλως ἔχειν οὗ ἐστιν ἐπιστήμη ἁπλῶς, ἀναγκαῖον ἂν εἴη τὸ ἐπιστητὸν τὸ κατὰ τὴν ἀποδεικτικὴν ἐπιστήμην. ἀποδεικτικὴ δ' ἐστὶν ἣν ἔχομεν τῷ ἔχειν ἀπόδειξιν· ἐξ ἀναγκαίων ἄρα συλλογισμός ἐστιν ἡ ἀπόδειξις. ληπτέον ἄρα ἐκ τίνων καὶ ποίων αἱ ἀποδείξεις εἰσίν. πρῶτον δὲ διορίσωμεν τί λέγομεν τὸ κατὰ παντὸς καὶ τί τὸ καθ' αὑτὸ καὶ τί τὸ καθόλου.

Κατὰ παντὸς μὲν οὖν τοῦτο λέγω ὃ ἂν ᾖ μὴ ἐπὶ τινὸς μὲν τινὸς δὲ μή, μηδὲ ποτὲ μὲν ποτὲ δὲ μή· οἷον εἰ κατὰ παντὸς ἀνθρώπου ζῷον, εἰ ἀληθὲς τόνδ' εἰπεῖν ἄνθρωπον, ἀληθὲς καὶ ζῷον, καὶ εἰ νῦν θάτερον, καὶ θάτερον, καὶ εἰ ἐν πάσῃ γραμμῇ στιγμή, ὡσαύτως. σημεῖον δέ· καὶ γὰρ τὰς ἐνστάσεις οὕτω φέρομεν ὡς κατὰ παντὸς ἐρωτώμενοι, ἢ εἰ ἐπί τινι μή, ἢ εἴ ποτε μή.

Καθ' αὑτὰ δ' ὅσα ὑπάρχει τε ἐν τῷ τί ἐστιν, οἷον τριγώνῳ γραμμὴ καὶ γραμμῇ στιγμή (ἡ γὰρ οὐσία αὐτῶν ἐκ τούτων ἐστί, καὶ ἐν τῷ λόγῳ τῷ λέγοντι τί ἐστιν ἐνυπάρχει)· καὶ ὅσοις τῶν ὑπαρχόντων¹ αὐτοῖς αὐτὰ ἐν τῷ λόγῳ ἐνυπάρχουσι τῷ τί ἐστι δηλοῦντι, οἷον τὸ εὐθὺ ὑπάρχει γραμμῇ καὶ τὸ περιφερές, καὶ τὸ ἄρτιον καὶ περιττὸν ἀριθμῷ, καὶ τὸ πρῶτον καὶ σύνθετον καὶ ἰσόπλευρον καὶ ἑτερόμηκες· καὶ πᾶσι τούτοις ἐνυπάρχουσιν ἐν τῷ λόγῳ τῷ τί ἐστι λέγοντι ἔνθα μὲν γραμμὴ ἔνθα δ' ἀριθμός. ὁμοίως δὲ καὶ ἐπὶ τῶν ἄλλων τὰ τοιαῦθ' ἑκάστοις καθ' αὑτὰ λέγω, ὅσα δὲ μηδετέρως ὑπάρχει συμβεβηκότα, οἷον τὸ μουσικὸν ἢ λευκὸν τῷ ζῴω. ἔτι δ' μὴ καθ' ὑποκειμένου λέγεται ἄλλου τινός, οἷον τὸ βαδίζον ἕτερόν τι ὂν βαδίζον ἐστί, καὶ τὸ¹ λευκόν, ἡ δ' οὐσία καὶ ὅσα τόδε τι σημαίνει οὐχ ἕτερόν τι ὄντα ἐστὶν ὅπερ ἐστί. τὰ μὲν δὴ μὴ καθ' ὑποκειμένου καθ' αὑτὰ λέγω, τὰ δὲ καθ' ὑποκειμένου συμβεβηκότα. ἔτι δ' ἄλλον τρόπον τὸ μὲν δι' αὑτὸ ὑπάρχον ἑκάστῳ καθ' αὑτό, τὸ δὲ μὴ δι' αὑτὸ συμβεβηκός, οἷον εἰ βαδίζοντος ἤστραψε, συμ-

βεβηκός· οὐ γὰρ διὰ τὸ βαδίζειν ἤστραψεν, ἀλλὰ συνέβη, φαμέν, τοῦτο. εἰ δὲ δι' αὑτό, καθ' αὑτό, οἷον εἴ τι σφαττόμενον ἀπέθανε καὶ κατὰ τὴν σφαγήν, ὅτι διὰ τὸ σφάττεσθαι, ἀλλ' οὐ συνέβη σφαττόμενον ἀποθανεῖν. τὰ ἄρα λεγόμενα ἐπὶ τῶν ἁπλῶς ἐπιστητῶν καθ' αὑτὰ οὕτως ὡς ἐνυπάρχειν τοῖς κατηγορουμένοις ἢ ἐνυπάρχεσθαι δι' αὑτά τέ ἐστι καὶ ἐξ ἀνάγκης. οὐ γὰρ ἐνδέχεται μὴ ὑπάρχειν ἢ ἁπλῶς ἢ τὰ ἀντικείμενα, οἷον γραμμῇ τὸ εὐθὺ ἢ τὸ καμπύλον καὶ ἀριθμῷ τὸ περιττὸν ἢ τὸ ἄρτιον. ἔστι γὰρ τὸ ἐναντίον ἢ στέρησις ἢ ἀντίφασις ἐν τῷ αὐτῷ γένει, οἷον ἄρτιον τὸ μὴ περιττὸν ἐν ἀριθμοῖς ᾗ ἕπεται. ὥστ' εἰ ἀνάγκη φάναι ἢ ἀποφάναι, ἀνάγκη καὶ τὰ καθ' αὑτὰ ὑπάρχειν.

Τὸ μὲν οὖν κατὰ παντὸς καὶ καθ' αὑτὸ διωρίσθω τὸν τρόπον τοῦτον· καθόλου δὲ λέγω ὃ ἂν κατὰ παντός τε ὑπάρχῃ καὶ καθ' αὑτὸ καὶ ᾗ αὐτό. φανερὸν ἄρα ὅτι ὅσα καθόλου ἐξ ἀνάγκης ὑπάρχει τοῖς πράγμασιν. τὸ καθ' αὑτὸ δὲ καὶ ᾗ αὐτὸ ταὐτόν, οἷον καθ' αὑτὴν τῇ γραμμῇ ὑπάρχει στιγμὴ καὶ τὸ εὐθύ· καὶ γὰρ ᾗ γραμμή· καὶ τῷ τριγώνῳ ᾗ τρίγωνον δύο ὀρθαί· καὶ γὰρ καθ' αὑτὸ τὸ τρίγωνον δύο ὀρθαῖς ἴσον. τὸ καθόλου δὲ ὑπάρχει τότε, ὅταν ἐπὶ τοῦ τυχόντος καὶ πρώτου δεικνύηται. οἷον τὸ δύο ὀρθὰς ἔχειν οὔτε τῷ σχήματί ἐστι καθόλου (καίτοι ἔστι δεῖξαι κατὰ σχήματος ὅτι δύο ὀρθὰς ἔχει, ἀλλ' οὐ τοῦ τυχόντος σχήματος, οὐδὲ χρῆται τῷ τυχόντι σχήματι δεικνύς¹· τὸ γὰρ τετράγωνον σχῆμα μέν, οὐκ ἔχει δὲ δύο ὀρθαῖς ἴσας). τὸ δ' ἰσοσκελὲς ἔχει μὲν τὸ τυχὸν δύο ὀρθαῖς ἴσας, ἀλλ' οὐ πρῶτον, ἀλλὰ τὸ τρίγωνον πρότερον. ὃ τοίνυν τὸ τυχὸν πρῶτον δείκνυται δύο ὀρθὰς ἔχον ἢ ὁτιοῦν ἄλλο, τούτῳ πρώτῳ ὑπάρχει καθόλου, καὶ ἡ ἀπόδειξις καθ' αὑτὸ τούτου καθόλου ἐστί, τῶν δ' ἄλλων τρόπον τινὰ οὐ καθ' αὑτό· οὐδὲ τοῦ ἰσοσκελοῦς οὐκ ἔστι καθόλου ἀλλ' ἐπὶ πλέον.

Posterior Analytics – Book (chapter) 4
– Aristotle

Aristotle's original introduction (in Attic Greek) to the concept of distinguishing between Essential and Accidental Attributes in the design of Relational Databases, first presented to the world more than two thousand years ago. Although largely forgotten over time, these are still very relevant today. See "Grammar: Verbs and Adjectives" on page 72 for more information.

"The secret lies in keeping a steady course between the waves of madness and the straight lines of logic."
— Salvador Dali (1904-1989)

"Intelligence itself may have evolved as a means to organize memories."
— Dr. Joel Fagot; London Guardian; November 2006

Illustration: Reverend Charles Lutwidge Dodgson (1832-1898)
(more well known as Lewis Carroll)

5 - GRAMMAR, SETS, AND (PREDICATE) LOGIC – PART 1

Introduction

LOGIC, although given a token level of lip service when discussing software creation, doesn't seem to be viewed as being at all germane to the design of databases. GRAMMAR, save for the syntax requirements of our programming languages, is often considered even less relevant to our designs. It is the intent of this chapter to show that common database design practices currently reflect the Egyptian Rule (see page 17). Current database design practices are sclerotic – still heavily influenced by the many technical inadequacies of early computer technology[86] – inadequacies known by our predecessors but accepted in order to take advantage of the benefits that technology could still bring to Business.

For the most part, those early technological constraints are no longer with us and, in order to mature (and move to our Greek phase), we need to begin exploring and taking advantage of the fundamental underpinnings of data management – to acquire a more detailed understanding of why we should be doing things a certain way, and what improvements this added maturity can bring to both our databases and our software.

---

86   This will be discussed and clarified in the chapter "Recent History of Data Management."

Logic, particularly Predicate Logic – the foundation of the Relational Model – must be based on the ability to precisely define the "Things" we need to deal with in a Business Database, and must drive, or at the very least inform, our decisions regarding the data models we use so that we can avoid the many business traps (and their accompanying costs) presented as examples in several chapters of this book[87].

Grammar, for its part, is fundamental to Logic of any sort. Grammar forms the basis of Propositions, which themselves are the basis of Predicate Logic – a tool that not only permits us to design better database structures, but allows us to more easily identify even subtle flaws in our existing database designs.

The Skeptics Corner

"Most of the occasions for the troubles of the world are grammatical."

Lord Michel Eyquem de Montaigne (28 Feb 1533-13 Sep 1592). Montaigne is known as the Father of Modern Skepticism

So in this chapter, we will begin with some basic Grammar, show how logical thought proceeds from grammar, and eventually show how an elementary form of Predicate Logic is used in real-world database design.

Although the idea of wading through basic grammar sounds like something you might want to skip, it isn't. For one thing, it's actually quite encouraging to realize that there is some science and logic that can be applied to assist in the often chaotic assembly of the tables we create for our databases; for another, when the few elements of grammar presented here are related to Aristotle's pronouncements on the organization of facts, you'll find a surprising amount of enlightenment on how to approach the design of a business database.

Basic Grammar Elements used in Database Design

Luckily, the level of grammar that we need to deal with when analyzing and correcting database designs consists of fairly basic elements and constructs (we'll revisit the implications of that at the end of this chapter.) The ones you need to be familiar with are covered below, along with commentary from our some of

---

87   For instance: "A Corporate Merger – Part 1," "Playing with Trucks – Part 1," as well as other incidental examples scattered throughout the book.

our esteemed predecessors about how these relate to the design of databases. First are the fundamental Parts of Speech[88] in which we have an interest:

Grammar: Nouns

▶ **Noun**: A Noun refers to a person, place, or other "Thing" (for example an object, concept, idea, or event). There are three generally recognized types of Nouns: Proper Nouns, Common Nouns, and Collective Nouns.

▼ *Proper Nouns* name specific persons, places, or things (for example: "Lewis Carroll," "Baltimore," "The John Hancock Building," the "Spirit of Saint Louis," and the "Chicago Bears"), and are generally capitalized in English.

 Aristotle, in "Categories," Book I, part 5.14, refers to such unique and individually identifiable "things" as **Primary Substance**s, and tells us there are many things that help characterize Primary Substances: a Primary Substance can never be subdivided into equivalent things; a Primary Substance has no possible contrary, although it may have contrary qualities over time, etc.

 Lewis Carroll, in "Symbolic Logic," Book 1, Chapter II, adds that an individually identifiable Thing or any Class to which it might belong need not be "real" or physical.

Although perhaps not obvious from this definition, it isn't the naming itself that makes these items uniquely identifiable. A random man on the street, for example, is obviously a specific and unique person, but we don't need to know his name to determine (or at least suspect) that.

When contemplating database design, we extend the usual grammatical definition to any uniquely identifiable "Thing" whether it has its own name or not. What Aristotle refers to as a Primary Substance might be anything with a serial number or other unique identifier, for example (an "instance" in OO terms).

It seems intuitive that Primary Substances – those things that qualify as Proper Nouns – will always be data elements in a well-designed database, and never entities, tables, or the like. Surprisingly, however, examples where this happens are not that rare[89] and should be examined carefully if encountered.

---

88 And, yes, parts of speech are not specific to database design, so you are welcome to pull out your old grammar textbooks for further illumination of these and other parts of speech.

89 A typical case is where a database contains a table for the Company itself separate from other companies it may track. While this may seem useful in some circumstances, it presents logical inconsistencies in managing a database and any applications that use it. But this isn't

Aristotle tells us several things about **Secondary Substances** in 2.2 of his Categories:

...that we predicate (that is, infer the existence of) a general Class such as "Person" (a Common Noun) from the existence of specific examples of a Person (such as "Lewis Carroll" listed above).

... that any Class (Secondary Substance: a Set described by a Common Noun), and in fact anything that is not a Primary Substance, is "predicable of" (that is "can be inferred from the existence of") at least one (even theoretical) instance of a Primary Substance.

... that it must be true that any Primary Substance (one identified by a Proper Noun) can be categorically classified as either "being in" or "not being in" the Secondary Substance (identified by a Common Noun), and if this isn't possible, the Set doesn't qualify as a Secondary Substance or a Class.

▼ ***Common Nouns*** identify a general class of persons, places, or things (for example "employee," "city," "building," "plane," "team"). In Logic, or in Database Design specifically, this type of Noun can refer to either a SET or a CLASS. (we'll defer the important distinction between the two until we get to Collective Nouns below). In addition to the commentary on the left, Aristotle also tells us that, in order to qualify as a Secondary Substance (a "Thing" that we identify with a Common Noun), the "Thing" **must have no possible contrary** other than the theoretical set "not a Thing." For example, there is no contrary to "Person" other than the artificial "not-a-Person" set – which includes every other possible existing "Thing"; if such a contrary exists, the Noun is not a Common Noun, the Set being described is not a Class, and it doesn't represent a Secondary Substance. While there may be exceptions based on specific business reasons, Classes identified by Common Nouns should always be implemented as tables within a database unless there is a very good reason for not doing so.

Because of its critical importance to database design, assigning Names to Common Nouns will be discussed separately in "Naming our Things" below.

Aristotle Categories 2.3

Any Set is a "collection," and never a "composition." This of course applies to Classes and Common Nouns, since they are Sets. A Person may have two arms, two legs, and so forth, but such a list of body parts defines a composition, not a collection. A Person missing a leg is still (logically and legally) a Person.

▼ ***Collective nouns*** give a name to identifiable groups, but groups that are ultimately arbitrary or transient. A Collective Noun may refer to a group of persons (but not all persons), places (but not all places), or things (but not all things). In Logic, a Collective Noun always describes a Set, but since it doesn't necessarily include all members of the Set, it doesn't represent a

the place to discuss such arcana.

Class. Examples of Collective Nouns include "Staff," "Fleet," "League" and so forth).

▼   Other types of Nouns and Pronouns, including Abstract, Concrete, Appositives, Gerunds, and others, are identified in some grammar texts, but these can be viewed for our purposes as subsets of Proper, Common, and Collective Nouns. For purposes of database design and analysis, we generally have no need to make these additional distinctions.

Sets and Classes – The Crucial Difference

So, what is the distinction between a Class and a Set? The first thing to note is that, while a Class must always be a Set, a Set is not necessarily a Class.

A Class[90], as noted above, includes (by definition) all Primary Substances from which the existence of the Class can be inferred (or predicated, as Lewis Carroll would say), whether they are known to us or not. A Set *might* include all such substances (in which case it would qualify as a Class), but doesn't need to.

For example: All Persons we know of (as well as those we don't) are members of the Class called by the Common Noun "Person." While some Persons will be members of the arbitrary Set called by the Collective Noun "Staff," it will rarely be the case that all Persons known to us, much less those we aren't aware of, will be members of the Set called "Staff."

The distinction between Common Nouns (Secondary Substances or Classes) and Collective Nouns is therefore very important to logical database design[91]. It will generally always be true that a set identified as a Class – that is a Set identified by a Common Noun – should end up after our analysis and design processes as a physical database table. Whether those sets identified by a Collective Noun become tables or simply transient results sets is far too dependent on a specific implementation to allow us to provide a general rule-of-thumb but it is

---

90   The term "Class" as used in object-oriented programming is defined much more loosely, but the implications of this important distinction will not be discussed until a later chapter.

91   It bears repeating that, throughout this book, I am using the word "logical" literally, and not as distinguished from "physical."

hard to argue that anything good will result from creating a physical database structure based on an arbitrary definition (essentially hard-coding the result set).

Grammar: Verbs and Adjectives

► **Verb:** Verbs are words or groups of words that express a state of being, an action, or a condition. For purposes of database design, we will limit our discussion of verbs to those most commonly used in Predicate Logic, and those will be introduced in that section.

► **Adjective**: Adjectives describe or modify any of the noun types mentioned above. Grammar texts identify a wide variety of adjective types (demonstrative, indefinite, interrogative, possessive, limiting, and so forth), but for database design, it is far more helpful to view these from a different perspective:

 In Book (chapter) Four of "Posterior Analytics," Aristotle says:

"Things, then, not predicated of a subject I call Essential; things predicated of a subject I call Accidental or 'Coincidental'."

Aristotle gives us definitions of two Classes of what, in database design, we refer to as Attributes: "Essential" and "Accidental." The ramifications of this distinction are quite significant when analyzing or initiating the design of data structures. The descriptions below will help clarify the distinctions:

▼ **Essential Attributes** are those that are fundamental to the definition of any member of a Class. As an example, Aristotle uses the Class "Triangle," and says "the very being or 'substance' of TRIANGLE consists of three sides and three angles." If the Thing we are examining doesn't have these essential attributes, it isn't, by definition, a TRIANGLE. If the Thing possesses these attributes, it is, by definition, a TRIANGLE.

▼ **Accidental Attributes** on the other hand are not fundamental to the definition of a Class. A Triangle might have both Color and Size as attributes, but whether the triangle is yellow or green makes no difference at all to the fact that it is a TRIANGLE. If the size is large or small, or even if we have no knowledge of the value of these attributes, the Thing is still a TRIANGLE.

Likewise, we may have an attribute called appearance that we apply to the Class "Bird," and we could say that any particular BIRD is "pretty" or "ugly," but whether a particular bird is "pretty" or "ugly" has no bearing whatever on whether it is, in fact, a BIRD.

In later examples, we'll see how not recognizing the critical distinctions between Essential and Accidental attributes can lead us astray when designing logical databases. Suffice it to say for the moment that, regardless of your position on the permissibility of Nulls in database tables, it is logically insupportable to ever permit any Essential attribute to be Null.

We will revisit the subject of Adjectives in a later section.

Naming our Things

As Aristotle, Lewis Carroll, and others make very clear, properly and logically naming the Things of interest is critical to any Logical endeavor. Three major things to consider when giving Names to our Classes, Entities, Tables, or whatever are the following:

☑ Always beware of using any sort of Homonym.

☑ Always beware of using any sort of Synonym or generalization. This occurs in more ways than one might expect, such as Naming something with anything other than the most narrowly defined Class to which it belongs.

☑ Beware of more subtle differences in the definitions we use for naming.

We'll discuss each of these in turn.

Homonyms, including Homographs, and Homophones

► A **Homonym** is a word that has the same pronunciation and spelling as another word, but a different meaning. As humans, we are able to use context to determine which definition is intended, but with technological systems, Homonyms are always equivocal and imprecise.

▼ A "bat," for instance, might refer to something used when playing baseball or it may refer to a type of nocturnal animal. The phrase "loaded" might mean "rich" or "drunk," but might also indicate that a weapon is filled with ammunition. Other examples include "club," "fine," "rock," and "lie."

Subcategories of Homonym include Homophones and Homographs.

▶ A **Homograph** has the same spelling as another word, but a different meaning and, typically, a different pronunciation. While not as often a problem as Homonyms, Homographs are, by definition, imprecise, and are better avoided if possible.

▼ "Dove," for instance, might be a noun referring to a certain type of bird, or a verb that is the past tense of dive. Some examples are more imprecise than others: A **bow** is used to shoot arrows, while the **bow** is the front of a boat on which we might affix a yellow **bow** to celebrate its maiden voyage. We might **bow** down before the **invalid** Tenor and **Bass** who entered a fishing contest and caught the two top contenders for prize **bass** that were later ruled **invalid**.

▶ A **Homophone** has the same pronunciation as another word, but a different meaning and spelling. Since homophones are only detectable by ear, they don't present a problem to our technology, but can make for humorous conversations, and should also be avoided if possible.

▼ Examples are Sea–See; Right–Write; There–Their–They're; Which–Witch; Steel–Steal; Pair–Pear; Cell–Sell; To–Too–Two; Air–Heir; Blue–Blew; Bass–Base. The operatic **bass** wore his **steel** cleats in the baseball game and that helped him **steal** third **base**.

Synonyms and Class Distinctions

▶ A **Synonym** is simply a word that has the same meaning as a different word. Although it would seem natural to immediately consider a synonym when faced with avoiding the use of a word that might be a homonym or similar, we need to consider that many of the Things we encounter and need to record in our databases may legitimately be known by synonyms.

Nash on Classes

"The cow is of the bovine ilk; one end is moo, the other milk."

– Ogden Nash (1902-1971)

When we encounter the three sentences "A cow is a mammal," "A dolphin is a mammal" and "A person is a mammal," the word "mammal" has an identical meaning in English in each of the three sentences. Likewise, when we encounter the sentences "A cow is an animal," "A dolphin is an animal," and "A person is an animal," the word "animal" likewise has an identical meaning. It is tempting, therefore, to say that "mammal" and "animal" must be synonyms, but it isn't logically correct to say so, and it is important to understand that in order to avoid falling into a common entity naming trap.

As we demonstrated in the "Accidents often occur at Intersections" section of the previous chapter, the two companies that were planning to merge had each used the name **Customer** for data related to their respective Customers. In each case, it was considered a reasonable name although, as it turns out, "Customer" was a synonym used to name two entirely different entities. Although either could likely be considered a grammatically "correct" name, neither

The Appropriate Level of Precision

In Categories Book I, part 5.5, Aristotle says "... the species is more truly substance than the genus ..." and continues to say that someone would "give a more instructive account by stating the species rather than the genus."

He reiterates this in part 5.8 when he says "we shall make our definition more exact by stating the former (species or class) rather than the latter (genus/generic or super-class).

was a logically correct name, since it wasn't as precise as it could be. In the chapter "Playing with Trucks – Part 1," we will present an example of how using an overly generic name – one commonly used by the business personnel – caused serious difficulties as the company attempted to add capabilities to their system.

Recognizing Purpose in Naming – Beyond Synonyms

Another more subtle mistake in database design results from assuming that if two separate entities have the same name, the same pronunciation, the same general meaning, and contain what appears to be identical data, they must be the same. This isn't always the case, however, and it is important to also consider the **purpose** of each element during design. The following example will illustrate how overlooking this can result in a complete loss of data integrity even when assiduously attempting to follow the design guidelines in the popular press.

In an earlier chapter, we introduced an interesting book[92] that contained, among some very good advice, a few surprising departures from logical database de-

---

92 Welling [1]; see page 385. The previous mention of this book was on page 38.

sign. The book contains a very good example of what happens when the **purpose** of a data element is ignored.

The authors assume a **Customer** table containing the name of each customer and that customer's address[93]. – an unfortunate but not uncommon table design – and then present the following **Order** table as an example of the redundancy that can occur when there is no foreign key reference back to the address which they had placed (inappropriately, of course) in the **Customer** table.

OrderID	Amount	Date	CustomerID	Name	Address	City
12	199.50	25-Apr-2000	1	Julie Smith	28 Oak Street	Airport West
13	43.00	29-Apr-2000	1	Julie Smith	28 Oak Street	Airport West
14	15.99	30-Apr-2000	1	Julie Smith	28 Oak Street	Airport West
15	23.75	01-May-2000	1	Julie Smith	28 Oak Street	Airport West

Orders Table from Welling [1], page 174 and 175, purportedly illustrating redundancy.

They then claim that making **CustomerID** a foreign key will eliminate the redundant entries in the **Name**, **Address**, and **City** fields. On the surface, this seems like a perfectly good idea, but for the fact that these columns are ***not redundant!***

Although the **Customer** table contains "28 Oak Street" and "Airport West" as portions of the "Address" for Julie Smith, and the identically named columns in the **Order** table for Ms. Smith contain apparently identical data, the purpose of these data elements differs. They, in fact, represent **different information**:

▶ In the **Customer** table, it is quite clear that the purpose of the **Address** column is to record the **current** address for customer number 1, who is named Julie Smith.

▶ In the **Orders** table, it is equally clear that the purpose of the identically named **Address** column is meant to record the location to which each **Order** was shipped.

The same observation can be made, of course, for the **Name** and **City** columns, but we'll ignore that for simplicity. To show why this is significant, consider

---

93 We will later show how this is a very poorly designed, decidedly non-relational, and improperly named table. But those arguments can be deferred for the moment.

what would have happened if, for instance, Order #12 was shipped on April 27th, Order #13 was shipped on April 30th at 2:00 pm, and on that same day Ms. Smith changed her address, but didn't call to notify the company until 3:45 pm. Now suppose that Order #12 was never delivered. If the Foreign Key had been used as suggested in the book, the Company's data would show that the order had been shipped to the new address on April 27th – three days before the company had ever been notified of the address change. The data is obviously incorrect (a fact which, unfortunately, would be far more obvious to the customer than to the company or its I/T department), and it is easy to imagine many more serious difficulties that could arise. The lessons are these:

> ▪ *When assigning Names to elements within a database, even deliberate efforts to avoid homonyms and such when naming attributes is not enough; the purpose of the element must be considered as well, and*
> ▪ *Because two elements contain identical data, this doesn't necessarily suggest that the two elements themselves represent the same "Thing" or information.*

McNaming and other Travesties

There is another type of situation where lack of early consideration of Names can result in later confusion, and that is with composite names. In 1972, Mc-Donald's introduced the "Egg McMuffin"™, which consisted of a slice of Canadian Bacon, a slice of cheese, and an egg on an English muffin. Some years later, they introduced a variant called the "Sausage McMuffin"™, in which the Egg was obviously replaced with Sausage so that the sandwich now consisted of a slice of Canadian Bacon, a slice of cheese, and a slice of sausage.

Or at least that is how a computer might have interpreted it from the name change alone. Only as humans are we capable of thinking of the original product as a single entity, and realizing that sausage, being a meat, had likely replaced the original meat component of the sandwich. Computers can't infer this!

Of course, this seems silly, but only until you run across an analogous situation when changes need to be made to a table (and the applications that use it) that had earlier been named with the same inconsistent regard for logic. Computers simply can't resolve inconsistencies like humans can!

The lesson is that composite entity set names should be complete, something we discussed in the previous chapter when giving names to Intersections.

Obscure Naming

Having once spent time correcting structural flaws in a table with the dubious name of **MC324A2**, it also seems necessary to point out that if the name of a Thing doesn't quite clearly state what it is intended to be or be used for, it should probably come as no surprise when, over time, it morphs into a trash bag of sorts. As we already saw in "Accidents often occur at Intersections" on page 54, even seemingly precise names like **Customer** are used inappropriately, so time spent on naming things unequivocally (as Aristotle dictates) is seldom wasted.

Lazy Naming

The sample database schema (scott/tiger) included with Oracle's RDBMS in the early generations of the product had a table named **Emp**, which was a terrific example of lazy naming[94]. When developers are too lazy to spell out the word "employee," this could suggest that they may also cut corners on the analysis needed to design a logical data model, leading to any of the consequences outlined in this book. Abbreviating the name of a very complex secondary result set may be appropriate (and even necessary given the arbitrary name-length limits

> In Praise of Laziness
>
> Although the term is used somewhat tongue-in-cheek in many instances, "Laziness" is often recommended as an objective of good design – both for programmers and database designers – and I fully support this.
>
> The meaning needs to be considered in context, however. When upfront effort is expended in order to reduce subsequent ongoing and often repetitive activities (the conditions under which errors and mistakes flourish), the subsequent "laziness" is a result of good design and the term simply means the avoidance of such unproductive effort.
>
> Laziness such as shortening a name (and often obscuring it unintentionally) serves no objective but saving programmers a little typing; it contributes nothing to the Business.

---

94   This particular schema was also a great example of how to build a non-relational database using a relational database management product. As I've suggested many times, the interests of Oracle (as well as other vendors who provide similar examples) seem to be to demonstrate the "mechanics" of using their product rather than the "art" or "science" of using it.

of many RDBMS products), but seldom provides any help or clarity to the business.

But, we now need to finish covering the basics of grammar before proceeding.

Quasi-Mathematical Naming

Relational Model theoreticians are appropriately fond of discussing their example table designs with quasi-formulaic shorthand, and when reading these – which you should take every opportunity to do – you will often encounter entity set names that are very reminiscent of the "x" and "y" found in mathematical textbooks. This might lead you to believe that, if entities can be identified with single letters by the theoreticians, abbreviations such as Emp on the previous page are not so bad, and might even be considered an improvement.

The well known author Chris Date gives us some examples of this in his book on Business Rules[95]:

He presents his classic supplier-parts schema consisting of the following tables: S, P, and SP. To which I can only comment IDAWTAAA!![96] If you read the actual book, you'll learn that S is a table containing Supplier data, P is a table containing Parts data, and SP is – not a Supplier-Parts intersection as you might infer – but a table containing Shipment data. He concedes, however, that:

> "By the way, there's nothing wrong with using more user-friendly names such as SUPPLIER, PART, and SHIPMENT in place of the rather terse names S, P, and SP … rightly or wrongly, I felt it would be better to stick to very short names. Long names tend to become irksome with much repetition."

Apparently "user-friendly" isn't that high of a priority in the theoretical world. My view is somewhat different, since I consider "user" to include application developers, report writers, auditors, business analysts and so forth.

---

95 Date [3]; see page 382 for additional information.

96 Oh sorry, that means "I Don't Agree With This Approach At All."

Grammar: Simple Sentences and Propositions

► A **Sentence** is a group of words that expresses at least one complete thought and usually (for our purposes) is made up of at least one **Subject** and one **Predicate**.

  ▼ Any grammar book will outline a wide variety of Sentence types (e.g. Declarative, Interrogative, Imperative, Exclamatory, and so forth) but our interest here is the simple Declarative sentence that states a single fact, has a single Subject and a single Predicate.

  ▼ Sentences may also contain Clauses of various types, Phrases and Modifiers, but those aren't of concern when discussing Logic or Database design.

► A **Subject** is the topic of the sentence.

  ▼ Once again, grammar books provide us with many types of Subject, such as Full Subject, Complete Subject, Simple Subject and Compound Subject. For discussions of Logic and Database Design, we will limit ourselves to a Simple Subject that consists of a single Noun.

► A **Predicate** is what is said about the Subject.

  ▼ Although Grammar books discuss Full, Complete, Simple and Compound Predicates, our focus will be entirely on Simple Predicates that always contain a verb and consist of, at most, one noun (as an Object) or adjective.

► A **Proposition** is, in fact, the very type of Sentence that we are interested in when discussing Logic and Database Design. The definition of a Proposition may be further refined as follows:

 Book II, Chapters 1-3 of Lewis Carroll's "Symbolic Logic" provide a more detailed explanation of Propositions, how they are reduced to Normal Form, and so forth.   Carroll [1]

  ▼ The subject must be a Common Noun, although a Proper Noun is permissible.

  ▼ The subject may not be a Pronoun. (e.g. "he," "she," "it," or "they")

  ▼ A Proposition is a statement. As such, **it may be True or False**. It may also be incomplete on its own and need to be considered alongside another Proposition in order to draw any logical conclusion.

► A **Corollary** is a Proposition following so obviously from another that it requires little or no proof. In Mathematics, corollaries are often inferred from other proven facts and, assuming that no one can prove them incorrect, are often accepted. If we have proven that "3 = 1 + 2," the corollary "1 + 2 = 3" can certainly be accepted without much discussion.

The difficulty with using Corollaries in Programming or Database Design is that, since the average Human's ability to draw logical inferences seems to be quite limited, we are better served by relying on more formal logic.

► An **Invalid Corollary** is a Proposition that, while it may seem to follow logically from another, is actually incorrect – usually because of faulty inference. Designs resulting from Invalid Corollaries are rampant in the world of Business Databases, and many examples are scattered throughout this book.

► **Normal Form** of a Proposition

Because any sentence, and therefore any Proposition, can be stated in many forms, it is desirable (some, including Lewis Carroll, say necessary) to reformat them into a consistent form in order to utilize them in Logic.

▼ In Book II, Chapter 1, §2, of *Symbolic Logic*, Carroll describes this format as:

Sign of Quantity + Name of Subject + Copula + Name of Predicate

The **Sign of Quantity** must be one of the following adjectives:

"All," "Some," or "No."

Propositions beginning with the word "All" are called **Universal Affirmatives**.

Propositions beginning with the word "Some" are called **Particulars**.

Propositions beginning with the word "No" are called **Universal Negatives**.

A **Copula** simply means a type of Verb that links or indicates dependence between a subject and a predicate. In the section Grammar: Verbs and Adjectives on page 72, it was mentioned that only certain types of verbs will be discussed as predicates in this book. Those are:

"to be" (e.g. "is," "are," "might be," "may be," "must be"), and

"to have" (e.g. "has," "possesses," "includes")

For example, the following valid Propositions

T "Every Company **is** an Organization."
T "A Company **must always be** an Organization."
T "Any Company **is** an Organization."
T "Any Company **must be** an Organization."

would all be normalized to become the single Universal Affirmative Proposition:

T "A Company **is an** Organization."

We already introduced some examples of Propositions on page 57, three of which are repeated here in their Normalized forms:

T "An Employee **must be** a Person" is TRUE.
F "A Person **must be** an Employee" is FALSE.
? "An Employee **may be** a Person" is INCOMPLETE.

We'll return to the use of Logic in database design shortly, but in order to understand the extent of the fight we are about to undertake, we need to examine the environment in which we exist.

Logic & Precision in Daily Life

In the next chapter, "Recent History of Data Management," we'll discuss how electronic computers eventually replaced human computers, providing us with greater accuracy, consistency, repeatability, etc. Accuracy, of course, depends to a great degree on how the machines are used. The acronym GIGO[97] dates back at least to the very early 1950s[98], so this tradeoff between power and intelligence was recognized very early on in the history of computing machines.

---

97   Garbage In; Garbage Out. Punch cards and paper tape have largely disappeared since those days, but bad data is still quite prevalent and still continues to breed like Asian Carp.

98   Although the existence of the GIGO phenomenon was a closely guarded secret in the Data Processing world, a 1963 syndicated newspaper article about problems with a new IRS system finally introduced the term and its acronym to the general public.

Unfortunately, Logic is often foreign to our normal lives. Our easy acceptance and comprehension of the meaning of the name Sausage McMuffin™ illustrates the innate superiority of the human mind – even one at the lower end of the bell curve – over a computer. Because this sort of "background" logical analysis isn't usually under our direct control, it is absolutely necessary that, as database design professionals (even if we have no pretensions of being "computer scientists"), we become able to recognize when our brains are providing us with more understanding than we will be able to impart to our machines.

Although this need has been recognized by Programmers for decades, new practitioners still struggle with this. Each novice programmer must typically learn first-hand that computers will do precisely what they are told, and care not one whit what the programmer actually *meant*. This usually takes several fights with the machine, and only after many endless loops or similar experiences does the lesson really begin to sink in.

This typical progression in the development of a programmer isn't surprising since, as humans, we have become completely immune to a lack of common sense, logic and precision in our lives. We have learned, in fact, to adapt to and live quite comfortably with this lack – and it takes a continuous and conscious effort to give our systems the precise, ordered and unambiguous instructions that they need (which we've learned to do with a fair degree of success), and to organize and structure our data in a logical and consistent manner (which is still an unfamiliar skill, and one we don't seem to do with any consistency). Consider some examples of things that sneak easily past our ears and into our brains without causing the slightest frown:

► Due to its polyglot origins, the English language itself, particularly as used in the United States, is terribly inconsistent, but we seldom notice. Pronounce "ough", for instance[99]. And what logic makes us pronounce the "o" differently in the words "woman" and "women?"

---

99 Does knowing the rules for pronouncing "ough" in the words "bough", "cough", "rough", "through", "though", and "thought" help you determine the pronunciation of the words "bought", "brougham", "dough", "enough", "ought", "sought", or "tough?"

► The marketing industry (for one) constantly clobbers us with logical gaffes:

▼ From a radio ad series: "Seattle Sutton's Healthy Eating provides your fresh fruits, salads, *and everything!*" Obviously set theory and logic, to say nothing of grammar, are not among the ad writer's strong points. Having never tasted Ms. Sutton's products, I can't comment on their quality, but hopefully most programmers and database designers intuitively cringe when they hear this ad.

▼ From television ads for Kay Jewelers: "Every kiss begins with Kay." Every kiss? Even if it were assumed that this refers only to the specific relationship in which the targeted viewer is embroiled, it still paints a rather sorry state of affairs (no pun intended – really). If someone wishes to learn logical thinking, pondering the possible corollaries and implications of this tag line and how they relate to the advertiser's intended message is a good start.

▼ From commercials for a mortgage service: "get your mortgage here… and pay less points…"[100] A similar flaw appears in ads for the introduction of a two door version of a new Mercedes-Benz vehicle: "More Power, Less Doors!"

▼ Casinos have been steadily siphoning gambling business from horse racing tracks. Hawthorne, a Chicago-area Race Track, ran an ad not long ago to recapture some of this business by suggesting that horse racing offers a 1 in 9 chance of winning whereas a roulette wheel only offers a 1 in 36 chance. What are they implying (or more correctly, what do they hope you will incorrectly infer?) with this statement? Does this represent a valid mathematical or logical comparison?

▼ It seems as if every automobile insurance company is now advertising that you can save a significant percentage on your premiums if you switch to one of their policies. Based on the clear implications of these ads, it seems quite reasonable that you could quickly reduce your premiums to a rather miniscule token amount by simply rotating through the group back to the company you started with.[101]

---

100 Proper handling of measures and quantities is extremely important in database design. Anyone who doesn't recognize the difference between "less" and "fewer" should not be permitted to access a database, much less to participate in the design of one.

101 Reviewing the fine print on these, it appears the assertions are based on the amount of money saved by those customers who switched to a particular company's policy AND SAVED MONEY. Strictly speaking, this seems more akin to a lie than a logical flaw.

▼ From a clear shrink-wrap sleeve around a bottle of generic pain reliever: "Do not use product if this seal has been tampered with or is missing."

Certainly, as computer *scientists*, we cringe at such things, don't we? Nevertheless, our immunity is compromised by constant exposure to this infectious sort of marketing nonsense and we need to take continuous precautions to cleanse our brains prior to engaging in designing systems for our inanimate targets.

More nefarious is the incessant barrage of Invalid Corollaries[102], whose success results from our logical naivete and masochistic willingness to be tricked into making unwarranted inferences:

► Lotteries, government-sanctioned and commercial, continuously use this Reader's Digest tactic:

> *"...in fact, when people receive their chances to win in our sweepstakes ... they often decide to throw them away, thinking that 'no one ever really wins.' And the fact is – if you receive prize entries and choose to ignore them, you will never have the chance of winning anything in our sweepstakes."*

You are clearly meant to infer that by responding to these mailings, you *will* have some meaningful chance. According to the Reader's Digest themselves, though, the odds range from 1 in 4,875 for the smallest prize to 1 in 120,000,000 for the largest, so is the chance really worth your time and the cost of a stamp? This is similar to the many state lottery ads that proclaim "You can't win if you don't play," clearly encouraging you to infer that, if you *do* play, you *do* have some meaningful chance.[103]

---

102 Because we can say "3 = 1 + 2" is equivalent to "1 + 2 = 3", and the word "is" is often used as an incorrect substitute for "equals," we are easily led into a belief that saying "An Employee is a Person" is equivalent to saying "A Person is an Employee". It isn't, of course; The second statement is an invalid corollary.

103 State lotteries are sometimes referred to as "stupidity taxes" – i.e. taxes based on someone's level of innumeracy rather than on income, property value, or other more typical criteria. Making such decisions on one's own behalf is perhaps acceptable, but we in I/T have a professional obligation to avoid being conned into making invalid inferences that cost our employers money.

Other examples abound and are trivially easy to find[104], so those given above should be sufficient to make the point that we need to be constantly vigilant to prevent our normal suspension of logic and reason from contaminating our efforts at achieving (among other things) logical organization and categorization of information and data. The computers we use today and for the foreseeable future are incapable of identifying and overcoming sloppy logic on their own, particularly the insidious use of invalid corollaries, and it is incumbent upon us to be sufficiently critical.

There is some evidence that, as an industry, we have made progress in utilizing logic when writing application programs, but inexplicably can't or don't manage to do so when designing databases[105].

Optional Homework Assignment

Take a break from reading this book for a while, but pay close attention to all the advertising and newscasts you encounter over the next 24 hours. Give yourself 5 points for each logically dubious claim that you encounter.

SALE – SALE – SALE – SALE
Our best Blue Balloons and Red Balloons – 50 percent off!!
Blue or Red: **YOUR CHOICE**!!
How many choices are available?

Categorize each gaffe, paying particular attention to identifying Invalid Corollaries (stated or meant for you to infer), mixed domains, and improper use of comparative measures. You should first, of course, make sure that you understand exactly what is wrong with the examples provided in the paragraphs above. You need to score at least 25 points if you aspire to be a good data architect, database designer or software developer.

---

104 An interesting book describing ways we are duped (sometimes by ourselves) in many areas of life is Savant [1] (see page 384 for more information).

105 To be fair, it probably helped that endless loops are a marvelous teaching aid for programmers, but there seems to be no corresponding didactic equivalent for database designers.

Set Theory and Predicate Logic

Both Set Theory and Predicate Logic are quite important when logically formulating queries against complex collections of properly organized data, but the truth is that we barely need to skim the surface of these subjects when discussing database design. Those who are more than superficially knowledgeable in either of these subjects will likely be disappointed by the limited discussions that follow. On the other hand, those who wish to avoid these subjects will probably be delighted. For what it's worth therefore, here are some fundamentals:

Aristotle's views on Sets and Classes, discussed under "Grammar: Nouns" above, began a period of several millennia during which philosophers and scientists were able to apply these principles to address a wide variety of problems.

But the use of Sets didn't make a full transition from its "Egyptian"[106] phase until 1874, when Georg Cantor formalized his *Theory of Sets* – establishing "Set Theory" as a formal branch of mathematics, with a rigorous notation and the variety of theoretical proofs that typically characterize these endeavors.

Lewis Carroll's writings on the subject of Sets and Logic were an introduction to the subject for a wider and not necessarily scientific audience, and he became for Georg Cantor what Chris Date later became for Ted Codd (the "Great Explainer").

The earlier section "Sets and Classes – The Crucial Difference" discussed the fundamental differences between a Set and a Class, but didn't explore how either was

 Caution about studying Lewis Carrolls Symbolic Logic.

Although this classic text presents the fundamentals of Predicate Logic in a simple and straightforward manner, it is important to be aware of the following:

Since our philosopher, logician, photographer and early gaming enthusiast didn't need to make such distinctions for his discussion of Logic, Carroll's book doesn't distinguish between Attributes and their Values, nor does he distinguish between Class and Set.

When discussing the use of Logic for the design of databases, however, it is absolutely necessary that we make such distinctions.

We have already discussed the distinctions between **Class** and **Set**. As for **Attributes** and **Attribute Values**, the following examples should suffice:

Color, for instance, is an **Attribute**, while "Blue" is an **Attribute Value** of Color. Similarly, **Gender** is an **Attribute**, while "Female" is an **Attribute Value** of **Gender**.

---

106 See "An Aside – The Egyptian Rule" on page 17 for the meaning of "Egyptian Rule."

formed. As humans, we are often able to do this quite intuitively, but it is worthwhile to discuss the process just a little more formally.

► A Set is a collection of Things – "Elements of the Set" – that share some common attributes or attribute values.

► A key requirement for the definition of a Class is that we must be able to state categorically that any arbitrary "Thing" **is** or **is not** an Element of that Class.

Carroll tells us more in Book II, Chapter 1, §2 of *Symbolic Logic*:

► One Thing may have many Attributes.

► One Attribute may belong to many Things.

► A Set of Attributes unique to a certain Thing is called an Adjunct. As he puts it: "This Adjunct is said to be **peculiar** to the Class (sic) so formed."

To further refine the distinctions we need to make between CLASS and SET – which we must do when designing data structures – note that while a Set may be defined by any arbitrary criteria, it is always formed of Things that share common attributes or even common attribute values, such as "all blue fish" or "all female persons." A Set may even be formed from combinations of attribute values, such as "all blue salt-water fish longer than four inches."

A Class, on the other hand, is much more narrowly defined, is never arbitrary, is always inclusive, and is always based on shared **Attributes**, but not shared **Attribute Values**. This latter distinction is generally true of well-designed OO Classes as well, although the dangers of ignoring the stricture can usually be minimized in software so long as they are recognized.

► If we identify a Set (whether a Class or not), a subset is formed by picking out those things from the Set that share a unique Adjunct.

► In this case, Carroll's statement is somewhat incomplete for our purposes. A subset may be formed from either a Class or a Set "by picking out those things from the Set that share a unique Adjunct." It is important for us to recognize whether a subset thus formed from a Class qualifies as a subclass, however. This is done by applying the same rules given above for defining a

Class (never arbitrary, always inclusive, based on shared **Attributes** rather than simply shared **Attribute Values**). If the Adjunct is formed with one or more essential attributes, it is a subclass; if not, it is merely a subset.

Cantor reiterates what we have already learned from Aristotle: a Set (and by inference, a Class) is a collection of Things, and not a composition and, further, that a Set (and by inference, a Class) is an entity set that is separate and distinct from the Elements that are its members, and may actually have attributes of its own that are not shared by any of the Members[107].

Like Aristotle, Carroll makes a point of acknowledging the importance of identifying class hierarchies (loosely equivalent to taxonomies), and being aware of the relation of what he refers to as "individual" (what Aristotle calls "primary substance"), "species" and "genus." Like Aristotle, he also indicates that Species and Genus are simply relative terms – a Species always being a particular subclass of some Genus. Looking at the diagram presented under "Deja Vu" on page 61, we can consider that an individual employee would always be considered an "individual" by Carroll and a "primary substance" by Aristotle. In the same drawing, the Employee Class would be considered a Species of the Genus Person, while a Person could be considered a Species of the Genus Party[108].

> But What about Compositions?
>
> Most Businesses will need to model a number of entities that are compositions – anything from the common elements that make up (compose) a customer's address to detailed bills-of-material.
>
> Although a Relational Database must, by definition, represent its key Relations (e.g. Parties, Employees, Customers, etc.) as Relational Tables, not all tables in a Relational Database will themselves be Relational.
>
> Simply put, a Composition is not a Relation*, and therefore should not be modeled as such. Other non-Relational tables may include Domain tables, tables that define many-to-many relationships, and similar constructs.
>
> * See Date [1] for a good discussion of the term Relation, from which the Relational Model gets its name, and which is not at all the same thing as a relationship. Think of a Relation as resulting from the Adjunct formed of Essential Attributes that define a particular Class, such as Employee or Customer.

---

107 One more reason why it is safer to give Classes (and therefore Tables) a singular name.

108 It needs to be said that this discussion only relates to Logic and Database Design, and not to natural science as a whole. In Natural taxonomies, Linnaeus (see "Early History of Data Management") classified Life into eight major ranks, which he called Domain, Kingdom, Phylum, Class, Order, Family, Genus, and Species. Since there is typically no distinction

The practical and immediately useful importance of Set Theory to Database Design, however, lies in the sorts of diagrams typically used to make Set (and therefore Class) Hierarchies apparent[109]. This is something that can't be said of Entity-Relationship Diagrams or UML Data Structure Diagrams which, although they may be immensely useful at a later stage of the design and construction process, allow fundamental logical errors to remain hidden until far too late in the development cycle to do much good.

Turning the Proper and Common Nouns we identify during analysis into suitable tables and columns presents us with a "chicken and egg" quandary. Do we work upward from various Primary Substances – cataloging their Essential Attributes – to determine what Classes we are dealing with, or do we first identify all the Classes we have an interest in and build up the details from there?

Actually, we can (and usually do) use both methods: The "Top Down" approach was illustrated in "Party Seating Chart" on page 3 when we identified many types of Party that our business dealt with. The "Bottom Up" approach was illustrated in "Deja Vu" on page 61 when we discovered enough common attributes in several of the entities we were analyzing to realize that this was a strong indication that these entities were in fact subsets of a larger entity set.

Both of these discoveries were actually examples of how simple set theory and predicate logic can assist in the discovery of the entities of interest and how to scientifically (logically) organize them. Another implicit lesson in these examples was that we should redo each such analysis exercise in both directions to ensure that we aren't missing anything. The top-down and bottom-up analyses should give us the same conclusions if our thinking is logical.

---

made between members of a species (except for humans and the odd pet), he ignored the idea of Individual or Primary Substance. Luckily, there is no need to use this many levels of rank in either Logic or Database Design, since those who can't be bothered to spell out "employee" probably couldn't be motivated to remember all eight terms – some of which, as you may note, already have other meanings in the world of Information Technology.

109 Popular diagram types include Euler, Venn, Carroll, and even those used in Barker [1]. Any of these are far more suitable for initial database design than Entity-Relationship Diagrams.

Aristotle's Help with Adjectives as Attributes

Aristotle provides a breakdown of the possible types of Attribute (each of which can be related to one of the grammatical categories of Adjective), and posits that every part of a verifiable statement, or Proposition, falls into one, and only one, of these types. These, in fact, are the Categories referred to in the title of his treatise[110]. The following list provides very limited descriptions of these Categories:

► 1. **Substance** (discussed in Categories, Part 5: 1-22) is that which exists in and of itself – a uniquely identifiable Primary Substance – discussed earlier. The remainder of the categories state something about the substance. Unlike the remainder of the Categories, Substance is never an Attribute.

► 2. **Quantity** (Categories, Part 6: 1-15) refers to the physical size of something and is the basis for much later mathematical thought. Nearly any concept that is physical in nature and can be measured in numbers would fall into the quantity category, such as descriptions of height, weight, and width.

► 3. **Relation** (Categories, Part 7: 1-19) describes how one object relates to another. This may express cause and effect, physical relativity (near or far, larger or smaller) or temporal relativity (earlier or later, before or after).

► 4. **Quality** (Categories, Part 8: 1-27) describes the inherent nature of an object. Although Quality can include physical descriptions, it would only include those that cannot be described mathematically or by Relation.

► 5. **Place** refers to the object's absolute (but not relative) physical location.

► 6. **Time** refers to the object's absolute (but not relative) temporal location.

► 7. **Pose** or Posture[111] refers specifically to the placement of different parts of the object in relation to each other.

---

110 Aristotle [1]; because the descriptions here are very limited, it is useful to read his original.

111 Some English texts translate this as "position" which, while technically a valid translation, is a misleading one, since "position" is a homonym.

► 8. **State** is an ongoing but not inherent attribute of the object. This is different than Quality: Whereas an adjective like "green" may fall into the quality category, one like "sleeping" would be classified as a state.

► 9. **Action** (Categories, Part 9) refers to how changes to this object affect some other Thing or the influence this Thing has had on some other Thing.

► 10. **Affection** (Categories, Part 8.8 and 9, sometimes translated as Passion) refers to the effect or influence that some other Thing or Action has had on this subject. Example: "John was **injured** by the falling rock."

Aristotle's ten Categories can be used to identify both the subject and the predicate of a Proposition. The Predicate is that which can be proven true or false about the subject. In the sentence "All men are mortal," for example, "All men" is the subject and "are mortal" is the predicate.

According to Aristotle, every part of a verifiable statement or proposition falls into one, and only one, of these categories.

Any of the Attributes (2 through 10 above) Aristotle describes might be Essential or Accidental (see Grammar: Verbs and Adjectives on page 72). It is the responsibility of a good designer to determine which are Essential and model them appropriately.

Aristotle as a Database Designer – Really?

Database design, at its heart, is or at least should be a logical organization of facts. Lest you remain unconvinced of the applicability of Aristotle's writings[112] to modern day database design, consider a few examples.

Aristotle's take on NULLs

If you've read more than one book, magazine article or blog on database design, it is apparent that the question of whether to permit NULLs in a database design is viewed by many designers as confusing, and assumed to be a matter of

---

112 ... or those written by any other of our illustrious forebears.

belief or philosophy: The arguments against ever permitting NULLs are compelling because they seem to be based on a solid theoretical foundation. That such theories are questionable is also apparent from the many realistic examples provided where NULL values should reasonably be supported.

I'm unaware of any writings other than those of Aristotle that provide a logical and well-reasoned resolution to this quandary, but he himself resolved it more than two thousand years ago.

Were Aristotle to create a table to store data about Triangles[113], his writings make it perfectly clear that the columns he created for each side length[114] would certainly be NOT NULL, while he would have felt perfectly justified in permitting NULLs in any columns he created for Color based solely on his requirements.

In short, he recognized the clear distinction between what he termed ESSENTIAL ATTRIBUTES and ACCIDENTAL ATTRIBUTES – specifically: an ESSENTIAL ATTRIBUTE value cannot logically be NULL. If the value were unknown, you would simply have no idea whether or not the Thing in question actually was a Triangle. As for Color – it may or may not matter if it contains a NULL value.

Normalization: Carroll, Codd, and Nixon

Yup, that Nixon – the thirty-seventh President of the United States.

I believe Ted Codd is the first to define what we call the "Normal Forms."[115] For reasons that are unclear, he has also been credited with the idea of normalization itself, although Carroll, as we have seen, discussed it at length long before Codd was born. In 1993, an interviewer from DBMS Magazine asked

"Where did [the term] 'normalization' come from?"

---

113 See the "Adjectives" section in "Grammar: Verbs and Adjectives" on page 72.

114 ... and he would have undoubtedly created corresponding columns to specify the units of measure for each of these lengths, but we'll get to that in a later chapter

115 As with the use of Entity-Relationship Diagrams (ERDs), the determination of Normal Forms often detracts from logical database design if considered at too early a stage, but we'll discuss the reasons for that in later chapters.

Codd replied:

> " … because then President Nixon was talking a lot about normaliz-ing relations with China. I figured that if he could normalize rela-tions, so could I."

It seems beyond coincidence that Dr. Codd would have chosen the term "nor-malization"[116] so frivolously, and it sure sounds as if he may have been playing a little prank to vent some understandable frustration with all the misrepresenta-tions of his work over the years – a bit of sarcasm that, unfortunately, whizzed right by the interviewer as well as other writers who have repeated this quote as if it were to be taken seriously. Personally, I find great comfort when discovering that historical figures had a sense of humor.

Grammar - Revisited

One conceptual difficulty some developers have with Grammar as the basis for Logic is the idea that English Grammar – used for the examples in this chapter – differs from that of other languages. To clarify this, consider that Logic is related to the *Essential* attributes of any Grammar, not the *Accidental* ones.

Grammar, as I am using the term here therefore, refers to the superset of all language-specific grammars. While this may suggest some interesting philo-sophical discussions, those are quite out of scope here.

Back to History and On to the Future

For the moment we'll let the ideas of predicate logic simmer while we cover other aspects related to database Triage. We'll continue to explore some more subtleties of Predicates, Sets, and Classes in a later chapter, and learn how these can rescue us from some tricky design dilemmas.

---

116 Sad experience suggests that it isn't necessarily patronizing to point out that if Dr. Codd based the Relational Model even partially on Predicate Logic, he must have been quite fa-miliar with Normalization as Carroll and others used the term.

LESSONS FOR CHAPTER 5
GRAMMAR AND (PREDICATE) LOGIC

► Good grammar is a necessary underpinning of good logic.

► Correctly identifying even basic parts of speech can enlighten and improve database design.

► Various types of Nouns, for instance, correspond to terms used by I/T: Proper Nouns are analogous to Instances and Common Nouns are analogous to Classes.

► Logic is the underpinning of Science and Technology, and should be applied far more rigorously in Database design than is typically done.

► "Relations" should not be confused with "Relationships." The term "Relational Database" refers to the fact that the key tables should always represent "Relations," which are not the same as "Relationships."

► Not all tables in a relational database will be "relational tables" (i.e. tables representing a Relation[117]), but all the entities of importance to a Business must be represented as relational tables.

► Correctly distinguishing Essential attributes from Accidental attributes during analysis will prevent developers from falling into many common data modeling traps. This is an essential (no pun intended) responsibility of the database designer!

---

117 Again, a "Relation" is not the same as a "Relationship." Don't confuse the two.

Illustration: Rear Admiral Grace Hopper (1906 – 1992): Admiral Hopper and her team created the first language and compiler for high-level computer programming.

Admiral Hopper ended her career as the oldest serving officer in the United States Military, having become an I/T Legend.

Her legendary wall clock is showing the time 10:07.

6 - RECENT HISTORY OF DATA MANAGEMENT

In the "Early History of Data Management" we talked about the centuries of philosophical and scientific developments that would eventually lead to what we now call Information Technology. This chapter reviews the birth and early life history of I/T – suggesting how rapid growth, as it often does with humans, resulted in the gangly, uncoordinated adolescent we now live with.

Computers and their Caretakers

As World War II was brewing in the late 1930s, computers, as they had been for many years, were working fulltime to handle the repetitive calculations required by Government, Science, and a few selected Industries. Central computers combined the outputs of many independent computers, permitting completion of large calculation projects that would otherwise have been impractical or extremely time-consuming.

Computers were rapidly becoming obsolete by this time, however, and were beginning to be replaced by more accurate and tireless electromechanical counterparts. Today, more than a decade into the twenty-first century, almost no one remembers that the word "computer" once referred exclusively to a human being.

Steady advances in electronics during the second half of the twentieth century soon transformed these early electromechanical beasts into smaller but more powerful and increasingly more capable systems. Methods for "programming" the actions of these machines beyond pure calculations were steadily improving, and by the mid-1980s, few businesses remained that were not reliant to some degree on the electronic computer (now simply "computer").

A new profession, as well as a highly competitive industry, grew up around these machines to support their programming, care, and feeding. Over the years, this profession has been labeled, among other things, as: Data Processing (DP), Electronic Data Processing (EDP), Management Information Systems (MIS), Information Systems (IS), and Information Technology (I/T). We won't mention the many other names given by the profession's beneficiaries and detractors!

Nash on Progress

"Progress might have been alright once, but it's gone on too long."

– Ogden Nash (1902-1971)

One must, of course, consider the reprehensible misuse by the IT industry of the word "Progress" as a euphemism for "Change."

Whatever anyone calls it, it is an exciting and dynamic profession. For those who strive to "keep current" by regularly reading trade literature and examining the continuous stream of upgrades and improvements emanating from the multitude of vendors, it seems that each day brings new advances. Many I/T practitioners consider themselves to be highly sophisticated – using "leading edge" techniques to provide flexibility and power to their operations, or to make their companies into "agile businesses" – something impossible to achieve with illogical database designs by the way, as we shall see.

From a business perspective, however, things don't seem all that impressive. Although many I/T departments seem to have some very bright, dedicated and hard-working people, progress toward fulfilling business needs and requests continues to be Sisyphean. Companies expend enormous time, effort and expense to obtain "enterprise views" of their pockets of disparate, redundant, and often conflicting data, to integrate their internal processes and, increasingly, to coordinate inter-company information and transactions. Periodic attempts to consolidate systems, create common data stores or even models, to share functionality, or achieve even minimal levels of reuse or repeatability are often abandoned after a short time as impractical or too expensive. I/T-project horror stories continue to abound – many even making it into the general press.

Few business managers would deny that computer automation has been beneficial, but few are not perturbed (if not astonished) by the costs. Many will admit that, while they tend to believe time and cost estimates provided by building contractors or vehicle repair shops, they generally mistrust (and often double) the estimates provided by their I/T professionals. Ironically, their I/T managers may have already doubled their own developers' time and cost estimates[118].

Nonetheless, it is still rare for an I/T project to be completed in the time required, or to fully implement all that had been promised – the practice of adjusting project objectives to match what has been completed by the end of the projected schedule being a commonly accepted practice. Interestingly, as the I/T profession has "matured" over the years, this has only become more of a problem.

To be fair, it can be argued that business and technology managers bear some blame for these problems by their seeming inability to clearly state their needs, by changing them during the development process, or by a naive belief in the hype and nonsense promulgated by vendors and consultants who are eager to capitalize on the business community's frustrations. But sharing the blame for these issues doesn't accomplish anything useful, and these issues must be addressed by I/T professionals themselves by rigorously segregating data definitions from business issues and treating each appropriately, preventing cross-contamination. But more on those critical distinctions later.

We'll now continue the capsule history of data management that we left off with the introduction of Bertrand Russell at the end of chapter 2.

---

118 A typical example: In "Bumpy Ride - Data Migration still plagued by problems", Intelligent Enterprise, March 20, 2003, page 10, there is a survey reported that concludes "the median cost of a data migration project was 10.7 times the amount budgeted." It should be quite clear that difficulties in "migrating data" suggest a fundamental design flaw somewhere!

Information Technology Time Line (from 1940)

The Modern Computer Era Begins

► 1940

By 1940, the world was in turmoil and the German and Japanese governments were using military might to aggressively expand their empires. Of specific interest to I/T history, these countries had developed mechanical devices to enable fairly complex methods for encrypting their communications in order to prevent potential opposition forces from realizing their intentions or, more importantly, their immediate tactics.

Primitive special-purpose computers had already been built in several countries, most notably to automate the tedious calculation of trajectory tables for Artillery[119] units, but there was now a need to apply the unique computation speeds of these devices to breaking the German and Japanese ciphers. The teams at Britain's Bletchley Park[120] devised automatic machinery to help with this. Because the encryption keys and even the algorithms used for encryption changed periodically, these efforts eventually led to the development of Colossus, the world's first programmable digital electronic computer. The first Colossus, designed and built by Tommy Flowers and his team at the Dollis Hill Post Office Research Station, was delivered to Bletchley Park in 1943. More followed, and the enhanced Mark 2 Colossus was in operation by D-Day[121].

---

119 Such tables had been provided to military personnel for at least a century because the computations, which used the weight of the shells to calculate the trajectories needed to reach specified target distances, were too time-consuming to be used in the heat of combat, even assuming that the gunners had the requisite mathematical skills.

120 These teams included a "who's who" of legendary names in Information Technology, such as Alan Turing (of "Turing Test" fame, and considered by many to be the "Father of Computer Science"), Dilly Knox, John Jeffreys, Gordon Welchman, "Doc" Keen and others.

121 Because of the Egyptian Rule, the ENIAC, completed in early 1946 by the University of Pennsylvania for the U.S. Army's Ballistic Research Laboratory, is generally considered the first fully-programmable electronic computer designed expressly to meet Turing's rules.

Chapter 6 - Recent History of Data Management

► 1950

Admiral Grace Hopper and her U.S. Navy team create the first "high-level" programming language, which they called FLOW-MATIC. This gave them the ability to write instructions in a quasi-English (albeit quite formal) language and have their "compiler" program translate the instructions into the tedious low-level, machine-specific, instructions that were quite different for each new computer or processor that was introduced.

This was a very significant breakthrough for the automation of processes since, in principle, when a newer, faster machine was introduced, a high-level program could simply be recompiled – a significant savings in time and effort. Admiral Hopper and her team had thus established the first "write once, run anywhere" applications and reuse was born. This problem continues to be "re-solved" every few years or so with a new language.

► 1951

The first UNIVAC computer introduced the use of half-inch wide metallic strips on reels as a storage mechanism; this scheme never caught on commercially, but became the precursor of magnetic tape technology once more flexible films with ferrous oxide coatings (by that time already commonly used in the audio recording industry) were adapted to computer use.

► 1953

A group of engineers at IBM's San Jose research laboratory develop a magnetic random access data storage medium that would eventually become known as a "hard drive." After several years of refinement, IBM introduced the first commercial product using this technology in 1956.[122]

See "Serendipity" later in this chapter (page 114) for more details.

---

122 The IBM 305 RAMAC system, which included their Model 350 "Disk Storage" units. The system could store 5 megabytes if all fifty 24" disks were installed in the 350 unit. Just about thirty years later, when IBM introduced their Personal Computer, a 5 megabyte drive was an option.

Business Joins the Modern Computer Era

► 1954

Computers slowly began to appear not only in Government and Military service, but in very large businesses, handling what today are considered rather mundane chores such as payroll processing, summary reporting, and the like. The "punch card" became ubiquitous as a means for storing data records as well as application program instructions. This created a very serious "good news – bad news" situation. The good news, of course, was that it allowed a nascent industry to fulfill some significant business needs and thus to develop and mature. The bad news is that it set the rather strange precedent that it was acceptable and even normal for attributes to have arbitrary limitations on size and character set placed upon their storage, leading to numerous time-wasting discussions about whether a last-name field should be 30, 35, or 50 characters long.

Admiral Hopper and her team introduced the idea of "subroutines" to promote consistency in their "software" as well as more efficiently utilize the limited amount of memory available to these programs.

► 1957

For scientific and mathematical software, the FORTRAN (FORmula TRANslating) language, developed by John Backus and his team at IBM was introduced to the market in April 1957.

In the same year IBM also introduced its COMTRAN (COMmercial TRANslator) language with the novel "Picture Clause." The picture clause permitted programmers to define the layout of data files to their programs, saving them from having to write elaborate routines to parse data streams into individual data elements themselves.

The Real World in the 1950s – A Business Perspective

In the 1950s, if anyone noticed that department A's card deck contained information on Customer Mary Smith that didn't quite match the information about Mary that was in department B's card deck, the most they could do was sigh, be thankful for the time savings of automated processing of the data on their cards, and wait for the sixties.

The good news is that much nicer furniture for storing 80 column cards began to appear – although Programming was beginning to develop and mature, the new furniture and the Picture clause in COMTRAN represented the only real progress in Data Management.

► 1959

The wider business world was now taking notice of computers, and commercial programming languages were being developed to bring the same benefits enjoyed by the military to the civilian world.

COBOL (an acronym for **CO**mmon **B**usiness-**O**riented **L**anguage), based largely on the Navy's FLOW-MATIC language, quickly became the most prominent and widely supported language in business computing. COBOL also incorporated COMTRAN's concept of the Picture Clause.

► Although the art of programming was now entering its adolescence, for most businesses, the idea of "permanent" random access storage and effective data management was still many years away.

► The Decade of the 1960s

The major breakthroughs of this decade, at least regarding what we call Information Technology, include:

> The Real World in the 1960s – A Business Perspective
>
> In the 1960s, if anyone noticed that department A's tape reel contained information on Customer Mary Smith that didn't quite match the information about Mary that was on department B's tape reel, the most they could do was fume, be thankful that dropping card decks no longer caused a crisis and wish for the seventies to come along.

▼ Magnetic Tape, prompted by advances developed by IBM and Digital Equipment Corporation, began to be used more frequently in Business due to its significantly lower cost and convenience.

▼ Development of smaller scale electronic devices (e.g. integrated circuits) continued, enabling second tier businesses to join the computer revolution as more cost-effective hardware became available.

▼ With the introduction of the Bryant 4000 Series, the "state of the art" in storage had now reached about 200 megabytes, although this was only affordable for government or very large corporate use.

▼ The very first hints of what later became known as Object-Oriented programming appeared in the Algol-60 programming language, whose other innovative features included the idea of "code blocks" and the ability to nest functions.

▼ Creation of the ASCII[123] standard coding that was touted as finally solving once and for all the difficulties of exchanging data between computers – a somewhat naive expectation, given what we've subsequently learned, but this assertion doesn't quite qualify as hyperbole, since it was apparently unintentional. It would be speculative to wonder what Aristotle would have thought of a universal standard that didn't include any characters other than English (which most authorities agree he was unfamiliar with), so I won't attempt to hazard a guess. One of the most important features of ASCII, by the way, was that upper case and lower case (English, of course) characters were coded exactly the same but for one bit, providing an easy means for case-insensitive sorting and the like by simply masking that bit.

▶ 1967

Ole-Johan Dahl and Kristen Nygaard of Norway introduced a mature version of their programming language Simula – a superset of earlier Algol language variants. Some credit this with being the first actual Object-Oriented programming language, but this claim is not generally accepted because the approach was entirely pragmatic and unaccompanied by any of the later theoretical discussions of the merits of Object Orientation[124].

▶ 1969-1970

Birth of the Relational Model: Dr Edgar F. (Ted) Codd, an IBM researcher, figured out an approach for applying predicate logic and set theory[125] to information systems – in particular, to the design of databases. His original

---

123 The American Standard Code for Information Interchange, in which many parties agreed that, henceforth, the letter "A" would always be represented by the binary equivalent of the number 65 (0100-0001), "B" by 66 (0100-0010), "a" by 97 (0110-0001), etc. This was certainly a major agreement, but since the largest vendor of the day (IBM) didn't buy into it, and there was as yet no agreement on the voltage value of a 1 or 0, and no agreement on the order in which the bits were sequenced, the effects of ASCII's adoption were not as significant as they might have been. The level of hyperbole regarding standards for data exchange capability increased as each subsequent step at standardization was concocted, and has reached its highest level yet with XML and its sibling variants. Santayana was right.

124 In other words, this is a variant in the Egyptian Rule. See "An Aside – The Egyptian Rule" on page 17 for more information. Also see the entry for the year 1988.

125 Well, a subset of set theory, if that makes sense.

publication of this approach[126] is still enlightening. While predicate logic and set theory were represented nicely in the model, Codd inexplicably minimized the importance of Classes and Taxonomies in the overall mix – an oversight that still causes some confusion today[127].

▶ 1973

This year saw the introduction of the first "Winchester" hard disk drives in sizes of 35 megabytes and 70 megabytes. The availability of Random Access data storage at this scale would eventually have a dramatic impact on the practice of Information Technology.

▶ 1974

C. J. (Chris) Date (the "Great Explainer", doing for Codd and the Relational Model what Lewis Carroll had done earlier for Georg Cantor and Set Theory) begins his ongoing, but largely quixotic, attempts to help I/T folks understand what "relational" is all about, and why it matters. An Introduction to Database Systems[128] is his most important work, and is currently in its eighth edition. Date didn't always agree with Codd, and there are many highly respected database professionals who don't agree with either Codd or Date on everything, but anyone claiming knowledge of business database design who is unfamiliar with some vintage of this indispensable work can safely be considered a fraud.

The Real World in the 1970s – A Business Perspective

In the 1970s, if anyone noticed that department A's disk pack contained information on Customer Mary Smith that didn't quite match the information about Mary that was on department B's disk pack, the most they could do was wonder about the data entry savings and marketing opportunities they had been promised for twenty years, and hope that the eighties would bring a way for both of Mary's records to be on the same disk.

▶ 1976

Dr. Peter Chen introduces and popularizes the use of Entity-Relationship Modeling[129] as a tool for database design and construction.

---

126 Codd [1]; see page 381

127 See the chapter "Freedom of the Press - Impedance Mismatches" for more information.

128 Date [1]; see page 382.

129 He is often credited for inventing it, but he never claimed that, and the germs of this tech-

Because this form of modeling was well suited to the limited capabilities of the early products being developed to support the relational model, it soon became entrenched and is still in wide use as a design tool (unfortunately, in my view, although it remains a very appropriate construction tool) today.

► 1977-1979

Software Development Laboratories (SDL – later Relational Software, Inc,[130] then simply Oracle) first introduces the Oracle Relational Database Management System. Although Ted Codd, who proposed the Relational Model, was an IBM employee, IBM was a market leader in non-relational systems and didn't develop its own relational product until many years later.

► The State of the Database Management Art in 1980

While the largest businesses had begun using Database Management Software, the average operation still handled their data stores with custom programming. Data was still stored as sequential records on cards and tapes and, although there were a number of programming tricks, the basic operations were similar to those described below:

▼ Assume that we have developed a record that is N characters in length.

▼ If there is an index[131] and we know that what we want is in record 43, we multiply 42 times N and add 1, placing us at the beginning of record 43. We may also need to add another value to account for any header that is present at the beginning of the file (sometimes used to identify how the records are organized into fields, etc.)

▼ We then need to perform a similar process to get to the particular field that we wish to read within a specific record. Of course, since the fields in each record are a fixed length, we often need to strip off the blank spaces at the end of each field, so that when, for example, we combine a customer's first and last names for an invoice we print "John Smith" instead of "John   Smith   ".

---

nique had appeared in earlier articles by other writers.

130 At least in those early days, RSI admitted that they were a software company. Oracle still is, of course, but now touts themselves as a database supplier – something they aren't.

131 ...and it should be mentioned that building and maintaining indexes was no trivial task.

▼ If there is no index, we may have to read a particular field from each record until we've located the one we want, then back up to the record's beginning to read the entire record.

▼ If we want multiple records meeting certain criteria, we do all the above, writing each record that meets our requirements to another "file" until the search is completed. We may then need to place these records in something other than their physical order, requiring many passes as we either create a new index, or write the records to yet another file.

▼ Then we select an appropriate sorting algorithm (quick – how many can you name by the way?) for the type and distribution of our data (do you know which algorithms are best suited for specific criteria?) and proceed with "processing" the data a little further.

A basic awareness of these common "data processing" steps (the descriptions of which have actually been simplified from what often needed to take place) is quite important when attempting to understand what happened after the introduction of the Relational Model. It is also critical to realize that, up to this point in time, Data Management was accomplished almost exclusively by Programming, and much of the effort expended by Programmers was related not only to "Data Processing," but to actual Data Management. Since both were accomplished in the same manner, I/T personnel got into the habit of making no distinctions between the handling of BUSINESS RULES and DATA RULES.[132]

The word "Relational" becomes Popular

► 1980 to 1990

Early adopters of the first "relational" tools began reporting good results and products such as SDL's RDBMS (Oracle) and the "me too" products that quickly followed began to garner significant market share. Because of this initial and continuing success of relational database management systems, it is often assumed quite incorrectly that this somehow indicated the industry's understanding and acceptance of the Relational Model. In a very

---

132 This reflects the "Hammer" Rule – if all you have is a hammer, everything looks like a nail.

few cases, this might have been so, but the acceptance of such products really had nothing much (if anything) to do with logic or anything of the sort.

As it happened, a product could not begin to support the relational model at all if it did not offer a number of features, among which are:

▼ ...the ability for a programmer to request data elements by name without having to know anything about the structure of the underlying database;

▼ ...the ability for the programmer to specify the order in which various data elements were presented, eliminating the need to understand or write custom sorting routines;

▼ ...elimination of the need to remove extraneous spaces from the ends of fields that had widely varying sizes;

These capabilities, and these capabilities alone, were responsible for most of the initial and continuing success of RDBMS products in the mass market. That these capabilities were only incidental to the relational model didn't seem to register with most developers who used the products. The attractiveness of these capabilities to developers did not escape the notice of other vendors, however, and the many non-relational products that subsequently provided some version of these unrelated features then began touting themselves as relational, leading to the mass confusion that still exists.

▶ October 1981

The first customer delivery of a multi-gigabyte hard drive, the IBM 3380, was made. As shown to the right, the unit weighed over 550 pounds and was about the size of a refrigerator. At a cost of between 80,000 and 150,000 dollars, the 2.5 gigabyte drive could be connected to other similar drives to provide even greater storage. Businesses now had significantly more random access data storage space – a necessity for beginning to treat data as a corporate asset – but the means for doing so responsibly were only just 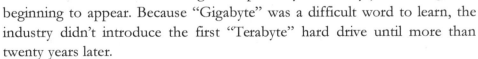 beginning to appear. Because "Gigabyte" was a difficult word to learn, the industry didn't introduce the first "Terabyte" hard drive until more than twenty years later.

▶ 1982 -

As both "relational" and "pseudo-relational" products began to be taken seriously, relational terminology began to be misappropriated by the great unwashed horde of bandwagon-jumping I/T vendors and self-proclaimed experts; technical concepts became obfuscated and relational terminology began to be recycled

The Real World in the 1980s – A Business Perspective

In the 1980s, both of Mary's records were finally on the same physical disk but, since each of the records were on separate virtual disks (an IT invention developed to hinder data integration), things hadn't really improved much.

as buzz-words with a wide variety of conflicting uses and meanings. People in and out of I/T began to lose sight of the distinction between the relational model, what it represented, and the RDBMS products that were provided to help make its implementation possible. Even today, no RDBMS product provides full support for the relational model!

▶ 1985

In the latter part of 1985, the confusion over what a database management system needed to be in order to qualify as "relational" became so prevalent that Dr. Codd introduced his now classic "12 rules" intended to clarify the subject.[133]

It was also about this time that the growing capabilities and power of the many existing RDBMS products (at least the real ones) gave rise to the need for specialized Database Administrators (DBAs). The new powers of these software products required increasingly complex management to realize their performance potential. The productivity gained by the use of these products – even when they were used to develop non-relational databases, which most were and still are – obscured the fact that such uses did not permit the maximum return on investment (ROI) that could be achieved.

Many in business assumed that Database Administrators, like "Key Operators" (who were widely utilized to handle the operational complexities of copiers at the time) would soon disappear as technology improved.

---

133 See Codd [2] on page 381. It is still very informative for designers of data structures.

► 1987

David Patterson, Garth Gibson and Randy Katz at UC Berkeley introduced the technology they originally called RAID (Random Array of Inexpensive Disks) to allow even very small businesses to obtain larger volumes of random access storage at a much lower cost and in a more incremental fashion than could be obtained by commercial products from the large vendors of the time. These general techniques were widely adopted, even by many of those same vendors, and heralded a new era of affordable storage[134].

Coupled with the increasing capabilities and market penetration of RDBMS products, 1987 can probably be singled out as the year that the "Management of Data" – one of Information Technology's primary responsibilities – became a viable possibility. Relative to the art of Application Programming, now leaving its adolescence and about to enter a new era of maturity, corporate Data Management was just beginning to crawl.

► 1988

A number of people who grasped what Codd was doing realized that set theory and predicate logic didn't need to be restricted to databases, but would provide a very useful approach to creating and maintaining extensible applications – sort of a culmination of the long path that began with the introduction of callable subroutines, the earlier development of Algol and Simula, and the concept of modularity. In 1988, Sally Schlaer and Stephen Mellor "introduce" Object Oriented approaches to the world outside AT&T[135], although the clear implications of the book's subtitle, "Modeling the World in Data," seem to have escaped most readers to this day. Schlaer and Mellor incorporate the idea of object taxonomies in addition to set theory and predicate logic; these eventually result in the concept of inheritance.

If Dahl and Nygaard had built a pyramid (see the 1967 entry on Simula), Schlaer and Mellor had begun to aim for the elegance of the Parthenon.

---

134 Of course, the acronym now means "Random Array of Independent Disks" because of its application to larger and more sophisticated storage systems. Most vendors consider "inexpensive" anything a clear and present danger that needs to be quashed immediately.

135 Schlaer [1]; see page 384.

► 1990 -

Many others began extending "OO" concepts, and products start becoming available to support this new approach to programming.[136] Application Programming was now entering late adolescence.

► 1991 -

Shortly after "OO" products appear, object terminology began to be misappropriated by the great unwashed horde of bandwagon-jumping I/T vendors and self-proclaimed experts; technical concepts were obfuscated and object terminology began to be recycled as buzz-words with a wide variety of conflicting uses and meanings.

The Real World in the 1990s – A Business Perspective

In the 1990s, Mary's two records were now on physical rather than logical discs. The good news is that all the company's computers were now networked; the bad news that was departments A and B now had data models that were way too dissimilar to justify the effort involved in integration.

► The mid 1990s

By this time, most of the imitation RDBMS products and those that temporarily survived by simply grafting on the "incidental" features described above, had faded away. Unfortunately, the continuing commercial success of the remaining RDBMS products caused marketing to move to the forefront in these companies, and further development of their product's relational capabilities (still incomplete) faded into the background in favor of other more easily understandable (and therefore easier to sell) capabilities.

► 1996 – 2000

Obfuscation and hyperbole reach new heights of foolishness with terms like "object-relational impedance mismatch"[137] and "post-relational database" along with a nearly constant stream of outlandish promises from vendors.[138]

---

136 Rumbaugh [1] on page 384 is a good example.

137 This will be discussed in more detail in Chapter 9, but properly designed relational databases (fairly uncommon) are quite compatible with properly designed object-oriented applications (slowly becoming more common).

138 I'm obviously somewhat of a cynic; some of the Vendors' hyperbole may just be ignorance in the guise of opportunistic drivel.

Somewhere in this period, the term "unstructured data" - a specialty term – was adopted as a euphemistic obfuscation for "disorganized data." I hope that the examples in various chapters of this book, along with a careful reading of some of the sources mentioned, will counter such silliness.

► The 21ˢᵗ Century

By 2007, terabyte-level hard drives had become commodity items even for consumer use, although data management for Business applications was still suffering from arrested development. Typical business operations still endured the constipation of multiple redundant data stores, and applications continued to spend a significant amount of their processing power because of the need to handle data management issues.

The decade-by-decade Business Perspective scenarios such as the one to the right and earlier are, of course, quite tongue-in-cheek, and would never happen in any business with a well-run I/T shop.   Right.

The Real World at the Turn of the Century – A Business Perspective

Early in the year 2000, Mary passed away from stress related to worries about her bank's handling of the Y2K crisis, and Department A deleted her record when Mary's daughter called to cancel her account.

In the year 2002, Department B tagged Mary as inactive, since she had unaccountably not responded to any promotions or made any purchases for the past two years.

In the year 2003, in the spirit of sharing information, Department A acquired a complete mailing list from Department B, merged it with their existing list, and mailed a large promotion to all customers who had previously dealt with the company. Mary was now reincarnated in Department A's database.

There is a point to this silliness, however. Historically, our technology has been unable to handle data sets large enough to support an entire enterprise. In the 1950s of course, even a reasonable sized customer record might need to occupy more than one card. Storage technology has advanced significantly since the mid-1980s, however and, for all practical purposes, **technical limitations to the implementation of large scale business databases no longer exist for most companies.**[139]

---

139 See the "The Single Operational Database" chapter beginning on page 345.

Inevitable Conclusions

Computer users realized quite early on that special purpose machines represented a dead end – becoming obsolete very quickly. Thus, general purpose computers appeared fairly early and, once altering the instructions for a computer changed from a hardware configuration process to one utilizing "software," "programming" was born as a profession and began its growth. At that time, and for many decades to come, data storage capabilities remained insufficient for any but token efforts to manage corporate data as a single entity.

Thus, "process management" (software development and programming) began maturing much earlier than "data management" and, in spite of the relative importance of the latter[140], the entrenched position of software development in the I/T pecking order has been difficult to overcome – even in the face of vast improvements in storage capacity – resulting in situations where, for instance, it still isn't deemed at all unusual for major business applications to each have its own database – something clearly not in the interests of the overall business.

General purpose computers appeared more than half a century ago, but general purpose databases – logically organized collections of randomly accessible data that could support an entire organization – really weren't feasible until the past two decades, and have still not penetrated Business I/T departments to any significant extent. As Relational database management software has become prevalent in business, databases were still viewed simply as aids to programmers. Businesses that are supported by a single Relational database are seldom seen. Business has yet to benefit fully from advances in data management capabilities.

So long as business database designs continue to follow process designs rather than being based on factual analysis of the Things about which a Business desires to retain data, responses to change requests that are most often related to new or altered processes are certainly going to take much longer to implement, and illumination of the overall state of the Business will remain elusive.

---

140 See "Relative Importance of an I/T Department's Two Primary Functions" in Chapter 1.

Serendipity

Although the RAMAC[141] is considered a breakthrough in the quest for a large scale random access storage device, this only became apparent years later. The truth – that the product was actually conceived and developed as a means of making the use of punched cards more efficient – has been studiously ignored.

IBM Model 305 Random Access Method of Accounting and Control (RAMAC)

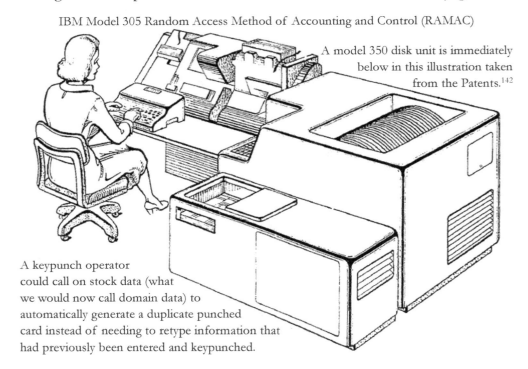

A model 350 disk unit is immediately below in this illustration taken from the Patents.[142]

A keypunch operator could call on stock data (what we would now call domain data) to automatically generate a duplicate punched card instead of needing to retype information that had previously been entered and keypunched.

Punched card decks were the means by which data was prepared for processing. When a new order was placed, for instance, a series of cards regarding the order were punched, and previously prepared stock cards for things like product and customer information[143] were pulled from storage to be inserted into the deck

---

141 See the 1953 entry earlier in this chapter.

142 Patents 3,134,097 and 3,503,060; also see the file http://files.asme.org/ASMEORG/Communities/History/Landmarks/5573.pdf for further history of this interesting invention.

143 Somewhat analogous to the foreign key data referenced in today's orders.

before it was sent for processing. The stock of duplicate cards for common data such as the products and customers in this example needed to be replenished periodically by having an operator either duplicate the cards that were being used up, or even retyping a new card if the last one had inadvertently been used.

This new system permitted the elimination of what were then called "tubs" that contained the collection of duplicate data cards.

If the company was busy enough to support more than one RAMAC, data management consisted of insuring that any new cards created on one machine needed to be copied onto the disk of the second machine. I know of no comparative data that would match this method of cross-database synchronization with that in most current businesses, so any cynical suspicions I have about which system worked better would merely be speculative.

So, even in the decade of the fifties, while programming techniques were beginning their growth, habits had already been ingrained in the I/T world that data was associated with a program, and that redundancy was pretty much the norm.

In the next chapter, we'll return to Wonderful Widgets Corporation (WWC) and their acquisition of Corporate Widgets Experts (CWX) to see how Triage and logical data redesign not only permitted a successful merger, but led to significantly expanded business opportunities not readily supported by the data models of either company.

Why it's taken so long for enterprise data viewpoints to be taken seriously!

A Perspective on Data Storage Costs over the past 32 Years

1981
IBM 2.5 GB
$100,000.00 +
(in 1981 dollars)
~7 feet high

State of the Art in 1981

2013
SanDisk 8.0 GB
$ 6.99
(in 2013 dollars)
~ 3 inches high

Very Low End in 2013

LESSONS FOR CHAPTER 6
RECENT HISTORY OF DATA MANAGEMENT

► "Programming" changed very early from a hardware configuration process accomplished by engineers to software written by member of a new profession called "programmers."

► The inconsistent progress of technological development in the twentieth century led to several unfortunate consequences:

  ▼ The ability to automate business processes far outpaced the development of the ability to store, much less automate the management of, data.

  ▼ A number of "habits" and "traditions" resulted from this imbalance that need to be excised from our DNA in order to improve our support for business.

► The development of the Relational Model, although it had the potential for improving our ability to handle data logically and correctly, has yet to provide the benefits that it could bring to Business.

  ▼ In order to support the Relational Model, early products needed to provide certain facilities that, while having little if anything to do with the Relational Model per se, were of enormous utility to I/T personnel. It was the introduction of these capabilities that drove the success of RDBMS products.

  ▼ As a result, the rapid success of "relational" products obscured the advantages of their underlying model. The utility of most business databases still could be improved significantly by adopting relational design principles.

► The second tier status of database design and architecture relative to "programming" needs to be changed

I always give myself such very good advice, but I very seldom follow it.
- Alice (Lewis Carroll via Walt Disney)

It would be so nice if something would make sense for a change.
- Alice; Ibid.

7 - FREEDOM OF THE PRESS: THE CUSTOMER

Business Perspective

The Customer is a key component in any Business, but much data modeling literature more often confuses rather than clarifies the issues involved in correctly (that is, realistically) modeling this entity. As we've seen in "A Corporate Merger – Part 1," any variant of "Customer" is (and must be treated as) an INTERSECTION in order to permit data structures that reduce redundancy and permit rather than impede Business expansion.

In "Recent History of Data Management," it was pointed out that valid concepts are often obfuscated over time or misunderstood to begin with. Because those tasked with designing databases are not usually specialists, they often need to rely on published material concerning techniques and methods for implementing these designs. Unfortunately the quality of material available varies widely, and it is difficult for those with limited exposure to formal logic, database design or even data modeling[144] to separate sound advice from nonsense. Although the examples in this book should assist in such evaluations, it is not easy to do much in a book of this scope but point out that this situation exists.

---

144 And, at the risk of being repetitious, data modeling deals with construction, not design.

The "customer-as-organization" versus "customer-as-person" issue illustrated in A Corporate Merger – Part 1 under "Accidents often occur at Intersections" on page 54, for instance, provides one example of the differences between good and bad material, and what to look out for.

In his excellent data modeling book[145], David Hay makes it very explicit that an "order" is essentially a contract between parties, and that a party may be (actually "must be") either a person or an organization of some sort. Although not as explicit, the authors of The Data Model Resource Book[146] likewise address this correctly. These two books (and certainly others) can safely be used as learning material, but many other authors present some solutions that, while possibly workable for single isolated applications (and is there really any justification for any of those anymore?), lead inevitably to poor data architectures not only across the enterprise but also beyond it, and certainly add unnecessary complexity to any applications written to utilize these data structures.

What is a Customer? - Misguided Literature

Presented with an identical "customer-as-organization or customer-as-person" scenario, one author, in what is an otherwise generally useful book[147], and one of the relatively few that are non-product-specific, suggests creating the class structures shown to the right.

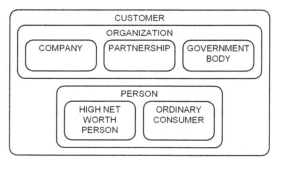

Poor Modeling of Subtypes and Supertypes.
Don't accept this !

This may or may not represent a convenient *view* of these entities from the standpoint of some particular application, but it clearly conflicts with reality. Consider *some* of what this diagram states in logical terms:

---

145 Hay [1]; see page 383. Chapter 6 of his book (Contracts) begins on page 95.

146 Silverston [1]; see page 384. See Chapter 4 of his book.

147 Simsion [1]; see page 385. See "Subtypes and Supertypes" on page 92.

Derived (Normalized) Proposition	Alternate Equivalent Propositions
T All Companies are Organizations	T Every Company **is an** Organization T A Company **must always be an** Organization T Any Company **is/must be an** Organization
F All Organizations are Customers	F Every Organization **is a** Customer F Any Organization **is/must be a** Customer F No Organization **is not a** Customer
Therefore: (based on the above) F All Companies are Customers	F Every Company is a Customer F Any Company must be a Customer
F All Persons are Customers	F Every Person **is a** Customer F Any Person **is/must be a** Customer F No Person **may not be a** Customer
T All Partnerships are Organizations	T Every Partnership **is an** Organization T Any Partnership **is/must be an** Organization
F No Partnership is a Company	F No Partnership **is a** Company F No Partnership **can be a** Company F No Company **is a** Partnership F No Company **can be a** Partnership

In "Mildly Offensive Beliefs" on page 36, I referred to the author's quote "*there is usually more than one way of doing this (classifying data into tables and columns)*" and suggested that the way he selected for his classification of data into tables and columns was logically incorrect.

By reading the author's diagram as if it were a group of Propositions[148], it is easy to see that this analysis is fundamentally flawed and should be summarily rejected as a basis for any further design.

As seductive as it may sound outside of a larger context, Organizations and Persons cannot logically be considered subclasses or subtypes of Customer. A further difficulty with the model is the author's introduction of "High Net Worth Person" and "Ordinary Consumer" as sub-Classes, which presents the following logical difficulties.

---

148 As mentioned repeatedly in this book, this is an extremely useful logical quality-control measure – far more useful in most cases than determining the "normal form" of a table.

▶ The definitions are arbitrary given the transient nature of "high net worth" (e.g. was this before or after the depression of 1929, the dot com boom of 2000, or the economic downturn of 2009?). Arbitrary distinctions should not be "hard-coded" into any database structure. Ever!

▶ These distinctions constitute a BUSINESS RULE rather than a DATA RULE and, as such, should not ever be "hard-coded" into any database structure.

▶ These distinctions might qualify as arbitrary subsets, but they certainly don't qualify as Classes. This is because the Person's net worth, however precisely we can measure it, is merely an Accidental[149] attribute and plays no part in determining whether or not a particular Person (e.g. John Smith – a Primary Substance) belongs to the Customer Class.

▶ Furthermore, the categories "High Net Worth Person" and "Ordinary Consumer" are clearly intended by the author to be mutually exclusive and, as Aristotle has pointed out, they therefore do not constitute (and should not be treated as) individual entities, and certainly not end up as tables in any logical database schema.

 Recall from chapter 5 that Aristotle tells us a "Thing" **must have no possible contrary** other than the theoretical set "not a Thing." Since "High Net Worth Person" and "Ordinary Consumer" are clearly contraries, these Sets are not valid Classes, and don't represent Secondary Substances.

Were we to replace some of the author's false assertions as presented by his diagram, we might (for example) end up with the Propositions:

T Any Organization may be a Customer

T Any Person may be a Customer

Note the significant distinction between the Author's implied "*is a* Customer" predicate and the more correct "*may be a* Customer" predicate. Also note that, if the correct predicates had been acknowledged during analysis, the diagram would have looked quite different[150].

---

149 See "Grammar: Verbs and Adjectives" beginning on page 72 for a discussion of the key differences between Essential and Accidental Attributes.

150 See the diagram in "Deja Vu" on page 61 for an idea of what a fact-based analysis would

It is also important to note that each of these Propositions is a DATA RULE, and is valid whether a more limiting BUSINESS RULE such as "we will never have an individual Person as a Customer" exists or not.

Interestingly enough, the author himself, although never explicitly rejecting it, apparently seems to realize there is something untenable about this model, and reduces the whole schema to a single Customer entity set, with a "Customer Type" attribute defined by the table to the right[151]:

Customer Type	Indicator
Company	Organization
Partnership	Organization
Government Body	Organization
High Net Worth Person	Person
Ordinary Consumer	Person

Bizarre and Illogical Taxonomy – Don't accept this !

Even without considering the lack of clear definition of "ordinary consumer" or the volatility of the "high net worth" attribute, this approach not only ignores logic, but adds complexity with no offsetting benefit and arguably makes the model even less realistic, less useful, and more prone to forcing application code to waste time dealing with data definition issues.

> *In what is referred to in logic as a "reductio ad absurdum," it may be helpful when analyzing such designs to apply similar distinctions to other rows in this table: Could we, for instance, divide the Customer Type "Government Body" into two separate categories called "Democratic Government Body" and "Dictatorship Government Body" and, if not, why not? And if two categories are helpful, why not three or six?*

The author attempts to rationalize his solution with the statement "relational data organization doesn't provide direct support for subtypes or supertypes."[152]. I suspect the author may have meant that current RDBMS *products* don't provide such support in an obvious manner, since the relational model, being heavily influenced by set theory, most certainly does, but this is nonetheless a flimsy excuse for creating an illogical model that is not likely to be compatible (or even

---

have produced.

151 One of the first rules for surviving when lost is, unless there is a clear danger in doing so, remain in place. It is less likely that you will be located and rescued if you wander off.

152 Simsion [1]; page 90.

congruent with) other data models in the enterprise, thus leading to substantial headaches in the future.[153] The fundamental flaw in the design presented, however, doesn't have as much to do with subtypes and supertypes but with the lack of recognition that any sort of "Customer" is a logical INTERSECTION.

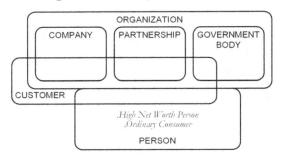

Ignoring the silliness of the domain table solution, the original schema can be partially "corrected" as shown to the left, but even this is not sufficient. Several issues remain to be resolved. The original Partnership set, for instance, should really be a subset of Company if normal legal definitions are accepted. Whether or not it becomes an entity set on its own or simply a type attribute of Company still needs to be clarified during the analysis and design processes.

The very arbitrary "High Net Worth Person" and "Ordinary Consumer" characteristics are dependent virtual attributes that should be inferred from other data. Although in a transactional system, such attributes might be physically realized for system performance reasons, this would be an implementation issue, not a design issue, and therefore the province of a DBA, not of a database designer.

The bottom line is that neither of the author's solutions to this issue reflect reality, and to suggest that this unrealistic view be used as the basis for an actual implementation of data structures is extremely troublesome[154]. Given the limitations these structures would place on even the application for which they were intended, not to mention the difficulty of integrating the information with

---

153 This is not to suggest that it might not be necessary at the physical layer to have some views which mimic such a structure, particularly if one is attempting to support a "legacy" application with read-only data, but that is an implementation decision, not a design one, and cannot and should not be made on the basis of a faulty logical design.

154 The logically supportable way of handling the Customer entity set as an Intersection will be discussed in the next chapter "A Corporate Merger – Part 2."

other systems, utilizing such a design comes very close to professional negligence.

Customer Semantics – Pseudo-Synonyms

In this chapter, we've seen how even the most straightforward examples of the Customer entity are often handled in such a way as to eventually lead to system constipation.

Because, as stated on page 1 of Chapter 1, "Business ... includes any interactions between two or more PARTIES, and is based on some form of implied or explicit contract," any given Business may need to deal with, and perhaps even supply products or services to entities that don't always meet the traditional definition of a Customer as "a Party that pays for goods or services received."

Effective Triage, therefore, needs to ensure that each specific "customer-like" entity be identified, and defined clearly enough to isolate the differences in ESSENTIAL ATTRIBUTES of each, as well as the proper level of each in any class hierarchy that may be uncovered. Generic pseudo-synonyms to watch for include "User," "Patron" and "Client", as well as domain-specific terms such as "Subscriber" or "Patient."

Conversely, good triage must ensure that any entity called "Customer" actually meets whatever specific criteria is appropriate for the business being analyzed.

Consider, for example: When buyer-seller contracts are implied, it is quite possible that not all, if any, customers can be individually identified. The person who purchases a single candy bar for the posted price could conceivably be identified if the transaction was made with a credit card, but such identification would generally be impractical if cash were used.

Be sensitive when the business uses terms such as "paying customer." Although this might simply be a typical example of marketing-speak (for example "our drug provides relief for a **full** twenty-four hours"), it might indicate that there are two separate entities, and the attributes of "paying customers" must be carefully compared to those of the implied "non-paying customers" to ensure a robust and extensible model.

A "User" might not actually be a paying Customer at all. In the case of Google, it is fairly obvious that someone performing a search would not be a Customer – it is the advertisers after all who are paying for the services – but the user may share certain attributes with a traditionally defined Customer.

The bill for a hospital stay may be paid partially by one or more insurance companies and partially by one or more private parties who may or may not include the actual patient. How many expressed or implied contracts are involved, and how are the various Parties distinguished from one another?

In the case where a college contracts with an outside company to supply cable television and various internet services to each room in a student dormitory, a much greater level of detail may be required for each student (User) than for the entity paying the bills (the College). This becomes even trickier if the Supplier also directly contracts with individual students for the provision of additional services such as premium television channels or additional internet bandwidth. The definitions and data model for such a business must be well defined in terms of sets and/or classes before any development begins if the resulting database and related applications are to meet ongoing business needs in an extensible and efficient manner.

LESSONS FOR CHAPTER 7
FREEDOM OF THE PRESS - THE CUSTOMER

► Freedom of the Press is desirable, but results in us having to accept an increased responsibility for validating the information available.

► Some information we encounter can be very useful, but much is flawed for any of several reasons.

► Not all entities that might qualify for the term "Customer" are equivalent, and care must be taken to distinguish these from one another.

► This Chapter provides examples of how:

▼ Customer, arguably one of the most critical entities in a Business Database, is defined illogically or inconsistently in much available literature.

▼ In almost any Business, many intersections across Parties, Customers, People, and Organizations (as well as many subclasses of these entities) will be identified. Many of the published solutions for handling these are quite demonstrably illogical. Proper formulation and use of formal Propositions will not only easily identify the flaws in these purported solutions, but will lead to models that will better serve both the application developers and the business.

"The conventional view serves to protect us from the painful job of thinking." – John Kenneth Galbraith

Introducing the Base Table/View Approach.

We now revisit the merger between Wonderful Widgets Corporation and Corporate Widgets Experts to get a glimpse of how the theoretical solutions described earlier were successfully implemented in practice.

8 - A Corporate Merger – Part 2

Resolution of the Merger

We concluded chapter 4 "A Corporate Merger – Part 1" with the basic logical model shown to the right that identifies some core classes/ entities of the integrated database used by Wonderful Wid-

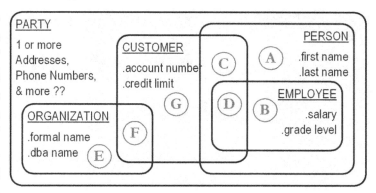

gets Corporation (WWC) and Corporate Widgets Experts (CWX) after their merger. Before proceeding to describe how the data integration was completed, we'll discuss the Members of the sets (letters A-H) to make sure the relationships among the various Classes, sub-Classes, and Intersections are clear:

► (A) represents an individual Person. We may or may not care about Persons who are not also members of some sub-class (such as Employee) or intersection – (such as Customer-Person), but we certainly haven't accounted for all possible sub-classes of Person for which we may have a business interest. A sales lead or a contact for some other organization we deal with, perhaps – so if we have sub-classes of such an entity, that entity must be modeled.

► (B) represents an Employee who, by definition, is always a Person. Because Employee is a PROPER SUBSET (and Subclass) of Person, anything that can be said about a Person is also true of (and can be said about) an Employee. Things that can be said about an Employee, however, are not always true of a Person and are, in fact, the very attributes[155] that distinguish a particular Person as an Employee in our database (in this case **Salary** and **Grade**).

► (C) represents an individual Person who is also a Customer. Anything that can be said about a Customer (and this refers to an actual Customer, not the poorly named intersections one sees in many databases[156]) is also true of (and can be said about) this Person, and anything that can be said about a Person can be said about this Customer. Again, however, what is always true of a Customer may or may not be true of any Person or Organization.

► (D) represents an Employee who happens to be a Customer and, by virtue of the fact that Employee is a PROPER SUBSET of Person, is also a Person.

► (E) represents a specific corporation that we care to keep information about. A specific organization represented by (E) is not a Customer, so we can assume that, although it may become one in the future or may have been one in the past, there is some other reason why this data is present. Typically, it may be a potential Customer or even a Competitor we are tracking, a Vendor that we are dealing with, or similar. It may, in fact, be data that we maintain on our own Business.

► (F) represents a specific corporation that is also one of our Customers.

► (G) represents a Customer that falls into some category other than Person or Organization. Perhaps it may be a Government, whose set of attributes may distinguish it from other Organizations, or it may belong to a subset of

---

155 This particular group of attributes is what Lewis Carroll calls the Thing's Peculiar Adjunct (see the chapter titled "Grammar, Sets, and (Predicate) Logic – Part 1").

156 Reread "Accidents often occur at Intersections" on page 54 if that isn't perfectly clear.

a typical Organization – such as a non-profit that we need to deal with differently. From the diagram, we don't know – we only know that it is logically possible for (G) to exist and the model should not preclude this.

▶ There is, of course, an implied set (H) – a Party that doesn't fall into any of the other sets, but considering such a possibility here would be a distraction.

Movement of Data to the Consolidated Schema

The diagram below shows, in very basic form, how the component elements of the various example sets in the two original WWC and CWX data structures were migrated to the new consolidated schema.

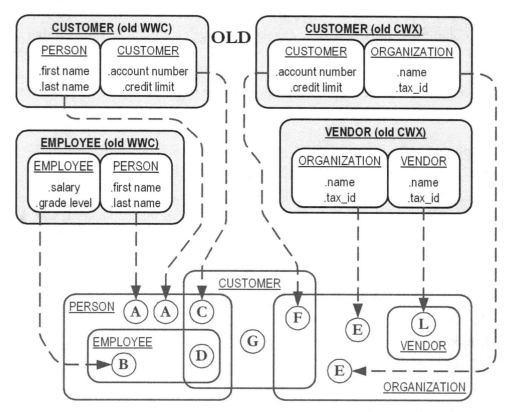

After an offline matching process to identify Parties that may have been customers and/or vendors of both WWC and CWX[157], new Party IDs were assigned to each Party – recall that Party encompasses any and all entities of interest to either business – and data was copied into the new structures. For simplicity's sake, the Party Class is not shown in the diagram.

For example, attributes in WWC's original **Customer** and **Employee** tables that were peculiar to Person (exemplified by **first_name** and **last_name** – vague terms that we will be renaming[158]) were copied to the new **Person** table with, of course, the same primary key each element had been assigned in the new **Party** table.

The remainder of the transfers were accomplished in similar fashion, with the columns in each company's original database tables transferred to the appropriate columns in the new database tables. Although it should be obvious that there had to have been many more Entities (or Classes if you will) in the merged company's database (as there would be in any "real-world" database), we will restrict our discussion to just these few in order to keep the following discussions manageable.

Application Changes

Once the data migration had been completed, and the many inevitable data duplications and conflicts resolved, the database was well-organized and able to fulfill all the criteria desired of a good business relational database. It was necessary, of course, that significant reworking of application code (much of which would be simplification) would be required to take advantage of the new model.

The core data model consisted of the six representative tables described in the form of grossly simplified SQL statements on the next page. Note particularly that four of the expected table names (Person, Organization, Customer, and Employee) have been prefixed with the abbreviation "bt" (meaning "base table"). The significance of this convention will be addressed in the next section.

---

157 A relatively straightforward (albeit complex) process, but out of scope for this example.

158 See "Renaming the Name Attributes – Who's on First?" on page 140 for details.

The Party table, on which all else depends, is created as follows:

```
CREATE TABLE PARTY
    (ID              NUMBER (2)       NOT NULL,
    CONSTRAINT PK_ID PRIMARY KEY ( ID ) );
```

The various base tables discussed below are created with statements similar to the following:

```
CREATE TABLE bt_PERSON
    (ID              NUMBER (2)       NOT NULL,
    Given_Name       VARCHAR2(12)     NOT NULL,
    Surname          VARCHAR2(12)     NOT NULL,
    CONSTRAINT PK_pID PRIMARY KEY ( ID ),
    CONSTRAINT FK_ID FOREIGN KEY ( ID )
            REFERENCES PARTY ( ID ) );

CREATE TABLE bt_ORGANIZATION
    (ID              NUMBER (2)       NOT NULL,
    Name             VARCHAR2(35)     NOT NULL,
    CONSTRAINT PK_oID PRIMARY KEY ( ID ),
    CONSTRAINT FK_oID FOREIGN KEY ( ID )
            REFERENCES PARTY ( ID ) );

CREATE TABLE bt_CUSTOMER
    (ID              NUMBER   (2)     NOT NULL,
    Account_No    VARCHAR  (5)     NOT NULL,
    Credit_Limit NUMBER (9,2)      NOT NULL,
    CONSTRAINT PK_cID PRIMARY KEY ( ID ),
    CONSTRAINT FK_cID FOREIGN KEY ( ID )
            REFERENCES PARTY ( ID ) );

CREATE TABLE bt_EMPLOYEE
    (ID              NUMBER (2)       NOT NULL,
    Salary           NUMBER (7,2)     NOT NULL,
    Grade_Level NUMBER (1)       NOT NULL,
    CONSTRAINT PK_eID PRIMARY KEY ( ID ),
    CONSTRAINT FK_eID FOREIGN KEY ( ID )
            REFERENCES bt_PERSON ( ID ) );
```

A Note on Naming Conventions

There are many opinions on how tables and classes should be named and, without attempting to establish "rules" it needs to be emphasized that whatever approach is taken, it should be consistent across the enterprise. The conventions I use are explained below:

Singular Class Name: There is only one singular Class "Person." The plural "Persons" refers to the collective members of that Class. Although some refer to a Class by the plural, I don't do that since, as both Aristotle and Carroll point out, it is quite possible for a Class to have some attributes that are not shared by any of its members. Therefore it must be clear that the Class and its collective membership are not the same thing. (Remember that, as earlier explained, Carroll didn't distinguish between "Set" and "Class.") I therefore ignore ISO/IEC 11179 naming guidelines, which result in non-grammatical Predicates: e.g. John is a Persons.

Intersections: I have chosen to call the two intersections discussed in this chapter "Customer_Organization" and "Customer_Person" rather than "Organization_Customer" and "Person_Customer." Although the point is made in the text that "Person" and "Organization" are not "types" of Customer, they do serve as informal descriptors for Customer, which is the primary entity of interest in these intersections. Plurals are never appropriate for intersections, by the way, since such entities are seldom inclusive.

Although easy to comprehend because of its similarity to an object model, this collection of tables seems to be perversely difficult to use from the standpoint of an application designer. The following sections, however, will discuss how a judicious use of database Views can simulate the Object

Classes (**Employee, Customer_Organization,** and **Customer_Person**) needed by the application developers. Although View creation is straightforward, it is critical to determine whether we will be creating Views against a PROPER SUBSET (such as **Employee**) or an INTERSECTION (such as **Customer_Organization** or **Customer_Person**) since these are handled differently.

Proper Subsets as Views

We'll begin with the **Employee** entity set, which we would like to treat as if it simply "inherited" all the attributes of its superset – in this case **Person**. The most straightforward method of doing this is to establish the proper subsets as "base tables," which we'll prefix with the notation "bt" for this exercise. We then create a View[159] called simply **Employee** which, for all practical purposes, is what our applications and reports will access. This is shown below:

BT_PERSON		
ID	Given_Name	Surname
----	--------------------	----------------
33	John	Smith
35	Rebecca	Apple
37	Steve	Banana
39	Theresa	Caramel
41	Victor	Donut
43	Adam	Eclair
45	Beth	Frosty
47	Denise	Gelato
49	Frank	Hamburger

From the base tables **bt_Person** and **bt_Employee**, we can create a working VIEW simply called **Employee** that can be used for the day-to-day operations of reading and maintaining (updating) our data. With the sample data shown in the **bt_Person** and **bt_Employee** tables, the working **Employee** View will show the data below:

BT_EMPLOYEE		
ID	Salary	Grade
----	-------------	---------
35	23456.98	1
37	34567.96	2
39	45678.94	3
41	56789.92	3

```
CREATE VIEW Employee AS
   SELECT p.ID
        , Given_Name, Surname
        , Salary, Grade_Level
     FROM bt_PERSON p
        , bt_EMPLOYEE e
    WHERE e.id = p.ID
    WITH CHECK OPTION
```

EMPLOYEE (working View)				
ID	Given_Name	Surname	Salary	Grade
----	--------------------	----------------	-------------	---------
35	Rebecca	Apple	23456.98	1
37	Steve	Banana	34567.96	2
39	Theresa	Caramel	45678.94	3
41	Victor	Donut	56789.92	3

---

159 Here (below) and elsewhere, the queries shown do not use the current INNER JOIN syntax in order to be as compatible with as many products as possible. Feel free to substitute the current form if your RDBMS supports it.

With virtually all RDBMS products[160], day-to-day management of the employee data can be handled exactly as if the **Employee** view were a table and, by using this technique, we will have eliminated the redundancy of having (for instance) **Given_Name** and **Surname** in many tables. Since attributes belonging to any element in the Class hierarchy of a PROPER SUBSET[161] like Employee are easily accessible for reading and updating, this technique also has the benefit of permitting cleaner use of realistic object hierarchies within a Company's applications, thus removing further redundancy from the system.

What seems at first blush to be bad news is that there are no RDBMS products that will permit creation and/or deletion of records from this view. The good news is that we really don't care! The simple reason for this is that the rules for adding or deleting such records turn out to be more dependent on BUSINESS RULES than DATA RULES and, as we have stated earlier, implementation of business rules needs to have a strong procedural rather than structural component.

To understand why this is so, let's first look at what needs to be done to delete an Employee record. In actual practice, most companies would, and indeed are required to, keep the employee data intact, and thus would simply change a status code and update a departure date (for simplicity, none of this is shown). But for the sake of argument, assume that we decide to delete the Employee. The following points discuss the business process choices necessary:

▶ Determine if the Person represented by the Employee record is also referenced by another sub-Class; is this Employee-Person, for instance, also a Customer-Person? In this circumstance, we might simply delete the entry in the **BT_Employee** table above and allow the entries to remain in the **BT_Customer**, **Person** and **Party** tables. The Person might in fact have been a poor employee, but a good Customer who will continue purchasing from us using the proceeds of any severance pay we offered.

---

160 It should go without saying that you need to confirm that your own RDBMS can do this; the sample scripts (using Oracle SQL) shown here can be used as a guide.

161 For Employee, this includes Party and Person attributes and relationships, as well as those of Employee (contained in the base table bt_Employee in this instance).

▶ We have already established that there is a **Party** table providing, among other things not yet discussed, the primary key for this **Person** and **Employee**. As we have mentioned previously, any contact information such as addresses and telephone numbers should be implemented as attributes related to Party. We still need to determine, therefore, if there is any Employee-specific contact data, such as a company-issued cell phone[162]. If so, we would need to sever the connection between that phone and the Party rather than simply deleting the phone data. And, of course, we need to determine whether we permit other contact information for this Party to remain.

If deletion of the Person record is deemed appropriate, determine whether the Party record represented by the Person and Employee record should be deleted as well. Laws promulgated by different government and industry bodies and so forth may also affect the design of processes that handle deletions.

For Business Managers who have read this far:

The term "Atomic Transaction" refers to handling several actions as if they were one, and insuring that either **all** of them are completed or that **none** of them is completed.

The classic example of such a need is when you transfer funds from one account to another at an ATM, all of which usually takes place via some communications channel.

Withdrawal from one account and deposit to a second account are separate transactions against separate accounts, but completing only one of these transactions would result in very significant accounting complications.

As you think of other similar circumstances in your own business (e.g. shipping an item and also removing it from inventory), ask your IT personnel how these activities are handled as atomic transactions – show them you care. Should you be met with blank stares, though, you need to worry.

While deletion of data from various levels of PROPER SUBSET Views involves business-driven procedures, these must be handled as a single ATOMIC TRANSACTION (see the sidebar). Although there are various means for accomplishing this, the simplest and most cost-effective approach is to use the inherent capabilities of the Company's RDBMS to handle this.

Addition of records to a PROPER SUBSET View is also a BUSINESS RULE issue and not a DATA RULE issue, but we'll postpone the discussion of additions until after the next example.

Intersections as Views

Creating Views for common intersections is similar, as shown below:

---

162 Of course, if the company has its act together, such data will be used as part of any departure check-list, but let's not get ahead of ourselves.

From the base tables **bt_Organization** and **bt_Customer**, we can create a working VIEW **Customer_Organization** that can be used for reading and maintaining our data. With sample data as shown in the base tables **bt_Organization** and **bt_Customer**, the working View will show the data below:

BT_ORGANIZATION

ID	Name
53	Wonderful Widgets Corporation
55	Corporate Widgets Experts
57	Phenomenal Widget Masters
59	Widgets for All, Inc.
61	The Widget Factory

BT_CUSTOMER

ID	Account_No	Credit_Limit
37	IL421	1000.00
39	TX715	1000.00
43	MO158	1000.00
45	FL622	1000.00
47	CT841	1000.00
49	MD359	1000.00
53	CA833	120000.00
55	MS587	120000.00
57	DE923	120000.00
59	WA385	120000.00
61	TX774	120000.00

```
CREATE VIEW Customer_Organization AS
SELECT o.ID
     , Name
     , Account_No
     , Credit_Limit
  FROM bt_ORGANIZATION o
     , bt_CUSTOMER c
 WHERE o.ID = c.ID
  WITH CHECK OPTION
```

CUSTOMER_ORGANIZATION   (working View)

ID	Name	Account_No	Credit Limit
53	Wonderful Widgets Corporation	CA833	120000.00
55	Corporate Widgets Experts	MS587	120000.00
57	Phenomenal Widget Masters	DE923	120000.00
59	Widgets for All, Inc.	WA385	120000.00
61	The Widget Factory	TX774	120000.00

BT_PERSON

ID	Given_Name	Surname
33	John	Smith
35	Rebecca	Apple
37	Steve	Banana
39	Theresa	Caramel
41	Victor	Donut
43	Adam	Eclair
45	Beth	Frosty
47	Denise	Gelato
49	Frank	Hamburger

From the base tables **bt_Person** (left) and **bt_Customer**, we can create a working VIEW called **Customer_Person** that can be used for reading and maintaining our data. With the sample data shown in the **bt_Person** and **bt_Customer** tables, the working View will show the data below:

```
CREATE VIEW Customer_Person AS
  SELECT p.ID
       , Given_Name
       , Surname
       , Account_No
       , Credit_Limit
    FROM bt_PERSON p
       , bt_CUSTOMER c
   WHERE p.ID = c.ID
    WITH CHECK OPTION
```

CUSTOMER_PERSON   (working View)

ID	Given_Name	Surname	Account_No	Credit Limit
37	Steve	Banana	IL421	1000.00
39	Theresa	Caramel	TX715	1000.00
43	Adam	Eclair	MO158	1000.00
45	Beth	Frosty	FL622	1000.00
47	Denise	Gelato	CT841	1000.00
49	Frank	Hamburger	MD359	1000.00

As with the earlier **Employee** View, the **Customer_Organization** and **Customer_Person** Views have eliminated a good deal of redundant data storage, and can easily be used for most normal business transactions. Also, however, as with the earlier **Employee** View, no RDBMS products will permit creation and/or deletion of records from these views. Also, again, we really don't care, because the decisions that need to be made when such records are created or deleted depend on BUSINESS RULES – not DATA RULES – and these rules are largely procedural.

Addition of Records

Procedures for adding new records to Views like those described above are a bit more complex, but still quite straightforward from a logical standpoint. Returning to the **Employee** View[163] above, let's consider the basic approach necessary when adding a new Employee which, as we have seen, requires the existence of its primary key in both the Person and Party tables.

▶ Does the Person we intend to hire already exist in our database, perhaps even as a Customer?

▶ Did someone in the Human Resources department already have this person's data entered under the guise of another PROPER SUBSET "Potential Candidate," with several distinctive attributes of its own?

Remember, the very existence of a PROPER SUBSET carries with it the implication that a member of that set might already exist as part of the super-set. Logically, we can't predict this and it needs to be determined for each transaction.

We certainly don't want to add a second, duplicate row to the **bt_Person**[164] or **Party** tables, so we need to simply make a new entry into the **bt_Employee** base table using the primary key of the Person whose resume impressed us. It should

---

163 The general approach for Employee, Customer_Person and Customer_Organization are similar but, since Employee is conceptually simpler, I've used that as the example.

164 If we're very lucky, there may be an opportunity to place a Unique index on the superset entity to help prevent this, but Person attributes (such as names) don't usually present such opportunities. An approach to this that fits with the company's needs must certainly be considered during analysis, however. See the chapter "Handling Constraints" on page 169 for a discussion of the wide variety of methods and locations for doing this.

be relatively clear that the possibilities to be considered are numerous and, as stated earlier, the appropriate actions are not inherently data-dependent, but are dictated by the needs and procedures of a particular corporation.

The steps needed to locate an existing Person with the same identity as the new Employee we are attempting to insert (using the above example) might involve checking for any Person with the same or similar proper name, surname, address, phone number or birth year (to avoid confusing a son with a father, for instance). All these elements (and possibly others) would likely be checked and a ranked set of possible matches provided to the person doing the data entry. A certain level of exact matches might be set to bypass any human intervention, but this step is crucial to avoid contamination of the corporation's data.

Routine Usage of Views

As demonstrated by the **Employee** view, Proper subsets can be most appropriately named using the name of the subclass, so long as the base table for that subset isn't given that same name. Hence the use of "bt" (base table) as a prefix.

To experiment with this approach, create and populate all the data objects described in the diagrams for "Proper Subsets as Views" and "Intersections as Views" by using the sample SQL DDL shown on page 388.

```
INSERT INTO PARTY (ID) VALUES (39);

INSERT INTO bt_PERSON
     (ID, Given_Name, Surname)
   VALUES (39, 'Theresa', 'Caramel') ;

INSERT INTO bt_CUSTOMER
     (ID, Account_No, Credit_Limit)
   VALUES (39, 'TX715', 1000.00) ;

INSERT INTO bt_EMPLOYEE
     (ID, Salary, Grade_Level)
   VALUES (39, 45678.94, 3);
```

A Note about Transaction Control

It will always be the case that a new entry into the **Party** table and the related entry into the **bt_Person** table must be handled as an atomic transaction.

Whether inserts such as the 3rd and 4th shown on the left are included in the transaction depends largely on the circumstances of the activity being recorded.

Transaction control must always be considered when handling data related to Class Hierarchies in a relational database.

Normal day-to-day use and maintenance of PROPER SUBSET views such as **Employee** or INTERSECTION views such as **Customer_Person** is quite straightforward. We can query the **Employee** view easily and retrieve all the attributes of the higher Classes to which it belongs. For example, a simple employee query for Theresa Caramel (ID=39) looks like:

```
SELECT ID, Given_Name, Surname, Salary, Grade_Level
  FROM EMPLOYEE
  WHERE ID = 39;
```

and will return the values from both the **bt_Person** and **bt_Employee** tables:

ID	Given Name	Surname	Salary	Grade Level
39	Theresa	Caramel	45678.94	3

Likewise, the customer query for Theresa Caramel:

```
SELECT ID, Given_Name, Surname, Account_No, Credit_Limit
  FROM CUSTOMER_PERSON
  WHERE ID = 39;
```

will return values from both the **bt_Person** and **bt_Customer** tables:

ID	Proper Name	Surname	Account	Credit Limit
39	Theresa	Caramel	TX715	1,000.00

Updates to data in either sort of View are also just as straightforward; if our employee Theresa Caramel marries and changes her name to Theresa Butterscotch, we could just update the **Employee** view with a statement such as:

```
UPDATE EMPLOYEE SET Surname = 'Butterscotch' WHERE ID = 39 ;
```

and both the Employee and Customer queries used above for Theresa will return the new Surname value:

ID	Given Name	Surname	Salary	Grade Level
39	Theresa	Butterscotch	45678.94	3

ID	Given Name	Surname	Account	Credit Limit
39	Theresa	Butterscotch	TX715	1,000.00

Additional testing of your own will confirm that the frequency of redundant and inconsistent data (in this example, the name) can be significantly reduced and, in many cases, eliminated as a concern[165]. Theresa's surname change from Caramel to Butterscotch was made in one location, and since it is actually stored in only one location (in this particular example, the **bt_Person** table), consistency across the enterprise is guaranteed. Observe that, had the name change been made in the **Customer** View instead, the results would have been the same.

As it turns out, whether we add to any superset or not during data entry, or delete from any superset during data removal depends on many things – our company's own policies, rules promulgated by many different government and industry bodies and so forth. All these "rules" are arbitrary and not fact-based. The excuse that current database management technology doesn't give us the flexibility to handle them in a strictly declarative manner turns out to be some-what irrelevant.

Clearly, the decisions that need to be made when creating or deleting data in a PROPER SUBSET or INTERSECTION include a significant dose of procedural issues and, as I have pointed out earlier, these are the proper provenance of applica-tion code. The location of this code, however, is a major consideration, but it should be accomplished as close to the data as possible, and certainly in a serial fashion. We will discuss these issues more thoroughly (and explain "in a serial fashion") in the chapter on "Handling Constraints," beginning on page 169.

Some Comments on "Base Tables"

Generally speaking, the Base Tables are not typically used by, or even accessible to, most users and applications. The intent is that only a few trusted routines – mainly those tasked with handling insertions and deletions on behalf of the Views – would be permitted access. Ideally, these would be stored procedures within the database itself. Again, the chapter titled "Handling Constraints" pro-vides a more comprehensive discussion on placement of such routines.

---

165 … unless of course your company is still saddled with multiple redundant databases.

Renaming the Name Attributes – Who's on First?

While it is possibly obvious to those who perused the chapter titled "Grammar, Sets, and (Predicate) Logic – Part 1" (and particularly the short paragraph on page 73 titled "Naming our Things") why the original attributes First_Name and Last_Name were retitled Given_Name and Surname respectively, it is perhaps worth some further discussion[166].

We know of course that, at least in the United States, the term "Last Name" represents the name of a person's "family," although in truth this is a bit misleading. Because our society defines the concept of "family" in a patrilineal fashion, it actually identifies the family name of a person's father and his direct line of male ancestors. In order to support the world at large, however, we need to understand that not all societies have the same view; family names of a few cultures reflect matrilineal descendancy, and the family names of many more cultures reflect the descendancy of both parents.

A more immediate concern, however, is the use of terms such as "first" and "last." Although we consider it perfectly normal to place the family name "last," we certainly don't find it abnormal when some government form instructs us to "Enter the Last Name first." This of course begs the question of where the middle name fits in, but that brings up even more complications.

More to the point, many cultures such as the Chinese[167] place their family name first rather than last. The traditional practice among some Hispanic societies is to hyphenate the family names of both parents as their "Last Name." In a few commercial software packages, however, the database or application designs (or possibly both) prohibit the use of hyphens in name fields, leaving the user to use the "Middle Name" field for one parent's family name. Sometimes, of course, the "Middle Name" field just contains a middle name – a situation that breeds inconsistency and potential misinterpretation of data.

---

166 To be honest, I suspect that many readers automatically skipped over a chapter titled "Grammar, Sets, and (Predicate) Logic – Part 1" as irrelevant. Go back and read it; it's not!

167 Is it necessary to point out that the Chinese alone outvote us on this convention?

As stated earlier, this book is not intended as a design text, but simply to illustrate the issues database designers need to consider. The use of **Given_Name** (name given at birth, Proper Name, Personal Name, Forename, etc.) and **Surname** (Family Name, whether Patronymic, Matronymic, or both, etc.) should not be considered a "solution" to this issue, but merely to rid the illustrations of vague and misleading terms like "first" and "last."

As repeated often in this book, good database design should ensure that, even if you don't need to implement a fully universal model, your model should not preclude or hinder any future migration to such a model.

Revisiting Proper Attribute Placement in Classes and Tables

In "A Corporate Merger – Part 1," before renaming them, we moved the "First Name" and "Last Name" attributes from both the **Employee** and **Customer** tables and placed them in the common superset table **Person**.[168] This was done to conform to Aristotle's maxim that we would "render a more instructive account by stating the species rather than the genus."[169]

In "Grammar, Sets, and (Predicate) Logic – Part 1," we saw some of the logical underpinnings for this decision and, in this chapter, discussed the resulting benefits to our company's data integrity. Nonetheless, the idea that **Given_Name** and **Surname** (and similar attributes) are not valid attributes of, for instance, the class/set Employee, doesn't sit well with some. It is helpful, therefore, to approach the placement of such attributes from another perspective.

> A Core Principle about Redundancy
>
> Storing identical attributes (in this example, for instance, the Given Name and Surname) for the same individual presents an inherent threat to data integrity.
>
> Even the *potential* for storing "John" and "Smith" in several different tables such as Employee, Patient, Customer, and so forth when John is the same person in all cases should be avoided. Period.

Take any group of closely related attributes proposed as part of a particular entity. As an example, use the various name attributes we've already mentioned (Proper Name, Surname, Middle Name, and so forth). Then, acknowledging the

---

168 In this chapter, we renamed them more correctly, but that isn't relevant to this section.

169 See the sidebar on page 75. Other eminent logicians have endorsed this maxim as well.

potential for loss of integrity should they be duplicated, look at them with an eye to the "best fit." Specifically, make a decision as to which table in any hierarchy these attributes "definitely" belong, since they should only be in one place.

Entity/Class Suggested by Attribute set:	Possible but Uncertain (this attribute set *might* represent this entity)	Certainly / Definitely (this attribute set *always* represents this entity)	Not Possible (this attribute set is never applicable to this entity)
Corporation	---------------------	---------------------	**Not Possible**
Customer	**Possible but Uncertain**	---------------------	---------------------
Employee	**Possible but Uncertain**	---------------------	---------------------
Party	---------------------	---------------------	**Not Possible**
Patient	**Possible but Uncertain**	---------------------	---------------------
Person	---------------------	**DEFINITELY**	---------------------

A combination of attributes Proper Name, Surname, Middle Name, in other words, indicates definitively that we are dealing with a Person. While it is possible we may *also* be dealing with a Customer, Employee, or Patient, *we cannot be certain from these attributes alone*. But this attribute combination makes it a certainty that we are not dealing with a Corporation or Party[170].

Now consider the implications of an attribute set for contact mechanisms, such as Mailing Address(es), Telephone Number(s), e-mail address(es), and so forth.

Entity/Class Suggested by Attribute set:	Possible but Uncertain (this attribute set *might* represent this entity)	Certainly / Definitely (this attribute set *always* represents this entity)	Not Possible (this attribute set is never applicable to this entity)
Corporation	**Possible but Uncertain**	---------------------	---------------------
Customer	**Possible but Uncertain**	---------------------	---------------------
Employee	**Possible but Uncertain**	---------------------	---------------------
Party	---------------------	**DEFINITELY**	---------------------
Patient	**Possible but Uncertain**	---------------------	---------------------
Person	**Possible but Uncertain**	---------------------	---------------------
Shipment	---------------------	---------------------	**Not Possible**

170 This is important. We might be dealing with a sub-Class of Party, but that isn't sufficient!

Given this particular attribute set, all we can say for certain is that any element of the set must be associated with a Party, since it is possible for any or all sub-Classes of Party to have all or part of this attribute set.

Aristotle's dictum concerning proper placement of attributes[171] has been proven over time in every scientific discipline that relies on formal categorization and organization of data. Our only excuse for not incorporating these proven rules is that, until recently, the state-of-the-art in storage technology[172] prevented us from taking full advantage of scientific and logical principles for handling our data. Those days are over, and it's time for database design to catch up.

Conclusion

Although it took a bit longer to complete than Worldwide Widget Corporation's board anticipated, their acquisition of and technical integration with Consolidated Widget Experts was ultimately able to be accomplished without a great deal of headaches because, although neither of the company's data models represented reality properly, neither conflicted with reality substantively.

In this example, correction of the data structures discussed, and the modifications needed to permit the applications to support the corrections[173], made subsequent changes to I/T's implementation of new or changed business processes much easier to handle.

Whether obvious or not, this discussion of Views has presented only the basic approaches. More subtleties of implementing such a scheme[174] will be addressed in the next chapter "Freedom of the Press - Impedance Mismatches" as well as with further elaboration in several subsequent chapters.

---

171 ...as well as similar instructions by many of our other distinguished predecessors.

172 See "Inevitable Conclusions" on page 113 in "Recent History of Data Management."

173 It is important to point out that many of these (as usual) were actually simplifications!

174 The use of Views to support Intersections (see Intersections as Views on page 134), for example, will drop us right into the middle of an often intense religious dispute within the OO community, but that will just add to this book's entertainment value.

► A fundamental step in the integration of I/T systems is not only to match program (process) functionality, but to match and correct the data class hierarchies – both actions that are part of Business Database Triage.

► The common objections that RDBMS products don't support insertion or deletion against their Views isn't at all the show-stopper it is sometimes made out to be. In fact, it seldom makes much difference at all when dealing with the type of Business addressed by this book.

Although Views as implemented by existing RDBMS products do not fully support the definition of View in the Relational Model, it turns out that this is not an impediment to judicious use of such views that serve to provide a better match between databases and applications than is typically found in business. This is because creation and deletion of such data involves arbitrary BUSINESS RULES, not DATA RULES – a critical distinction.

► Properly identifying subclasses and intersections and implementing them as relational views leads to database structures that mesh quite nicely with well-designed classes in modern object-oriented programming languages.

Sample PL/SQL scripts demonstrating the techniques discussed in this chapter can be found beginning on page 388.

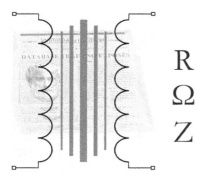

Popular Myths behind the concept of "Impedance Mismatches."

Although part of the "Freedom of the Press" series, this chapter also continues the discussions begun in "A Corporate Merger – Part 2."

R

Ω

Z

Illustration: Electronic symbol for a Transformer, an Impedance Matching device used to "transform" voltage and current levels between different sections of an electronic circuit.

9 - *Freedom of the Press - Impedance Mismatches*

Background

At the end of "A Corporate Merger – Part 2", the integrated company's data model looked more like a hierarchical object model than one designed using the more common ERD (Entity-Relationship Diagram)[175] approach, suggesting that "real" relational database designs can actually be quite compatible with good OO designs. The closer each reflects reality, the more likely it is that the design will accommodate extension and change, and integrate easily with other systems. The real issue with many so-called "Object-Relational Impedance Mismatches" is the same as that of most data conversion or migration difficulties: – when either or both models ignore reality or represent an invalid view of reality, there will always be difficulties as business processes need to change over time.

As noted in "Recent History of Data Management," the theories behind object-oriented programming are closely related to those underpinning the Relational Model. Nonetheless, a type of tension between the two is undeniably evident to those creating interfaces between object-oriented programs and relational data-

---

175 Not an "Entity-Relation Diagram," which is a silly, but common misnomer. Although not equivalent, Entities and Relations are conceptually on the same plane, whereas relationships occur between Relations (usually, but not always, in different Entities).

bases. In what can be regarded as yet another unhelpful example of Freedom of the Press in action, the term "Object-Relational Impedance Mismatch" has become commonly used to describe the issues involved. Further, this has led to a common perception that Object and Relational technologies have some inherent differences that prevent them from working well together.

There are, in fact, quite a few differences[176], but not at all for the reasons most commonly bandied about, and it is important for practitioners to clearly understand the distinctions between Object and Relational approaches in order to use them effectively and avoid being led astray by rumors. To address this misunderstanding, it is quite helpful to first dissect the "impedance mismatch" analogy by discussing a little bit about electronics – the reference against which the analogy is made – to show how the term might seem to apply, but really doesn't.

Origin of a Misleading Analogy

When we turn on a flashlight, DIRECT CURRENT ("DC") – essentially a flood of free electrons – begins flowing in one direction from the battery, through the bulb and back, causing the bulb to glow; the amount of this current is described by Ohm's Law, which states that for a given voltage (force), the resulting current (volume of electrons) will be inversely proportional to RESISTANCE – the lower the resistance of the bulb, therefore, the more current will flow through it[177].

ALTERNATING CURRENT ("AC") however, such as that available from our wall sockets, reverses direction on a regular basis, and the calculations get a little more interesting. Simple Resistance is joined by several types of REACTANCE – akin to resistance, but very dependent on the rate at which the current switches direction (i.e. its frequency). It will still be true that the more force (voltage) is applied, or the less resistance exists, the more current will flow, but the frequency of the

---

176 The most obvious are the Scope of Data Management and the Handling of Processes; we'll discuss each of these in "So What are the Real Mismatches?" later in this chapter.

177 Since a battery, as we all know, has only a finite charge, this relationship among voltage, resistance, and current falls apart as the battery becomes depleted, of course, but that need not concern us for this explanation.

current's change in direction is now a significant part of the equation. This combination of the effects of Resistance and Reactance is known as IMPEDANCE.

We have all experienced frequency-dependent effects in action, and we are used to the fact that higher frequencies[178] act differently than lower ones. Inside a night club, for instance, we hear all the sounds produced by a band, from the highest guitar notes to the lowest bass notes. Once outside, however, we hear only the lower frequencies. The power of the music's higher frequencies is impeded more than that of its lower frequencies by both simple distance as well as the presence of intervening materials such as walls, curtains, and even air.

If we wish only to maximize the transfer of power from one device to another, we match the impedance of the output device to that of the input device as closely as possible. It might seem, therefore, that matching impedance is always desirable and, from the way the term "Object-Relational Impedance Mismatch" is used, that certainly seems to be what many writers believe or at least seem to be implying. Matching impedance by value alone isn't always desirable, however, and a common example will show why that is a simplistic assumption.

Looking at the back of an amplifier, for example, we usually see some sort of warning label suggesting that any speakers or headphones we connect should have an input impedance in the range of 4 to 16 ohms. Many people assume therefore that the output impedance of the amplifier is in that range as well. It isn't, and for many good reasons.

If a drummer slaps his stick against the drum and then quickly silences it by placing his hand on the skin, we hear quite a different effect than if he had not silenced the drum. If, when reproducing that sound with a speaker whose impedance value matched that of the amplifier, the speaker cone, unlike the drum

---

178 For those who are not familiar with physics, our perception of sound results from alternating changes in the direction of the air pressure at our ears; in an amplifier the same sound is represented by analogous changes in direction of the current flow. The current from our wall sockets changes direction sixty times a second. The air flow direction when we are listening to music changes anywhere from about twenty times per second to fifteen thousand times per second or more. The radio waves to and from our cell phones switch direction at a rate that can be several billion times per second.

skin, would continue to vibrate, resulting in a distortion of the drummer's intent. The same phenomenon occurs throughout the whole spectrum of the music, and such a system would sound terribly muddy and quite unsatisfactory.

Fidelity to the original sound is increased by what is known as damping – which greatly increases the amplifier's control over the speaker's independent vibrations. The amplifier is designed to have a low output impedance relative to the speaker's input impedance. An "8 Ohm" marking above the amplifier's speaker terminals indicates the impedance at which the designer's intended damping factor (the ratio of the speaker's impedance to that of the amplifier's) will be achieved, which is usually well above 400.

The Benefits of Deliberate Impedance Mismatches

Numerical "impedance mismatches" are neither good nor bad, but depend exclusively on how, where, and for what purpose they exist. An "ideal" match does not always mean identical values. Indeed, if a speaker with an impedance only slightly lower than the recommended value is attached to the amplifier, the sound quality will suffer – and if the impedance is significantly lower, the possibility of destroying the amplifier's output circuitry becomes very real.

We've seen that object-oriented designs and relational designs were developed from the same (and quite ancient) logical underpinnings. In "A Corporate Merger – Part 2" we've also seen that they can be quite compatible. The "impedance mismatch" myth mostly stems from the common attempts to match illogical data models (relational or not) with correctly (or at least better) designed object models. Consider the two class models discussed earlier:

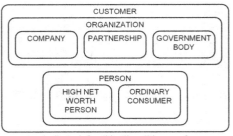

Logically Indefensible Class Diagram from "What is a Customer? - Misguided Literature" on page 118 as published in Simsion [1].

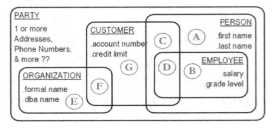

Logically Correct Class Diagram from "Déjà Vu" on page 61.

Suppose, following the advice given in Simsion [1], we built database tables using the class structures on the left. Further suppose that the class definitions shown on the right (whether the Party class was included or not) were used to build class structures in an application[179].

The upside down (inside out?) hierarchy on the left conflicts with reality and isn't going to mesh very well with any application. This is not, however, due to an "impedance mismatch!" *It is simply bad design!* Database designs can be used successfully even if they don't fully reflect reality, but if they conflict with reality, they should be discarded. As demonstrated in "What is a Customer? - Misguided Literature," when class diagrams are written out as formal Propositions, it is obvious that many formed from the diagram on the left are demonstrably false, while those formed from the diagram on the right are all true.

So What are the Real Mismatches?

Two so-called "mismatches" (but simply differences) between the Object and Relational paradigms are their differing approaches to Data Management and Handling of Processes.

...Data Management

While an Object is an aggregation of closely related data elements[180] that are potentially retrieved and aggregated from multiple locations, a Database contains very discrete elements. This distinction reflects the purpose of each:

► an Object contains all the data needed to describe a specific instance of a Thing; an instance of the Employee object shown to the right should aggregate all the data required to deal with the specific Employee

```
class Party {
   int ID;
   void new(); // methods
   void add-contact()
   void edit-contact()
   et cetera;      }

class Person
      extends Party {
   String Given Name;
   String Surname;
   void new(); // methods
   void edit-name()
   et cetera;      }

class Employee
      extends Person {
   Float salary;
   void new(); // methods
   void hire();
   void promote();
   void fire();
   et cetera;      }
```

---

179 This reflects the likelihood that knowledgeable programmers are far more prevalent than knowledgeable database designers, who often are unaware of relational database design principles, much less the importance of class hierarchies to successful designs.

180 Usually along with some methods, but that's a separate subject for later discussion.

---

identified by a particular ID, including most, if not all, elements of any super-classes (Person and Party) to which it belongs.

▶ a Data Structure must store data elements at their most discrete logical level. As we have seen, Person data is utilized for many other classes, and storing it in the database as part of an Employee structure not only confuses that, but inevitably leads to data redundancy and potential integrity issues.

A casual reading of many object-oriented design texts should convince one that the class structures above (Party, Person, and Employee) would be a good example of how objects can reduce code maintenance, reduce redundancy, promote reuse, etc. While certainly true, there is no justification for constructing poorly designed and illogical database structures to achieve these benefits. This was demonstrated (albeit in a primitive fashion) in "A Corporate Merger – Part 2."

At first blush, the base table/view mechanism from that chapter would seem to render all the class structures given on the preceding page unnecessary and even redundant. A little reflection, however, will show that this mechanism merely simplifies the process of interfacing an OO application with the database[181], and doesn't at all conflict with the use of Class structures, particularly with regard to managing the methods of the various Classes.

For those who contend that using the base table/view mechanism can be slightly tedious, I would argue that:

▶ The data structures are logically defensible, and very extensible.

▶ The object/class definitions are logically defensible.

▶ The mechanism is certainly not as tedious as maintaining and extending software that is based on a poor data model.

By using this mechanism, both the database's structures and the object's instance variables can correctly model[182] their respective spheres of influence. The base

---

181 Of course this assumes that the class structures used to build the database and those used to build the application are congruent – and that neither conflicts with Reality. Note, by the way, that the phrase is "**the** database" and not "**its** database."

182 "Modeling the World in Data" Schlaer [1]; see page 384.

table/view mechanism can be viewed as a transformer that bridges the "mismatched impedance" between the discrete data of the Relational world and the aggregated encapsulated data of the Object world.

This approach, by the way, is also far, far, less costly than commercial solutions that purport to solve the mythical impedance mismatch and, in fact, is often easier to implement and provides more operational flexibility. Remember that the level of analysis that needs to be done to implement either is identical.

...Handling of Processes (Location, Location)

A second significant difference between the Relational and Object paradigms is that, in object-oriented software, each class has associated methods – including processes that act on the data classes we've discussed. Thus, in object-oriented software, an Employee would not only inherit the Name attribute, but any methods (processes) that were defined for Person as well[183]. Although there may or may not be any "methods" (triggers, stored procedures, etc.) associated with the tables in a Relational database, there is no requirement that they exist.

So, where should the methods related to Person management (for instance) reside? The answer is conceptually fairly simple. If the processes are meant to manage BUSINESS RULES, they usually belong in the methods for the Person Class. If any of the methods differ for the various subclasses of Person, they would be "overridden" by methods in the subclass. If the processes relate to DATA RULES, however, they should almost always be implemented within the database.

The chapter "Handling Constraints," although specifically addressing the location of Data Constraints, has a more involved discussion of determining the logical placement of shared software routines.

---

183 Depending, of course, on the programming language used, some of which don't actually allow for the inheritance of the methods themselves, but merely the method's signature, requiring separate implementations for each level of the class hierarchy – an approach that carries its own benefits and (sometimes serious) penalties, but that's another subject.

Conclusion

The supposed Object-Relational Impedance Mismatch originated with an analogy that elevates an incidental and irrelevant observation to a wholly undeserved status of a supposedly meaningful Truism. It just ain't so!

Other similar myths are considered to be "common wisdom" because they are perpetuated through Freedom of the Press. Some of these are:

▶ [FALSE] A database built using relational database management software is a relational database.

This is an Invalid Corollary. The truth is that it is extremely difficult, time-consuming and, from a business standpoint, quite impractical to build a relational database without the support of Relational Database Management System software, but simply using such software to build the database does not make that database "relational."

It's difficult to determine, of course, but my own experience suggests that, of all databases built with Oracle, DB/2, Informix, etc., those qualifying as relational databases are a small minority.

▶ [FALSE] Many-to-Many relationships can't be handled directly by relational database designs, so they are unsuitable for most businesses.

Many writers tell us this, but it is somewhat akin to saying "Dissimilar fractions can't be added directly using traditional arithmetic"[184] so we should avoid traditional arithmetic.

▶ [FALSE] The name "Relational Database" comes from the fact that relational databases implement relationships[185] between tables.

This is simply nonsense; (re)read Date [1]. The term Relational derives from the word "Relation," and the only commonality is that both "relationship"

---

184 For those who have forgotten, an example of such addition would be "x = 1/3 + 3/7." Hopefully you remember how to arrive at the correct answer of, uh, uh, uh, … 16/21.

185 Example: In the article "Base: Planning Your Database" is the statement: "Relationships put the 'relational' in relational databases." (Full Circle Magazine; Issue 66; October 2012)

and "relation" start with the same eight letters. Any single row in a well-designed relational database table represents a single Relation.

As a hint of where we're heading in future chapters, we'll add one more Myth to stew over:

▶   [FALSE] Multiple Inheritance is best avoided when developing Object-Oriented applications.

Consider that the sheer volume of opinions – both pro and con – on this subject and the examples given by both camps to support their views both suggest that – just perhaps – not only there might be some truth to the arguments given by each side, but that some level of logic might assist us in determining whether there are some situational characteristics we can identify to help determine the efficacy of using multiple inheritance and resolve these differences of opinion in any given instance.

Later on, in Grammar, Sets, and Predicate Logic – Part 2[186], we'll use grammar and logic to address some of the more humorous myths that underpin both the belief in object-relational impedance mismatches as well as the confusion surrounding what is or isn't valid multiple inheritance.

Before delving into such issues, however, we need a useful example to work with – one that is simple enough to provide a limited scope, but complex enough to qualify as "real-world." So before any further exploration of intersections and matrix objects (those that would seem to suggest using the pesky and controversial multiple inheritance in our applications), we'll introduce a realistic and not-so-trivial example in the next chapter, "Playing with Trucks – Part 1."

---

186 … which begins on page 235.

► The incredible amount of baloney written about the so-called impedance mismatch between object oriented programming and relational database systems largely misses the salient points completely.

► Programming and Database design serve entirely different purposes. This inevitably makes it appear that there is some "conflict" between them.

  ▼ Programming, whether traditional or object-oriented, is the automation of a company's processes; programming may be used to create and manage data more easily, but it is a separate effort that is only incidentally related to the structure or organization of the data.

  ▼ Database design, whether relational or not, is intended to effectively categorize, organize, store and protect the company's data and make it accessible.

► The Relational and Object paradigms share the same heritage, and there is no inherent conflict between them.

► The real, and only significant, difference between Relational databases and Object-oriented software is the level of granularity.

  ▼ The most useful form for an object is to have all its relevant data encapsulated and treated as a single entity.

  ▼ The most useful form for a database and for the Enterprise (however that is defined), is to have all data maintained in the most granular form practical.

► When either the Data Model or the class structure of an Object don't conform to physical reality (use Predicates!) there will always be difficulties getting applications to mesh smoothly with databases.

How data integrity declines over time when a growing business is saddled with an illogical and non-relational data model.

To some readers, this chapter may read like a parody of poor database design practices – perhaps even a pastiche of examples from several companies, but it is quite real and I still have a few of the company's sweatshirts as sad reminders to prove it.

10

10 - PLAYING WITH TRUCKS – PART 1   ----

This chapter will show by example how ignoring the grammatical and logical guidelines presented in "Grammar, Sets, and (Predicate) Logic – Part 1" – well understood by philosophers and scientists for centuries – lead inevitably to what can only be termed "business constipation" – viral growth of difficult-to-maintain application code, loss of data integrity, lost business opportunities, and the like. By concentrating on mostly a single poorly named and designed table, we will show how and why ignoring logical class taxonomies not only limits flexibility, reuse, etc., but can strangle even seemingly innocuous business expansion efforts.

Background and Business Model

The business model for the company in this example, which we'll call Trux-M-Us (or TMU), was essentially to fill unused space in long haul "semi-trailers" – the closed trailers that we're all familiar with from our own highway driving – by offering that space on the open market to other shippers who could take advantage of already committed routes and thus save money. Whether this space was in a partially loaded truck making a delivery or an empty truck returning from a delivery made no difference to the model. The carrier would derive extra revenue and efficiency by maximizing use of its assets, the shipper would save money, and TMU, as matchmaker, would earn a commission. As with the previous example, some business details have been changed to protect the guilty and avoid any appearance of divulging embarrassing or proprietary information.

The non-powered trailers initially targeted by TMU were vehicles designed to be easily attached to motorized "tractors" so they could be moved to a location, disconnected, and left for as long as necessary without tying up the tractor. Later, another (or even the same) tractor would pick up the trailer and move it again. The whole independence between storage space (the trailer) and locomotion (the tractor) permitted the tractors and drivers to remain productive regardless of how long it took for loading or unloading.

What made the model attractive was that it is well known within the transportation industry that few of these trailers are filled to capacity and, in fact, many are completely empty during return trips. A manufacturer, for instance, might own a fleet of such trailers and, as each was filled – perhaps over several hours or even days – would assign a tractor to pick up the shipment and deliver it to an intermediate distribution center or directly to one or more retail stores. Although there might be defective or returned products on board as the trailer was being transported back to its origin, generally speaking, it would be empty.

TMU would allow shippers to register the origin, destination, size and weight for items requiring transportation, and have these matched to similar listings registered by the carriers as described above. It appeared to be a profitable concept for all concerned, and one that seemed as if it would be even more successful as more carriers and shippers signed up for the service, since an increased pool would represent more opportunities for attractive "matches."

A Sad but Common Mistake

In preparation for an eventual public offering, TMU's management was persuaded to enhance its "high tech credibility" by moving from a proprietary database to a recognized "industry standard" – in this case, Oracle. To keep costs down, however, TMU elected to simply clone their data structures in the new RDBMS without any effort to effect a redesign. Because no distinction was made between having a robust database management system and a robust database, however, this public relations effort was technically pointless and wasteful.

Original Data Model

In order to understand how this system degenerated over time, we'll use a single representative table from the company's database schema, the Trailer table.

TRAILER (v1)		TRAILER Table: A short description of each Column's purpose
Trailer_ID	pk	.......The matchmaking Company's (TMU's) primary key for this trailer – not null
Carrier_ID	fk	.............ID of the Carrier that owns or controls this Trailer; foreign key – not null
Carrier-Trailer_ID		.........................The owning/controlling Carrier's own ID for this Trailer if known
Length	not null	.....................The outside Length of this Trailer, assumed to be in feet – not null
Width	not null	....................The inside Width of this Trailer, assumed to be in inches – not null
Door_Height	not null	........The Door Height opening of this Trailer, assumed to be in inches – not null
Available_Floor_Feet	not null	...The inside Length of available (unused) space in this Trailer, in feet – not null
LBS_Available	not null	......................The remaining weight capacity of this Trailer, in pounds – not null
Pallets_Available	not null	...........Varied: Sometimes the number of pallet positions available in this Trailer
Et cetera		....................Mostly related to administration, routing, schedule availability, etc.

Many design flaws are (or should be) obvious even from this very abbreviated table schema; I'll leave the structures of the other tables to the reader's imagination. The first, and probably most important blunder was the table name Trailer.

The name "Trailer" is a generic term, but was used here to describe a specific sub-class or sub-set of trailer types – specifically the one with closed sides that was targeted in the company's original business model. There is little doubt that the original developers, most of whom were, or at least were guided by, transportation industry veterans, knew of other dissimilar trailer types such as tankers, flatbeds, and so forth, but apparently were unaware of the implications of their choice of generic naming, which will become painfully apparent as this chapter unfolds.

Thoughts from Aristotle

In Book I; Part 1.2 of Categories, Aristotle's second sentence describes the need for unambiguous naming.

In Categories Book I, part 5.5, Aristotle says "... the species is more truly substance than the genus ..." and continues to say that someone would "render a more instructive account by stating the species rather than the genus."

It was therefore a serious design mistake to have used the generic term "Trailer" when a more specific subclass name could (and should) have been used.

Data in the **Length** column was intended to determine if the Trailer could fit in certain enclosed docks, but gradually became used for other purposes, with an implicit assumption that inside and outside lengths were effectively equal. The **Length** value was assumed to be in feet – an assumption that, in itself is a very limiting design flaw[187].

The original purpose of the **Width** value was unclear, but in practice it was used to represent both inside and outside values, the former to determine whether shipments would fit in the trailer, and the latter to confirm that a particular trailer would fit in a particular loading dock. (Data related to the characteristics of origin and destination facilities was kept in equally silly table designs, by the way.) The **Width** value was assumed to be in inches, once again a design flaw, albeit a more interesting one because it was inconsistent with the assumption for the **Length** value's unit of measure (feet), and users of the system were expected to just "know" that.

RED
FLAG

Pallets, at least those used in the United States, come in several standard sizes, but it is quite common for the contents placed on any particular pallet to "overhang" the sides of the pallet by varying amounts depending on the material being shipped.

The **Red Flag** in this instance is the fact that it is the width of the pallet *plus* any overhang that actually needs to fit through the trailer door, not simply the pallet itself.

Various industry groups, of course, recognized the need for limitations on permissible overhang values, but their recommendations were often ignored.

The **Door_Height** value was matched against data given for a shipment's **Height** to ensure the cargo could be placed into the trailer. This value was also assumed to be in inches, and the same comments regarding design flaws apply to this element as well.

Once our team was engaged, one of our many questions was why there was no value for "Door Width" in the schema. We were told that door widths were "standard" because of the need for "standard pallets" to fit in the trailers. It later turned out that the lack of precision in defining "standard" would lead to some interesting situations where drivers arrived to pick up cargo that could not fit through their trailer's doors.

---

187 The reasons for this, as well as the techniques for handling weights and measures in a logical, flexible, and extensible manner are discussed at length beginning on page 201.

Available_Floor_Feet was only vaguely defined, with a general assumption that the value represented the length (in feet of course) of the full-width remaining space in the rear of the trailer. Although this was known to result in "missed opportunities,"[188] this definition was deemed acceptable and caused no apparent difficulties.

Trailers of any type have weight limits – based both on their designs and by various legal entities. LBS_Available represented the unused weight capacity available for additional shipments and was another element of the matching process.

Had the company made any effort to have consistency in their naming conventions, LBS_Available might have been called Available_Weight – still logically unacceptable, but at least consistently so. In this case, since a key piece of data – the Unit of Measure – is embedded in the attribute name, they made an existing design flaw even more serious. Since this subject will be discussed at length in the chapters devoted to handling Weights and Measures, we'll ignore it for now.

Interestingly, the company had developed a demonstration of its capabilities for their Sales and Marketing personnel to use. In that application, developed by a contractor that apparently had no communication with anyone outside the marketing department, Pallets_Available was touted as as a complex calculation to determine how many pallets could be placed in the remaining empty space of a particular trailer. In the actual application, however, Pallets_Available simply represented the number of empty pallets that the driver of a particular trailer had with him that a shipper could use for any additional cargo he wished to ship.

Keep in mind that this was simply one table in TMU's database. Shipments, of course, had similar weight and size attributes to allow for finding potential matches, and there was a wide variety of other tables – each of which appeared to be designed to some degree of ineptness and without any apparent attempt at logical structure, consistency of naming, common definitions, etc. But, the com-

---

188 For instance, if the existing cargo didn't take up the full width or length of the trailer, the calculations used by the company would sometimes not recognize that a particular additional shipment might fit alongside the existing cargo rather than just to its rear.

pany was in business, their service could be marketed and sold and to some extent even executed usefully, so the management was eager to grow.

The Slippery Slope to Business Expansion

As Trux-M-Us perceived an opportunity to provide the same service for its Clients' Flatbed (i.e. unenclosed) Trailers, TMU's management, having such a high level of confidence in their programming staff that they felt no need to solicit the programmers' opinions on the timing, saw no difficulties at all in promising to offer this service within a very short time frame. In the misguided spirit of rapid response, and with apparently no recognition of the dangerously weak data structures, several quick modifications were made to the database schema and to the applications that used it. Again, this discussion will present a very simplified description of the progression of just the Trailer table as the designers attempted to respond to their management's enthusiasm.

TRAILER (v2)	
Trailer_ID	pk
Carrier_ID	fk
Carrier-Trailer_ID	
Length	not null
Width	not null
Door_Height	not null
Available_Floor_Feet	not null
LBS_Available	not null
Pallets_Available	not null
Flatbed_Indicator	*Y or N*
Tarp_Available	*Y or N*
Chains_Available	*Y or N*
Et cetera...	

As shown in the revised table layout on the left, a **Flat_Bed_Indicator** column was added to instruct the application to handle the exceptions and changes required for handling flatbed trailers and their shipments. A key point to note here is that this attribute clearly doesn't describe the entity *as it is being used*[189], but merely indicates an exception to the entity's use, a clear sign that this database design is flawed.

Beyond the flatbed indicator itself, the addition of flatbed-specific columns indicating whether a given trailer carried its own tarp, chains, etc., necessitated modification of most data access code.

---

189 The general name "Trailer" doesn't indicate that the entity set was really intended to record only a specific type (subset) of trailer, i.e. an enclosed non-powered vehicle with door heights (see "Naming our Things" on page 73). More disturbing from a design standpoint, the schema doesn't make it clear what is affected by the exception.

Since the concept of Door Height is irrelevant for a flat bed, the Not Null constraint on this column was no longer possible, leaving what would normally be a database-level constraint to be implemented (hopefully identically) in every portion of the application that dealt with inputs to this table. This, of course, made the system just a little bit more difficult to maintain.

Load sizes on a flat bed trailer are not limited by the length and width of the trailer as they would be for a closed van, but are allowed to "overhang" the trailer bed by a certain amount. Since the amount varies depending on where the trailer is traveling, more conditional code and some hard-coded parameters were needed to handle that.

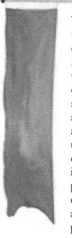

DOUBLE
RED
FLAG

Whenever you encounter a situation where data from a particular column in a data table (in this case Flatbed_Indicator) is used to determine whether or how another column (in this case Door_Height and Available_Floor_Feet as well as to a lesser extent Tarp_Available and Chains_Available) is to be used or interpreted, you can conclude that a) your database design is seriously flawed and b) your application code is (or is going to be) quite unnecessarily complicated, and more prone to system constipation.

A further red flag is that whenever changes to the system result in the need to remove a NOT NULL constraint, this invariably reflects a poor initial database design.

Since it was now obvious to management that their system was "flexible and extensible," the next step was to offer the service for refrigerated trailers, or "reefers" as they are known in the industry. In management's view, this required just a few more simple changes to the database and code base.

Refrigerated trailers obviously need to be insulated, since the outside shell of a normal trailer is surprisingly thin. This meant that the clever trick of using the Width field for both inside and outside dimensions was no longer valid. Therefore an Inside_Width column was proposed but, in the end, rejected because that would have meant far too many changes to existing applications and reports than the specified development time frame allowed. So the application code for the matching process was modified to obtain the inside dimension in the case of a refrigerated trailer by reducing the available inside dimension by 8 inches, a reasonable compromise (compromise was needed since insulation widths vary).

TRAILER (v3)	
Trailer_ID	pk
Carrier_ID	fk
Carrier-Trailer_ID	
Length	~~not null~~
Width	~~not null~~
Door_Height	ww
Available_Floor_Feet	not null
LBS_Available	not null
Pallets_Available	
Flat_Bed_Indicator	Y or N
Tarp_Available	Y or N
Chains_Available	Y or N
~~Inside_Width~~	
Max_Temperature	*number*
Min_Temperature	*number*
Et cetera ...	

Since refrigerated shipments need to be held within specified temperature ranges, the **Max_Temperature** and **Min_Temperature** columns were added (ideally not null whenever the record was for a refrigerated trailer, but that could only be implemented at the database level by a trigger rather than by the more ideal declarative means). These were *assumed* to be in Fahrenheit.

Non-Zero entries in the **Max_Temperature** and **Min_Temperature** fields were deemed sufficient to indicate that the Trailer was temperature-controlled, so no new attribute was necessary for this purpose – lucky, since that would have meant substantial changes to existing code. There was the slight[190] disadvantage that *different types of trailers were now detected in quite different manners*, but that just made the code all that more interesting for future programmers to understand and maintain. Sadly, it wasn't discovered for quite some time that **the default value of zero was actually a legitimate temperature limit for certain types of cargo**.

Another factor not handled by the code at all was that the addition of a refrigeration unit to the trailer sometimes altered the inside height of the trailer along portions of the inside length (**Available Floor Feet**) depending on where it was located. On the surface, this would not seem to be a problem, but all code to that point had been written with the assumption that the entire length of the inside of a trailer was the same height. But, how risky was that anyway?

Of course at this point, in addition to the fact that zero was a valid temperature value, it was now possible to make entries into the database specifying that a flatbed trailer was refrigerated, but that was considered a small risk to take to acquire the additional business. Code was added to several of the more commonly used applications to help prevent this, but as one might expect of a company that accepted this caliber of database design, this coding wasn't done consistently or very well.

---

190 Yes, this is a sarcastic use of the word "slight," so I hereby offer my insincere apologies.

Europe Beckons

At this time, the company had been exploring the possibility of licensing what its management considered to be a highly sophisticated system (called, with the cute hyperbole of that particular year, its "engine") to countries in both Europe and Asia. Although it is far beyond the scope of this example to explain the technical reasons why, this effort fortunately died as potential licensees thought through the effort and expense of what would have essentially been a complete redesign of the database and software. Development of internationalized systems is virtually impossible without a strong relational database as the foundation, and certainly isn't economically possible for one with such logical gaffes and inconsistent use of often unspecified measures.[191]

With the improbable safely off their radar, the company's management looked for the next potential business opportunity that could take advantage of its "transportation engine." Because their system had for some time been finding loads for empty trailers on their return trips, it was not at all a significant step to begin actively marketing to carriers for all vehicles in their fleets. Since the system had been designed from the ground up on the assumption that origins, destinations, and scheduled pickup and delivery times were known, this presented some interesting challenges to both the application and database designs but, again, we'll skip those in the interests of brevity.

Chaos Reigns

It was around this time that some shippers began questioning whether it was really appropriate to ship certain commodities in the same trailer (sacks of fertilizer with Prom Dresses for example). Oops. The customer service department was tasked with reviewing all the potential matches produced by the system in order to determine if they were appropriate.

---

191 Ok, it's out of scope, but just one example: the "engine", when calculating the cost of going "out of route" to accommodate additional pickups and deliveries, made numerous assumptions in code that were based on a relationship between miles traveled and gallons of fuel consumed – a relationship which is not the same as that between kilometers and liters.

When reviewing the potential development costs of adding industry-standard commodity coding (which, in any case, wasn't typically supplied by the shippers) to both data structures and application code, human intervention was deemed to be more cost-effective over the short term. Admiral Hopper (see page 97) would have been bursting with pride.

TRAILER (v4)	
Trailer_ID	pk
Carrier_ID	fk
Carrier-Trailer_ID	
Length	not null
Width	not null
Door_Height	ww
Available_Floor_Feet	not null
LBS_Available	not null
Pallets_Available	
Flat_Bed_Indicator	Y or N
Tarp_Available	Y or N
Chains_Available	Y or N
Max_Temperature	Number
Min_Temperature	Number
Volume	*Number*
Number_of_Cells	*Integer*
Et cetera ...	

With the potential for inappropriately intermingling various types of shipment now having been addressed, and due to slower than anticipated growth, the company's management now wanted to turn its attention somewhat simultaneously to both the tanker market and what is referred to as inter-modal transportation. We'll discuss the issues related to integrating tankers first.

Since tankers generally carry liquid or material which "fits" into any convenient shape, and are thus categorized in terms of volume rather than size, all the inner dimensions in the overly generic Trailer table become completely irrelevant with a tanker. To support tankers, therefore, a Volume attribute was added, as shown on the left. Following the technique used to add refrigerated trailers discussed above, the presence of any entry in a Volume attribute was used to indicate to the applications that a particular trailer was a tanker. (at the time, no one suspected that hopper trailers might ever need to be supported.)

Of course, NOT NULL constraints were now completely absent, further compromising the integrity of data in the system. Furthermore, shipments in tankers could not safely be combined to take advantage of empty space (as they were with other types of trailers), necessitating the addition of new exceptions in the software.[192]

---

192 Combining milk with gasoline in a tanker was rightly considered to be potentially more offensive than shipping Prom Dresses with fertilizer (aka manure).

Needless to say, the Program Logic had now become frightening! One primary reason for the resulting complexity of the program logic is that it needed to compensate for what had become an almost complete absence of logic in the table design. This is readily apparent when looking at the applicability of the individual columns to each of the trailer types, as illustrated below.

Applicability of Trailer Table Attributes to Actual Trailer Types

TRAILER		Closed Trailer	"Flatbed"	"Reefer"	"Tanker"
Trailer_ID	pk	applicable (PK)	applicable (PK)	applicable (PK)	applicable (PK)
Carrier_ID	fk	applicable (FK)	applicable (FK)	applicable (FK)	applicable (FK)
Carrier-Trailer_ID		applicable (AK)	applicable (AK)	applicable (AK)	applicable (AK)
Length		applicable	sort of applicable	sort of applicable	not applicable
Width		applicable	sort of applicable	sort of applicable	not applicable
Door_Height		applicable	not applicable	applicable	not applicable
Available_Floor_Feet		applicable	sort of applicable	applicable	not applicable
LBS_Available		applicable	applicable	applicable	not applicable
Pallets_Available		applicable	not applicable	applicable	not applicable
Flat_Bed_Indicator		not applicable	applicable	not applicable	not applicable
Tarp_Available		not applicable	applicable	not applicable	not applicable
Chains_Available		not applicable	applicable	not applicable	not applicable
Inside_Width		redundant usage	not applicable	modified usage	not applicable
Max_Temperature		not applicable	not applicable	applicable	not applicable
Min_Temperature		not applicable	not applicable	applicable	not applicable
Volume		not applicable	not applicable	not applicable	applicable
Number_of_Cells		not applicable	not applicable	not applicable	applicable
Et cetera ...		(crap shoot)	(crap shoot)	(crap shoot)	(crap shoot)

Forget normalization: it is quite obvious that this design no longer has even a pretense of being organized, sensible or logical, and that there is no single "Thing" this table is representing (a fundamental premise of good organization of facts and therefore of good database design). When consideration is given to the addition of other transportation MODES, e.g. rail, sea, air, etc., each of which brings its own attributes, yet is still segmented across the already identified "Closed", "Open", etc. categories, it is also obvious that any system built in this manner will soon collapse of its own weight.

The matrix technique used above, by the way, is a useful analysis tool, although its main message here is that there are simply way too many entities stuffed into a single table. Of the seventeen columns we've shown in the Trailer table, and the four types of trailer stored in the table, only thirty-one of the sixty-eight elements – barely 45% – are applicable to anything in any given row! And even the most minimal data integrity constraints have been removed!

Interestingly, the "Applicability of Trailer Table Attributes to Trailer Types" matrix carries with it many of the clues necessary to determine the natural taxonomy that exists and which would need to be implemented to organize and categorize the data properly and permit the software to concentrate on process (its actual purpose) rather than data definition and integrity constraints.

Matching Shipments and Trailers

The key business benefit provided by TMU to its clients was the ability to find suitable matches between the empty space tendered by its carriers and the cargo tendered by its shippers. In a perfect world, with a well-designed database, this should have been possible by using a single (albeit complex) real-time query against the database.

Sadly, with the non-relational design and the resulting requirement that many data elements could only be interpreted by referencing the values of other data elements, the matching process could only be done in a quite ponderous procedural manner. This was compounded, of course, by the fact that, as with the Trailer table, TMU's Shipment table was as ineptly designed and had suffered similar deterioration (directly due to the poor and illogical initial design) over time.

For reasons we never could determine, the matching routine had been designed from the earliest days of the company as a procedural batch process that ran overnight against all available data. Since no attempt had been made to redesign the database structures when the company's database was migrated to Oracle, this inefficient approach had to be carried forward. The process was, however, rewritten as a stored procedure. Extant evidence suggested that what was even then a rather large and complex procedure may have been the programmer's first exposure to SQL in general and to Oracle's PL/SQL language particularly.

By the time the company had acquired programmers with the appropriate skills and experience, business changes due to the expansion described above were coming fast enough that there was little choice but to make continuous adaptations to this fragile and almost unreadable code. Further, as suggested earlier, rewriting any code to run against such poorly designed data structures would likely have provided little benefit to the business.

A Sobering Perspective

The situation in which the company found itself at this point was actually worse than is apparent from the foregoing description.

Consider that the word "Trailer" assumes a lack of locomotion, which will obviously cause difficulties or at least confusion should motorized vans need to be accommodated in the future. (A failed tractor can usually be replaced on short notice, but if a motorized van fails it must be repaired or its contents unloaded and reloaded into some other vehicle – a serious and potentially dangerous operation if it must be done on the open road.)

Consider, also, that the bulk of this chapter has dealt with *only one table*! If you've ever wondered how apparently competent programmers can be forced into a situation where they use the latest tools and technologies to produce incomprehensible and difficult-to-maintain spaghetti code, this chapter should give you an idea. By this point in Trux-M-Us's history, having recognized but not exactly acknowledged that their system was ill, the company had collected a very experienced and capable group of both programmers and database designers. Sometimes, though, even with the best surgeons, a seriously ill patient isn't diagnosed in time (or isn't very cooperative) and the only thing that can be done is to provide comfort and pain management during the inevitable passage to whatever awaits bad information systems when they take their final breath.

Some would say that this example simply demonstrates the inability of the relational model to handle very complex data, so we'll take a look at how the business might have been approached in a later chapter. Keep in mind, however, that no possible argument can be made that this company used a relational database, even though the tables I've described were all built using the Oracle RDBMS.

LESSONS FOR CHAPTER 10
PLAYING WITH TRUCKS - PART 1

► Redesigning a constipated or difficult-to-maintain software system (or even a single application) without first identifying and addressing any underlying database design defects is usually an irresponsible waste of corporate resources and is unlikely to bring significant benefits.

► This Chapter provides examples of how:

▼ Simply rewriting software without considering the underlying database design or determining how it may have contributed to the need for such a rewrite is not likely to be a very cost-effective endeavor for a business.

▼ While the use of a general term (in this example "Trailer") can legitimately be used to refer to what the company was dealing with, it is by definition less precise than it needs to be for a logical and sustainable database design.

▼ Poor sensitivity to class hierarchies during database design results, more often than not, in a substantial decline in data integrity over time.

▼ Poor sensitivity to class hierarchies during database design results, more often than not, in procedural code that is much more convoluted and difficult to maintain than it needs to be.

► Relational Tables must be utilized for all fundamental business entities (such as Employees, Customers, Products, and so forth) in order for a database to be considered "Relational," but not all tables in a relational database need to be (nor should be) relational.

► Although acquisition of an RDBMS to replace an older system will undoubtedly provide benefits to many businesses, much of the investment will be wasted if the product's relational capabilities are not utilized.

An Overview of Constraints
Distinguishing Business Rules from Data Rules
Intentional and Accidental Constraints
A Little History of Constraints
Myths about Use and Placement of Constraints

11

---

11 - HANDLING CONSTRAINTS

In "The Two Primary Functions of a Business I/T Department" on page 6, it was noted that one of an I/T Department's most important responsibilities is to take whatever steps are necessary to ensure the integrity of corporate data assets. Leaving aside physical and other security measures, one of the most effective ways to accomplish this (assuming removal of data redundancies) is through the use of what are called CONSTRAINTS.

Constraints, intended to minimize entry of invalid, illogical, inconsistent, or simply impossible data into our systems, are sometimes viewed by novice programmers more as Restraints (as, for example, handcuffs). In one sense, they are, but only in the same manner that an Employee is a Person. In other words, Constraints, as the term is intended to be used in database management, merely constitute a sub-class of Restraints – a desirable subclass that is meant to protect the consistency and integrity of our data and, often, protect us from ourselves.

In "Playing with Trucks – Part 1," we were able to see one common mechanism by which constraints in a poorly designed database inevitably became progressively watered down as new functionality was added. The lack of logic in the Trux-M-Us database design made its constraints appear to the designers as impediments that were arbitrarily interfering with their ability to add features and capabilities to their company's applications, thus leading to their removal.

The lesson of the Trux-M-Us fiasco (described in painful detail in "Playing with Trucks – Part 1" beginning on page 155), which is always true, is that if, in the normal course of business (including attempts at expanding service offerings), it appears that a database constraint needs to be removed in order to proceed, this is a clear indication that the underlying database design is logically flawed. The design should ideally be corrected before proceeding.

RED FLAG

The subject of Constraints is yet another area where we need to provide more than a general level of detail in order to show exactly how misuse or lack of constraints can harm a business, and offer some practical, and hopefully actionable, approaches to preventing this.

If the explanations presented in first part of this chapter appear patronizing to I/T practitioners, I can only remind them that business managers are another important target audience of this book, and I believe that presenting a simple, but still thorough[193], explanation will foster better communication between these groups. Even more importantly, it has been my experience that many I/T practitioners seem unaware of the wide variety of locations and methods of establishing Constraints, **particularly unintentional ones**. Like the many examples of unintentional and undesirable business rules enforced by illogical designs presented as examples in "Data Structures as Unintentional Business Rules" (beginning on page 44), a keen awareness of this variety is necessary before beginning to plan any redesigns of an ailing system.

Two Primary Purposes of Constraints

When considering any particular Constraint and how best to implement it, we should always consider its basic purpose, which generally is one of the following, but not both:

▶   DATA RULE: A data rule is intended to strictly define a fact whose definition is based on objective reality. An example of such a rule might be any of the Propositions given in the "Grammar, Sets, and (Predicate) Logic – Part 1" chapter. For example "an Employee is a Person" is an inviolate Data Rule.

---

193 Though hopefully not too technical and informal enough to be useful.

► BUSINESS RULE: A business rule is an arbitrary, subjective, and quite possibly transient limitation on the scope or value of certain data elements based on the current needs of your particular business. Although "volatile" is probably too strong a word for many of these rules, it isn't entirely inappropriate. "Our business will only deal with individual Customers as opposed to Corporate Customers" is an obviously arbitrary Business Rule.

In order to achieve an effective and flexible design, the distinctions between DATA RULES and BUSINESS RULES must be kept in mind when considering where and how Constraints are to be implemented. In the following discussions, therefore, we'll comment on the suitability of particular methods and locations for each of these types of rule.

Common Approaches to Handling Constraints

Without regard to the purpose of the constraint as discussed above, there are two broad approaches typically taken – alone or in combination – when using Constraints to protect the corporation's data. As illustrated in the diagram on the right[194], there are two Proper Subsets of IMPLEMENTATION LOCATIONS (set A in the accompanying figure) which are "Inside the Database" (set C) and "Outside the Database" (set D).

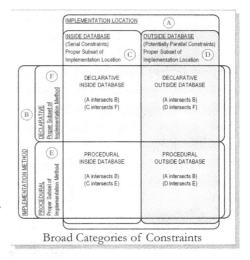

Broad Categories of Constraints

Similarly, there are two Proper Subsets of IMPLEMENTATION METHODS (set B), which are "Declarative" (set F), typically implemented within the database itself, and "Procedural" (set E), which may be implemented in either external programs or within the database itself. These implementation methods, of course, are independent of the implementation location.

---

194 There is a larger copy of this diagram on page 195 near the end of this chapter.

As can be seen, this results in four rather broad intersections of location and method that need to be considered, each of which covers a variety of more specific techniques that will be discussed below. The four intersections are:

▶ **Declarative** Constraints implemented **Inside** the Database (C ∩ F[195]).

▶ **Procedural** Constraints implemented **Inside** the Database (C ∩ E).

▶ **Declarative** Constraints implemented **Outside** the Database (D ∩ F).

▶ **Procedural** Constraints implemented **Outside** the Database (D ∩ E).

An awareness of the wide variety of Constraint Types and Locations possible is necessary in order to properly assess the integrity of a company's business data since, as we will show, that:

▶ It is quite possible for different Constraints to be in conflict.

▶ It is quite possible for Constraints to be unrecognized.

▶ It is quite possible for Constraints to be unintentional.

The good news, as it turns out, is that only three of the four intersections of type and location will usually need to be considered when deciding how and where to implement Constraints.

The bad news is that these conclusions assume that the enterprise being analyzed has only one "Business Database." If that isn't true, it should be reasonably obvious that the potential for inconsistencies in the handling of Constraints, as well as the potential for logical errors in the Enterprise, rises dramatically. Further details on each of the type and location intersections are given over the next several pages.

Primitive Declarative Constraints in the Database (C ∩ F)

Declarative Constraints, available in most modern database management systems, are appropriate for defining individual data elements at their most fundamental level. As one might expect from the name, Declarative Constraints are simply "declared" to the system. In other words, we instruct the computer (in

---

195 In Set Notation, this is read as "the intersection of sets C and F."

this case, our database management system) "what to do" and it then decides "how to do it."[196] There are several types of these to be aware of and, of course, these may vary slightly from product to product. Some examples follow:

▶ The NOT NULL clause

It seems unfortunate to me that the NOT NULL specification was implemented to appear as a "negative," since that presents a subliminal implication that having empty elements in the database represents the norm, and that we therefore need to go out of our way to specify that this isn't allowed. Actually, in any database, especially a relational database, NULLs should ideally be permitted only in cases where the presence or absence of such data is completely irrelevant to the definition of a particular record – i.e. in Accidental attributes[197] not required to distinguish the row it is in from others, or not being needed to fully identify or describe the entity defined by the record. A valid example of a data element that could be Null might be a column for Nickname[198].

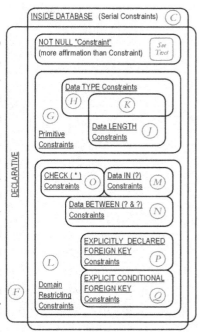

Declarative Constraints
in the Database

---

196 Of course, the computer was previously "programmed" by the DBMS to know how to do this and, as we all know, computer programs are pretty much infallible. Cynicism aside, though, modern database management systems are quite reliable in this regard.

197 See "Grammar: Verbs and Adjectives" on page 72 for a definition of "Accidental."

198 Some will certainly object that the NOT NULL Constraint precludes entry of partial records as "placeholders." An example would be a new patient record in a medical office, where we know the name, but not much else until we've taken blood pressure readings, etc. Discussing "placeholders" here would be a distraction, but a little thought will show that proper classification of Parties and the proper use of relationships will eliminate many of these concerns. NULL values have their place, but they should not be very common in a Relational table. Blood pressure is not only a transient measurement and an accidental attribute, but is not required to identify a patient and logically belongs to a separate entity.

► The DATA TYPE specification (set H in the accompanying figure) is not always considered a Constraint in popular literature, but certainly can and does serve that purpose, albeit sometimes unintentionally. Although not a complete listing, which would vary by product, examples of data type specifications include:

▼ **Character** (also known as String, Alphabetic, Text, Variable Character, and similar names); these are most often intended to prevent anything other than what typically appears on a keyboard from being accepted. Note that, although the term Alpha is still in use with certain products, characters other than those in the actual alphabet are typically permitted.

▼ **Number**; an arithmetic value on which some mathematical operation can be performed, such as addition, subtraction, and the like. Examples of Number data types include Integer, Floating Point, and similar. This data type should not be confused with "numeric characters," which include the characters "0" through "9," both by themselves and in various combinations. The English language includes a wide variety of terms in which the distinction between "numbers" and "numeric characters" is blurred, such as "post office box number," "serial number," and other similar examples. Although out of scope of this discussion, any failure to recognize this distinction can and often does lead to humorous[199] results.

One particularly interesting and not all that uncommon example of the misuse of "numeric" data is the definition of a United States Postal Code (also known as a "Zip Code"[200]) as an integer value between 1 and 99999 (the BETWEEN clause and its other misuses are discussed below), which results in Zip Codes for some northeastern states having fewer than five displayed digits; further, the postal bar codes derived from these are not consistently recognized by USPS scanners. Addition or multiplication of Zip Codes is meaningless, therefore they should be implemented as numeric characters – not numbers.

---

199 Humorous to me but, as I said earlier, I'm retired. Your management or user community may not be as amused.

200 Some may notice that the name "Zip_Code" itself indicates that the database design is less than flexible (there is an assumption, as well as country-specific data, contained in the data element name). This will be discussed in a later chapter on handling contact mechanisms.

▼ **Date**. Date data types in many modern systems store data in such a way as to permit easy determination, manipulation and formatting of dates, times, and intervals. For those who haven't dealt more than superficially with this subject, the definition of dates and times can be surprisingly arcane.[201] If your business is concerned with some of these issues, it is very important to evaluate the capabilities of your database management system, as these vary considerably.

Depending on the database management system in use (as well as its age), there are likely a variety of other data types for specialized needs, but the three listed above will suffice for the later discussions in this chapter.

► The DATA LENGTH specification (set J), also not always considered a Constraint by some references, often accompanies many data type constraints. Generally speaking, it limits the length of data that can be placed in a data element. The definition of Length, of course, sometimes varies depending on the data type. Examples of a data length specification might include:

▼ A data element called **First_Name** might be defined simplistically as alphabetic data with a maximum length of twenty-five characters. Although out of scope for an introduction of this type, Data length declarations sometimes seem to be misused about as often as they are correctly or appropriately used. Countless wasteful planning sessions have been devoted to determining the optimal sizes for data elements like names, although there hasn't been a compelling technical reason for limiting these for at least two decades.[202]

Data Length was an extremely important consideration in the early days of "data processing," when each of the eighty positions on a punched card needed to be carefully conserved. This sort of restriction is still part of the I/T genome, however, in spite of the fact that, with modern systems, it is far less critical. Arbitrary data lengths often present themselves as unintended constraints, such as when your best customer's name (or even your

---

201 An interesting and informative discussion of these issues appears in chapter 9 of Celko [1].

202 Should you find yourself in such a meeting, either use the time to take a nap, or demand to know why there need to be any restrictions on the size, then stomp your feet and leave. "There isn't enough space on our reports," a commonly cited excuse, simply doesn't stand up to scrutiny. Be snide and point out that "The Artist Formerly Known as Prince," while a silly but lengthy moniker at 35 characters, was just as valid a name as "Cher."

first foreign customer's name) won't fit in the limited number of characters you've defined.[203]

► COMPOSITE TYPE AND LENGTH specifications (set K) are common, but because this is simply an intersection of Type and Length, aren't discussed separately.

Higher Level Declarative Constraints in the Database (C ∩ F)

► DATA DEFINITION LANGUAGE (usually known by the acronym DDL[204]) Various Constraint capabilities are provided with virtually all database management system products used in business today. Examples, which vary somewhat by product, include:

▼ The IN Clause (set M), for example, specifies that a particular element can only be one of a few values. For example, if the definition of a data field for **Color** is created, and followed by something that looks like: "Color IN (Blue, Yellow)", this has the effect of preventing entry of anything other than the values Blue or Yellow. If another data element in the table requires the same IN clause or if any external application might need to access this Constraint domain, it is more appropriate to use a Foreign Key so redundancy is avoided.

Another common example of how the IN clause is used might look something like "Answer IN ('Y', 'N')" if the designer wished to make certain that a single character answer value could only be the letter "Y" or the letter "N." For various reasons beyond the scope of this explanation, this certainly isn't the best way to accomplish the objective, but can sometimes be acceptable.

▼ The BETWEEN Clause (set N) is similar to the IN clause, but is intended to set a contiguous range of valid values, e.g. "Quantity BETWEEN (1 AND 30)."

---

203 Of course if your Customer's name is Φρηνκ Ωβερλε or á¿Ã¹¤ÿ âÍàºÍÅÕ, the length of the data element may be the least of your worries, but such niceties are out of scope here.

204 Data Definition Language is a term for the syntax used to instruct the database management system to follow certain rules when creating data structures. DDL is somewhat analogous to what a programming language is to software. Many, though not all, database management systems consider Data Type and Data Length to fall under the general category of DDL. In the latter part of this chapter, I classify Data Type and Data Length as "primitive constraints" and, since they predate DBMS systems, I have treated them separately.

The BETWEEN Clause is often used quite inappropriately to approximate the range of a domain that should really be explicitly defined. A common example of this would be a declarative constraint such as "Zip_Code BETWEEN ('00001' AND '99999')," which permits all sorts of invalid values.

As with the IN clause, if another data element in the table uses the same BETWEEN clause or if any external application might need to access this Constraint domain, it is more appropriate to use a Foreign Key.

The major difficulty with the IN and BETWEEN clauses is is that this type of constraint can't easily be seen by users or applications. An example of this is given in the discussion of Unconditional Foreign Keys in the next point.

► FOREIGN KEY A foreign key constraint (usually known by the acronym FK) instructs the database management system to allow the entry of only those data elements that are already present in a separate DOMAIN TABLE, which can be viewed informally as a list of valid or permissible values. Such tables can and should be used extensively in any well-designed Relational Database, but do not always qualify as "relational tables" themselves. Though not usually classified this way in most instructional material, it is helpful to consider that Foreign Keys may fall into either of two classes:

   ▼ Unconditional Foreign Keys (set P) are based on a single piece of data. Rather than using the IN Clause as described above, the same effect could be achieved by specifying the data field **Color** as a Foreign Key to another table that contained a list of valid colors. There are clear advantages for utilizing Foreign Key Constraints over IN Clauses: not only can the Constraints be viewed and directly used by users and applications (thus promoting Enterprise consistency), but they may also be used by other columns in the table, as well as other tables in the database. This will be discussed in more detail later in this chapter.[205]

   ▼ Conditional Foreign Keys[206] (set Q) are based on a combination of more than one piece of data. If, for instance, your company wished to establish constraints on a data element that were dependent on some other value in the table, a conditional foreign key might be established to accomplish this. An ex-

---

205 See "Sharing Domain-based Constraints – The Ideal" on page 191.

206 I'm not aware of any product that uses this term, but a multi-part foreign key can certainly be viewed as a Boolean conditional, so it isn't inappropriate.

ample would be to establish a postal code domain based on the Country of the addressee, so that a U.S. Zip Code couldn't be used with a Canadian address.

Conditional tests are usually considered to be in the domain of procedural programming and are often implemented outside the database with code such as:

```
IF the country value is 'USA'
THEN use Postal_Code values (or formatting) from (A-list)
    but
IF the country value is 'CAN'
THEN use Postal_Code values (or formatting) from (B-list).
```

This fairly common situation[207] is more easily handled by declarative conditional foreign keys than error-prone code that is likely to be duplicated across an enterprise, and code, by the way, that is likely to become much more complex and dissimilar over time as more conditions are added.

In the example figure, the available choices and formatting of the **Postal_Code** column in the **Address** table varies based on the Country just as they are in the procedural pseudo code shown above. All valid postal codes for each country would, of course, need to be listed in the **Postal_Code** table for this to be useful.

A simpler alternative use of a Conditional Constraint, although obviously not so comprehensive, would be to have a format mask provided in the **Postal_Code** table against which entries in the **Address** table could be validated. Some techniques for approaching this are discussed in a little more detail later in this chapter. See "Contact Mechanisms" for more realistic handling of addresses.[208]

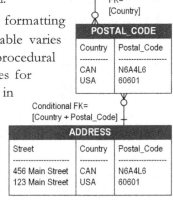

The foregoing can only be considered a very high level introduction to Declarative Constraints. Consult the manuals for your own database management system to see the variety of methods available for specifying declarative constraints.

---

207 Having mentioned postal codes twice in two pages, it may seem as if I have some bias against common methods of validating these, but you can't prove that conclusively.

208 "Contact Mechanisms," which begins on page 311, provides a more thorough approach to handling addresses, as well as a general approach to handling "flexible constraints."

Declarative Constraints outside the Database (D ∩ F)

Earlier in this chapter, I stated that only three of the four intersections of Constraint types and locations will usually need to be considered when deciding how and where to implement Constraints. This is the fourth.

Because programmers often "declare" a variable within a program, some assume that these are declarative definitions, more or less equivalent to those "declarations" made within a database management system. Since the scope of such programming language definitions is limited to an application, however, these cannot be considered "declarative," particularly for purposes of this discussion. When there is any reference to "Declarative Constraints" in the rest of this chapter, therefore, such references will always be to DDL Constraints that are declared and implemented in the Database.

This is not to suggest that programming language type and length definitions cannot conflict with or unduly restrict those made within the database, however. It only states that such mismatches and conflicts will not be addressed here. Certainly, if you declare a floating point number in an application and attempt to write it to a database element that was declared as an integer, you will cause data integrity violations – some, sadly, subtle enough that they may go undetected for a very long time, while others will become apparent immediately.

Procedural Constraints Generally (C ∩ E) and (D ∩ E)

Procedural Constraints (set E) can generally be implemented in a wide variety of locations. These are essentially sections of programming code that might be implemented in external applications, or contained within the database itself. Unless there are very good reasons, Procedural Constraints for DATA RULES (as described earlier) should normally be implemented in the database. Determining where to implement Procedural Constraints for BUSINESS RULES depends to a great deal on whether the particular business rule is (or can be made to be) data-driven or not.

▶ Procedural Code may be embedded in the database itself – most RDBMS software has at least one procedural language with which code can be written for triggers, data input utilities, and the like. Examples include the PL/SQL and JAVA languages used in Oracle, Sybase's TRANSACT-SQL (or T-SQL, in Microsoft's implementation), and so forth.

► Procedural code can, of course, also be contained in one or more external applications that access and manipulate the company's data, as well as in macro languages that reside in spreadsheets and other applications. The number, suitability, and capabilities of these languages is far beyond the scope of this discussion, but an awareness that this variety exists, and may have an impact on the consistency with which corporate data is handled, makes it incumbent on any data analyst to consider this alternate universe when evaluating their company's overall handling of data assets.

Summary of Constraint Approaches

In far too many corporate databases, we either begin with or eventually end up with very few or very inconsistent constraints. We'll begin with examples of Applications that use procedural code exclusively to enforce any desired constraints before writing new data into the database. Following those examples, we'll discuss declarative methods for constraints that began to become available with the advent of database management software. As we shall see below, the choices for where and how to apply or, sadly, to violate Constraints are more diverse than many designers consciously realize.

The Gamut of Constraint Practices

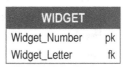

To illustrate various ways that constraints have been implemented over time in typical databases, consider the contrived **Widget** table to the right. The requirement to be enforced is that the **Widget_Letter** attribute for each Widget recorded in the table must only be permitted to contain a single character value that falls between "G" and "L" inclusively.[209]

---

209 Obviously there are some perhaps unwarranted assumptions here, such as the order of the letters in the alphabet, the use of a western alphabet, etc., but ignore those for now.

Early Programming of Database Interactions

In the dark but exciting early days, before the advent of database management systems, the sole means to ensure that only valid data was stored in "permanent" memory, which over time may have been a cuneiform tablet, 80-column card, magnetic tape or hard disk drive, was to write a section of code that looked something like the following, depending on the programming language:

```
IF  the Widget_Letter character is equal to or greater than "G"
    AND it is also less than or equal to "L",
THEN let it through
ELSE (otherwise) block it.²¹⁰
```

Since this approach still survives in a few musty corners of I/T practice, it would be remiss to ignore it. In the application depicted below, there were five sections of code capable of writing data into the data storage mechanism in use.

As the business requirements changed over time, it became necessary that the **Widget_Letter** attribute had to be reprogrammed to recognize only the letters that fell between "F" and "K" as valid, and the changes were duly made by members of the programming department. As sometimes happens, not all of them were fully informed, and the results are shown below:

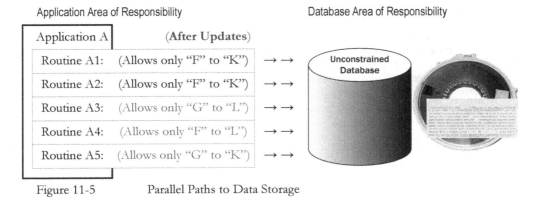

| Application Area of Responsibility | | Database Area of Responsibility |

Application A	(After Updates)
Routine A1:	(Allows only "F" to "K")
Routine A2:	(Allows only "F" to "K")
Routine A3:	(Allows only "G" to "L")
Routine A4:	(Allows only "F" to "L")
Routine A5:	(Allows only "G" to "K")

Figure 11-5   Parallel Paths to Data Storage

---

210 ...and, hopefully, return a useful error message explaining why it was rejected. In the early days, of course, memory was far too scarce and valuable to waste on storing intelligible error messages, so users were generally accused of violating long numbers that only those with a secret book owned by the I/T Department could interpret.

Several programmers attacked the changes and, while routines A1 and A2 were converted correctly, routines A3, A4, and A5 were not.

Most contemporary application designers will recognize the presence of multiple routines (five in this contrived example) that are intended to perform the same function as a "Bad Practice." The reasons are fairly obvious,[211] but generally revolve around the ideas that a) multiple copies of code waste space and, far more importantly, b) updates to these pieces of procedural code based on changes to business requirements need to be made in multiple locations. The common need to efficiently adapt to such changes over time is exactly what originally led to the invention of the Subroutine[212] and its later descendants (functions, methods, et al.). If one of these routines is done incorrectly or is inadvertently "overlooked" during the update, the omission isn't always obvious and may not be discovered until long after corrupted data has infected the system. Reviewing these errors, we find that:

The Cynics Corner

What Ἀντισθένης (Antisthenes), might have thought:

The important role of pre-release testing has been ignored in this discussion, but it should be observed that, when any business changes have not been adequately explained to or understood by developers, there is almost certainly less of a chance that they have been adequately explained to or understood by Testers.

Of course, you do have technically capable independent Testers, right?

▶ The incorrect change to the A3 code, where the domain of acceptable values has been extended at the wrong end, will obviously not allow the new "F" value and will still permit incorrect "L" values into the data. The former condition will certainly be discovered sooner rather than later and will likely result in the need to do a complete review of the upgrade process. The latter condition may or may not ever be discovered.

▶ The incorrect change to the A4 code, where the domain of acceptable values has been extended at both ends, will seem to function correctly, but will obviously still permit invalid "L" values into the data. As with the incorrect A3 modification to the code, this may remain undetected indefinitely.

---

211 If the reasons are not obvious, you should read a good programming book – any language created after 1960 has means for avoiding this.

212 See the chapter "Recent History of Data Management" that begins on page 97.

▶ Routine A5 seems to have been overlooked entirely, with the result that the domain of acceptable values has the same restrictions it started with. As with the A3 modification, it will likely be discovered eventually, but require more intervention than desired.

In any case, the only constraints one finds in a database where this sort of programming practices exist are very minimal constraints regarding data type and data length. In the very early days, even those data type constraints were often ignored.

Thankfully, the presence of redundant routines in a single application that are functionally identical has become the exception rather than the norm over the past forty years or so. Unfortunately, it is still not all that uncommon to encounter databases (even supposedly "relational" databases) that have minimal or no constraints whatever on many key data elements.

What's even more disturbing is that it isn't uncommon to discover that the database originally had constraints that were removed over time as illustrated with the Trux-R-Us example given in "Playing with Trucks – Part 1" that begins on page 155. We'll discuss another common (albeit pathetic) reason for constraint removal later in the section titled, naturally enough, "Common (and Loud) Objections to Such Heresy" that begins on page 188.

The examples on the following pages will continue to follow our deliberately innocuous requirement that a certain alphabetic character value needs to be limited to a specific range.

The implementation of this requirement can obviously be accomplished in a variety of ways, but the choice of location and the determination of whether any constraints we define should be serial, parallel, or both can have a significant impact on the flexibility of the system.

Flexible Constraints

There are many circumstances where we would like to have our Constraints vary depending on the value of a particular piece of data. An example would be to restrict postal codes (types, values, formats, etc.) based on the country for which data is being entered.

This is appropriate in more situations than typically recognized and, since it is quite possible to do so in a fairly straightforward manner, examples will be provided, but not in this chapter, which is more concerned with placement of Constraints.

The use of Flexible Constraints will be deferred until the "Contact Mechanisms" chapter.

Corrected but Redundant Programming of Database Interactions

While contemporary programmers are generally astute enough to remove redundant routines from their applications (or never create them), in many organizations where "architecture" is treated as a vague theoretical concept with little practical application, and where different groups are responsible for different applications, the identical situation can occur, as illustrated in the figure below:

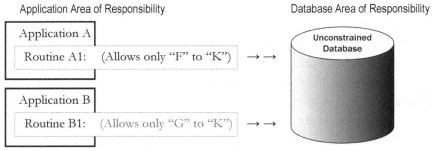

Figure 11-6   Parallel Paths to a single Database

The situation in figure 11-6, although architecturally flawed, seldom occurs. It is far more common, unfortunately, for different groups within a single business to have separate databases, as illustrated in the next figure. Sadly, from a corporate perspective, having multiple databases is a more serious architectural flaw.

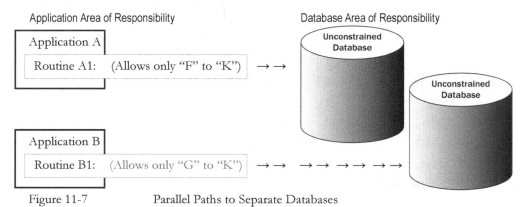

Figure 11-7   Parallel Paths to Separate Databases

If our company has data about its Widgets (or anything else) in multiple databases or tables, we still exhibit the same deficiencies in our stewardship of the corporation's data. The data in each of the independent systems is internally consistent (an amateurish, but not at all uncommon objective for department-level I/T groups but, from a corporate perspective, rather myopic and ultimately useless). Continuing to accept the idea that similar data is present in multiple business repositories is understandable, but barely tolerable. Building new business applications with independent data repositories is absolutely **in**tolerable, and can't be considered professional or responsible I/T support.

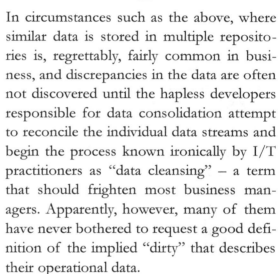

RED FLAG

When diverse Constraints are present across the Enterprise, data synchronization and cleansing are, by and large, logically impossible without significant human intervention and a large helping of assumptions. The best that can be done is what magicians refer to as "misdirection" or "sleight of hand."

The best way to understand this is to consider which department's (or application's) rules must be followed and which must be ignored.

In circumstances such as the above, where similar data is stored in multiple repositories is, regrettably, fairly common in business, and discrepancies in the data are often not discovered until the hapless developers responsible for data consolidation attempt to reconcile the individual data streams and begin the process known ironically by I/T practitioners as "data cleansing" — a term that should frighten most business managers. Apparently, however, many of them have never bothered to request a good definition of the implied "dirty" that describes their operational data.

One Routine – One Database

Even when we have removed all the deficiencies described above, and all our Widgets are recorded in the same database and all programmatic interactions with the database are handled through one shared routine, we are still left with a potential threat to the integrity of our data.

Even if there is (as there should be) only a single database and a single table within that database where Widgets appear, and all the external applications share a common routine for evaluating the validity of the data being placed in the database, we are still left with a situation where it is possible through non-programmatic means to add, modify, or delete data without having to be concerned about or protected by Constraints. This is illustrated below.

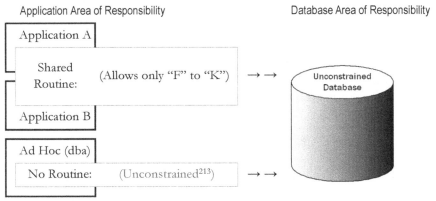

Figure 11-8   Parallel Paths to a single Database

In many circumstances, a DBA or some other person with DBA-type access privileges from a variety of tools is easily able to bypass (and, in fact, might be quite unaware of) constraints that are embedded in applications. This not only presents a risk of inadvertent data integrity violations but, in many situations, might also present a significant security risk that can affect not only the data, but the integrity of the business itself.

Summary of Constraints Implemented Outside the Database

All the approaches described so far share a common characteristic: they are based on procedural code that is separated from the database itself. They likewise share a common flaw in that they allow parallel (and therefore potentially different) paths into the corporate data stores whose consistency can't therefore be guaranteed. Having multiple access paths is never a good control mechanism and, if there is even a single unconstrained access path to the data such as that in figure 11-8, there is an unnecessary risk to the integrity of that data.

---

213 Strictly speaking, any database specifications regarding type (for example, alphabetic only) and/or length can be considered, at least from a primitive standpoint, as Constraints.

As discussed in the chapter "Recent History of Data Management," prior to the advent of database management systems (of whatever type), there was little point in making distinctions between DATA RULES and BUSINESS RULES, since they were each handled with the same techniques. This lack of differentiation is another holdover from the early days of computing that needs to be excised, since not accounting for the distinctions (or even recognizing them) can lead to both data integrity and system maintenance problems in the future.

The Funnel Effect

So far, as may have been annoyingly overemphasized, all the approaches described have been characterized by parallel paths into the database. A much better, and logically more defensible approach is to place any protective mechanisms in series with any data update or access paths. In military terms, we need to force any attacks to the integrity of our data to be made through a single avenue, which, as tacticians have known for thousands of years, is far easier to defend.[214]

A Single Entry Point!
Bridge and Portcullis of the Engenthal Castle in Alsace.

An inescapable conclusion is that, to assure the best protection for the corporation's data, Constraints must ideally be implemented in a guaranteed serial fashion – that effectively means that, at least for Data Rules (and many Business Rules as well), the Constraints must be implemented within the database itself. Of course, there are many obvious objections to this, particularly from application programmers, but these will be addressed as we examine the various methods of implementing Constraints within a modern database.

---

214 This is why old fortresses and castles generally had only entrance and were surrounded by moats (wet or dry), drawbridges, and reinforced gates. This was in spite of the inconvenience to those who lived outside the walls, but conducted much of their daily business inside. (Tradesmen lived near the gate, but laborers and domestics lived well to the rear)

Across the Moat and through the Portcullis

The figure below illustrates the general topology of the methods by which parallel paths into a database are restricted to a single serial approach. The block marked "The Moat" might represent any sort of database constraints described earlier from primitive declarations to conditional foreign keys.

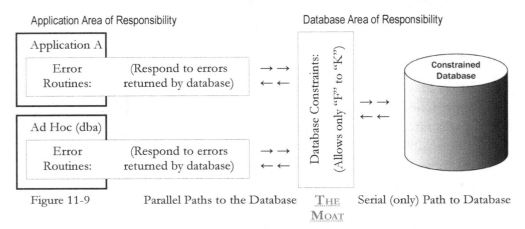

Figure 11-9   Parallel Paths to the Database   THE MOAT   Serial (only) Path to Database

The applications implement no Constraints themselves, and simply respond to errors returned by the database. Assuming that the Constraints in the database are implemented in such a way as to avoid easy bypass, such a topology provides very good protection of our data, but there will still be (and should be) objections to this approach.

Common (and Loud) Objections to Such Heresy

Objections to having strong data constraints embedded in and managed by the database generally fall into the following categories:

▶ **Performance**: Concerns about the performance of Constraints that are implemented within the database, although actually related more to speed than overall performance,[215] are often legitimate. The speed issues of concern include the round-trip timing of queries and updates, delays in being able to provide

---

215 See footnote 40 on page 29 for comments on speed versus performance.

user feedback, and so forth. Since integrity concerns often dictate the use of serial constraints, options for helping to mitigate these delays will be addressed in later examples.

► **Poor System Design**: If the design of the database structures was incompetent, or based on application needs rather than reality, Business Rule changes often can't be implemented without removing constraints.[216]

► **Control**: In some organizations, particularly in those where poor system design and/or unreasonable deadlines are also factors, declarative constraints in the database are perceived as impediments, since the requisite coordination among multiple groups inevitably increases the workload. This issue is exacerbated if the constraints were improperly intended to enforce Business Rules, rather than Data Rules.

Designers must always question why unconstrained access is deemed necessary or desirable, and address the objections appropriately.

RED
FLAG

A particularly insidious reason (at least from a business perspective) for resisting efforts to impose constraints on data comes from certain types of individuals within the IT community who relish the need to be viewed as "go-to" persons, "team players," or "operational problem solvers."

While often innocuous, most reasonably sized IT departments have at least one clueless (or worse) person who is willing to alter data by using dba privileges to bypass constraints – perhaps as a favor for a sales manager who can't place a major order into the system because the client doesn't meet the credit criteria established by the company's finance department.

Redundant Constraints in Series

Before dealing with the most common objections to maintaining Constraints within the database, it is first necessary to point out a common, but invalid corollary that is based on the following Propositions:

T Good programming guidelines dictate that functionally redundant routines are "Bad."

T Good data management guidelines dictate that Data Constraints must be in the Database.

Many people assume, therefore, that if Constraints are placed in the database, the same Constraints should not also be implemented in Applications outside the Database. They draw an invalid corollary from the two premises above that they are dealing with an either/or choice. Consider the following diagram:

---

216 A quick review of the chapter "Playing with Trucks – Part 1" will illustrate why this is so.

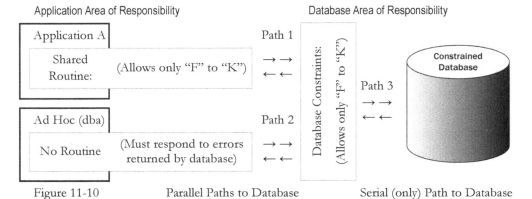

Figure 11-10   Parallel Paths to Database   Serial (only) Path to Database

At first glance, this seems to reintroduce the same issues of redundancy that we disparaged earlier in this chapter but, because our ultimate protection is in series with any external Constraints, there are three very important differences:

► **Serial vs Parallel** – the parallel nature of the external constraints such as those described above is what gives rise to the legitimate concern that we may be dealing with an either/or decision here. Closer examination shows that the data entry path is (Path 1 OR Path 2) AND (Path 3) – in other words, Path 3 will always be the final arbiter.

► **Effects on the Database** – If external constraints are more restrictive than those of the database, some valid entries may not be permitted. The good news, however, is that no invalid entries will be permitted, and the more significant this mismatch may be, the more quickly it will be exposed.

► **Effects on the Application** – if the application permits entries that are rejected by the database constraint (which is in series) the discrepancy will be exposed immediately – the good news again is that no invalid entries will be permitted. If the application is more restrictive than the database, the discrepancy may not be as immediately obvious.

Unfortunately, while the issue of redundant Constraints isn't the logical problem it first appears to be, the potential for performance (if this is defined solely as "response time") issues remains. One way of addressing response time, as well as reducing network traffic, is to share (rather than duplicate) the Constraints. This can be accomplished in several ways: we'll begin with the most appropriate.

Sharing Domain-based Constraints – The Ideal

As discussed earlier, data driven Constraints are the ideal way of maintaining integrity and consistency across the enterprise, and these can often be shared very easily as in the following diagram.

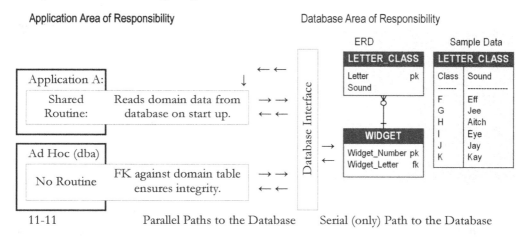

11-11   Parallel Paths to the Database   Serial (only) Path to the Database

This reaffirms the superiority of domain tables (e.g. **Letter_Class**) over IN and BETWEEN constraints, which really couldn't be conveniently handled in this manner. If, however, there are multiple databases (ugh!), there are still parallel paths into the "Company's Data." If there seems to be a justification for having multiple databases, even temporarily, the use of shared constraint tables should at least be contemplated, and these domain tables must be considered the "References," with all other external instances considered and treated as "copies."

Loading the data at start-up in effect replaces the cumulative overhead of multiple calls (one for each INSERT or UPDATE) with a single call when the application begins. More sophisticated techniques (e.g. for the database domain to automatically notify "subscribing" applications of domain table changes are beyond the scope of this book, but should be explored if needed.)

Sharing Pattern-based Constraints – Possibly Acceptable

A less robust method of constraining data that always has a known format is to make use of pattern definitions; although these would typically take the form of regular expressions, there are many alternatives that can be used. Such a scheme would look very similar to the previous diagram:

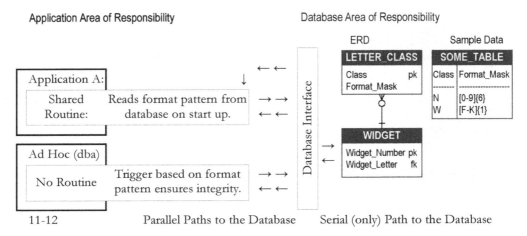

11-12   Parallel Paths to the Database   Serial (only) Path to the Database

In this example, however, we validate the input data based solely on format. A trigger reads the regular expression " F-K]{1}"[217] from whatever table contains the validation mask for our **Widget_Letter** attribute value. Examples of how this approach can be used are given in the chapter "Contact Mechanisms."

The drawbacks? While " 0-9]{3}" is a valid pattern for matching a North American telephone exchange, finding a "555" exchange in a delinquent customer's data might not please your credit department.[218] Furthermore, not all database management systems handle regular expressions and, given the variation in standards for regular expressions, those used in your systems might not be easily shared. Luckily, it isn't all that difficult to "roll your own" routine that can handle the limited types of uses to which this capability might apply.

---

217 This particular sequence is Oracle's form of a regular expression and is interpreted as one instance ("{1}") of any letter between "F" and "K." See page 323 for examples.

218 The "555" exchange, commonly used in television and movies, is never used for active lines.

Sharing Process Based Constraints – One Approach

Of course, not all Data Constraints can be purely data-driven[219], resulting in the need for procedural Constraints. As described earlier, most modern database management systems have at least one language with which such Constraints may be coded.

Depending on the particular environments and products used to build a given system, actual procedural constraints stored and used in the database can sometimes be called externally and even shared in more or less the same manner as in the domain table example above. We'll first illustrate, obviously in very general terms, how a database routine can be "called."

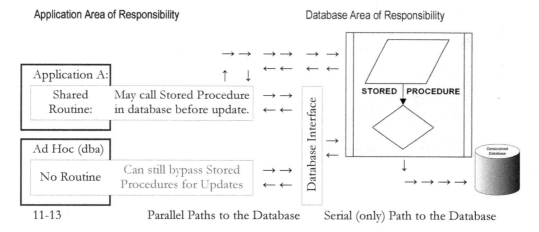

11-13   Parallel Paths to the Database   Serial (only) Path to the Database

Such a called procedure might simply validate data to eliminate the need for an application to be aware of the data structures and rules, but unless the procedure does the actual data entry for the application (rather than simply validating the data for later entry), this approach can result in reduced performance and unnecessary network traffic. Also note that, once again, there is a separate parallel access path into the data that can bypass procedural Constraints.

---

219 ... although competent analysis will show that this can be done far more often than is generally realized, albeit with sometimes more complex data structures. Data-driven Constraints are almost always the best method to use for Business Rules when a choice is available, and are appropriate for Data Rules as well.

Sharing Process Based Constraints – A Better Approach

Although "write-once, run anywhere" claims for programming languages as far back as COBOL in the 1950s have always turned out to be mostly empty promises, it sometimes happens that, depending on the particular environments and products used to build a given system, actual procedural constraints stored and used in the database can sometimes be utilized by external applications in more or less the same manner as the domain table example above.

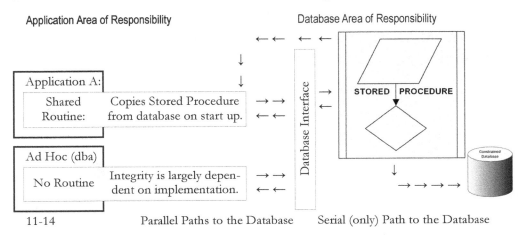

11-14   Parallel Paths to the Database   Serial (only) Path to the Database

Whether this can be accomplished depends, of course, on a wide variety of factors, including the particular programming languages in use, whether they are compiled or interpreted, the RDBMS in use, the operating systems of the various components, and so forth. Even if it is possible, consideration should still be given to what is referred to as "vendor lock-in" in the longer term.

In effect, this replaces the cumulative overhead of multiple calls (one for each insert or update) with a single (albeit longer) call at application startup. More sophisticated techniques, such as having the database notify all "subscribers" of changes made to the stored procedure, are out of scope for this book, but should be explored if warranted (e.g. for systems that shouldn't ever be halted).

Even if it is necessary to both read and compile source code routines for an application at each start-up, it may be worth it. Your mileage, as they say, may vary.

Informal Taxonomy of Constraint Types and Locations

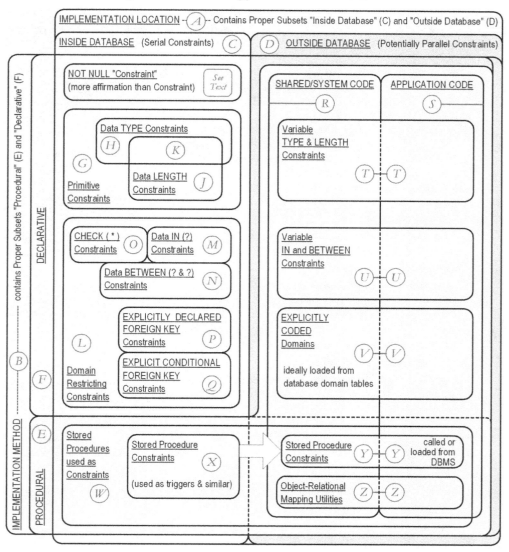

The figure above provides a useful reference for the descriptions of various types and locations of Constraints that follow: Capital Letter references to each set, subset and intersection are used in the following discussions of the applicability of any particular set to handling BUSINESS RULES or DATA RULES. As with the tables given in the chapters discussing Weights and Measures, it is expected that analysts will make any modifications or additions appropriate to their particular situation.

	Constraint Type and Location Taxonomy	Comments on Suitability for:	
	General Description	Data Rules	Business Rules
A	*Implementation Location • (all)* Consists of two mutually exclusive Proper subsets "Inside the Database" (C) and "Outside the Database" (D). This assumes, of course, that there is only one Business Database; if that isn't true the potential for Implementation Location as well as the potential for logical errors in the Enterprise rises dramatically.	See C & D	See C & D
B	*Implementation Method • (all)* Consists of two mutually exclusive Proper subsets "Procedural" (E) and "Declarative" (F).	See E & F	See E & F
C	*Implementation Inside the Database • (all)* Proper subset of Implementation Location (A) that represents a Constraint that is implemented inside the database. Whatever subclass (G, L, or any of their subclasses) is used, this will be a serial Constraint.	Ideal	Only subset W is acceptable and then only to the extent that its procedures are visible to application developers.
D	*Implementation Outside the Database • (all)* Proper subset of Implementation Location (A) that represents a Constraint that is implemented outside the database.	Unsuitable as the only Constraint due to parallelism	Not Applicable
E	*Implementation Method • Procedural • (all)* Proper Subset of (B); intersects with (D)	Suitability varies on the particular subset used (W through Z)	Only subset W is acceptable and then only to the extent that its procedures are visible to application developers.
F	*Implementation Method • Declarative • (all)* Declarative Constraints are always implemented in the Database. Because a Programmer often "declares" a variable within a program, some assume that these are declarative definitions, but since the scope of the programmer's definition is limited to the application, these are not considered "declarative" in this discussion. Declarative Constraints form a Proper Subset of (B)	Suitability varies on the particular subset used (G through Q)	Not Relevant since Business Rules should never be hard-coded into the database structures.

| Constraint Type and Location Taxonomy | Comments on Suitability for: | |
General Description	Data Rules	Business Rules
G *Implementation Method • Declarative • Primitive • (all)* Primitive Constraints form a Proper Subset of both (C) and (F).	See subsets (H) and (J)	Not Relevant (same as above)
H *Implementation Method • Declarative • Primitive • Type* Data Type Constraint	Required by any Data Store	Not Relevant (same as above)
J *Implementation Method • Declarative • Primitive • Length* Data Length Constraint	Avoid unnecessary restrictions.	Generally Not Relevant
K *In Database • Declarative • Primitive • Type & Length* This is an intersection of (H) and (J)	See (H) and (J).	Not Relevant (same as above)
L *In Database • Declarative • Domain-Restricting Constraints* Domain-Restricting Constraints form a Proper Subset of both (C) and (F).	Suitability varies on the particular subset used (M through Q)	Suitability varies on the particular subset used (M through Q)
M *In Database • Declarative • Domain-Restricting • IN()* Data IN Constraints are a Proper Subset of (L).	Less acceptable than (P) or (Q)	Completely Unsuitable
N *In Database • Declarative • Domain-Restricting • Between()* Data Between Constraints are a Proper Subset of (L).	Less acceptable than (P) or (Q)	Completely Unsuitable
O *In Database • Declarative • Domain-Restricting • Check* Typically used to incorporate IN and BETWEEN constraints in DDL Some products permit other uses.	See (M) and (N).	See (M) and (N)
P *In Database • Declarative • Domain-Restricting • Foreign Key* Simple Foreign Key Constraints are a Proper Subset of (L).	Preferable to (M) or (N)	Always Acceptable; can be Desirable
Q *In Database • Declarative • Domain-Restricting • Conditional FK* Conditional (i.e. multi-part) Foreign Key Constraints are a Proper Subset of (L).	Preferable to (M) or (N)	Always Acceptable; can be Desirable
R *Outside Database • Procedural • Shared/System Code* Subset of D + E	Not Relevant so long as Database and Application data types are the same	Not Relevant so long as Database and Application data types are the same
S *Outside Database • Procedural • Application Code* Subset of D + E that intersects with W, Y, & Z	Only subset Y is acceptable and only so long as Database and Application data types are the same	Not Relevant so long as Database and Application data types are the same

	Constraint Type and Location Taxonomy General Description	Comments on Suitability for:	
		Data Rules	Business Rules
T	*Outside Database ● Procedural ● Data Type & Length* Subset of D + E that intersects with R + S Data Type Constraint "Declaring" a variable's characteristics within a piece of software should not be compared to doing the same within a database as the implications are different.	Could be required in some circumstances, but difficulties may arise if there are any conflicts between the Database constructs and the Application code	
U	*Outside Database ● Procedural ● IN & BETWEEN* Pseudo IN or BETWEEN Construct intersects R + S. See comment under T regarding declarations.	See text	
V	*Outside Database ● Procedural ● Explicit Domains* Intersects with R + S See comment under T regarding declarations.	Ideal if the domain is loaded from Database. Acceptable as long as Database and Application data types are the same.	
W	*In Database ● Procedural ● Stored Procedures*	Can reduce redundancy so long as the routine can be loaded or at least called from the database, but it leaves an open unconstrained access path to the data.	Only subset Y is acceptable.
X	*In Database ● Procedural ● Triggers and similar uses* Proper Subset of W; subset of (C+E) Note that triggers which simply access external domain tables for business rules are acceptable, since it is actually the external table that defines the rules as data.	Sometimes necessary, but undesirable unless being hidden from application code is desirable for some reason.	Undesirable unless referring to external domains, since triggers themselves are not easily visible to applications or developers.
Y	*Outside Database ● Procedural ● Database Stored Procedures* Remotely loaded from RDBMS special case of W; intersection of (W+R)	Can be acceptable for elements that require very low response times.	Acceptable, but carries a risk of RDBMS vendor lock-in due to language

Chapter 11 - Handling Constraints

| Constraint Type and Location Taxonomy | Comments on Suitability for: | |
General Description	Data Rules	Business Rules
Z *Inside or Outside Database • Procedural • OR Mapping*	Can be acceptable for elements that very low response times.	OR Mapping tools generally map only Data, and hence are Unsuitable for business rules.

Generally, the rules for constraints are:

DATA RULES should always be implemented as structures or declarative constraints, even if any such constraints duplicate those in external software.

BUSINESS RULES can and often should be stored as **Data** in a database (e.g. the contents of domain tables), but should **never** be reflected in the Structure, including IN and BETWEEN clauses and triggers that contain such rules internally.

This is one area in which I believe even Chris Date drops the logical ball. In "Database Design and Relational Theory,"[220] he discusses "the familiar employees-and-programmers example, in which all programmers are employees but some employees aren't programmers." After evaluating several options, he concludes "But on the other hand, if we record all employees in EMP, we have some redundancy in our design: If e is a programmer, e is certainly an employee, so why say so explicitly?". This is actually a Proposition: F: A Programmer is (certainly) an Employee. But this Proposition is False, and therefore has no place in a design.

All that's needed to prove that this Proposition is False is to locate one contract programmer or subcontractor. This Proposition may be true for some particular business, but it isn't always true (meaning of course that it is False), making it – at best – a Business Rule. That's why this particular situation appears intractable.

Date argues – rightly – for the correspondence between Propositions and RelVars; when we attempt to regenerate the Propositions behind the tables he is describing, it becomes clear that these tables were based on False Propositions.

Correct the Propositions and the logically correct design appears like magic. A more logical approach is presented in "Triaging the Triangle" on page 245.

---

220 Date [2]; example 4 of Chapter 15. (see page 382 of this book for publication details).

► Constraints can be used to enforce Business Rules as well as Data Rules, and if we don't clearly distinguish between the two when designing a database, the oversight will eventually lead to serious problems.

► Constraints on natural Data Rules are absolutely necessary to protect data integrity, and tend to be factual, specific, and immutable. See "Playing with Trucks – Part 1" to see how poor database design conflicts with this.

► Constraints on Business Rules are likewise necessary, but tend to be arbitrary and subject to change over time.

► Constraints can and often are implemented unintentionally.

► Constraints can be implemented …

  ▼ … in a variety of ways

  ▼ … in a variety of locations

  ▼ … in parallel with other Constraints or in Series with them

► For Data Rules, the "gold standard" for Constraints is that they are

  ▼ implemented in a Declarative manner,

  ▼ implemented in the Database, and

  ▼ implemented in Series with any other Constraints

► From a business perspective, the effectiveness of any Constraints is severely and negatively impacted if there are multiple databases.

Supporting the handling of weights and measures at an enterprise wide level is perhaps the easiest (i.e. least politically sensitive) enhancement to undertake. It is thus recommended as a suitable "first step" towards introducing developers to the many benefits that can accrue from a logical approach to database design.

"Est Modus in Rebus" ("There is Measure in all Things") – Quintus Horatius Flaccus (Horace): Satires i,1

12 - WEIGHTS & MEASURES – PART 1

Weights and Measures[221] of various sorts are a key component of most business databases and, indeed, of many types of databases beyond the scope of this book, so it would be remiss not to discuss how these are typically handled and contrast that with how they should be handled. Although at first glance, this manner of properly handling data in accordance with the relational model and predicate logic might seem convoluted, it actually allows both businesses and applications to achieve a much higher level of flexibility, increases data integrity, reduces development time needed to implement future changes, and achieves other objectives dear to the hearts of both I/T and business professionals..

Logical approaches for reorganizing other types of data structures to better reflect reality have been presented earlier, but at a rather more general level than many developers might consider useful. As I mentioned earlier, this is not primarily intended to be a database design book, but lack of actual example code can certainly contribute to the idea that the ideas presented here are more theoretical than practical.

---

221 In the spirit of being precisely "logical," it should be admitted that a Weight is, of course, a specific form of Measure, but given the common acceptance of the term "Weights and Measures" throughout physics and science textbooks, as well as in U.S. and international standards, that term will be used here with only this insincere token apology.

In order to lend credence to the idea that implementing logical data structures is not only possible in the "real world," but actually quite straightforward, the subject of Weights and Measures will be dealt with in much greater detail over several chapters, even going so far as to discuss analysis and implementation strategies and to provide pseudo-code[222] examples.

The Business Issue

In "Playing with Trucks – Part 1" (beginning on page 155) as well as in many other scenarios where a business contemplates removing some of the strictures placed on their operations, or even actively joining the global community, implementation of designs based on the approach outlined over this and the next few chapters permits a much higher degree of flexibility and a more rapid and painless response to similar business needs in the future.

Although the scope of this book has been specifically limited to "Business[223] Databases," proper and explicit handling of measurement data is certainly applicable to other fields where data is "explored." Consider the following anecdote, for example:

> In 1999, NASA conducted a research mission in which its Polar Lander was to explore the surface of Mars. Another craft, the Climate Orbiter, would circle the planet and serve as the intermediate navigation and control station, and relay data between the Polar Lander and Earth.
> On September 23, 1999, after a 286 day journey, the Climate Orbiter, which cost about $125 million, fired its engine to achieve the desired orbit according to instructions transferred between the Lockheed Martin Corporation in Colorado and NASA's Jet Propulsion Laboratory in California.
> Unfortunately, the Orbiter came about 100 kilometers closer to the planet's surface than the engineers intended – and actually about 25 kilometers closer than the altitude at which the Orbiter could even function. As a result, the craft's propulsion system overheated, ultimately causing the Climate Orbiter to be lost.
> When looking into the causes for this, it was determined that all data was handled as

---

222 Well, it's actually very simple (albeit working) PL/SQL code used to test the functionality while writing these chapters, but for non-Oracle users it may as well be pseudo-code.

223 "Business" as defined in Chapter 1, (Definition of "Business"), beginning on page 1.

absolute values – that is, with no stated unit-of-measure. NASA assumed that distances were in kilometers but, unfortunately, the Lockheed Martin engineering team supplied the absolute values with an assumption that the distances were in miles. Oops![224] No Harm, no Foul, apparently. On September 30, 1999, according to CNN[225], the JPL administrator said "No one is pointing fingers at Lockheed Martin."

Of course this was just taxpayer money. Most business managers are not so forgiving; the lesson is that removing any assumptions can never hurt.

The Objectives of this Exercise

Earlier anecdotal chapters, such as "A Corporate Merger – Part 1" and "Playing with Trucks – Part 1" illustrated some of the difficulties resulting from poor database design. These examples emphasized the necessity for both designing data structures that closely fit the taxonomies of the real-world Things being represented by the data they contain, as well as avoiding hard coding of assumptions into database structures. Both of these practices invariably lead to severe system limitations. Furthermore, hard coding of assumptions into database structures causes these same assumptions to be implicitly hard coded into any applications utilizing them, since there is very little that software developers can do to effectively mitigate this. Unfortunately, the implications of this hard coding are seldom recognized, much less addressed.

Handling of Weights and Measures in typical information systems is one particular area in which hard coding of assumptions occurs quite frequently. This discussion should help expose the extent of these assumptions.

Aristotle Speaks

Remember that the second sentence in his Categories describes "univocal" (unequivocal or unambiguous) naming. The need for this is very close to the root of Philosophy, Logic, and Science, and was recognized as so by Newton, Carroll, etc. Are any of us wise enough to simply ignore this?

Categories; Part 1; Section 1.2

Over the next few chapters, we will discuss what specific data elements are required to

---

224 ...and this isn't an acronym for Object-Oriented Programming.

225 http://articles.cnn.com/1999-09-30/tech/9909_30_mars.metric.02_1_climate-orbiter-spacecraft-team-metric-system?_s=PM:TECH

unequivocally define the information elements needed for a representative sampling of weights and measures. We will demonstrate that there are numerous steps that can be taken to model this data more effectively in relational databases, and show how to make the transition from existing practices to designs that are more reliable, flexible and extensible, and to do this in discrete phases if necessary. To accomplish these objectives we will, over this and several additional chapters do the following:

In this chapter, we will:

▶ Outline the design principles and objectives used to guide development of models and processes for storing and manipulating weights and measures.

▶ Define the various classes of weights and measures that are in and out of scope for this exercise.

▶ Discuss what data elements are needed to completely and unequivocally define any particular measure.

▶ Construct a generalized logical model for handling most types of data related to weights and measures.

In "Weights & Measures – Part 2" we will discuss the mathematics required for correctly manipulating data relating to weights and measures. See page 225.

In "Weights & Measures – Part 3" we will describe the desired end state of our system(s) once changes have been made. See page 271.

In "Weights & Measures – Part 4" (See page 279.) we will:

▶ Outline a process for migrating from typical database and application designs to extensible designs in manageable stages.

▶ Discuss some factors that will need to be specified for any company-specific implementation of these methods.

▶ Discuss some issues encountered when creating applications that utilize logical data models such as the one presented here.

Finally, in "Chapters 12 & 13 - Weights & Measures Parts 1 & 2" of Appendix B, (page 393) we will:

► Provide some sample (functional, but not production-ready) database structures and code illustrating some of the principles and techniques described.

► Provide a sufficient number of test cases to prove the recommended approach and which can serve as models for creating test cases that more closely match the specific needs of your own organization.

Although the concentration in the four "Weights and Measures" chapters is on remediation of existing database structures and applications, all the techniques discussed here are applicable as well to new development and, in fact, will make future development much easier when handling these types of structures.

The Scope of this Example

Measures that fall into the following classes, to be defined later, are discussed in this example:

Angular	Dry/Solid Volume	Pressure	Temperature
Apothecary	Force	Quantity	Troy
Area	Frequency	Solid Volume	Weight/Mass
Consumption	Linear (L, W, H)	Speed	
Distance	Liquid Volume	Surveyor's/Gunter's Chain	

Although the classes of measurement listed above sound like they might be "standard" definitions, they do not quite meet that level. Two of them, in fact, are quite arbitrary.[226] The justification for this will be explained later.

Design Principles

The following principles[227] and objectives are intended to guide the design and implementation of general methods for handling the "Weights and Measures" classes developed in the following sections.

---

226 Go ahead! Guess which two; given what's been covered so far, it should be fairly easy.

227 Good Architects, of course, always work to a set of Guiding Principles.

► 1. As with all database designs, the primary considerations should be for data integrity and business flexibility. Thus, the data structures must be designed to accurately, completely, and unequivocally reflect the information of interest, and not be bound by the transient needs of a particular application or environment.

► 2. Business flexibility, as well as extensibility of information systems, is best served by maximizing opportunities for reuse, thus requiring that any design for handling weights and measures should be as consistent, general and universally applicable as possible.

To ensure that all participants in an enterprise are consistent in their use of units of measure for their particular needs without utilizing a flexible and inherently reliable database design, we would likely need a large government-sized bureaucracy to continuously cross check the data and perform sophisticated quality control on applications and reports. As we've seen with the Climate Orbiter example, however, that isn't actually all that reliable.

► 3. No assumptions should need to be made for any measurement information represented in a well-designed database or application.

> *For example: Nothing weighs 16. Something may weigh 16 lbs or it may weigh 16 oz, but a measurement always requires at least two pieces of information (and therefore two data elements) in order to be meaningful.*

► 4. A fundamental principle of logical[228] database design is that each data element must be atomic, or contain only one piece of information.

> *For example: A data element called "Weight in Pounds" actually represents two distinct pieces of information - the weight's absolute value and the weight's unit-of-measure, one of which cannot be directly queried. Such constructs are therefore amateurish and unacceptable.*

► 5. The original information related to each weight or measure accepted into the system must be retained exactly as it was entered for audit and documen-

---

228 This refers to the use of formal Logic as described earlier in this book. It does not refer to the distinctions made between "logical data models" and "physical data models" which, in many corporations, aren't very obvious. I want there to be no doubt that the approach described here is intended to be implemented physically.

tation purposes. This information should remain available so long as the data record in which it exists remains.

> *For example: A U.S. company may sell widget powder by the ounce, and fulfill all orders for this powder in ounces. If an order is received from another country for a specified number of grams, this requested measurement value and unit-of-measure should be retained as the original value of the order even if that order is ultimately filled with an amount in ounces.*[229]

▶ 6. The design of the system should not result in any loss of capabilities normally present in less universal systems that are customized for some particular purpose or application. It is very likely that meeting the criteria in Principle 5 will satisfy this principle, but they are different in intent.

▶ 7. The design of the system should adhere to National and International Standards for Weights and Measures, including conversion factors, names of units of measure, abbreviations for units of measure, etc. Although there are certain internal inconsistencies across measurement classes in these Standards, they are well established and agreed upon. This falls under the useful business maxim of "Don't reinvent the Wheel."

▶ 8. A general rule outlined earlier is that, while database designs may not always need to completely reflect reality, it is imperative that they never conflict with reality. Practical considerations may require compromises in the completeness of certain implementations of the approaches for handling weights and measures outlined in this book. While this may be acceptable within limits, any data structures or coded procedures that conflict with these approaches are not acceptable, and Triage should identify them.

Design Objectives

▶ 9. The design should be such that, eventually, all measurement values will be forced to have explicitly specified units-of-measure upon entry — even if such specifications are provided by default values rather than user inputs.

---

[229] Similarly, of course, the actual amount shipped should then be expressed in ounces!

▶ 10. Measurement Classes and Units of Measure, along with any related conversion information (formulas, values, offsets), must be domain controlled at the database level[230] in order to ensure data integrity and internal consistency and allow us to detect any nonsensical data inputs.

▶ 11. For each Unit-of-measure defined in a domain, a base or reference Unit-of-Measure (UOM) will be established for use in internal calculations; these will be referred to as Root Units of Measure or "Root UOMs" in the remainder of this document. For example, if the base or reference for distance were to be defined as kilometers, all system calculations, including the implicit calculations, comparisons, aggregations, etc. involved in summary queries, would be done on values that had been converted to kilometers.

▶ 12. Units of Measure used for input and/or display purposes should be independent of the units used for internal storage or calculation - whether or not they happen to be the same - since these represent different pieces of information.

▶ 13. The design of the system must not permit cumulative conversion errors or value changes when successively converting back and forth between or across multiple units of measure.

▶ 14. The data structures should be designed such that the number of formulas required to handle any required conversions is kept to a minimum — preferably one. Furthermore, the defined calculation method must be available to all database users to ensure consistency.

▶ 15. The system design should not require any specialized knowledge on the part of typical users. To the extent that any implementations require users to have knowledge of formulas, values, standards, or even the proper case of standard abbreviations, such implementations are undesirable.

---

230 Remember the insidious nature of Invalid Corollaries! This principle should *not* be taken to mean that domain control may not also be implemented at the application level, simply that it *must be* implemented, preferably through declarative constraints, in the database. See the discussion of why such dual implementations can safely be implemented and how this should be done in "Handling Constraints," particularly the section "Redundant Constraints in Series" on page 189.

▶ 16. To the extent possible, implementation of the design should not require that changes be implemented in a "big bang" fashion although it should not restrict that. Changes to the database structures should be decoupled from application changes such that system enhancements can be adopted incrementally.

▶ 17. The design should be such that as many future changes as possible can be implemented by adding or altering data rather than changing and recompiling code.

Classes of Weights and Measures

There are numerous classes of weights and measurements that are important to the worlds we model in data and for which we build software. These range from size to distance, from weight to cost, from temperature to time, and so forth. As with many broad subjects, there are several possible taxonomies of measurement class that can be developed, so for our purposes, the tables in this section will list and define the measurement classes that will usually be encountered when conducting business.

Defining the class of a measure is important because conversions can only take place between units of measure (UOMs) within the same measurement class.[231] It would make no sense, for instance, to attempt a conversion between gallons and inches, but only explicit measurement class data would allow a system to detect this as invalid. Likewise, the conversion between a quart and a liter would use a different mathematical factor depending on whether the measurement class is dry volume or liquid volume, since a dry quart differs from a liquid quart. These examples of a dual use of a single standard Unit of Measure is another reason why a measurement class is usually[232] required for clarity.

---

231 As part of Design Objective 10. There are exceptions to all such rules, of course, but they needn't be of concern here. An example is given in the section "Conversion between Measurement Classes" on page 306.

232 Even if you suspect you can get away without the Class, for instance by convincing users to always think in terms of "fluid ounces" for liquids and just "ounces" for dry measurements (and good luck with that, by the way), you will soon be thwarted by human nature.

Measurement Classes in Scope

All measurements that fall into the general Measurement Classes listed below are considered to be in the scope of this document, and can be handled for most enterprises using some or all of the design approaches and techniques discussed in this and subsequent chapters:

	MEASUREMENT CLASSES IN SCOPE
Class	**Description**
Angular	**Angular** units of measure are used by mathematicians, engineers, physicists, and anyone dealing with trigonometry. Angular units of measure include degrees and radians. When handled using the techniques in this book, Angular measurements are expressed as decimal numbers, although in common usage, they are more typically expressed as combination measures: Degrees, Minutes and Seconds for degrees, and relative to π (e.g. $3\pi/2$ radians instead of 4.71 radians). Conversion to and from such combination measures is not in the scope of this discussion, however. *Although the Angular measurement class falls within the scope of this discussion, and can easily be handled by adding the necessary conversion factors, it is not commonly used in business, so no conversion factors are given in the examples in this book.*
Apothecary (two classes: Liquid Solid)	**Apothecary** units of measure are used by pharmacists, and are actually divided into two classes: liquid (traditionally called apothecary measures) and solid (traditionally called apothecary weight.) Apothecary units of measure include grains, scruples, drams, ounces and pounds (although a pound consists of twelve, rather than sixteen, ounces.) *Although the Apothecary measurement class falls within the scope of this discussion, and can easily be handled by adding the necessary conversion factors, it is not commonly used in business, so no conversion factors are given in the examples in this book.*
Area	**Area** measures define the two-dimensional space on a plane occupied by any material, and are typically given in units of measure such as square feet, square meters, acres, etc..
Consumption	**Consumption** is a measure of the *rate* at which something is utilized, and is typically given using two units-of-measure. Fuel consumption, for instance, is measured in Miles-per-Gallon. Conversions between consumption measures typically involve differences in both units-of-measure, such as a conversion between Miles-per-Gallon and Kilometers-per-Liter.

MEASUREMENT CLASSES IN SCOPE	
Class	**Description**
Distance (also see Linear) (Spatial only, not Temporal)	Strictly speaking, **Distance** is a measure of the interval between any two points in space or time. For the purposes of this discussion, only space is covered by this class, however, and time measurements are given their own class. Given this segregation of space and time, distance could just as easily be considered as a Linear measure but, since the typical scale is quite different between measurement of Things and measurement of Distances, it is more convenient and useful to treat Linear and Distance classes separately. Additionally, it would be quite unusual for there to be an ongoing need to express the distance between cities, for example, in inches, a typical Linear unit. (Also see **Linear**) Distance measures are usually given in units such as miles, kilometers or other units of similar scale. See the comments immediately below this table for a discussion of the distinction made here between Linear and Distance Measurement Classes.
Dry Volume or **Solid Volume**	**Dry Volume** measures define the space displaced by a known collection of solids, given in units of measure specific to solids. These may be three-dimensional measures, such as cubic feet or cubic yards, or amorphous space measures such as gallons or liters. Viewed from another perspective, **Dry Volume** defines the Capacity of a container.
Force	**Force** is a measure of power or energy – something that changes or tends to change the state of rest or motion of some body. (Also see **Pressure**). *Although the Force measurement class falls within the scope of this discussion, and can easily be handled by adding the necessary conversion factors, it is not commonly used in business, so no conversion factors are given in the examples in this book.*
Frequency	**Frequency** is a measure of how often something occurs. Specifically, it is primarily the number of vibrations or waves occurring in a specified time period, typically one second. **Frequency** is the inverse of Period.
Linear (also see Distance) (Spatial only, not Temporal)	**Linear** measures provide the length of a straight one-dimensional line between two points. Names of linear measurements, such as "length", "width", "height", "depth", etc. are simply conveniences to distinguish across multiple simultaneous aspects of the same item. (Also see **Distance**) Linear measures are usually given in units such as inches, millimeters, yards, meters or other units of similar scale. See the comments immediately below this table for a discussion of the distinction made here between Linear and Distance Measurement Classes.

Class	Description
Liquid Volume	**Liquid Volume** measures define the space displaced by a known amount of liquid, and are given in units of measure specific to liquids, such as gallons or liters. Viewed from another perspective, **Liquid Volume** defines the Capacity of a non-permeable container.
Pressure	**Pressure** is a measure of Force (q.v.) applied uniformly over a defined surface, measured as force per unit of area. Surface, as defined here, includes not only plane surfaces, but measures such as atmospheric pressure as used in meteorology.
Quantity (non-absolute)	**Quantity** is normally given as an absolute value but, in certain specialized cases, there may be magnitude-related units of measure associated with this Class. For instance, an electronic device may have sixty-four million Bytes of memory; for convenience, we would use units of measure such as Bytes, Kilobytes, Megabytes, etc. Such units of measure are not considered in this paper, but the approach outlined would support such units. Of course, in the example given, one needs to determine whether a Kilobyte is equal to 1,000 bytes or 1,024 bytes. Who says that we don't adhere to standards in our own industry? *Although the Quantity measurement class falls within the scope of this discussion, and can easily be handled by adding the necessary conversion factors, it is not commonly used in business, so no conversion factors are given in the examples in this book.*
Solid Volume	See **Dry Volume**
Speed	**Speed** is a measure of the rate of movement across a defined distance during a specified period of time, and may be given in both two-part measures (such as miles-per-hour, kilometers-per-hour) and single measures (such as knots.)
Surveyor/ Gunter (Chain)	**Surveyor**'s or **Gunter**'s Chain units are used to handle segmented or irregular perimeters, specifically those used in describing plots of land. *Although the Surveyor measurement class falls within the scope of this discussion, and can easily be handled by adding the necessary conversion factors, it is not commonly used in business, so no conversion factors are given in the examples in this book.*
Temperature	**Temperature** values give a measure of the degree of heat (molecular motion) within or around an object, usually given in units of measure such as degrees Fahrenheit or degrees Celsius (also known as Centigrade). The example formulas discussed in this paper will not handle conversions to and from absolute zero or the Rankine scale, although extensions to do this are discussed in the "Offset(s)" section beginning on page 227.

Class	Description
Troy	**Troy** units of weight are utilized by jewelers; typical units of measure include grains, pennyweight, ounces and pounds (although, as with the apothecary class, a pound is twelve, rather than sixteen, ounces.) *Although the Troy measurement class falls within the scope of this discussion, and can easily be handled by adding the necessary conversion factors, it is not commonly used in business, so no conversion factors are given in the examples in this book.*
Weight (Mass)	**Weight** is the mathematical product of a solid object's mass and gravity, given in pounds, kilograms or similar units of measure. These discussions do not distinguish between weight and mass, since the distinction isn't generally relevant to business.

It was mentioned earlier[233] that some of these Measurement Class definitions were arbitrary. You will note above that the definitions of Linear and Distance are similar enough to suggest that they may, in fact, be the same thing. And indeed, you would be correct in that observation. However, since the range of what might be encompassed by these definitions could easily be several orders of magnitude in many businesses, I have arbitrarily separated them. It is certainly recommended that you make your own determination of how these are defined, although unless your business has some reasonable ongoing need to express the distance between cities in inches or millimeters, you may want to follow my example here.

Other similar circumstances may arise in specialized systems. In a system meant to handle, for instance, cosmological measurements, Einstein's Theory of Relativity may need to be considered, in which case, the separation of Distance, Linear, Speed and Time may no longer make sense. For most businesses, however, the Class taxonomy given here will prove quite adequate.

Measurement Classes Not In Scope

The general Measurement Classes listed below are considered to be out of the scope of this document:

---

233 In "The Scope of this Example" on page 205.

Class	Description
Calendar	**Calendar** mathematics is specialized and, although the rules are reasonably well defined, most operating systems provide sufficient native support for common contemporary business calendar operations. Therefore, there will usually be no need for additional conversion support unless the enterprise has very specialized requirements.[234] **Time** and **Calendar**, which would seem to be related, differ primarily in the facts that Calendar measurements can be arbitrary: Differences in minutes and seconds (Time-related) are absolute, while differences in elapsed number of months and years (Calendar-related) are quite dependent on the identification of specific start and stop points.
Currency or **Money**	The primary distinction between **Currency** and the measures considered to be in-scope is that the conversion factors for the latter remain fixed and the procedures for performing the conversion consist of straightforward, unchanging, and universally agreed upon standards. Currency value conversions, on the other hand, fluctuate continuously, require continuously updated external data (exchange rates), and are often complicated by arbitrary regulations that change from country to country and over time.
Global Positioning	**Latitude** and **Longitude** measurements are universally agreed upon and require no conversions of the types considered in this chapter.

---

234 When dealing with historical data, for instance, it may be necessary to adjust between calendars used by different cultures, or calculate elapsed time periods in a single culture, particularly since science and astronomy have improved the accuracy of calendars over the centuries. Politics has also played a significant role in complicating calendar calculations. Following the French Revolution in 1789, for instance, the government implemented an all new calendar consisting of twelve 30 day months with an uneven number of "floating days" at the end of each year. Although this lasted less than a quarter century, determining the timing of historical events in France during this period involves some rather arcane calculations. In many professions (e.g. historical, genealogical, archeological, etc.), the need to handle date approximations (year ranges, years with no month, sorting approximations or dates that are non-aligned across cultures properly), and similar circumstances isn't handled at all by non-specialized commercial products. Were you aware, for instance, that nothing at all happened in the American Colonies between the 3rd and 13th of September 1752 and why? (See "An Unexciting Period of History" on page 223). Consult Celko [1] for additional discussions if your business might be affected by such considerations.

MEASUREMENT CLASSES NOT IN SCOPE	
Class	**Description**
Time (of Day: Clock)	**Time-of-day** measures themselves are universal and, except for the differences in twelve and twenty-four hour notation, need no conversions. See Time Zone for additional time-of-day considerations.
Time (elapsed)	**Elapsed Time** is a measure of the difference between two defined times, and is typically given in hours, minutes, and seconds (and occasionally in larger or smaller units).
Time Zone	**Time Zone** handling is usually accomplished by use of the UCT[235] but requires some specialized reference data and conversion techniques that do not fit in well with the general scheme provided here. This is because of the inconsistent and often uncoordinated use of daylight savings time across the world, and even within the United States.

Expressing Measurement Information as Data

This section could just as easily have been titled "Modeling Data Elements for Weights and Measures", and is intended to illustrate how information that is trivial for humans to process is quite a bit more complex to present unequivocally to a machine-based system.

To repeat the example in the design principles, nothing weighs sixteen! Something may weigh sixteen pounds or it may weigh sixteen ounces, but a measurement always requires at least two pieces of information in order to be meaningful: an absolute numeric value (e.g. 16) and a unit-of-measure (e.g. pounds.)

An American would dress more warmly when his local newscaster says that the temperature is 40 degrees than a Frenchman would when his own local broadcaster says the exact same thing.[236] When an American says that something weighs six pounds, or an Englishwoman says that something costs six pounds, they mean entirely different things, and any attempt to compare the two is meaningless. Also, as we have already seen, there are liquid "ounces," dry

---

235 Universal Coordinated Time, formerly known as Greenwich Mean Time.

236 Presumably, the second announcer would really have said "quarante degrés" ("forty degrees" in French), but the point is that 40 degrees Celsius is 104 degrees Fahrenheit.

"ounces," and Troy "ounces." Therefore, the Class of measurement is also required to unequivocally define any measurement.

As can be seen, most colloquial uses of measurement rely on context as well as knowledge and, often, a few assumptions – the absence of these attributes are a common cause of complexity in our I/T systems. A little thought suggests that the following data elements are required to completely capture these attributes in a database or information system.

Many are undoubtedly wondering whether it is really necessary to take something seemingly so simple, and that is so "intuitive" to us as humans, and make it so "complicated." My answer is fairly straightforward: machines are not humans – able to make logical inferences[237] to determine meanings from context and so forth. Once this is recognized, it is evident that the "complications" arise in the system from our failure to properly define the complexity. "Complex" and "Complicated" are entirely different concepts; when dealing with machines (and many humans) we need to recognize complexity and define it accordingly.

DATA ELEMENT	Purpose of the Data Element
Value	To a human, the **Value** is the most significant data element in a measure. This is because it is the only unique element we need to consider, and we are able to make assumptions as to its meaning from the context of a conversation. When a U.S. highway patrolman asks "How fast do you think you were going?," we can safely respond "fifty-five" knowing full well that, although we are telling a bald-faced lie, the patrolman knows that we are referring to the unit-of-measure *miles-per-hour*, and not *feet-per-second* (55 feet-per-second is about 375 miles-per-hour).
Unit of Measure (... of input value or user value)	The **Unit-of-measure** is necessary whenever the context is, or might not be, clear, or the communicating parties may not share the same assumptions (a situation, it should be strongly emphasized, we are usually unaware of, as with the Climate Orbiter example given earlier). Thus, once we cross over into Canada, and the speed limit signs say "80" instead of "55", our presumed knowledge that Canada uses the metric system (meaning that the "80" represents kilometers-per-hour) will suffice. In a computer system, however, this knowledge and the assumptions

237 Actually, I'm not all that convinced many humans are that skilled at recognizing such logical inferences but, for the sake of argument, will concede that as a legitimate possibility.

DATA ELEMENT	Purpose of the Data Element
	that derive from it, must be explicitly conveyed by means of a data element, specifically the unit-of-measure.
Class of Measure (… of input value or user value)	In many circumstances, the **Class of Measure** seems to be even more obvious to us as humans, and therefore something we seldom consider. Grocers (and most of us) know that there are sixteen ounces in a pound. Pharmacists, however, who use a different measurement class, believe that there are only twelve ounces in a pound.[238] A truly general-purpose system needs to be aware of this. Generalized data structures and software routines, both of which are not only possible, but highly desirable, need the information that allows them to distinguish among identically named but semantically and mathematically different units of measure that exist across the different measurement classes. Keep that last point in mind, however (that Class is needed only because units of measure are duplicated across measurement classes), since this will impact your design decisions.

One implication of Design Principle 3 ("no assumptions should be made for any measurement information represented by a well-designed database or application")[239] is that, for each measure, there must therefore be at least the three distinct data elements described above. Doing so will: – produce a system that allows our businesses to have the maximum flexibility in handling weights and measures; – provide information systems that are very easily extensible and; – permit us to produce software routines that have excellent reuse opportunities.

But we still need to consider a critical performance implication of storing measurements in arbitrary units, and that is the need for efficient sorting by the measure's magnitude, for totaling, averaging or performing other mathematical aggregations of the measurements. Since performing the necessary conversions during any such processing would be unacceptably expensive in terms of processing speed, it follows that, in order to achieve the system flexibility we desire,

---

238 Does an apothecary's pound have the same weight as a grocer's pound (meaning their ounces don't have equivalent weights) or are the ounces the same and the pounds different? Or is there no correspondence whatever? If you don't know the answers to these questions, consider how likely it is that your software or database does!

239 See "Design Principles" beginning on page 205.

each measure should be converted to a standardized value upon entry and stored separately[240] as an additional data element for use by internal processes. Therefore, we can add the following three information elements to consider when designing generalized data structures:

DATA ELEMENT	Purpose of the Data Element
Internal Value	The **Internal Value** is the calculated value of the data element of interest when stated in the unit-of-measure we have selected as our internal standard. For many (and perhaps most) applications, this value may in fact be equal to the value described in the previous table, but it represents a different piece of information. This value is used when totaling line items in an order or a shipment that are given in different units of measure, totaling route distances across countries with different standards, for example a trip from Mexico to Canada through the United States.
Unit of Measure (of internal value)	Knowing the **Unit-of-Measure** for the internal value is necessary for the same reasons described above. As with the internal value, the internal unit-of-measure may be the same as the input unit-of-measure, but is a different data element because it represents different information.
Class of Measure (of internal value)	A little thought will show that the **Class of Measure** for the internal value must, by definition, always be the same as that of the input or user value. Thus, while this represents a different piece of information, it is logically defensible that it shares the same data element and can always be safely inferred from that element.

Yet Another Taxonomy, and a possible Subset

DATA ELEMENT	Purpose of the Data Element
Measurement System	A **Measurement System** is a collection of units-of-measure that are typically used together as a group in, for instance, a country, region, or specific industry. Inches and Centimeters, for instance, while both in the same Class, are in different Systems (English and Metric).

For applications where it is desirable to permit entry of a single measurement value in multiple units-of-measure, e.g. "14 feet, 7.5 inches" in construction, Class of Measure may not be the only information required. In order to split

---

240 It is stored separately rather than replacing the input value in order to retain the original entry. This is in keeping with Design Principle 5.

measurements into component units, while still keeping within the same Measurement System (converting inches to a combination of meters and inches, for example, would make little sense), the System itself may need to be recorded as data. Again, as humans, we have no difficulty handling the choice of "next highest *relevant* unit-of-measure," but without explicit data, our information systems would! For the moment, however, we will not consider the use of the Measurement System.[241]

Interestingly, even within a Class such as Liquid Volume, some subsets may need to be defined for each Measurement System. The liquid volume of a Barrel of petroleum, which is equivalent to 42 gallons (U.S.) or 158.987 liters (Metric), is not equal to the liquid volume of a Barrel of proof spirits, which is equivalent to 40 gallons or 151.416 Liters — and a Barrel of beer is a different amount than either of these.

At this point, logic seems to be suggesting that a significant expansion in the number of data elements we will be storing in our tables is about to take place. Where in a typical system we previously had a single value, we might now have four or more data elements[242]. Many I/T folks recoil at such an idea, considering that this would result in "far too many" columns in their tables.

Too Many Attributes?

Emperor Joseph II of Austria, to Wolfgang Amadeus Mozart, after hearing a rehearsal of the latter's opera "The Marriage of Figaro:"

"Your work is ingenious. It's quality work, but there are simply too many notes, that's all. Just cut a few and it will be perfect."

To which Mozart supposedly replied: "Which few did you have in mind, Majesty?"

Recoil Example – A Dissenting Opinion

While Emperor Joseph didn't really have the musical chops for Mozart to take him seriously, the well-respected author Joe Celko certainly has the database chops to have his opinions taken seriously and, in most cases, I do.

---

241 An approach to handling this is discussed briefly under "Application Considerations and Caveats" on page 307.

242 As it turns out, it will not always be necessary to explicitly state the unit-of-measure for the internal value so long as the system design is such that the internal unit-of-measure can be queried. The approach proposed in this book supports such a query ability.

An exception to this is his argument in "Data & Databases"[243] against the recommendations I am making here, so I feel it appropriate to justify my position.

In chapter 12, in a section titled "Punctuation and Standard Units," he defines "punctuation" by saying that it "… serves to identify the units being used and can be used for prefix, postfix, or infix symbols. It can also be implicit or explicit." Examples of explicit punctuation that he uses include currency symbols, date formatting, and the inclusion of what I refer to as units-of-measure in this book. He notes as a matter of interest that "Databases do not generally store punctuation" and that "Punctuation is only for display."

He follows with this rather explicit paragraph regarding approaches apparently similar to what I am proposing (written, remember, in 1999):

> *"It is possible to put the units in a column next to a numeric column that holds their quantities. This is awkward and wastes storage space. If everything is expressed in the same unit, the units column is redundant. If things are expressed in different units, you have to convert them to a common unit to do any calculations, so why not store them in a common unit in the first place?"*

In 1999, I also found these arguments reasonable, but my belief is that the technological and business environments in which we operate have changed dramatically since then.[244] While I agree that "databases do not generally store punctuation," it is my contention that they should – not only for weights & measures, but for currency as well. The following table will summarize my arguments:

The Argument	The Counter-Argument
"Punctuation is only for display."	Since computers have less ability to infer the punctuation than humans, I can't agree. Punctuation permits humans to distinguish between 20 dollars and 20 euros, or between 20 ounces and 20 pounds. Punctuation is required for clarity and precision – both requirements for responsible data management.
[putting the units of measurement in another column]	Business managers as well as many I/T practitioners preach flexibility and adaptability. Admittedly they practice it much less

---

243 Celko [1]; see page 381 for more information.

244 1999, coincidentally, was the year of the Mars Climate Orbiter incident described earlier in "The Business Issue" on page 202 and, again coincidentally, caused by missing punctuation.

The Argument	The Counter-Argument
"is awkward and wastes storage space."	often, but restricting a business system to a single unit-of-measure for any given value seems in conflict with this objective. Flexibility in any form (including any of the punctuation examples given) demands the use of arbitrary units-of-measure in modern business. Any use of arbitrary units-of-measure without transparent support in their respective I/T systems would seem to be flirting with a lack of accountability at the very least, and presenting an open invitation for error, if not fraud, in the worst case.
	Is it really awkward to specify that you want 5 gallons instead of 5 ounces?
	As stated many times in this book, I no longer find storage space concerns to be very compelling now that I can carry more storage space on my key ring than I ever encountered in a data center in 1999.
"If everything is expressed in the same unit, the units column is redundant."	This would appear on the surface to be true, but only if the unit of measure is an independent data element; in fact it is only one component of the data element. This argument assumes that there is some inherent benefit to recording everything in the same unit[245] simply to avoid the appearance of redundancy. Without the storage limitations of the past, there is no longer any need to assume a single unit of measure and, in fact, quite a number of potential benefits to eliminating that assumption.
"If things are expressed in different units, you have to convert them to a common unit to do any calculations, …	This is certainly true, but calculations and summaries of weights & measures can be handled quite transparently with the design approaches recommended in this series of chapters. Similar but slightly more complex approaches can be used with currency.
… so why not store them in a common unit in the first place?"	… because it is more often necessary now than in 1999 to be able to recover or document the original input data.
	Since that time, the expansion of business opportunities to global markets has continued, while government regulations (often from multiple venues) regarding transparency and traceability have grown. These increased responsibilities of businesses (and therefore I/T departments) require more accurate data structures.

---

245 Any benefit to the business, that is. Of course there is a benefit to developers and database administrators, but that isn't relevant.

Disagreements aside, an expansion in the number of columns for each relevant data element would indeed be a major change for many organizations, but such an expansion is indeed the suggestion, although contemplating doing this should give us pause for a number of reasons that are quite legitimate:

▶ Database structures will need to be changed

▶ Existing data will need to be migrated

▶ Database stored procedures will need to be changed

▶ Application code will need to be changed

▶ Reports will need to be changed

▶ All these changes will need to be coordinated carefully to avoid operational disruptions.

In the following chapters, we will discuss in detail how to determine the extent to which such a migration may be required (including how many new elements are really needed in any given enterprise), how it would appear from a technical standpoint (e.g. some simplified entity-relationship diagrams, with query and code examples), and how a migration could be handled in realistic and controlled phases. First, however, it will be helpful to do a little homework – to perform a little Triage on your own data structures.

Homework Assignment

As a preliminary design exercise, identify all the "measurement" data elements within the business data schema with which you are most familiar and determine which of the above Measurement Classes applies to each of them, and whether there might be other Classes that are necessary.

Save this information for future reference, since it will be necessary to proceed with redesigning the data structures to fit the relational model and permit an eventual restructuring of your systems to increase flexibility, maintainability, extensibility, etc.

Determine which of these data elements place operational or marketing restrictions on your business (manual exception processing for instance) or, conversely, which data elements, if made more flexible, would present operational or marketing opportunities to your business. This information will help in prioritizing any efforts undertaken based on the migration techniques presented in chapter 17 (Weights & Measures – Part 4).

Keep in mind that these explorations should not be restricted to Information Technology personnel whose opinions are not the most relevant! Marketing, Finance, and other Management personnel should be actively engaged as well.

In the next chapter, before getting into the details of how data structures would be changed, we'll discuss some mathematics used in unit-of-measure conversions, since these are not quite as straightforward as the inside flap of your old grammar school book covers might have suggested, particularly if we wish to achieve the Design Objectives previously outlined.

An Unexciting Period of History

A brief look at the calendar on the right[246] should answer the question raised earlier about why nothing at all happened in the American Colonies between the 3rd and 13th of September 1752[247]. Of course, a lot of future rebels complained incessantly during that first week of September about the British government's

SEPTEMBER 1752						
S	M	T	W	T	F	S
		1	2	14	15	16
17	18	19	20	21	22	23
24	25	26	27	28	29	30

abrogation of their rights, and the shortening of their lives by eleven days. Of course, people had no such rights back then, but if your business deals with historical data, or with many disparate cultures, you may want to pursue calendar mathematics and date measurements, since they are not discussed here.

---

246 If you are on any Unix-like system that is installed in the United States or Great Britain, you may type in "cal 9 1752" or simply "cal 1752" at a command line to see this.

247 See Footnote 234 on page 214.

"The concept of Length is ... fixed only when the operations by which length is measured are fixed. The concept is synonymous with the corresponding set of operations. - Percy Williams Bridgman[248]

"A single accurate measurement is worth a thousand expert opinions"
– Admiral Grace Hopper

13

13 - WEIGHTS & MEASURES – PART 2   ▬ ▬ ▬

Prelude – The Mathematics of Weights & Measures

Converting a value from one unit-of-measure to another might seem to be a straightforward process. We may remember the conversion tables on the inside covers of our grammar school notebooks, and even our cell phones can provide easy conversions. Such conversions are, in fact, fairly straightforward, but need to be thought through a little more carefully than is first apparent, particularly if we wish to prevent cumulative conversion errors or value changes when doing multiple conversions between different units of measure (Design Objective 13). This chapter will discuss the pitfalls of using stock conversion factors and how to ensure consistent and repeatable conversion results.

The Gimli Glider

In 1983, Air Canada's Flight 143 left Montreal for Edmonton. Because the new Boeing 767 had a malfunction in its automated fuel measurement system, the ground crew calculated the fuel needed for the flight manually.

Traveling 469 knots at 41,000 feet over Ontario, fuel warning lights came on, and eventually both engines stopped. The plane's fuel tanks were completely empty. Oops ...

The 767 was now an unpowered glider. Luckily, one of the pilots was familiar with the relatively close, but abandoned and unoccupied RCAF base at Gimli, and was able to safely accomplish an emergency landing.

By the way, the 767 was the first of Boeing's aircraft designs to have been fully converted to the metric system. Hmmm. Look it up.

As you might suspect, the forty million dollar price of the aircraft itself was just one line item on the total cost to Air Canada.

---

248 Bridgman [1]; see page 381 for details.

Conversion Factors to Consider

Multiplier

All measurement conversions rely on multipliers and most conversion tables provide these for many possible pairs to be converted. For instance, a conversion table for distance might list the following useful multiplication factors:

```
1 mile     = 1.6093 kilometer (inexact, but often adequate)
1 kilometer = 0.6214 mile      (the rounded reciprocal 1/1.6093)
```

Such tables are, of necessity, not entirely accurate. If, for instance, we take an assumed distance of 38.5 miles (a reasonable decimal), and multiply it by 1.6093, we get 61.95805 km. This is not a reasonable decimal for general use, so we would probably round it for display to 62.0 km.

Converting the stored value of 61.95805[249] back to feet by multiplying by 0.6214, however, gives 38.500732, a very small error, but one that could accumulate with multiple conversions. It should be obvious, therefore, that the general practice of using different multipliers for converting in different directions between the same two units of measure will not always allow multiple conversions of the same value without introducing cumulative errors.

On the other hand, converting the stored value of 61.95805 km back to miles by *dividing* by the original 1.6093 gives exactly 38.50, since we are using the identical factor and exactly offsetting any lack of precision in that conversion factor. This provides the trick we need to achieve design objective 10.

To avoid any possibility of such rounding errors, our rule should be to establish ONE value as a conversion factor for each Unit-of-Measure pair and use the formulas [* factor] in one direction and [/ factor] or [* (1/factor)] in the other. This further implies that a "standard" unit be established for each measure we track, so that the correct conversion "direction" can be set. This "standard" unit will be known as the "root" unit-of-measure in this discussion.

---

249 Obviously we would not try to convert the rounded display value of 62, and if that isn't obvious, you really should retire or find some other line of work...

Offset(s)

Measurements with natural or physical reference points often require some fixed offsets as well as formulaic conversions. The best example of this is temperature, where various different systems in use throughout the world all have known points (and altitudes) at which water freezes or boils. In a Fahrenheit to Celsius conversion, for example, an offset of 32 is required in addition to the conversion of the size of a "degree" to account for the fact that water freezes at 0 degrees Celsius and +32 degrees Fahrenheit.

For most conversions, this offset value will be zero, which will allow a single formula to be used for all expected conversions, whether an offset is required or not. This will make life much simpler and help fulfill design objective 14.

In the case of absolute zero, it is necessary to utilize both pre- and post-formula offsets when converting to or from Fahrenheit or Celsius, but it doesn't seem necessary to implement this in normal business systems, so only one offset value will be needed in a practical implementation, and that is all that is shown in this discussion. It should be a straightforward matter to add a pre-formula offset if needed when developing systems for scientific organizations.

Sample Conversion Calculations

This section will illustrate how calculations of various measurement conversions would be done using the scheme described. Any calculation algorithm would first need to determine the direction of the conversion (i.e. whether the conversion is into or out of a root unit-of-measure and therefore whether to divide or multiply). The general forms of these calculations are shown below.

The following table contains sample conversion factors for three classes of Weights and Measures, and will be used in the calculation examples to follow. A table like this will be implemented almost literally as a database reference table, with the stipulation that for each measurement class, there must be one and only one unit-of-measure with a multiplier of 1 and an offset factor of 0; this will define the root unit-of-measure (our internal system standard) for a particular Measurement Class. See a more complete table in Appendix C on page 415.

Measurement Class	Unit of Measure	Root Unit of Measure	SAMPLE CONVERSION FACTORS	
			Multiplier	Offset
Liquid Volume	Gallons	Gallons	1	0
Liquid Volume	Liters	Gallons	3.7854118	0
Speed	Miles per Hour	Miles per Hour	1	0
Speed	Kilometers per Hour	Miles per Hour	1.609344	0
Temperature	Degrees Celsius	Degrees Fahrenheit	1.8	32
Temperature	Degrees Fahrenheit	Degrees Fahrenheit	1	0

As should be evident, `Gallons`, `Miles per Hour`, and `Degrees Fahrenheit` have been chosen as the root units-of-measure for their respective categories.

Converting from a root UOM to a non-root UOM:

Converting from a root unit-of-measure to a non-root unit-of-measure would usually be done for display or output purposes, and is accomplished by multiplication using the following general formula:

```
(Root Unit Input Value - Offset Factor) * Multiplier Factor
```

Examples:

1. Convert from a root unit measurement of 21.6 Degrees Fahrenheit to Degrees Celsius:

```
    (Root Unit Input Value - Offset Factor) *  Multiplier Factor
= (        21.6          -       32      ) *           1.8
= (                         -10.4          ) *           1.8
=                                          -18.72 degC
```

2. Convert from a root unit measurement of 2 Gallons to Liters:

```
    (Root Unit Input Value - Offset Factor) * Multiplier Factor
= (          2            -        0       ) *        3.7854118)
= (                          2              ) *        3.7854118)
=                                            7.57 liters
```

3. Convert from a root unit measurement of 55 Miles per Hour to kph:

```
    (Root Unit Input Value - Offset Factor) * Multiplier Factor
= (         55            -        0       ) *        1.609344
= (                         55              ) *        1.609344
=                                            88.51392 kph
```

4. To illustrate that the formula will not cause errors when attempting to convert like units of measure, convert from a root unit measurement of 55 mph to mph:

```
  (Root Unit Input Value - Offset Factor) * Multiplier Factor
= (          55          -       0       ) *          1
= (                     55               ) *          1)
=                                          55 mph
```

Converting from a non-root UOM to a root UOM:

Converting from a non-root unit-of-measure to a root unit-of-measure would usually be done upon input of a non root unit-of-measure, and is accomplished by division using the following general formula:

```
(Non-Root Unit Input Value / Multiplier Factor) + Offset Factor
```

Examples:

5. Convert from 44 Degrees Celsius to the root unit-of-measure Degrees Fahrenheit:

```
  (Non-Root Unit Input Value / Multiplier Factor) + Offset Factor
= (          44              /       1.8        ) +       32
= (                    24.444                   ) +       32
=                                          56.444 degF
```

6. Convert 100 kph to the root unit-of-measure mph:

```
  (Non-Root Unit Input Value / Multiplier Factor) + Offset Factor
= (          100             /      1.609344) +          0
= (                  62.13712                ) +          0
=                                          62.14 mph
```

7. Convert 684 liters to the root unit-of-measure gallons:

```
  (Non-Root Unit Input Value / Multiplier Factor) + Offset Factor
= (          684             /      3.7854118) +         0
= (                180.693683                ) +         0
=                                          180.693683 gal
```

8. To illustrate that the formula will not cause errors when attempting to convert like units of measure, convert from 65 Degrees Fahrenheit to the root unit measurement of Degrees Fahrenheit:

```
  (Non-Root Unit Input Value / Multiplier Factor) + Offset Factor
= (          65              /       1        ) +         0
= (                     65                    ) +         0
=                                          65 degF
```

Function Interface

Any system implemented using the conversion approach described above will require a generic function whose signature would look something like the following:

```
Function UOMConvert ( FromUOM
                    , ToUOM
                    , FromMeasurementValue
                    , MeasurementClass
                    )
```

The function would, of course, return the value expressed in ToUOM units. As mentioned earlier, the Measurement Class is used to distinguish between similar units of measure in different Measurement Class domains, such as liquid and dry volume that have different conversion factors. For a detailed example of how such a function might be implemented, see the example WM_UOM_Convert() on page 396.

Function calls for the example calculations given above would then look something like the following:

```
ToMeasurementValue
    = UOMConvert ('degF', 'degC',  21.6, 'Temperature')
ToMeasurementValue
    = UOMConvert ('gal', 'lit',    2,    'Liquid Volume')
ToMeasurementValue
    = UOMConvert ('mph', 'kph',    55,   'Speed')
ToMeasurementValue
    = UOMConvert ('mph', 'mph',    55,   'Speed')
ToMeasurementValue
    = UOMConvert ('degC', 'degF',  44,   'Temperature')
ToMeasurementValue
    = UOMConvert ('kph', 'mph',    100,  'Speed')
ToMeasurementValue
    = UOMConvert ('lit', 'gal',    684,  'Liquid Volume')
ToMeasurementValue
    = UOMConvert ('degF', 'degF',  65,   'Temperature')
```

From the descriptions so far, it may not be immediately obvious that the calculations shown do not directly support conversions between two non-root units of measure (e.g. liters and quarts.) If such a function is intended as a private means of converting to and from Root measurement values (i.e. for applications and internal procedures), and *not* intended to serve as a general purpose measurement conversion routine, this is of no particular concern. If, however, the function is also intended as a general purpose conversion utility, this can easily be accommodated by first converting the input value to a root unit and then converting that intermediate result to the desired unit on a second pass.

The example `UOMConvert()` function referred to above is such a generalized version, and can handle any conversion for which conversion factor data is available, whether either unit is a root unit or not. It can easily be simplified, however, to serve only internal needs if required, and if that offers any worthwhile performance benefits; an example of such a simplified function is also supplied under the name `WM_SYS_VAL()` under "Bare Bones WM_SYS_VAL Function in PL/SQL" on page 398.

Note that the units of measure are all given in the English language. It is quite possible, using the techniques shown in the chapter on "Contact Mechanisms", to have these available in multiple languages if desired, but a discussion of the techniques for doing so would be confusing at this stage. The important thing to note is that this technique does *not* preclude the use of multiple simultaneous languages in a database or application.

Naming Revisited

In "Naming our Things" on page 73, the importance of precisely naming entities and concepts was introduced as one prerequisite to the design of robust and extensible data structures. In this series of chapters on Weights & Measures, a key lesson has been the importance of specifying the Unit of Measure - both to clarify the meaning of the related data quantity and to permit more flexible data input and output.

Sadly, some commercial software packages and published materials confuse the term Unit of Measure with another concept more precisely known as Unit of Issue[250]. Reviewing the ill effects of this poor naming choice is enlightening.

---

250 Other terms for this include Unit-of-Sale, Pack Size, and the like.

We can buy, for instance, a single can of soda, or we can purchase a "six pack" or even a "case" of twelve or twenty-four cans of the same soda. The size of an individual can may be eight ounces, twelve ounces, two liters, or similar. There are two quite different pieces of information expressed here:

Unit-of-Measure

This chapter covers the meaning and necessity of **Unit-of-Measure** at length and so will not be repeated here. "Ounces" and "liters" in the preceding paragraph are Units-of-Measure, and give meaning to the quantities eight, twelve, and two.

Unit-of-Issue

In our soda purchase example, "single" (also known as "each" in logistics circles), "six-pack," "case," "carton," and such terms are the **Unit-of-Issue**, and refer to the quantity of the items that are treated as if they were a "unit" – that is the collection is issued, sold, or priced together. For products we purchase at a store, such groupings will have a different UPC than a single quantity of an otherwise identical item. Unit-of-Issue is known by other terms such as Unit-of-Sale.

Clarity

The important distinction between and **Unit-of-Issue** and **Unit-of-Measure** seems rather obvious when the two terms are used together, but good Triage will require particular sensitivity to such differences when only one concept is in use, which is often the case in packaged software or published materials.

In the book "Oracle – Building High Performance Online Systems,"[251] the section "Basic Data Base Design" illustrates a column labeled "Unitmeas"[252], a single character code for what is obviously a Unit-of-Issue. The deficiency in such a

---

251 W.H. Inmon; QED Information Sciences, Inc.; ISBN 0-89435-302-0)

252 (sic), page 4 – this column label itself is an example of poor naming. If a shorter name was desired, a standard abbreviation such as "UOM" would have been much more suitable, and far easier to guess for someone searching the schema. Then again, the author clearly defines "performance" as "amount of time required" (page xiii).

design is the difficulty that would arise if it became necessary to add an actual Unit-of-Measure to the schema at a later date. As we have seen, such data is critical if a corporation wishes to enhance rather than constrain its capabilities.

Hiatus

The discussion of how to handle Weights and Measures in a Business Database will be continued on page 271, but first we'll expand our exploration of logic, predicates, propositions, and the perils of multiple inheritance in order to see how a refurbishment of the Trux-M-Us database might be approached. If Triage of such a pathetic design can show the way to making improvements, there should be hope for almost any database design.

► Because management of corporate data is a primary responsibility of any group associated with Information Technology, unintended alteration, contamination or loss of data cannot be permitted.

► The approach taken to handle data elements that can be expressed in different terms is therefore quite important to the integrity of a corporation's data.

► The approach taken to handle data elements that can be expressed in different units is therefore also quite important to the ability of a corporation to expand its business without undue pain and expense.

► The handling of data related to Weights and Measures is one very good example of how this responsibility is regularly – although seldom deliberately[253] – abrogated by both database and application designers.

► During Triage, the handling of data related to Weights and Measures also typically provides many examples of the abhorrent practice of collapsing two pieces of information into one data element (Atomicity Violations).

► A good system design for handling Weights and Measures should therefore never result in cumulative conversion errors as data is manipulated, and it is incumbent on designers to provide a consistent means for insuring this.

---

253 Indeed, questioning such designs during Triage is almost always met with blank stares.

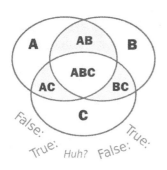

Having begun a discussion of why the concept of an "Object-Relational Impedance Mismatch" is largely mythical, and having suggested that multiple inheritance may not only be a good thing, but even a requirement for implementing a logically designed system, it only seems fair to continue this line of reasoning to see where it leads when applied to some real world examples.

So this chapter will begin to tie together many of the earlier concepts discussed in preparation for a serious Triage on the Trux-M-Us database table presented in Chapter 10.

14 - GRAMMAR, SETS, AND PREDICATE LOGIC – PART 2

In an earlier chapter, we introduced the analysis of classes and subclasses as a logical approach to designing core business entities in a Relational Database,[254] and suggested the viability, practicality and benefits of this approach using examples such as the class hierarchy of [Party→Person→Employee].[255]

Very briefly in that chapter, and in later chapters with a bit more detail, we suggested the inevitability of Intersections[256] in logical database design and used **Customer_Person** and **Customer_Organization** as examples. We mentioned in passing that Intersections implied multiple inheritance, but that OO theoreticians and programmers are of two different minds about the use of multiple inheritance. In fact, several popular object-oriented languages don't even permit multiple inheritance.[257] Logical Intersections occur quite commonly in the real world we need to model, and because it is naive and counter-productive to think we can avoid dealing with them, we will begin to do so in this chapter.

---

254 See "A Corporate Merger – Part 1" beginning on page 41.

255 See "Deja Vu" on page 61.

256 See "A Corporate Merger – Part 2," particularly "Intersections as Views" on page 134.

257 Humorously enough, there are numerous techniques described on the internet for "getting around" these strictures in most of those languages, which should tell us something.

Previous chapters have introduced many of the principles needed to resolve the issues of multiple inheritance related to database designs, but we need to review and refine those principles specifically for addressing Intersections. The next chapter will then present a more aggressive use of Intersections to suggest how the Trux-M-Us database[258] design could have been approached more logically.

Classes, Sets and Attributes Revisited

It was pointed out earlier that while a Class is always a Set, a Set isn't always a Class.[259] The difference, remember, is that a Class is taxonomic, and includes **all** Primary Substances – known or unknown – from which the existence of the Class can be predicated. Sets, on the other hand, are defined more arbitrarily.

 Aristotle was very concerned with collecting and recording facts about taxonomies of the Things he was studying;[260] he was therefore more of a data person, and considered a Class to be quite precisely defined (a common noun, predicated from the existence of primary substances, etc.)

Lewis Carroll, on the other hand, concentrated on Propositions and Logic, and would likely have been more comfortable as a programmer. As mentioned earlier, he not only wasn't concerned with the differences between Sets and Classes, but used the terms interchangeably in his writings.[261]

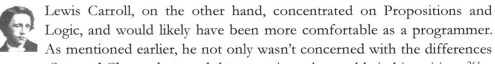

Sherlockian Observation #1

The Aristotelian view of Classes differs from the Carolingian view in the same manner as the relational database designer's view of data classes/elements differs from that of a programmer.

The sense of the word CLASS as it is used in Object-Oriented programming is, in fact, much broader than that of the taxonomic term CLASS as it is (or should be) used in relational database design. Relational Database designers deal primarily with taxonomic CLASSES to build the skeletal backbone of the database, while programmers deal with Carroll's more loosely-defined Classes, some of which are legitimate taxo-

---

258 See "Playing with Trucks – Part 1" which begins on page 155.

259 See "Sets and Classes – The Crucial Difference" on page 71.

260 We could have said he was "building a database" if there were computers in ancient Greece.

261 Remember the Caution about studying Lewis Carroll's "Symbolic Logic." on page 87.

nomic Classes, but some of which are just Sets. Recognizing the implications of this situation is quite important when addressing the use of multiple inheritance in software that interfaces with Relational Database Intersections, since such constructs are a significant part of the reality we need to model in our systems.

Recall that Aristotle distinguishes between Essential Attributes and Accidental Attributes while Carroll, given his particular interests, doesn't even consider the matter. As with the distinctions between Classes and Sets, application programmers tend to live in the Carolingian world and seldom recognize the differences. In object classes, a data member could be either type of attribute. In relational database design, however, while Accidental Attributes may appear variously as columns (but never keys), relationships to another table, or perhaps not be implemented at all, Essential Attributes must become Columns in a table – often serving as keys. These distinctions are important when analyzing Intersections.

Scope of this Chapter

While not eager to step into any religious discussions, nor to suggest that there aren't legitimate concerns for application programmers, avoiding multiple inheritance seems disturbingly myopic, particularly since this phenomenon clearly exists in the business world. As stated repeatedly, this book is not primarily a design manual, and because it is aimed at identifying common design flaws in **databases** (not **applications**), this chapter will be narrowly focused on interfacing the object classes required to support well designed relational Intersections.

The management of a company's data in a logical and organized fashion is, as described in the "Relative Importance of an I/T Department's Two Primary Functions" on page 6, more critical than many application programmers can accept. Relegating data integrity (whether through redundancy, arbitrary definitions or any other faults identified in this book) to a position where it becomes compromised for the "needs" of an application (or, worse, due to the arbitrary limitations of a programming language) does not serve the needs of our businesses well and, indeed, seems to me to represent some level of professional negligence. Building applications without compromising the integrity of the data structures, therefore, must always be a key design consideration.

Object Classes and Sets versus Relational Classes

Although originally conceived as targeting the same taxonomic classes defined by relational database theory (objects, remember, were intended to "Model the World in Data,"[262]) programmers quickly discovered that Object Classes were also useful for managing even loosely defined Sets in their applications. And of course, given that programming deals with the automation of Process rather than management of Data, it was inevitable that the programming world would adopt the more loosely defined Carolingian view of Classes.

While object class designs often result from programmer or application convenience, object classes that correspond to taxonomic data classes must never be permitted to conflict with reality[263] or they are just as likely to constipate a system as poor database designs do. They need to follow Aristotelian definitions, and Propositions derived from such Class diagrams must be logically True. We'll show examples of what this means after a discussion of some key reasons behind the OO community's ambivalence to dealing with multiple inheritance.

A Counterfeit Diamond of Death and its Triangular Sibling

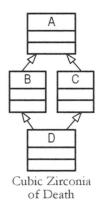

Cubic Zirconia of Death

The phenomenon known as the "Diamond of Death" and other pithy epithets is the basis for most objections to multiple inheritance in the OO world. A generic diamond-shaped[264] example commonly used to illustrate this is shown on the right.

Classes B and C both inherit from class A. Class D then inherits from both B and C. Potential ambiguities arise when there are identically-named data elements or methods in both B and C. The Base Table/View approach described earlier resolves data element ambiguities in the CREATE VIEW statement,[265] but ambiguities in object methods still need to be accounted for.

---

262 That is to Aristotelian or taxonomic Classes; see Schlaer [1] on page 384.

263 Repeat the mantra: "Data Classes (and therefore database structures) do not need to fully reflect reality, but *they must never conflict with reality.*"

264 Hence, of course, the name "Diamond."

The Cubic Zirconia of Death (as I've named it) is, of course, a less than useful example serving only to suggest how ambiguity **might** occur. Since we have no concept of what the "A," "B," "C," or "D" Classes[266] really are, it isn't possible to determine if the problem is contrived or realistic, so we'll ignore this layout.

A more useful example of potential multiple inheritance issues that does lend itself to meaningful analysis is the [Person→Employee→Teacher] layout.[267] This example illustrates multiple inheritance in the same manner as above, but with recognizable class names. Because it is subtly different in that it only shows three entities, I am calling it the "Triangle of Death" here.

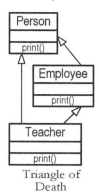

Triangle of Death

The potential ambiguity issues with this layout cannot be fairly or at least exclusively attributed to multiple inheritance, however, since the design is seriously flawed from a logical standpoint. We'll revisit this Triangle later (see page 245) to see how predicate logic can tell us something about the layout and how to correct it. First, however, we need to continue our review of Propositions and Predicates.

A Plethora of Propositions and Predicates

Beginning on page 80 of "Grammar: Simple Sentences and Propositions," we briefly introduced how Propositions are formed, and how they are normalized for use in Predicate Logic. Of particular interest in the discussions to follow are those Predicates formed from the verb "to be." Forms that this verb can

Presidential Precision with Predicates

"It depends upon what the meaning of the word 'is' is."

– William Jefferson Clinton, 42nd President of the United States, in his wide-ranging 17 August 1998 lecture on Predicate Logic to an awe-struck Federal Grand Jury.

take are "I am," "You are," "He is, She is, or It is," and their plural forms. Because "I," "You," "He" and "She" refer to Primary Substances, we will concentrate on only third-person Predicates in the form of "Something *is an X*."

---

265 Obviously, application architects or designers will participate in the design of such Views.

266 Remember, due to Carolingian views, these "Classes" might just as easily be simple Sets.

267 The Person-Employee-Teacher example appears in too many locations to easily attribute it to its original source. In any case, I suspect the author might wish to remain anonymous.

Clinton was correct. The meaning of the word "is" varies widely and, for this reason, it is important that we review the examples in the following table to ensure a level of comfort with the translations between user colloquialisms and more precise statements, as well as the Normal Forms of these Propositions.

The following table gives several examples of the meaning and interpretation of logical Propositions in the context of logical relational database design:

Propositions (True, False, or ???)	Commentary
T A Person is a Party. **(TRUE)**	The predicate is a Party[268] states the existence of a parent class structure and in order to be useful, must always be True. It can therefore also be understood as: T A Person is always a Party. T All Persons are Parties. T Any Person must be a Party. The sense of an "is a" Predicate in a Proposition is taxonomic – "Person," remember, is a Common Noun[269]; a Person not only **is a Party**, but has been a Party for the Person's entire existence and will always be a Party, even if the Person never inhaled.
F A Person may be a Party. **(FALSE)**	As a colloquial statement, this doesn't seem to be false but, logically, it is; this and the previous Proposition cannot both be True! Since we know the previous one is True, this one is False. The reason is that "may be" implies uncertainty. Recall that for a taxonomic Class, we must be able to state with certainty that a Thing (or subclass of Things) be categorically classified as either "being in" or "not being in" the Class.[270] While this Proposition is false, a "may be" predicate can be true in other circumstances. See the last Proposition in this table for an example.
T Mary is a Person. **(TRUE)**	"Mary" is a Proper Noun and a Primary Substance, one of many from whom the existence of a "Person" Class can be predicated.
T Mary is a Party. **(TRUE)**	This is True, and follows logically from the Propositions "Mary is a Person" and "A Person is a Party."

---

268 You'll recall that we inferred the existence of a Party Class in the first chapter with a top-down analysis, and confirmed its existence using a bottom-up analysis in "Deja Vu" (pg 61).

269 See "Grammar: Nouns" on page 69. I told you it would be important!

270 See the discussion of Common Nouns in "Grammar: Nouns" beginning on page 69.

Propositions (True, False, or ???)	Commentary
F Mary <u>is a Teacher</u>. **(FALSE)**	Although Mary may or may not *currently* be a Teacher, the statement is logically false because "Teacher" is a Collective Noun, and therefore cannot be a taxonomic Class to which Mary can belong. See "Grammar: Nouns" on page 69 for a definition of Collective Nouns. Further, based on her "Mary-ness" alone, we cannot state categorically that Mary is or is not a Teacher, and it is unlikely that Mary has always been a Teacher. Also note that "being employed as a Teacher" isn't logically the same as "being a Teacher." ("Being" here implying "essence") Mary "happens to be" a Teacher, but teacher-ness is not an inherent characteristic or attribute of Mary, event though it may be an attribute *value* of some other attribute, e.g. "Profession." In the world of Data, "Teacher" is a Set, not a Class. The implications of representing such Sets with OO "Classes" will be addressed further in "Classes versus Sets Redux" on page 253.
T An Employee <u>is a Person</u>. **(TRUE)**	This predicate is also stating the existence of a taxonomic class structure and in this case is always True. It can therefore also be understood as: **T** An Employee <u>is always a Person</u>. **T** All Employees <u>are Persons</u>. **T** An Employee <u>must be a Person</u>. "An Employee is a Person" is a more interesting Proposition than it seems because the subject (Employee) is a special (although not uncommon) case, and will be revisited in the next section, "Ambiguous Naming Revisited."
F A Teacher <u>is an Employee</u>. **(FALSE)**	While an Employee is always a Person, a Teacher may or may not be one of our Employees, and the statement is logically false simply because it may not always be true.
F Mary <u>is a Customer</u>. **(FALSE)**	Again, the Proposition seems true enough, but it is based on a single example (Mary). The Proposition is logically false both because Mary was not always (and may not always be) a Customer and because "Customer" is a Collective Noun, and therefore cannot be a taxonomic Class to which Mary can belong. Although Mary is a Person, she isn't inherently a Customer.

Propositions (True, False, or ???)	Commentary
T John <u>is a Customer-Person.</u> (**TRUE**, but ...)	Here the Proposition is true but, since it is based on a single example (John is a Primary Substance), merely allows us to predicate that a Class "Customer-Person" might exist.
Or, when further Normalized: T John <u>is a Customer.</u> [logical AND with] T John <u>is a Person.</u>	Care needs to be taken, however, to recognize that when the grammatical object of the Proposition is actually two objects, the Proposition needs to be further normalized (as shown). Propositions based on Primary Substances (e.g. John), whether true or not, cannot logically tell us anything about whether they are generally true of the predicated Class.
? A Customer <u>is a Person.</u> (**INCOMPLETE**)	While use of a Class rather than a Primary Substance as its subject makes this Proposition more useful for analysis, it is still logically incomplete because it may or may not be true in any given case. Although it can't be said to be false, we need more information to make a determination. It is equivalent to saying: **?** A Customer <u>may be a Person</u>. or <u>might be a Person</u>. ... and, based on the previous examples of Predicates in "What is a Customer? - Misguided Literature" on page 118: **?** A Customer <u>might be a Corporation</u>. Some obviously false Negative Predicates may help clarify the logic: **F** A Person <u>can never be a Customer.</u> **F** A Corporation <u>can never be a Customer.</u> Note that since these last two Propositions could only represent BUSINESS RULES rather than DATA RULES, neither Relational Database designs nor Object Class designs should rely on them as a basis for data structure definitions.

We'll begin utilizing Predicates in "Triaging the Triangle" below, but before doing that, we'll revisit the subject of Naming.

Ambiguous Naming Revisited

The proposition "An Employee is a Person" in the above table alluded to the idea that **Employee** is an interesting Class. The reason is that, in spite of the extensive[271] discussions about "Naming our Things" that began on page 73, the

---

271 And, admittedly, possibly tedious to some readers.

[Person→Employee→Teacher] hierarchy contains a subtle violation of that earlier chapter's caveats about naming.

While **Party** and **Person** are well-defined and appropriately named entity sets, the entity set called **Employee** can actually be considered somewhat ambiguously named, since it isn't typically predicated of "employees in general" or of "all employees," but only of your company's own employees.[272] Depending on your particular business, this ambiguity might never be noticed and may be of no consequence, but it further reinforces the importance of recognizing how common terms that "everyone understands" can lead to subtle difficulties,[273] and dealing with them appropriately.

As with many design issues, your own business circumstances need to be taken into account during analysis. A corporate health insurance company, for example, might record data on many corporate customers and those clients' respective employees. In such a situation, you would likely see an **Employee** table

Sherlockian Observation #2

Although Logic can help clarify an analysis, it doesn't necessarily provide a clear-cut solution.

Avoiding logical analysis, however, will more often than not impede the search for a solution and lead to other potential difficulties.

containing information about the Health Insurance Company's own employees, and a separate cross-reference table of their clients and their clients' employees. Naming both such tables "Employee" would obviously cause considerable confusion, since they are different entities with different attributes, etc.[274]

Recall from the Proposition "A Person is a Party" in the earlier examples that the predicate "is a Party" carries the implication that a Person has not only been a Party since it came into existence but will always be a Party. A subtlety of the Employee Class (and similar Classes) is that membership in the Employee Class might appear transient, disqualifying it from status as a taxonomic Class. Al-

---

272 Or perhaps more accurately, to employees of the company that owns the particular database being analyzed. This is true of most object classes named "Employee" as well.

273 Of course, if the Trailer table in "Playing with Trucks – Part 1" hadn't already convinced you of that, it may be time to find a less intellectually challenging profession.

274 Far-fetched as it may seem, there is an actual financial services company that, at least at one time, called the first table "Employee" and the second "Employees." Ugh.

though seemingly disingenuous, the reason Employee qualifies as a taxonomic Class is that "ex-employee" is simply another category of Employee. An Employee has been a Person since coming into existence and will always remain an Employee, albeit of the "ex" type.

Compare the following Propositions that use Mary as their subject:

Mary is a(n) ...

... Person *(a Taxonomic Class)*	Mary is a Person, and Mary will always be a Person. Mary is a member of the taxonomic Class Person.
... Employee *(a Taxonomic Class)*	This proposition states something that we can confirm as true. We can say categorically that "Mary is our employee" because (for one thing) we give her a paycheck. "Mary is an Employee" will always be categorically True or False.
... Teacher *(Simply a Set)*	This proposition states what is a matter of degree, an opinion, or an evaluation. The proposition as written can actually be interpreted in different ways. We can state that Mary is a Person fulfilling a temporary role as a Teacher, but we could never say Mary is a Party fulfilling a temporary role as a Person.
	Although Teacher certainly qualifies as a Set (or a Carolingian/OO Class), it can't be considered and should not be treated as a taxonomic Class when creating relational database tables.
... ex-Employee	This proposition also states something that we can confirm as a fact. We can say categorically that "Mary used to be our employee."
... ex-Teacher	This Proposition is vague: Does "Mary is an ex-Teacher" mean that Mary no longer has the skills to be a Teacher, or that Mary is no longer qualified as a Teacher, or that Mary is no longer serving in the Role of Teacher?"

So, in a strict interpretation of "taxonomic," **Employee** might not seem on the surface to qualify as a Class. Since any members of the Class will be permanently associated with that Class, however, it is, and must be treated as if it were, and database designs should reflect this.

There are, of course, other similar "gray-area" Classes such as **Patient, Prisoner,** and so forth, and we need to recognize those. A common characteristic of such pseudo-taxonomic Classes that we can look for may relate to legal (or simply bureaucratic) issues such as requirements for record retention or similar. Certainly in the United States, we provide year-end tax statements to those we employed during the year, regardless of their current status. Another characteristic is that the status change from "current" to "ex" isn't always permanent.

Because this sort of pseudo-taxonomic Class category presents some interesting database and application design issues that must be addressed in any Triage or subsequent cures, it seems useful to discuss some specific problems that can occur with them. Although that is a design issue, and thus somewhat off topic for this book, how this type of Class is handled is important, so it will be discussed at the end of this chapter in "Employees, Prisoners, and Patients" on page 254.

Triaging the Triangle

In order to bring it closer to the I/T Department, the Triangle of Death presented earlier in the chapter has been replaced with the logically identical but more relevant [Person→Employee→Programmer] hierarchy on the right. We begin our triage by formulating some Propositions from the UML diagram *without regard to whether the Propositions are true or false* (remember that we are basing the analysis on what the diagram **says**, not on what the designer might have intended). Once the list is complete, we can determine if each Proposition is logically true, false, or somewhere in between.

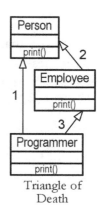

Triangle of Death

To aid with clarity, we'll assume that "John" is a Programmer[275] assigned to one of our Company's software development projects. The UML Class diagram above then suggests that:

---

275 See "Classes or Roles? – a Momentary Digression" on page 249 for a more logical model.

	Implied Propositions for Evaluation	Commentary
[A]	**T** John is a Programmer. **(GIVEN AS TRUE)**	This is our starting Proposition in the colloquial terms typically used.
[B]	- *A Programmer is a Person.* **(UNEVALUATED)**, therefore:	Proposition [B] is implied by the Programmer-to-Person inheritance line #1 in the figure.
[C]	- *John is a Person.*	Therefore, if we accept that John is a Programmer, he must also be a Person.
[D]	- *An Employee is a Person.*	Proposition [D] is implied by the Employee-to-Person inheritance line #2.
[E]	- *A Programmer is an Employee.* **(UNEVALUATED)**, therefore:	Proposition [E] is implied by the Programmer-to-Employee inheritance line #3.
[F]	- *John is an Employee.* - **(UNEVALUATED)**, and therefore:	If we accept [A] and [E] as being true, then we must accept that Proposition [F] is true.
[G]	- *John is a Person.* - **(UNEVALUATED)**	If we accept [D] and [F] as true, then we must also accept that Proposition [G] is true.

A cursory look at this chart reveals that Propositions [C] and [G] both indicate that John is a Person. A journalist might say that we have two sources for a story exposing John as a Person, so we might be forgiven for believing this redundancy to be a "Good Sign." In actuality, it isn't. It's just redundant. The implications of that will become clearer momentarily, but now, regardless of whatever Business Rules or traditions may be in place, and regardless of whatever processes we intend to automate, we need to add the following "real-world" Propositions to our analysis in order to "future-proof" our design:

	Propositions known to be True	Commentary
[M]	**T** A Programmer might not be an (our) Employee. **(TRUE)**, but we normalize it to:	Although this is a legitimate (and true) reflection on the Triangle model shown above, it states a negative, so we should normalize it to Proposition N.
[N]	**T** A Programmer may be an (our) Employee. **(TRUE)**	Since it is quite possible for us to utilize contract programmers that are not our own Employees, this statement is true. Note that, although a Business Rule may exist that says only our own Employees may work on our software, **Business Rules have no place in Data Definitions**. We must therefore acknowledge and

conform to this real-world Data Rule when defining our data structures, whether they are in our database or our key object classes.

Because we've established the truth of Proposition M, it therefore becomes obvious that Proposition E ("A Programmer is an Employee") is false. Propositions F and G therefore, being derived, don't merely become false – they simply cease to exist, because the basis on which they were proposed has disappeared.

But, we haven't yet completed our Triangle Triage. The figure on the right shows two Euler diagrams that could be inferred from this Triangle of Death.

To the right of each Euler diagram is a new UML diagram that would result from modeling its respective Euler diagram.

The top left Euler diagram is based on the original assumption that all the Propositions [A] through [G] are true.

Since, as we determined, Proposition [E] (a programmer is an employee) is false, the bottom left Euler diagram has been adjusted to reflect its removal.

Note that neither of the derived UML diagrams resembles the original Triangle. In Triage

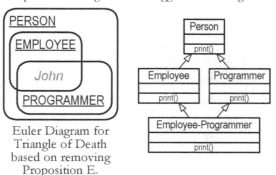

Implied Euler Diagram 1 ... Suggests UML Diagram 1

Euler Diagram for Triangle of Death based on Propositions A, B, C, D, E, F, & G

Implied Euler Diagram 2 ... Suggests UML Diagram 2

Euler Diagram for Triangle of Death based on removing Proposition E.

terms, this is known technically as a "Bad Sign," and is a clear indication that something doesn't make sense.

Design Objective 13 for Weights and Measures (see page 207) proposed that a system must not permit cumulative conversion errors when successively converting across multiple units of measure. Likewise, converting UML class diagrams to Euler diagrams and back should not result in changes either. When such alterations appear, this generally indicates some logical flaws in the design.

It was suggested earlier[276] that analysis of Entity Relationship Diagrams and UML Data Structure Diagrams can obscure a lot of logical flaws in taxonomic Classes, and that Euler diagrams such as those commonly used in this book are significantly more helpful in both design and Triage of data structures. As is evident from previous paragraphs, UML Class Diagrams can serve much the same purpose.[277]

Sherlockian Observation #3

UML Diagram #2 is logically correct, by the way. Sometimes the perceived difficulties of multiple inheritance are the result of implementing an Intersection without recognizing it. Some ambiguities attributed to multiple inheritance are actually the result of illogical designs. The fundamental logical flaws in any Object Classes meant to implement Taxonomic Classes should be addressed before drawing any conclusions about the supposed ill effects of multiple inheritance.

The whole sense of the original author's presentation of what I have titled the "Triangle of Death" was to illustrate how multiple inheritance leads to redundancy, but it is clear from the Euler diagrams that the redundancy is due to a logical flaw in the design itself. To be sure, it was presented in such a way as to frame multiple inheritance for the crime. Like medics performing Triage, however, you need to develop sufficient detective skills to convict the right party.

Business Rules and restrictions aside (which they must be when designing data structures), we can't logically state, as the "Triangle of Death" example implicitly does, that a Programmer or Teacher "is an Employee." The design statement is therefore flawed, and we shouldn't be drawing erroneous conclusions about any ill effects it might produce.

---

276 In "Grammar, Sets, and (Predicate) Logic – Part 1"

277 This shouldn't be a surprise given the similarities between Object and Relational approaches to data analysis and the shared theoretical foundations of each.

Classes or Roles? – a Momentary Digression

If Programmer (or Teacher, or any similar Set) doesn't qualify as a taxonomic Class, how then is it logically handled? Without going into great detail, the Euler diagram below will outline a fundamental and logically defensible approach.[278]

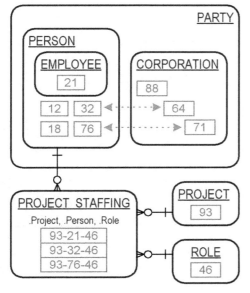

21: John Doe is an Employee (OUR Employee)
    ergo: John Doe is a Person
        ergo: John Doe is a Party
32: Mary Smith is a Person
    ergo: Mary Smith is a Party
    (but Mary Smith is not OUR Employee)
64: Mary Smith, Inc. (MSI) is a Corporation
    ergo: Mary Smith, Inc. is a Party
71: XYZ Consulting, Inc. is a Corporation
    ergo: XYZ Consulting, Inc. is a Party
76: Bill Jones is a Person
    ergo: Bill Jones is a Party
    (but Bill Jones is not OUR Employee)

93-21-46 John Doe (21), our company's employee, is working as a programmer on Project 93.

93-32-46 Mary Smith (32), MSI's only employee, is working as a programmer on Project 93.

93-76-46: Bill Jones (76), an employee of XYZ, is working as a programmer on Project 93.

46 - Role 46 is, of course, "Programmer."

Assume that **Party, Person, Corporation** and **Employee** classes are just as we've described them earlier. The **Project** class is simply a list of our company's projects, while **Role** is a listing of the roles any person might fill during their assignment to a project. The **Project Staffing** class is a three-way intersection, and each member contains data concerning one Person's assignment to one Project in one particular Role.

⊢◯< : This symbol, for those not familiar with Entity-Relationship diagrams, describes a relationship between the classes it connects. The short vertical line and the circle can be understood as "0" and "1" while the "crow's foot" suggests "many."

The text will describe how this is read for each of the three relationships shown.

---

278 It isn't considered traditional to intermingle Entity Relationship Diagram (or UML Data Diagram) symbols with Euler diagrams but, as I pointed out earlier, I'm retired, so I don't care. Sue me. The sidebar explains the meaning of the ERD symbol used here.

The three ⊥—O⊰ symbols on the Euler diagram are interpreted as follows:

The relationship between the **Person** and **Project Staffing** classes states that any Person (note that this connection is not to **Party** or **Employee**, since we've already established that not all programmers are necessarily employees) may potentially appear in multiple elements of the Project Staffing cross reference list, but any given Person might not appear at all in that list. If the symbol is read from **Person** to **Project Staffing**, it states that a Person may appear from zero to many times in the Project Staffing list; if read in the opposite direction (just as important) it states that each entry in the Project Staffing class may only refer to one Person and, in fact, must refer to at least one Person.[279]

When reading from the **Project** to **Project Staffing** classes, the relationship between the two specifies that any given Project might appear many times in the Project Staffing cross reference list, but any given Project might not appear at all in that list (e.g. if the project exists but has not yet been staffed). When reading from the **Project Staffing** to the **Project** class, our design states that each entry in the Project Staffing class may only refer to one Project and, in fact, must refer to at least one Project.

As should now be clear, the remaining relationship states that any Role may appear zero or many times in the Project Staffing cross reference list, but any given Role might not appear at all in that list. Additionally, it tells us that each Project Staffing entry must refer to one and only one Role.

Although our Company's projects are staffed with members of the Person class, they may or may not be (our) Employees. Nonetheless, they are someone's employees,[280] and a realistic design needs to account for this. The diagram is quite vague about how exactly Person #32 (Mary Smith) relates to Corporation #64 (Mary Smith, Inc.), and how Person #76 (Bill Jones) relates to Corporation #71

---

279 If it were optional (another common way to read the circle is as the letter "O"), there would be a circle at both ends of the relationship line.

280 Well, they may be volunteers, but that's a whole separate exercise for you to sleep on.

(XYZ Consulting, Inc.), since that would be unnecessarily distracting at this point.[281] Consider it an optional homework exercise.

With this useful and possibly even necessary digression out of the way, we can now return to the triage of potential multiple inheritance issues.

A Genuine Diamond of Death

The more realistic scenario to the right[282] shows how an amphibious vehicle might inherit data members and methods from both the Car and Boat classes, and how each of them in turn might inherit two copies of the same elements from Vehicle.

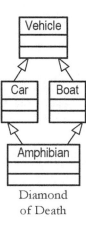

Diamond of Death

The author reasonably suggests that the Vehicle in his example[283] likely has several data members common to all vehicles, such as maximum speed, year of manufacture, and so forth. With a normal implementation, the Amphibian Class will end up with two copies of any data elements and two copies of any methods that were present in Vehicle. He also, correctly, points out that it may sometimes make sense for the inheriting class (Amphibian) to have both copies of the common elements, but sometimes it will result in ambiguity and potentially cause implementation difficulties.

As an example, the author notes that the subclasses Car and Boat would likely each have independent maximum speeds, since a single vehicle could have a different maximum speed capability[284] depending on whether it was operating on

---

281 Once again, although a fair amount of database design techniques have been presented, the primary purpose of this book is not to be a design tutorial.

282 Josuttis [1]; see page 383. This example was arbitrarily selected from many realistic ones that have been published simply because of its eerie similarity to the subject matter of "Playing with Trucks – Part 1," which will be revisited later.

283 Which, by the way, he has defined as an abstract Class, a concept that doesn't explicitly exist in the relational world. Whether this is important depends on your specific circumstances.

284 Although the author doesn't mention that each would have an independent unit of measure for maximum speed as well (perhaps miles-per-hour and knots respectively), likely just to keep his example simple. But if you've read this far, you already know that. Right?

land or in the water. It would therefore make sense for the Amphibian Class to inherit a `Maximum Speed` element from both parents, while it would make no sense to inherit more than one copy of `Year of Manufacture`.

Told You So

Perhaps, had the designers heeded Aristotle's advice, the "maximum speed" attributes of the Car and Boat classes might have been named more precisely (since they are really subtly different attributes), thus avoiding this dilemma. Although this observation, made in hindsight, is perhaps unfair, it does illustrate the validity of Aristotle's advice.

Determining which of the possible parent data element pairs are redundant (e.g. `Year of Manufacture`) and which should be interpreted individually (e.g. `Maximum Speed [on Land]` and `Maximum Speed [on Water]`) is made, as the author points out, quite problematic due to this ambiguity — especially when dealing with multiple inheritance in object-oriented software. For those data elements that we have determined are only to be inherited once, such as `Year of Manufacture`, selecting from which of the two parent classes it is to be inherited provides yet a further layer of difficulty.

As should be clear by now, a Diamond of Death is invariably associated with an Intersection of two or more[285] taxonomic Classes, and this particular author has provided us with a realistic example to analyze. Using a Euler diagram derived from the above example, we can begin by inferring the following Propositions:

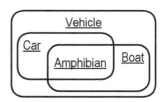

Propositions (True, False, or ???))	Commentary
T A Car is a Vehicle. **(TRUE)**	The Car class is a Proper Subset of the Vehicle class, and so long as there is at least one unique Essential Attribute in the set defining "Car," qualifies as a taxonomic class.
T A Boat is a Vehicle. **(TRUE)**	The Boat class is a Proper Subset of the Vehicle class, and so long as there is at least one unique Essential Attribute in the set defining "Boat," qualifies as a taxonomic class.

---

285 Yes, more! "In for a penny, in for a pound" as our British cousins say. Multiple Inheritance can provide much more entertainment than we have so far discussed.

Propositions (True, False, or ???))	Commentary
? An Amphibian <u>is a Car</u>. **(INCOMPLETE, ERGO NOT TRUE)**	This Proposition is incomplete. Although it isn't necessarily false in this case, it certainly isn't the "whole truth."
? An Amphibian <u>is a Boat</u>. **(INCOMPLETE, ERGO NOT TRUE)**	This Proposition is incomplete. Although it isn't necessarily false in this case, it certainly isn't the "whole truth."
T (An Amphibian <u>is a Boat</u> AND An Amphibian <u>is a Car</u>.)	Only when the previous two Propositions are combined with a logical AND can the pair together be considered true.
T An Amphibian <u>is a Vehicle</u>. **(TRUE)**	The diagram makes it clear that this is true, whether on its own, or through the Amphibian's membership in either the Boat or Car classes individually.

In taxonomic terms, the author's Amphibian Class must therefore be a logical Intersection. Following the scheme used in "Proper Subsets as Views" on page 132, we might have called this Intersection **Car_Boat** or **Boat_Car**.[286] The author chose the term Amphibian which, being an adjective, is less appropriate than the compound noun (and military term) "Amphibious Vehicle," and possibly somewhat confusing if sea-planes (a term that includes both float-planes and flying boats) are to be handled in the same system.

Nonetheless, the author has convincingly established that such an intersection is not only plausible, but quite realistic, rendering the pontifications of some authors that multiple inheritance should be avoided (or ignored or "worked around") quite disingenuous!

Classes versus Sets Redux

The idea that databases should be built to support a given business application is quite antithetical to the needs of a logical data architecture, since business requirements are, by nature, potentially transient and/or arbitrary. Data, being essentially fact-based, must be modeled to reflect this. As stated many times, it isn't necessary to completely model reality, but the data models must never be

---

286 Interestingly, these vehicles are called by such simple combination names in quite a few languages, as is the similar and even more common intersection "Boat-Plane."

permitted to conflict with reality. As we have seen, correctly modeling reality requires considerably more open-minded analysis of the business situations than the myopic concentration on specific applications that is usually the case.

For this reason, it is typically a serious mistake to use Object Modeling tools to generate database schemas. Automatic generation of data models from UML class diagrams is pretty much guaranteed to result in architecturally unsound and illogical database designs. This is because object modeling tools by their nature are not only process-centric, but centered around specific applications, and the resulting data elements simply reflect the myopic needs of the application.

Employees, Prisoners, and Patients

In the section titled "Ambiguous Naming Revisited" that begins on page 242, allusion was made to "gray-area" taxonomic Classes, exemplified by Employee, Prisoner and Patient. There is almost always a Hire Date, Admittance Date or similar essential attribute associated with this type of Class, and just as often some sort of Current Status code. There may or may not be, however, a Stop Date, Discharge Date or whatever. The primary key for an individual employee, patient, or prisoner could (and, ideally, should) be inherited from their Super-Class (e.g. Person in these examples). It might, however, be a completely separate Employee ID, Patient ID, Prisoner Number, or similar, since another characteristic of this type of Class is that the format of the primary identifier is defined by statute or convention or by the requirements of external systems not under the control of the business owner. A third-party payroll service, for example, might require a certain format for employee identifiers, a State legislature might dictate the formatting of prisoner numbers, and so forth.

In such instances, the primary key inherited from the superclass should be retained and used internally; where required for user interfaces or data sharing, the "dictated" identifier should be treated as an alternate key.[287]

---

287 Although true for most classes of the variety being discussed, it is particularly true for classes such as Patient; the formatting of such numbers is subject to change when specific hospitals or medical facilities are acquired by or consolidated with other similar facilities.

When a company rehires an Employee,[288] an Inmate returns for another term, or a Patient is readmitted to a hospital, there are two common approaches depending on the initial design choices made when the system was first created.

▶ Add an additional Start Date (start and stop dates should not be columns in an Employee table, but have a relationship to a (Party_ID, Start_Date, Stop_Date) row in another table. Why this is the case is hopefully obvious but, if not, review the earlier discussions of Normal Forms, particularly with regard to repeating elements and repeating groups.

▶ Have an Employee Identifier that is separate and distinct from the Party ID. On the surface, that would seem to make things easier but, as discussed briefly above, unless the Party ID is retained, any Party relationships that we might need, such as contact information and so forth will be lost. This second method, by the way, is what most Prisons do – on a return visit, each prisoner is given a new number.

Having elaborated on the usefulness of applying Predicate Logic to the Entities of interest to the business, the next chapter will explore how this technique can be applied to the Trux-M-Us Trailer table described earlier.

---

288 Remember once again that, even if there is currently a firm Business Rule stating that the company will never rehire an Employee, such a Business Rule should not be enforced by data structures, or subsequent changes to the rule will be extremely costly to implement.

LESSONS FOR CHAPTER 14
SETS, CLASSES, AND PREDICATES REVISITED

► One semantic disconnect between relational database designers and object-oriented programmers is that, while the distinctions between the terms Class and Set are (well, should be) critical to the former (the Aristotelian View), the terms are often used interchangeably by the latter when defining OO "classes" (the Carolingian View).

► We must keep in mind the relative importance of data categorization, organization, and integrity compared to the needs of our procedural efforts. Application code seldom needs to fully model the real world, but should never permit any models that conflict with the real world.

► In any realistic data model, the presence of Intersections is inevitable, and where there are Intersections, there will be multiple inheritance. Object-oriented software interacting with Intersections must therefore be capable of handling multiple inheritance cleanly and gracefully.

► We have seen examples, however, of how multiple inheritance can be (and typically is) misused.

► Just as poorly designed (and usually not-really-relational) "relational databases" have misled I/T practitioners for years, so can poorly designed object models mislead application programmers into specifying data structures that will constipate their systems as each inevitable change needs to be made.

Revisiting Trux-M-Us to see one approach to analyzing and reworking its Trailer table in a logical and extensible manner.

After analysis, the illustration on the left will no longer be seen as just a "Trailer," but as a five-way E:G:D:U:– intersection*, therefore leading to a much more flexible system.

* Shorthand for an Enclosed, Ground-based, Dimensional, Unpowered conveyance capacity having no Temperature control.

15

15 - PLAYING WITH TRUCKS – PART 2

Introduction

It is not the intent of this chapter to provide a "fix" for the partially illustrated database design in "Playing with Trucks – Part 1." Indeed, as mentioned at the end of that chapter, only one table (although, sadly, a representative one) from

TMU's system was presented, leaving too many unknowns to proceed. We can, however, use the detailed description of TMU's **Trailer** table to perform some level of database Triage in preparation for a redesign.

Recall that one fundamental flaw in the design of TMU's original **Trailer** table was that it was given too generic a name for its specific contents – a system-constipating error that isn't recognized often enough as a harbinger of difficulties to come. Consider how the business change progression described in "Playing

> **Naming: An Annoying Reminder**
>
> Again, as Aristotle has said "... the species is more truly substance than the genus ..." and continues to say that someone would "render a more instructive account by stating the species rather than the genus."
>
> Use of a more appropriate (i.e. specific) name than "Trailer" would have greatly improved TMU's ability to adapt to its desired business expansion, but there is no intention to suggest that this alone would have made much difference to the company's ultimate fate, as there were so many other inappropriate technical and business decisions that contributed.

with Trucks – Part 1" might have been handled with a more reasonable naming taxonomy – based on, for instance, the more appropriate term **Conveyance**.

With this new name for the universe of things TMU might use to carry freight, we can apply the Base Table/View technique (see "A Corporate Merger – Part 2") to model TMU's world, and see how its business fits into that world. This presents the minimal analysis and design activities needed to use that approach.

Conveyance

Conveyance will share some basic attributes of TMU's Trailer table, such as the Conveyance ID (primary key) and Carrier ID – coincidentally, the attributes marked as "applicable" under every conveyance type listed in "Applicability of Trailer Table Attributes to Actual Trailer Types" on page 165, and that form the PECULIAR ADJUNCT (so far)[289] for Conveyance. Although the four columns in that table (Closed Trailer, Flatbed, Reefer, and Tanker) aren't very useful (being derived from analysis of a flawed design), other taxonomies, each with unique attributes, suggest themselves as useful classes. A few are shown below:

Some Potential Subclasses of Conveyance

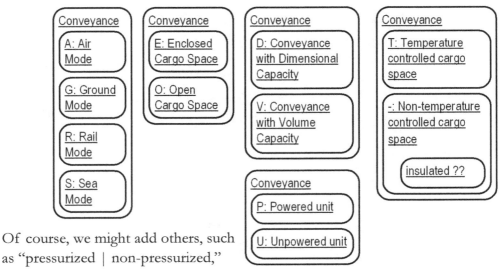

Of course, we might add others, such as "pressurized | non-pressurized," etc. and Volume Capacity could be subdivided into "Liquid | Dry" if needed.

---

289 See "Set Theory and Predicate Logic" on page 87 for a definition of Peculiar Adjunct.

Conveyance
A: Air Mode
G: Ground Mode
R: Rail Mode
S: Sea Mode

A primary example of a rather critical conveyance category is associated with one or more of what transportation folks refer to as Modes (shown to the left). Until interplanetary transportation becomes commercially feasible, assume that there are four of these modes – Ground, Air, Rail, and Sea – each with its own particular characteristics. Mode is a valid taxonomy of transportation conveyances that exists in the real world and, although it was never considered in the design we saw in "Playing with Trucks – Part 1," its potential usefulness should be obvious.

Conveyance
E: Enclosed Cargo Space
O: Open Cargo Space

The many differences between Open and Closed Conveyances discussed in "Playing with Trucks – Part 1" (e.g. bed length and width for open conveyances; inner as well as outer length, width, and height for enclosed ones) suggest that this is another valid taxonomy. Lacking a logically designed database, we saw how the company dealt with this fundamental but initially unrecognized difference (e.g. in its inconsistent handling of flatbed trailers), albeit in a rather poor and non extensible procedural manner. The Essential Attributes of Open and Enclosed cargo spaces are quite different – confirming the conclusion that they are independent and mutually exclusive subclasses of conveyance.

Conveyance
D: Conveyance with Dimensional Capacity
V: Conveyance with Volume Capacity

Yet another distinction can be made between the characteristics and attributes required for conveyances with dimensional capacity (i.e. those where the available capacity is measured in linear values such as feet, inches, meters, etc.) and those with capacity measured in volume (such as the tanker trucks TMU attempted to force-fit into their linear-centric model[290]).

Conveyance
P: Powered unit
U: Unpowered unit

Earlier in the book, we pointed out that no consideration had been given to the operational differences between powered and non-powered capacities. These are shown on the right as another valid taxonomy.

290 See the Trailer v4 table in the section "Chaos Reigns" beginning on page 163.

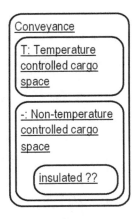

Conveyance

T: Temperature controlled cargo space

-: Non-temperature controlled cargo space

insulated ??

Among other possible groupings of subclass we might consider, the diagram on the left suggests that the requirements for temperature control might also be a valid breakdown of the general Conveyance class. A quick note might be made that even if there is no active temperature control in a particular conveyance, the knowledge of whether it is insulated may be an important attribute. **Whether these or any other taxonomies we conceive**[291] **make any sense is irrelevant at this point!**

We can now consider how the use of database intersections (as well as the inevitable appearance of multiple inheritance in applications that access this database) can be applied to mitigate the chaos of the Trux-M-Us database design:

Simple Two-Way Intersection

Conveyance	E: Enclosed cargo space	O: Open cargo space
A: Air Conveyance	E:A	O:A
G: Ground Conveyance	E:G	O:G
R: Rail Conveyance	E:R	O:R
S: Sea Conveyance	E:S	O:S

Looking at only the first two possible taxonomies considered, it is clear that there are eight possible two-way intersections. The intersection identified as E:G, of course, is the original concept of **Trailer** that TMU began with.

What is also obvious, though, is that if we consider each of the eight intersections in turn, we can probably ignore O:A and more than likely ignore O:S as well. It seems unlikely that we will need to model any open (unenclosed) space on an Aircraft or Ship!

---

291 Such as "Pressure" mentioned earlier, or Intermodal transportation, not considered here.

It would be inappropriate and extremely unwise to eliminate them at this point, however, since even if we don't ever foresee a circumstance where they might be implemented, any analysis or design we come up with should not preclude the possibility. Leaving the Matrix as is without implementing all its intersections costs us nothing, and will enable us to explore and evaluate the practicality of future alternatives much more readily.

Adding the third of our original taxonomies (Dimensional capacity versus Volume capacity) to the Euler diagram gives us something like this:

A More Complex Three-Way Intersection

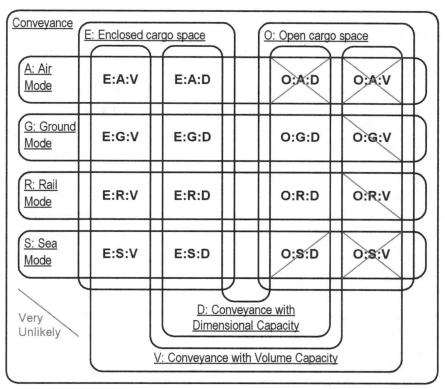

In this diagram we now have sixteen possible three-way intersections (the product of 4 for "mode," 2 for "enclosed vs open," and 2 for "dimensional vs volume"). Since we had originally crossed off O:A and O:S as unlikely, we continue in this diagram by crossing out O:A:D and O:A:V as well as O:S:D and O:S:V. Further, since all the Open space with (liquid) Volume capacity are highly improbable, those will be also be crossed out.[292] As before, however, we need to retain them in the diagram to ensure that we are building a complete picture of the world we are modeling. The original TMU concept of "Trailer" would, of course, be represented by the E:G:D intersection, while TMU's Flatbed Trailer would be located in the O:G:D intersection.

Complex intersections such as **Conveyance_Enclosed_Ground_Dimensional** (or whatever name your conventions dictate), although multidimensional, are no different in principle from the two-dimensional intersections **Customer_Person** and **Customer_Organization** presented in "Intersections as Views" (see page 134) and can be handled in a similar manner. Although the SQL `Create View` statements might be slightly more complex, the E:G:D intersection would have: All the attributes of an Enclosed Conveyance (and none of the attributes that are specific to an Open Conveyance); All the attributes of a Ground Conveyance (and none of the attributes that are specific to Air, Rail, or Sea Conveyances); All the attributes of a Conveyance with Dimensional Capacity (and none of the attributes that are specific to a Conveyance with Volume Capacity). And so forth!

As is the case with any Base Table-View constructs, queries and updates are quite straightforward; like such constructs, addition and deletion of new Conveyances would need to be defined by business rules and thus would be accomplished with procedural code that can be altered as operational needs dictate.

Although this may initially seem like an unusual way of viewing things, its benefits are that it can be implemented in a reasonably straight-forward manner using a valid relational database design. More importantly, only one of the intersections needs to be implemented for software development to proceed. If the software is also written to follow the model, future expansion into other types and modes of transportation would become driven largely by population of ad-

---

292 Two of those – O:A:V and O:S:V – have of course already been crossed out. To get an idea of what an O:S:V capacity would look like in the real world, picture an open-air swimming pool on a cruise ship. Although this is obviously feasible, evaporation would quickly render it unsuitable for transporting water, to say nothing of more volatile liquids!

ditional data elements. Additional software would need to be written for each new intersection supported but, if the original analysis and design is done carefully, very little of the existing software would need to be rewritten. The resulting improvements in business flexibility are compelling arguments for formal, logical database design; to see why this is so, simply assume that Trux-M-Us had begun its operations with the E:G:D intersection instead of its silly Trailer table, and then walk through the life cycle described in "Playing with Trucks – Part 1" considering how each new conveyance type would have been added.

The most important conclusion we can draw from the latest Euler diagram, however, and one that I've conveniently ignored until now, is that a three-way intersection probably represents the practical usable limit of this sort of diagram for analysis of intersections. While the Euler diagram of our first three potential subclasses outlined sixteen possible intersections, we would have sixty-four possible intersections once we included the five subclasses proposed on page 258 – a number that would likely render the diagram incomprehensible. Fortunately, a relatively straightforward grid can serve just as well.

An Alternate Approach – Tabular Analysis

A listing of the sixty-four possible intersections resulting from the various subclasses suggested for analysis of the "Conveyance" Thing serves much the same purpose as the Euler diagram while also providing a convenient location for recording other information relevant to each intersection. Such a listing (with each intersection numbered) would look something like this:

Enclosed; **Open** (E:O) 	Air; Ground; Rail; **Sea** (Mode) (A:G:R:S) 		Dimensional capacity; **Volume capacity** (D:V) 			**Non-powered**; Powered (N:P) 				Temperature-controlled or **not**: (T:-)	**Conveyance**: Possible Intersections Sample Attributes
^{01}E : A : D : N : T: e.g. a temperature-controlled container on an aircraft.	Min & Max Temp
^{02}E : A : D : N : -: e.g. a standard cargo container	
^{03}E : A : D : P : T: e.g. cargo in a temperature-controlled aircraft hold	Min & Max Temp
^{04}E : A : D : P : -: e.g. cargo in a standard aircraft hold	
^{05}E : A : V : N : T: e.g. temperature-controlled tank/vessel in aircraft hold	Min & Max Temp

Enclosed; **Open** (E:O) | **Air**; **Ground**; **Rail**; **Sea** (Mode) (A:G:R:S) | | **Dimensional capacity**; **Volume capacity** (D:V) | | | **Non-powered**; **Powered** (N:P) | | | | **Temperature-controlled or not**: (T:-)	**Conveyance:** Possible Intersections Sample Attributes

	Sample Attributes
[06] E : A : V : N : - : e.g. standard tank/vessel in aircraft hold	
[07] E : A : V : P : T : e.g. temperature-controlled tanker aircraft	Min & Max Temp
[08] E : A : V : P : - : e.g. standard tanker aircraft; usually only refueling or firefight- (can be ignored) ing aircraft and not used for transportation.	
[09] E : G : D : N : T : e.g. temperature-controlled semi-trailer (aka "Reefer")	Min & Max Temp
[10] E : G : D : N : - : e.g. TMU's original concept of "Trailer"	
[11] E : G : D : P : T : e.g. enclosed refrigerated ground powered delivery truck.	Min & Max Temp
[12] E : G : D : P : - : e.g. enclosed powered delivery truck.	
[13] E : G : V : N : T : e.g. temperature-controlled ground-based tanker trailer	Min & Max Temp
[14] E : G : V : N : - : e.g. ground tanker trailer with no temperature control	
[15] E : G : V : P : T : e.g. temperature-controlled powered tanker truck	Min & Max Temp
[16] E : G : V : P : - : e.g. powered tanker truck with no temperature control	
[17] E : R : D : N : T : e.g. temperature-controlled enclosed rail car	Min & Max Temp
[18] E : R : D : N : - : e.g. enclosed rail car with no temperature control	

- : R : - : P :   Rail-based capacities are not typically self-powered, so six
(6 possibilities)   intersections are not considered, including:
    [19] E : R : D : P : T;   [20] E : R : D : P : -;   [23] E : R : V : P : T;   [24] E : R : V : P : -
    [52] O : R : D : P : -; [56] O : R : V : P : -	

[21] E : R : V : N : T : e.g. temperature-controlled rail tanker car	Min & Max Temp
[22] E : R : V : N : - : e.g. rail tanker car with no temperature control	
[25] E : S : D : N : T : e.g. a temperature-controlled towed barge [293]	Min & Max Temp
[26] E : S : D : N : - : e.g. an enclosed unpowered (towed) barge	
[27] E : S : D : P : T : e.g. a temperature-controlled ship's hold	Min & Max Temp
[28] E : S : D : P : - : e.g. a typical ship's hold with no temperature control	
[29] E : S : V : N : T : e.g. temperature-controlled unpowered tanker barge	Min & Max Temp

---

293 The meaning and implications of "powered" and "non-powered" may be different for ships than for what we see with ground-based tractor-trailers (e.g. consider towed barges).

Enclosed; Open	(E:O)	Conveyance: Possible Intersections
Air; Ground; Rail; Sea (Mode)	(A:G:R:S)	
Dimensional capacity; Volume capacity	(D:V)	
Non-powered; Powered	(N:P)	
Temperature-controlled or not:	(T:-)	Sample Attributes

		Sample Attributes
[30] E : S : V : N : - :	e.g. unpowered tanker barge with no temperature control	
[31] E : S : V : P : T :	e.g. temperature-controlled volume based ship cargo hold	Min & Max Temp
[32] E : S : V : P : - :	e.g. volume based ship cargo hold; no temperature control	
O : A : ? : ? : ? : (8 possibilities)	Having open cargo space on an Aircraft makes no sense, so eight intersections are not considered, including: [33] O : A : D : N : T; [34] O : A : D : N : -; [35] O : A : D : P : T; [36] O : A : D : P : -; [37] O : A : V : N : T; [38] O : A : V : N : -; [39] O : A : V : P : T; [40] O : A : V : P : -	
O : ? : ? : ? : T (12 possibilities)	An open conveyance can't be temperature controlled, so sixteen intersections are not considered, including: [41] O : G : D : N : T; [43] O : G : D : P : T; [45] O : G : V : N : T; [47] O : G : V : P : T; [49] O : R : D : N : T; [51] O : R : D : P : T; [53] O : R : V : N : T; [55] O : R : V : P : T; [57] O : S : D : N : T; [59] O : S : D : P : T; [61] O : S : V : N : T; [63] O : S : V : P : T Furthermore, $(O : G : V : N : -)$, $(O : G : V : P : -)$, $(O : R : V : N : -)$, $(O : R : V : P : -)$, $(O : S : V : N : -)$, and $(O : S : V : P : -)$ would have been ignored anyway, since open conveyances aren't usually suitable for volume-based freight.	
[42] O : G : D : N : - :	e.g. a standard flatbed semi-trailer	
[44] O : G : D : P : - :	e.g. a powered flatbed truck	
O : ? : V : ? : ? : (4 possibilities)	Open conveyances can typically only handle volume-based freight if it is dry freight such as grain or coal[294], so four intersections are not considered, including: [46] O : G : V : N : - [48] O : G : V : P : - [62] O : S : V : N : - [64] O : S : V : P : - Should any open volume-based class be required, this may imply the need for an additional "liquid | dry" subclass.	
[50] O : R : D : N : - :	Open rail dimensional non-powered no temp control	
[54] O : R : V : N : - :	Open rail volume non-powered no temp control	
[58] O : S : D : N : - :	Open sea dimensional non-powered no temp control	
[60] O : S : D : P : - :	Open sea dimensional powered no temp control	

---

294 Remember to distinguish this from a "container" that can be independently loaded onto a ground trailer or water-borne conveyance or a conventional semitrailer that can be attached (and moved) by or loaded onto a Rail car or (another) flat-bed Trailer.

Compositions and Intersections

Remember to ensure that what you believe to be an Intersection is not actually a Composition …

Further, when reviewing each intersection that has been selected for implementation, it is important to determine as early as possible if the Intersection might have any attributes of its own.

Since an Intersection doesn't by nature possess any Essential Attributes (these being inherited from the parent classes), any attributes it does possess will be Accidental, and usually in the form of a relationship.

We've already selected which possible intersections would not be of interest to our business (and would therefore not be implemented unless business conditions changed significantly). What remains is to analyze the remaining intersections, determine what others might be ignored, which intersections would be the most useful to implement, and to set some prioritization for development.

The only sample attributes shown in the table above are **Minimum_Temperature** and **Maximum_Temperature**, which appear in fourteen of the rows. Using the techniques in earlier chapters, it quickly becomes clear that these are common to the "Temperature-Controlled" class, and should eventually become attributes of whatever base table is based on that class. Even without delving further into the analysis process for intersections, it should be reasonably clear how identification and development of database tables and views would proceed.

Constructing a table similar to the preceding can provide a very useful analysis tool for Triage of both existing systems and new designs. If used as a bulletin board of sorts, sufficient data can be collected not only to ensure logical data design but optimal software modularity and so forth. We can build base tables and views with confidence from this sort of matrix, and we can ensure accurate placement of attributes (at the highest possible level in the class hierarchy).

Taxonomies and Intersections

Many, if not most, database designers and application developers tend to balk at the consideration – much less the application – of taxonomies or even sets to their data structures, particularly to those structures considered trivial in the context of their local or immediate needs or responsibilities – believing that:

a) consideration of taxonomies and sets is too complex for the situation,

b) identifying taxonomies doesn't justify the analysis effort required,

c) available database modeling and development tools do not readily or directly support (or even recognize) class taxonomies, and

d) there is insufficient time allocated to design and development to consider taxonomies, and

e) because of the dysfunctional and short-term thinking in many businesses, there is no reward, and quite often a penalty, for taking the time to build structures that will withstand a change in business needs and make future modifications simpler, less expensive and less risky.

The following table considers each of these objections very briefly.

Objection	Response
a) Taxonomies and sets appear too complicated for the current situation or application.	There is a clear difference between the words "complex" and "complicated." Complex implies the presence of an order, whether immediately visible (easily grasped) or not. We usually end up *complicating* things when we *don't* understand such complexities – and if we don't understand them (or even realize that they exist), it is not likely that either the database or application designs will reflect reality sufficiently to allow for future straightforward expansion, reuse, integration, etc. Of course, one needs to take care not to go overboard with possible taxonomies. Even the world famous botanist Matthias de L'Obel, in his milestone publication "Stirpium adversaria nova" (published around 1570 during the reign of Queen Elizabeth I of England) presented one (ultimately embarrassing) taxonomy for classification of plants according to the characteristics of their leaves. The number of leaf segments of course turned out to have no general biological significance.
b) Taxonomies and sets are not worth the effort required to uncover and implement them.	Although this is a common objection, we need to recognize that what we are really implying here is that "the *benefits of* considering taxonomies and sets are not worth the effort," which certainly isn't true. Designing logically may (but doesn't always) take slightly more time, thus giving the impression that the same system (data structures and application code) was delivered at a higher initial cost. To fulfill our responsibilities to the corporations we serve, however, we must consider the time and effort required to maintain the system as well as the time and effort to develop it. Studies over many years have consistently shown that maintenance and upgrade costs for the I/T systems we produce far exceed those for development. Of course, the continuous pressure to deliver as quickly as possible by cutting corners will always be

Objection	Response
	with us unless and until we begin delivering extensible systems, and we need to recognize that this will be a difficult task.
	Many developers selfishly admit to being far more interested in new development than in the maintenance and upgrade of existing systems, yet the fact that the majority of I/T work seems to be in software maintenance is, ironically, mostly our own fault because of our myopic and illogical database analysis and design practices.
c) Available database modeling and development tools do not readily or directly support taxonomies or sets.	This is certainly true to some extent, and is mostly due to the failure of RDBMS and modeling tool vendors to continue the work they started. OO tools certainly support these concepts better than RDBMS tools do, but are completely under the sway of common misconceptions about the preeminence of application design over database design, if such comparisons are even considered at all.
d) There is insufficient design and development time to consider use of taxonomies or sets.	The response to this is very similar to that for "taxonomies are not worth the effort" above.
e) Short term performance is more rewarding to developers.	This is, unfortunately, true more often than not. But, ironically, short term performance with existing systems (e.g. in response to change requests, business expansion, etc.) will never improve much from what it is now without addressing fundamental design issues.
	Although business management might be persuaded of the merits of analyzing more than the very limited world of current business requirements, the belief that the result will, in most cases, lead to "analysis paralysis" has been inculcated in them over the seventy year history of system development.

Conclusion

An easily overlooked lesson from the Trux-M-Us example is that, while converting from a non-RDBMS platform to a relational platform offers a number of advantages (though primarily to developers), it can be and often is a complete waste of money from a business standpoint since there is far less than optimal return on investment unless the conversion is accompanied by a redesign of the data structures to take advantage of the relational model. For Trux-M-Us, sadly, the monetary investment in Oracle licenses, as well as the ongoing consulting and maintenance fees, was completely squandered.

► The importance of carefully naming our Things can't be emphasized enough, and will have a significant impact on the quality of the taxonomies we construct and, therefore, our data structure and class designs.

► Failure to carefully consider the place (i.e. its position in any hierarchy) of each Thing identified in any triage or analysis we perform will increase the possibilities of system constipation and unnecessary maintenance expenses should later changes be contemplated by the business.

▼ A Thing with a very general name should likely be considered as a high level class; further investigation is usually needed to determine what subclasses (particularly those with differing Attributes, and especially those with differing Essential Attributes) might exist.

▼ Any very precisely named Thing should be carefully examined to determine if it is, in fact, a subclass of a more general class.

► Converting to a relational platform without converting to relational database designs can be wasteful from a business standpoint because there is far less than optimal return on investment.

This chapter will describe a fully normalized and extensible system for supporting the correct handling of weights and measures in business databases. The chapter following this will describe how migration from traditional structures would be handled in an iterative fashion, and discuss the business benefits that might be gained by doing so.

16 - WEIGHTS & MEASURES – PART 3

Desired End-State Implementation

Starting Point – Existing Database Structures

Assume that the tables shown to the right are typical of the way that weights and measures are handled in an operational corporate database. The company is planning ahead, and wishes to offer its line of Things in a number of different countries, to sell its Widgets in consumer as well as industrial sizes, and to supply its Gadgets to a new overseas market segment with unique measurement standards.

Each of these objectives implies the need for generalization, and specifically the ability to support a variety of measurement units. Columns that will be affected by the company's generalization of weights and measures are highlighted on these simplified entity-relationship diagrams. In the Widget table design, for instance, there is obviously a system assumption as to the units of measure represented by the Length and Width values, and therefore these assump-

THING	
ID	pk
Height	not null
Width	not null
Other Attributes ...	

WIDGET	
ID	pk
Length	not null
Weight	not null
Color	fk, not null

GADGET	
ID	pk
Volume	not null
Temperature	not null
Other Attributes ...	

tions need to be separated and made explicit in order to remove the business and application restrictions these assumptions represent.

Using the Widget table as an example, a complete generalization using all possible additional elements discussed in "Expressing Measurement Information as Data" (page 215) would look like the diagram below. Also illustrated is a minimal set of supporting domain tables. The additional data elements in the Widget table are shown indented and colored for clarity.

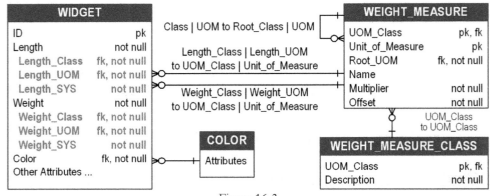

Figure 16-3

The additional **Length_Class** and **Length_UOM** columns are straightforward additions based on previous discussions.

Length_SYS represents the standardized internal or system value of the value contained in **Length**. The unit-of-measure for the system value is implied by (and can be queried from[295]) the **Weight_Measure** domain table.

A domain table for the Accidental Attribute **Color** is assumed, but not shown in any detail.

For each of the measurement values (**Length** and **Weight**) in our **Widget** table, the **Class** and **Unit-of-measure** are constrained as a pair to the **UOM_Class** and **Unit-of-Measure** columns in the **Weight_Measure** table. For the **Widget** table, that implies two foreign key relationships to the **Weight_Measure** table: one for the **Length** attribute and one for the **Weight**.

---

295 e.g. Select … where uom_class = whatever and unit_of_measure = root_uom

The purpose of the shared system **Weight_Measure** table is to store the multiplication factors and offsets required to convert from the system standard unit-of-measure (what we are calling the "root unit-of-measure") to other units of measure that are valid for a specific measurement class. Because of the asymmetric nature of the mathematics used in this scheme, it does not, and *must not* store a multiplication factor and offset required to convert from other units of measure back to the system standard unit.

Constraints on the **Weight_Measure** table ensure that, for any Class, there can only be one row with a Multiplier of 1 and an Offset of 0. This row defines the system reference unit of measure for that particular measurement Class. There should never be an instance where, if there is a Celsius to Fahrenheit conversion factor row, there is a Fahrenheit to Celsius row.

Therefore, the following query must return 0 for any insert to be valid:

```
SELECT Count(*)
  FROM Weight_Measure
 WHERE Unit_Of_Measure      = new:Root_Uom
   AND Root_Unit_Of_Measure = new:UOM
```

The following query must return 0 if new:Multiplier = 1 and new:Offset = 0:

```
SELECT Count(*)
  FROM Weight_Measure
 WHERE UOM_Class  = new:Class
   AND Multiplier = 1
   AND Offset     = 0
```

Since the method for accomplishing this varies from one RDBMS product to another, the use of these constraints on Insert and Updates may or may not be somewhat expensive. Since the table, once created and populated initially, is virtually static, however, this doesn't typically prove to be a drawback. This Entity Relationship diagram is discussed further in "Relational Constraints for UOM and Adding Standardized Values" on page 290.

Obviously, the **Weight_Measure** table should be protected from normal inserts and updates, and have most normal access restricted to a very few individuals who are fully aware of the implications of any changes.

Sample Data

To provide a better idea of what data looks like in a scheme such as that described above, the table below illustrates these structures with some representative sample data elements.

Again, a Color domain table is implied, but not shown.

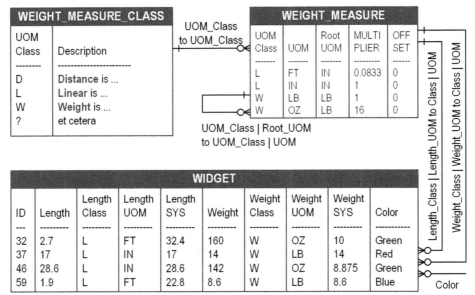

Figure 16-3

Use of Tables

The Weight_Measure table which, in a generalized design, should be common to (and used by) all other system tables that contain measures, is directly analogous to the abbreviated table given earlier in "Sample Conversion Calculations"[296] on page 227 and establishes the domain for units of measure that will be considered valid within the enterprise (or at least system.) The Class is constrained by the Weight_Measure_Class domain table. UOM_Class and UOM form the primary key for the Weight_Measure table. The UOM_Class and Root_UOM are constrained

---

296 A more complete table, as well as a model Oracle script to create and populate an actual database table, is given on page 403.

to already existing **UOM_Class** and **UOM** pairs (the system standard units of measure for each Class), which ensures that the data in the table remains internally consistent.

Other constraints on the **Weight_Measure** table ensure that, for any **Class**, there can be only one row with a **Multiplier** of 1 and an **Offset** of 0. This row defines the system reference unit-of-measure for each Measurement Class. A valid corollary to this is that not only may there only be one row for each measurement class where the **UOM** and the **Root_UOM** are the same, but that there *must* be such a row for each measurement class.[297]

Because of the non-symmetrical nature of this design approach,[298] another constraint should ensure that there will never be an instance where the contents of a **UOM** and **Root_UOM** pair are repeated as a **Root_UOM** and **UOM** pair. For example, if there is a "degrees Celsius" to "degrees Fahrenheit" conversion factor row for the Temperature Class, there must never be a "degrees Fahrenheit" to "degrees Celsius" row for that Class. One method for accomplishing this is left for the next chapter, which discusses implementation issues.

On entry or update of any data in the table, the standardized internal values in **Length_Sys** and **Weight_Sys** in the Widget table will be automatically calculated by a trigger using the conversion techniques described in "Sample Conversion Calculations" on page 227.[299] These internal values (**Length_Sys** and **Weight_Sys**) should generally be accessible to all queries, but direct updates to these columns should never be permitted. The Measurement Classes for the *_SYS values (the internal, standardized values) are, by definition, the same as for the respective input values, and the internal Units of Measure are implied by whichever corre-

---

297 Depending on the method of implementation, this may be useful in setting constraints and validating data.

298 The reasons for this approach, required to fulfill Design Objective 13 (see page 207) are described under "Multiplier" on page 226.

299 Conversion to system-standard values used for aggregations is best done during entry of the data — a much better — and less noticeable to a user — distribution of work than attempting bulk conversions during an aggregation or, worse, during an overnight update process.

sponding row for that Class in the **Weight_Measure** table contains the values 1 and 0 for the **Multiplier** and **Offset** respectively.

Stored Procedures

Conversion functions similar to those described beginning on page 228 must be available for use within the database during inserts and updates. A sample implementation of a conversion function (WM_Sys_Val) for the trigger described above is given on page 398. A sample general purpose stored procedure to perform unit-of-measure conversions (WM_Uom_Convert) is given on page 396; depending on the capabilities of the particular RDBMS in use, a routine like this may be designed to be called from external applications or even downloaded at application start-up[300] as described in "Sharing Process Based Constraints – A Better Approach" on page 194.

Applications and Reports

A generalized application based on such a normalized model would permit a user (or data loader utility) to supply a given widget's length and weight in any convenient and valid unit-of-measure. The application might accept the 2.7 ft and 160 oz values in the first row, for example, and an insert trigger and stored procedure would automatically convert these to populate the internal (SYS) values of 32.4 in and 10 lbs.

Summaries and aggregations would be done by using the standardized data in the **Length_Sys** and **Weight_Sys** columns rather than the raw original data in the **Length** and **Weight** columns. Totals can then, of course, be converted into any arbitrary Unit of Measure desired.

Obviously, the sections above only cover a small portion of what ultimately needs to be considered in making changes of this magnitude, but this explanation should suffice to continue with a discussion of how a migration to such a system can be approached. First, though, there is a little more homework.

---

300 This would require, of course, a different language than PL/SQL, such as a flavor of Java that can be run in both the database and application environments.

Homework Assignment

Be sure you can answer the following questions based on the sample data in the Widget table on page 274.

1. What is the internal system standard unit-of-measure for the linear class?

2. What is the internal system standard unit-of-measure for the weight class?

3. What is the simplest SQL WHERE clause that can be used to determine the internal system standard unit-of-measure for the weight class of measures? Are there other ways to determine this?

4. What column is used to query and calculate the total weight of all four widgets in the sample table?

5. Which Widget is the longest: ID 32 (length is given as 2.7) or ID 46 (length is given as 28.6)?

6. Which Widget is the heaviest: ID 37 (weight given as 14) or ID 46 (weight given as 142)?

Sample DDL

Sample Oracle DDL scripts to build and experiment with the Widget examples in this chapter are given in "WM_Widget Demonstration Table" on page 401.

Trivia

LB is actually a Roman Empire era abbreviation for the Latin word "Libra," a device that we today refer to as a balance scale[301]; this might be related to the ancient Greek word "λίβρα." The Latin word "Pondus" was the origin of our word "Pound," and "Libra" was eventually used as a shorthand for "Libra Pondo,"[302] a standard measure of weight that actually predated the Roman empire. Thus, it is evident that inconsistent handling of terminology related to weights and measures is apparently not a new phenomenon.

---

301 Hence the use of the balance scale as a symbol for the astrological sign of Libra.

302 Literally, a Pondus as measured on a balance scale.

"I always give myself such very good advice, but I very seldom follow it." Alice (a confused early database analyst)
- Lewis Carroll

This chapter provides a "real world" description of how migration from traditional measurement value structures can be implemented in an iterative fashion, and discuss the benefits that might be gained by doing so.

17

17 - WEIGHTS & MEASURES – PART 4

Implementation: Conversion Strategy and Progression

Weights & Measures Parts 1-3 discussed how data for various measurement values needs to be organized in order to provide extensible and reliable data structures and promote reuse of code and data related to weights and measures. For each element, we need to know both a value and a unit-of-measurement. In most cases, we need to maintain an "original" data value and unit-of-measure as well as a standardized measurement value that can be easily correlated with other values in our existing system. In many cases, we will also need to know the class into which a unit-of-measurement falls. Since, in most organizations, it is unlikely that an opportunity for a "big-bang" conversion will present itself, this section will discuss moving these ideas incrementally from theory to practice.

The first, and most obvious, concern is whether we actually need to go as far with generalization as the desired end state proposed in the previous section. Among other things, this technique adds significantly to the number of columns in the database, and those paying very close attention will also have noticed that the various Class values for any given column will all contain the same value, which might appear to the inexperienced as redundant.[303] There are probably concerns that this approach may introduce new system limitations or additional maintenance complexities, although these concerns are unwarranted.

The enhancements proposed in this document do constitute a change in system architecture, and specifically a change in data architecture. Because for many enterprises this represents a fundamental shift both in practice and in design philosophy, we will parallel the normal architectural migration planning methodology in this section. This classic Architectural approach consists of:

▶ identifying and presenting the initial state;

▶ outlining the stages required to reach the desired state (as summarized beginning in "The Migration Process" beginning on page 292);

▶ determining whether some intermediate level of the desired state will offer some business advantage.

These steps can be accomplished in an orderly manner, with minimal risk and disruption to system operations. At each step, we will also discuss the reasons for each design decision.

Levels of Generalization

So far, we have discussed only two levels of generalization: none and fully generalized, but in the process of explaining each intermediate state between these levels, we will encounter stages that might seem acceptable for some enterprises. The series of design iterations presented here will also mention commonly encountered, but misguided, attempts to solve some of the issues discussed, particularly one state in which a possibly well-intentioned design improvement seems intended to thwart any efforts at generalization. These poor approaches have been covered only so that they can be recognized and avoided.

---

303 The reason it's not is, of course, that Class is only a portion of a multi-part key.

Typical Starting Condition

The single non-generalized database table to the right (one of the examples presented earlier) is typical of the way weights and measures are handled in many corporate databases, and will serve as the basis for a hypothetical design upgrade path. As discussed earlier, the **Length** and **Weight** columns in this table are examples of the types of measurements that fall into the scope of this discussion. The company employees or application(s) using this table currently assume that Length is always given in feet, and Weight is always expressed in ounces.[304]

WIDGET	
ID	pk
Length	not null
Weight	not null
Color	fk, not null

Earlier, we mentioned some difficulties that can result from this type of design. The table below will summarize the characteristics of this design and outline its drawbacks:

	TYPICAL STARTING CONDITION
Subject	**Commentary on this Design**
Applications (Existing)	The primary failing of this approach to storing measurement values is, of course, the lack of business flexibility available, but there are more subtle failings as well.
	Applications built on this sort of data structure probably restrict input values to only those in the assumed unit-of-measure, which (hopefully) is made clear to the user. If there is a need to enter information that was provided in other units of measure, the user must do a manual conversion, leading to:
	▶ unnecessary user work and possible confusion
	▶ the potential for inconsistent and/or incorrect conversions
	▶ loss of the original information and any means of auditing/tracing input data errors
	▶ If, as in some cases, the application provides a utility to help the user calculate the conversions, this really only addresses the first of these issues, and unless all applications utilize the same conversion utility, the risk of inconsistency from differing levels of precision and conversion factors in the utilities will be high.

---

304 Now be fair! How would you know that if I hadn't told you? The Unit of Measure can't be queried. The Length could be in inches for all you know.

	Because input of each measurement value is treated independently, there is typically very little reuse of application code.
Applications (New)	Each new application built that relies on this same data will create an unnecessary and undesirable linkage between applications that share or exchange data – e.g. if the underlying unit-of-measure assumption needs to be changed in one application, the others must also change. The alternative is that the enterprise will be left with assumptions that are inconsistent from application to application, department to department, or organization to organization (like Lockheed Martin and NASA for example – see "The Business Issue" on page 202).
Assumptions (aka Risks)	Each assumption about the data that is not explicitly incorporated into a data structure presents risks. As implied earlier in this discussion, the assumptions for each measurement value contained in a table designed in the simple manner shown include: ► Unit of Measure ► Class of Measure ► Constancy of Measure (i.e. that consistent and repeatable unit-of-measure conversions will never be necessary) This lack of explicit clarity to both new developers and typicals well as users presents a serious business risk.
Data Constraints	If there are any constraints on values such as Length and Weight in the Widget table, they are most likely limited to establishing acceptable ranges for the absolute values (still assuming a particular unit-of-measure.)
Data Exchange	When it is necessary to share data with other applications, the options are limited to hard coding the assumed unit-of-measure, or assuming that the receiving system is making the same assumptions regarding the unit-of-measure (a double assumption!). When receiving data from other systems, conversions must be made if differing units of measure are used in the input stream, thus losing or possibly rounding the original information (i.e. we only retain an imprecise[305] conversion), or an assumption as to the unit-of-measure in use must be made.

---

305 The definition of "imprecise" is, of course, relative to some unknown future requirement for a certain level of precision. The intent of the word here is that the original absolute value can probably never be recovered precisely.

	TYPICAL STARTING CONDITION
Subject	**Commentary on this Design**
Data Integrity	Since this typical design (or lack of design) relies on assumptions that are not physically enforced, there are significant risks with regard to data integrity. These risks become more significant with each additional application or report that utilizes this data in any way. There is a potential for contamination of information. When the data is based on assumptions, the information it represents must be considered potentially contaminated or at least questionable.
Reports (Current)	Any reports that do not use the same unit-of-measure as that assumed by the creating application may not present consistent or reliable information to the users. There is a potential for contamination of information.
Reports (New)	Each new report built that utilizes this data will create an unnecessary and undesirable linkage between reports and application(s) (see the comments under Applications above). This makes future modifications to applications and reports unnecessarily expensive and time-consuming. There is little flexibility; when multiple reports or applications are forced to share the same assumptions, any attempt at changing these assumptions becomes incrementally more costly.

Units of measure should always be explicit. If this seems like a trivial matter, consider that different suppliers, industries, and even countries have different standards for what units-of-measure are appropriate for what purpose, what measures are available for ordering and shipping, etc. In summary, the existing Widget table design limits the business by imposing unnecessary constraints, is amateurish, and can lead to loss of information or incorrect information. Luckily, correction of this type of design flaw is fairly straightforward.

Ironically, however, it is often more difficult to handle correction of designs that attempted to overcome some of the flaws described above, but did so ineptly and without regard to good logical/relational design practices. The next section will discuss a common, but very poor, state from which to attempt addressing the lack of clarity regarding units of measure.

An Even Less Benign Starting Condition

A few database designers seem to have become aware of the difficulties of having built-in unit-of-measure assumptions like those in the original Widget design schema, but either ignore or don't recognize the real underlying problem (i.e. there are two pieces of information in one data element). A common solution in these cases, but one that is actually more difficult to correct, is shown in the table layout to the right, in which explicitly named columns have been substituted. In an apparent case of "friendly fire," the units of measure have been, as application programmers would say, "hard-coded," which is just as bad an idea in a database structure as it is in a section of code.[306]

WIDGET	
ID	pk
Length_in_FT	not null
Weight_in_LB	not null
Color	fk, not null

Please don't ever do anything like this!

In this case, all the difficulties described in the earlier example remain but the specification of unit-of-measure, but although the unit-of-measure has been "added" to the database, it is not typically visible to a user, nor can it be changed or queried.[307] However, any further efforts made in an attempt to generalize this table or make it more extensible will require significant changes to every application and report that uses this table. More importantly, all these changes would need to be rolled out simultaneously (unless, of course, you are willing to temporarily store a length in inches in a column titled **Length_in_FT**). Some products (e.g. DBMS utilities, language libraries, report generators) permit the creation of aliases to hide this. If you are the sort of person who likes to shove things under the rug, assigning an alias might work for a while, but I would not advise doing this.

It is strongly recommended that this sort of "solution" be repaired (removed) before attempting to proceed very much further with correcting the database design. In this example, one might add **Length** and **Weight** columns and update the primary source application to use them, while adding a temporary trigger to

---

306 One could argue that it is, in fact, worse, since hard-coding in an application generally affects fewer portions of a typical system than hard-coding in a database does.

307 Well, alright, maybe the user could browse the data dictionary to see this, but that really isn't much of an improvement.

automatically populate the Length_in_FT and Weight_in_LB columns on any insertions or updates. Broadcast the changes as widely as possible to report users and other developers that the "legacy" columns will be removed in some relatively short period (perhaps 30-60 days). If the number of such instances is small, these changes could be done in conjunction with the next step outlined below.

A Tempting (but very misguided) Design Enhancement

On the surface, it might appear that simply adding a second column for each absolute measurement to specify its unit-of-measure would suffice, since it seems to eliminate all the drawbacks of the previous designs. For the original example table, this simple change is shown to the right. Assume for this example that the units-of-measure have been constrained by using an SQL "IN clause"[308] since, as will be ex-

WIDGET	
ID	pk
Length	not null
Length_UOM	not null
Weight	not null
Weight_UOM	not null
Color	fk, not null

plained later, the use of domain tables and foreign keys to those tables presents some interesting issues if not handled correctly. If the table enhancement has been made friendly to application developers (i.e. to permit them to update applications without concern for the exact timing of the changes in the database), there will also be a default value inserted into any UOM columns that aren't explicitly populated during data entry. Inserting a default unit-of-measure must only be temporary, however – used to reduce inter-dependencies across the different development groups. It can't be considered a permanent measure, since it presents long-term issues that must be addressed. See the discussions in the table below, and note that we have actually *removed* what, for most businesses, was a very significant capability from the system – that of easily being able to total multiple values! See the various Drawbacks listed in the table below:

Subject	Commentary on this Design Approach	Business Impact
Applications (Current)	Applications may now be modified as needed to permit data entry in various different units-of-measure. With the database applying a default value for the unit-of-measure that matches the	Risk of simultaneous changes to data structures and application portfolio is reduced, while still permit-

---

308 For example "Length_UOM IN ('yd', 'ft', 'in')" or a similar construct.

Subject	Commentary on this Design Approach	Business Impact
	previous assumed value, applications will continue to function as they previously did until updates can be made and functional enhancements added.	ting as-needed enhancements.
Applications (New)	New applications can be written to permit users to enter data in whatever units-of-measure it is received.	Additional business flexibility is gained without incurring the labor and risks of users doing manual calculations.
Assumptions	The primary assumption – that of unit-of-measure – has been removed from each value in this design approach. Business flexibility only results, of course, from enhancing applications and reports to take advantage of the removal of these assumptions.	Some additional business flexibility becomes possible if applications add features.
Data Constraints	Data constraints, although limited, have been improved and are now more meaningful.	Better data integrity, but lurking problems.
Data Exchange	Output flexibility is enhanced: original data with original units-of-measure can be supplied, or normalized data (i.e. all in a single unit-of-measure) can be supplied – but at a cost. Although inputs can now be accepted in any unit-of-measure, intervention is probably still required. Unless and until all implicit assumptions are replaced by explicit data on both the sending and receiving ends of any data exchange process, there will still be a need for significant developer intervention. DRAWBACK: Comparisons or aggregations of the Length and Weight values become extremely costly and tedious to perform.	Generalized methods of passing data to other systems or businesses are now possible. This drawback alone is usually a "show-stopper."
Data Integrity	With any conversion from implicit to explicit data, integrity is improved.	Intangible, but important.

Subject	Commentary on this Design Approach	Business Impact
Reports (Current)	Reports may now be modified to utilize explicit units-of-measure rather than making assumptions. These may (and should) begin to be changed to utilize the actual data values. DRAWBACK: Comparisons or aggregations of the Length and Weight values become extremely costly and tedious to perform, since the units-of-measure differ. Also see the drawback under Data Exchange above.	Reports would most likely become *less* useful without extensive rework due to the lack of a common unit-of-measure in the data sets.. This drawback alone is usually a "show-stopper."
Reports (New)	Reports can be designed to provide information that meets the needs of those doing the analysis, rather than being constrained by the units required for business operations. DRAWBACK: Comparisons or aggregations of the Length and Weight values become extremely costly and tedious to perform. Also see the drawback under Data Exchange above.	This drawback alone is usually a "show-stopper."

The data structures as shown above have been improved primarily because the Unit-of-Measure assumptions have been removed: existing applications and reports can continue functioning with no changes, but developers and report designers can begin working on taking advantage of the new system flexibility these small changes allow. For some businesses, this simple addition of units-of-measure for each measurement value may seem to be sufficient in the short term, so long as the Unit-of-measure columns are each constrained in some manner to ensure consistency and data integrity. Unfortunately, the Constraint on unit-of-measure values achieved by using IN clauses presents its own dangers, since it is quite primitive.[309] There is no mechanism to ensure that all the various IN clauses start off or remain consistent across attributes in the same table, much less from table to table or even (shudder) from database to database.

The primary flaw introduced in this design, however, is that the **Length** and **Weight** values may (and likely will) have inconsistent units-of-measure values, which is a major failing. If the business seldom ever requires any comparisons

---

309 See the section "Primitive Declarative Constraints in the Database (C ∩ F)" on page 172.

between or aggregations of the data in this table,[310] and doesn't anticipate any need to ever do so, this simple approach might be appropriate, but it isn't recommended, since a more elegant and complete solution requiring only slightly more work is only a few steps away.

Non-Relational – and also misguided – Constraints for UOM

The previous examples removed the system limitations resulting from using assumed and/or unspecified units-of-measure. To further refine the system, it is now necessary to explicitly define the domains for units-of-measure in each measurement class rather than using individual (and, as we have pointed out, potentially inconsistent) IN clauses on each UOM column.

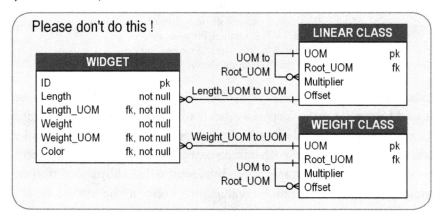

As with most design decisions, there are right and wrong ways to do this. It was mentioned earlier that the use of foreign keys to domain tables can present difficulties. The designers of the schema above have added domain tables to support each of the measurement classes in the hope of resolving any discrepancies

---

310 For example, if there is ever a need to calculate a total or average length value over more than one row, this can become quite tedious without the values being in a common unit-of-measure. This may well be acceptable in inventory tables, for instance, where each row represents a separate product, but isn't suitable for a generalized approach that can be commonly applied, and totaling length or weight values would have no meaning.

across their system and, in the process, provide a good example of the types of difficulties one might encounter.

At first glance, it appears that this approach will address the requirement for standardizing and constraining the Units-of-Measure for any given measurement class. For each measurement in any system table (e.g. the Length_UOM column above right), a foreign key would be established to the appropriate Class table. **Length_UOM** would be constrained by the **Linear_Class** table, and **Weight_UOM** would be constrained by the **Weight_Class** table and so forth for other tables throughout the schema.

Although this will "work," the primary advantage the designers saw was that this approach reduced the number of columns (i.e. the Measurement Class is not required for each column in the table that contains a measure) that would be present in each table, and naively perceived this as an advantage.

From a formal relational perspective, however, it's a poor design for several reasons. The primary flaw is that this schema utilizes domain tables that are not normalized; each value of an obvious attribute, Class, is treated as if it were a separate entity.[311] Accommodating additional classes of measure, therefore, requires that changes be made to the database structure rather than simply adding data to a single generalized table. Setting constraints can be error-prone (the correct table must be chosen for each foreign key), and determining which domain table is being referenced by any given column can be time-consuming for those without easy access to an entity-relationship diagram or data dictionary.

Further examination of the design will demonstrate that the only real benefit to reducing the number of columns[312] in the table by eliminating class (e.g.

---

311 This is somewhat akin to having two domain tables for Color – one for light colors, and another for dark. As a general rule, all attributes of a specific relation (in this case the Classes of Weights and Measures) should be considered as a single relation.

312 To reiterate a point made earlier in this book, there is nothing inherently good or bad about Schemas that have what may be viewed by some as "too many" or "too few" tables, and nothing inherently good or bad about "too many" or "too few" columns in any given table. (also see Emperor Joseph II's comments in Weights & Measures – Part 1). The real criteria should be the accurate and complete (or as complete as required) definition of the "Thing"

Length_Class and Weight_Class in the above example) is to the I/T department (less typing is involved). Not only does this not benefit users, it actually makes life more difficult for them by obscuring the domain.

Relational Constraints for UOM and Adding Standardized Values

The earlier Widget schema, repeated below, shows the correct[313] approach to placing Constraints on the various units-of-measure to be added to a schema.

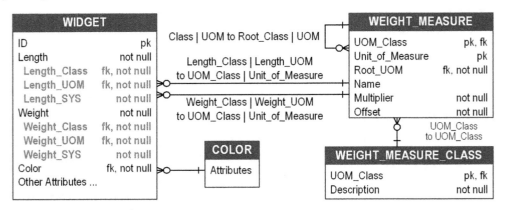

Compared to the original four-element table, this grouping of three tables can, at first glance, seem to be unnecessarily complicated. It is indeed more complex, but as pointed out earlier, that isn't at all the same thing as complicated, and it provides a much more powerful and flexible alternative to the primitive original.

The design completely reflects the reality of the two original attributes **Length** and **Weight**, and provides the system with all the data we humans use when interpreting information about weights and measures. It may seem cheeky to point this out, but if one has much difficulty understanding how this model functions,

---

being modeled. When you encounter books or articles that give rules of thumb concerning how big a table should be, throw them in the garbage, or at least recognize that such generalizations are not always applicable and recycle them responsibly.

313 By "correct," I mean it is a Logically defensible schema that adheres to the Relational Model; as mentioned more than a few times in this book, the Relational Model is one of the few things in our industry that is based on proven scientific and mathematical principles.

it is likely that one doesn't fully understand the unpleasant ramifications of handling weights and measures in a less than rigorous fashion.

In practice, columns like **Length_Class** and **Weight_Class** would most often be auto-populated by triggers or set as `Default` values when this schema is implemented. Columns like **Length_SYS** and **Weight_SYS**[314] would be auto-populated with standard values calculated by triggers using functions described earlier and in the "System Values Auto-Population Trigger" on page 403.

Those paying close attention so far will realize that, in this schema, the Class values in every row of each column will be identical. This, of course, raises all sorts of red flags about the need for the column. Such similarity, however, is limited to the point of view of the table in question; from the viewpoint of the Weight_Measure table to which each column is constrained, the value cannot be predetermined. We will address this apparent redundancy once the model is fully developed. (Note that Class values are only a portion of their respective Keys.)

There are some cute DBA tricks (not discussed here, but easy enough to figure out[315]) to store the universal Class value for each database unit-of-measure value, but they can be unnecessarily complex and obscure what is happening from a casual observer of the schema (e.g. a programmer, report writer, or casual user) – seldom a desirable characteristic.

What is critical for effective use of this schema is that no external updates should be permitted to any of the internal value columns; only the trigger and system conversion function should be permitted to do anything other than read from this column. Serious data integrity problems could otherwise result.

---

314 There is nothing sacred about these names. Actual implementations of this scheme in various of our client companies have been called Length_Standard, Standard_Length, Internal_Length, Root_Length, etc. Of course, all such root value columns in any enterprise should follow the same naming pattern.

315 Think of reference tables keyed to columns in the RDBMS data dictionary, as proposed by one cowboy I encountered. On second thought, don't think any such things, since they may be implemented in such a way that opens up the potential for subtle security violations.

The Migration Process

In almost any situation where database structures and application code could be made more extensible through generalization, weights and measures are likely to be high on the list of target elements because of the correspondingly high potential for payback. As with other generalization efforts, however, the transition from the existing state to the desired state must be handled in a very controlled and orderly fashion in order to avoid operational disruptions. Except for new development (which should always be designed in an extensible manner), "big bang" changes to a system are likely to be deemed too risky by many businesses so conservatism is in order when upgrading existing systems. This section provides a minimal outline that will guide the migration process by defining the stages needed to safely modify existing data stores, applications, reports and data exchange processes, and to do these things quite safely and incrementally.

Business Case Analysis

Before beginning the project(s) that will generalize the handling of weights and measures, it is of course necessary to do a Business Case Analysis. The steps that must be included in such an analysis are outlined below.

1) Analyze the needs of your business and determine which data elements could be generalized most profitably.

   a) Determine which of the columns in the database are used to record weight and measure data that is within the scope of this discussion. Answers to the homework exercise at the end of the "Homework Assignment" on page 222 can be used as a starting point.

   b) From the list of columns derived above, determine which, if remodeled, would present business opportunities (or remove business impediments) if they were to be generalized. Although the process outlined here is designed to minimize risk, particularly in relation to the enhanced capabilities it offers, there must still be some identifiable business drivers.

c) Determine the level[316] to which each column's data should be generalized. If there is any doubt whatever, the data structures should be fully generalized.

d) Determine which Classes of Weights and Measures are in use and whether the Class taxonomy given here is appropriate. Should Linear and Distance Classes be separated as done here, for example?

Preparatory Technical Analysis

2) Inventory all applications, processes and reports in order to determine how each interacts with each data column being considered for generalization. Divide the resulting list into insert/update (Data Creator) and output/query/report (Data Consumer) categories or, as is often the case, those that fall into both categories. This can be a tedious process, and use of a commercial tool that can analyze and report on all interactions of the system with each data element is recommended.

a) Identify all reports and applications that read data from the columns to be generalized. This class of processes is known as *Data Consumer Processes*.

   i. Identify the output processes that feed data from these columns to other systems (e.g. transmissions to trading partners through EDI or XML, ETL processes that feed data warehouses, etc.) Include other systems that simply read data from these columns.

   ii. Identify all reports that utilize the columns being considered for generalization.

   iii. Identify other uses of the data in these columns (e.g. database views,[317] value triggers, etc.) In enterprises where there is any signifi-

---

316 UOM only, UOM and System Value, fully generalized. See earlier portions of this chapter for more complete descriptions of these levels and a discussion of the benefits of each.

317 We know from earlier discussions, of course, that the "views" we use with RDBMS products are not really views as defined in the relational model, but this book is intended to be more practical than theoretical, so we'll continue with our vendors' blatant and shameless misuse of the term.

cant level of uncontrolled user access to the data, this may well involve publicizing the tables for which modification is being contemplated and offering assistance with correcting poorly constructed queries, etc.

    iv. Ensure that none of the above processes (i.e. anything used to read and/or otherwise acquire data) are affected by the presence of additional columns in the table structures.

> Regarding step iv, special attention must be paid to any database queries that utilize non-specific SQL statements (e.g. SELECT * FROM WIDGET). Such abominations (as well as any other structure-sensitive code) *must* be corrected (that is, made explicit by specifying column names) before considering generalization, much less actually altering any of the database structures.

    v. Subdivide all the above into those that are easily modifiable and those that are not. "Easily modifiable" refers to such things as availability of source code and compilers, not to the level of developer effort, since the ease of future modifications to a generalized system more than outweighs any developer effort.

  b) Identify the applications used to create or update the columns to be generalized. This class of processes is known as DATA CREATOR PROCESSES.

    i. As above, subdivide these into applications that are easily modifiable and those that are not.

3) Pre-modification Analysis

  a) Based on all information collected above, make a final determination as to which tables and columns will be generalized. It is not necessary that all tables be modified at the same time (i.e. in one single project) but, if the planning is thorough, there is typically no advantage to not doing so since the system will need to be closed off from user activity for a few of the steps.

  b) Determine the appropriate internal (root) unit-of-measure for each class; this will generally be the unit-of-measure previously assumed for the columns being modified, but there may be business or mathematical reasons (e.g. assuring reasonable scales) for selecting some other unit. Be aware that changing the root unit-of-measure choice later will require conversion of all system value measurements for that Class, and will need to be done simultaneously throughout the system.

c) Determine the level of precision required for each measurement class within the enterprise. See "Data Precision" on page 305.

d) Calculate all the required conversion factors for the root units of measure chosen. If the root unit-of-measure chosen happens to match that in the examples given in this document, and the precision used is appropriate to your needs, that value may safely be used.

e) At this point, the analysts can begin the activities described beginning in step 6 of "Modifications of Data Consumers" below while parallel design and development of new database structures is taking place.

Design and Development of New Database Structures

4) Initial Design and Development – this work does not affect existing database structures or applications, and constitutes preparatory work needed to put the system domain tables in place for later use.

a) Create the Weight and Measure Class domain table based on the model.[318]

b) Populate the Weight and Measure Class domain table with all relevant classes of interest.

c) Create the Weight and Measure domain table.

d) Populate the Weight and Measure domain table with all relevant conversion factors.

e) Create a comprehensive set of test cases for all affected weights and measures that emphasize the range limits and specific conversions of interest to the business.[319]

---

318 Sample build scripts for steps 4a through 4d are given in "Sample Data for Weights & Measures Test Cases" on page 404.

319 The sample test script given in "Table for Weights & Measures Test Cases" on page 403 may be used as a model or starting point, although test cases should be concentrated on areas of interest to the specific business, cover all boundary conditions, etc.

f) Build a stored procedure for unit-of-measure conversions that need to take place during inserts or updates to the database.[320] This is dependent on and will utilize the domain tables created above.

g) Build and test a generalized conversion function for use by applications and reports as either a wrapper around the stored procedure created above or as a standalone piece of code. The former is best for maintenance and standardization; the latter provides better performance.

These tables may be placed into production after suitable testing of the new structures, since there will be no interaction with any existing tables or applications until they are modified to make use of the enhanced capabilities.

Design and Modification of Existing Database Structures

Assume that the **Widget** table[321] is representative of the types of tables to be modified. Further assume that something like the following SQL statement was used to create the table (this is Oracle-specific DDL based on the earlier Widget example):

```
CREATE TABLE Widget
   (ID          NUMBER          NOT NULL,
    Length      NUMBER          NOT NULL
                CONSTRAINT chk_Length_Range
                   CHECK (Length BETWEEN 0 AND 100),
    Weight      NUMBER          NOT NULL
                CONSTRAINT chk_Weight_Range
                   CHECK (Weight BETWEEN 0 AND 20),
    Color       VARCHAR2(10)  NOT NULL,
    CONSTRAINT PK_WIDGET PRIMARY KEY (ID)
    )
;
```

5) Modify the structure of the tables selected for generalization to add new columns and constraints. By the end of this section, all the selected target database structures will be generalized, and triggers and temporary defaults will ensure that all the new columns will be populated with appropriate val-

---

320 A sample of how such a procedure might work is given in "Bare Bones UOM_Convert Function in PL/SQL" on page 396.

321 See the example in "Starting Point – Existing Database Structures" on page 271.

ues without any modifications to the applications and other processes that currently populate the database. This will allow developers to begin the process of modifying the applications and reports that utilize the data. This series of steps is of course done for each table to be modified.

a) If there were any existing range CHECK constraints on any of the value columns (as shown above), user and programmatic access to the affected tables should be blocked at this point until all alterations have been completed.

Remove any existing range CHECK constraints on **Length** and **Width** columns; the constraints will be replaced by identical ones (assuming the old Units-of-Measure have become the System Units-of-Measure) on the **Length_SYS** and **Weight_SYS** columns.

```
ALTER TABLE Widget
  DROP CONSTRAINT chk_Length_Range;
ALTER TABLE Widget
  DROP CONSTRAINT chk_Weight_Range
;
```

If the original constraints were not explicitly named according to some company standard, you will need to query the data dictionary for the name assigned by the RDBMS product.

b) Alter each table (first pass)

i. Add all needed unit-of-measure columns as *nullable* columns (this will be temporary).

ii. Add all needed measurement class columns as *nullable* columns

iii. Add all needed system standard measurement value columns as *nullable* columns

iv. Add default values for each new unit-of-measure column; this will automatically populate new columns with the previously assumed unit-of-measure. This is a *temporary measure* until all processes that insert or update data have been altered to provide this information explicitly. It is desirable to widely publicize that this is happening and that it is a temporary measure; setting a removal date, even if tentative, is desirable.

v. Add default values for each new measurement class columns; this will automatically populate new columns with the proper class.

vi. Example for steps b) i through b) v. above:

```
ALTER TABLE Widget
    ADD (Length_Class   VARCHAR2(15) DEFAULT 'Linear',
         Length_UOM     VARCHAR2(10) DEFAULT 'in',
         Length_SYS     NUMBER,
            CONSTRAINT chk_Length_Range
                CHECK (Length_SYS BETWEEN 0 AND 100),
         Weight_Class   VARCHAR2(15) DEFAULT 'Weight',
         Weight_UOM     VARCHAR2(10) DEFAULT 'lb',
         Weight_SYS     NUMBER
            CONSTRAINT chk_Weight_Range
                CHECK (Weight_SYS BETWEEN 0 AND 20)
        );
```

Astute readers, particularly those with a vindictive bent) will note the use of BETWEEN clauses in this statement, which, as indicated in the chapter on Constraints (see "Primitive Declarative Constraints in the Database (C ∩ F)" on page 172), often have drawbacks (e.g. they can't be queried directly). The use of BETWEEN here is simply a carry-over of the constraints that were already in the **Widget** table and, although you may want or need to address whether these particular Constraint values are appropriate, or whether they should be re-placed with Foreign Keys to separate range domain tables (highly recommended), that is outside the scope of this example.

c) If not previously done, user and programmatic access to the affected tables should be blocked at this point until all alterations have been completed.

d) Update all new system standard measurement values with existing measurement values.

```
UPDATE WIDGET SET
        Length_SYS   = Length,
        Weight_SYS   = Weight;
```

Note that **Length_Class**, **Length_UOM**, **Weight_Class** and **Weight_UOM** will have already been set by the DEFAULT statement (see 5 b) vi above) in most RDBMS products; otherwise they will need to be included in this statement as well.

e)   Add foreign key relationships for all unit-of-measure/measure value pairs.

Example:
```
ALTER TABLE Widget
   ADD (CONSTRAINT Widget_FK1 FOREIGN KEY (Length_Class, Length_UOM)
      REFERENCES WEIGHT_MEASURE (UOM_Class, Unit_of_Measure));
ALTER TABLE Widget
   ADD (CONSTRAINT Widget_FK2 FOREIGN KEY (Weight_Class, Weight_UOM)
      REFERENCES WEIGHT_MEASURE (UOM_Class, Unit_of_Measure));
```
These can certainly be combined with the earlier ALTER TABLE commands, but are shown separately here for clarity.

f)   Alter each table (second pass)

i.   Change all new unit-of-measure columns to Not Null

ii. Change all new measurement class columns to Not Null

iii. Change all new system standard measurement value columns to Not Null

Example for combining steps f) i. through f) iii. above:
```
ALTER TABLE Widget
   MODIFY (Length_Class   NOT NULL,
           Length_UOM     NOT NULL,
           Length_SYS     NOT NULL,
           Weight_Class   NOT NULL,
           Weight_UOM     NOT NULL,
           Weight_SYS     NOT NULL);
```

g)   Add triggers to convert inserted or updated measurement values into the internal standard unit-of-measure; this should be the only means of populating the internal values. Using a "before insert or update" trigger is a sufficiently effective means of enforcing this.

Example for the two measurement values in the **Widget** table:
```
CREATE OR REPLACE TRIGGER Widget_Measure_BIU
BEFORE INSERT OR UPDATE ON WIDGET
   FOR EACH ROW
BEGIN
   :new.Weight_SYS :=
   WM_SYS_VAL(:new.Weight, :new.Weight_UOM, new.Weight_Class);
   :new.Length_SYS :=
   WM_SYS_VAL(:new.Length, :new.Length_UOM,:new.Length_Class);
END;
```

h) Run the test procedures[322] developed for placing these changes on-line and, if successful, return the tables to an on-line state to permit user and program access.

Need for Patience

At this point in the migration process, *there are still no tangible business advantages*, but everything is in place to safely begin modifications to the processes that consume data output. Once that is done, the modifications needed to allow the system to accept arbitrary units of measure can begin, at which point the benefits will begin to appear.

Modifications of Data Consumers

Once changes have been made to all the weights and measures, there will be more information available to data consumers, providing the potential for an increase in power and flexibility. While adapting these data consumers to take advantage of this increased power can be considered optional in some cases (i.e. use of the additional information can be deferred or even ignored in some cases), the meaning of the existing values has changed,[323] and each data consumer process must be protected from the effects of having removed the previous system assumptions. In the case of the Widget table, for instance, the weight value can no longer be assumed to be in pounds, and applications that are not relieved of that assumption will become unreliable.

> **Caution: Data Consumers must be modified before any Data Creators are permitted to enter any data in other than the previous system units-of-measure!**

The following steps need to be taken to address this:

---

322 Testing procedures for the fundamental processes described here are covered separately in the appendix referred to earlier, but testing the integration into a specific system is, of course, impossible to discuss here without detailed knowledge of that system.

323 It is now more limited, and more precise or less vague depending on your world-view.

6) Analysis of information usage

   Now that there is a choice of data available for the generalized measurement values (i.e. both the entered value as well as a standardized value), each prior use of the affected data elements must be examined to determine what assumptions were made when the process was developed.

   a) Report designers and analysts must determine whether reports will utilize actual values, system standard values, or some combination of both (e.g. actual values and units of measure on each detail line, system values and units of measure on summary lines).

   b) For each application (and perhaps for each module or component) that reads, calculates, or displays data, application designers and analysts must determine which data value is most appropriate.

   c) All reports and queries must, at a minimum, change from reading (for example) Length and Weight to reading Length_SYS and Weight_SYS. This, of course, provides no enhancements whatever, but will permit the report or query to function normally until enhancements can be made.

7) Design and Development for information consumers

   a) Modify the processes that collect data to use the columns with the correct semantics

      i. Begin work on altering all reports to explicitly query units of measure rather than simply printing the assumed unit on the report as a constant or, even worse, not listing it at all. (Reports using system values will need to read the system unit-of-measure from the weight_measure table as in the example given in the query below.)

      Example of a report query reading only measurement values in system standard units:

```
SELECT ID                     "ID"
     , Length_SYS             "Normalized Length"
     , a.Root_Unit_of_Measure "Normalized Length Unit-of-measure"
     , Weight_SYS             "Normalized Weight"
     , b.Root_Unit_of_Measure "Normalized Weight Unit-of-measure"
     , Color                  "Color"
  FROM Widget, Weight_Measure a, Weight_Measure b
 WHERE Widget.Length_Class  = a.UOM_Class
   AND a.Unit_of_Measure    = a.Root_Unit_of_Measure
   AND Widget.Weight_Class  = b.UOM_Class
```

```
         AND b.Unit_of_Measure     = b.Root_Unit_of_Measure ;
```

Even though much of the total work and time required for a successful migration process has been expended by the completion of this stage, *there are still no tangible business advantages.*

> **Patience-2: While this is not a technical issue, handling of business and user expectations (as well as internal I/T expectations) becomes critical to eventual success, and the importance of this cannot be overstated.**

Once all data consumer processes are generalized to be able to accept weights and measures in arbitrary units, the processes that create the data can now be modified to begin accepting such arbitrary units, at which point the business benefits will begin to appear rapidly as each source of data is modified.

Modification of Data Creators

All activity prior to this stage of the migration process has been preparatory in nature – in a sense, all the previous work has prepared the system so that it can be generalized. In this stage, some or all system inputs can now be modified to take advantage of increased flexibility and, unlike previous stages, each modification that is placed into production will bring immediate increases in system flexibility.

Completion of this section is where the benefits of generalization change from theoretical to tangible, removing restrictions that previously constrained business expansion efforts, while simultaneously presenting new business opportunities.

8) Modify the processes that insert and update data to take advantage of increased flexibility.

   a) Modify applications used by humans to enter data, so that arbitrary units of measure may be chosen when entering data. For example, consider the screen segments on the following page:

   In this simplified example, a drop down list has been added to display the unit-of-measure, and it is preset to the normal system default (i.e. the system unit described earlier.) For the weight value, the user has chosen to enter the value in ounces, as she received it, rather than having to convert it to pounds. A non-editable display below the input boxes could show all the system values and units of measure for the user's convenience.[324] It is obviously beyond the scope of this paper to discuss all the issues involved with generalizing an application in this manner, although some are suggested in "Application Considerations and Caveats" on page 307.

```
┌──────────────────────────────────┐
│      Widget Specifications       │
│  Length (in)        Weight (lb)  │
│  ┌──────────┐      ┌──────────┐  │
│  │     28.6 │      │       10 │  │
│  └──────────┘      └──────────┘  │
└──────────────────────────────────┘
```

Data Entry Screen Before Generalization

```
┌────────────────────────────────────────────┐
│           Widget Specifications             │
│  Length . . . . . . .      Weight . . . . . . . .  │
│  ┌──────┬────┬───┐      ┌──────┬────┬───┐   │
│  │ 28.6 │ in │ ▼ │      │  160 │ oz │ ▼ │   │
│  └──────┴────┴───┘      └──────┴────┴───┘   │
│     ( 28.6 in )            ( 10.0 lb )       │
└────────────────────────────────────────────┘
```

Data Entry Screen After Generalization

b) Modify batch or message based data load procedures. In an ideal world, our information technology systems would be designed with few enough assumptions that we could respond immediately to changing business needs and opportunities, and possibly even become proactive in creating new opportunities. Unfortunately, I/T departments are generally reactive and it isn't unusual that generalization efforts such as those described in this paper are only precipitated by some external event (or the realization that the system is so arthritic that further modifications will produce no tangible results in any reasonable amount of time or without increasing the risks). It would not be atypical, for instance, for custom unit-of-measure conversions to be added to data load procedures

In addition to removing redundant and inconsistent processes and conversion factors, correcting (and thus simplifying) these load procedures will eliminate loss of information.

---

324 In certain circumstances, it might be more useful to display the values in the units of measure most convenient for a particular user or functional department.

9) At some point, it will probably be desirable to remove the default insertion values for all new unit-of-measure columns.[325] As suggested above, a reasonable deadline should be set for this in order to avoid procrastination. It must be emphasized that removing these defaults will force all input data to be explicit, and that this is a primary objective of this exercise. (Remember the Mars Climate Orbiter?)

The Testing Process

While a comprehensive discussion of testing these changes would likely double the size of this series of chapters, the changes envisioned here must be thoroughly vetted before being put into a production system. Aside from normal good testing practices, there are two areas that demand a fairly large suite of test cases or scripts: – conversion consistency and data integrity:

Conversion Consistency and Accuracy

There should be a series of iterative conversions to ensure that no degradation of the original value appears after multiple conversions into other units of measure. All measurements of interest to the company should be represented; both business management and accounting managers, as well as day-to-day users can easily contribute sample test values to this effort.

A very straightforward method of doing this is to create test tables (whether database tables or not is dependent on a particular business environment) containing some test values, the process to which they are to be subjected, and the expected/desired output value(s). Output from the test suites can be matched against the expected values and easily searched for differences.

Data Integrity

Procedures should be established to perform multiple iterative conversions between various units-of-measure to ensure that the input values remain stable.

---

325 See 5.b.iv earlier.

Other Issues to be Considered

Data Precision

There are a number of values for conversion factors used within this discussion as examples; these are summarized in "Sample Conversion Calculations" on page 227.[326] While these are all "correct," there is no intent to imply a specific precision, nor is there any intent to imply that the numeric precision for any one class of measures needs to be the same as for any other class.

Actual data values and necessary precision will need to be reviewed and validated prior to implementation based on whatever specific criteria are needed to meet your business requirements, any industry standards and the like. Generally speaking, there is little cost differential between low precision (one or two decimal places) and the highest precision that can be reached with the data types utilized in the database management system product and the programming languages. The choice of an appropriate data precision is significantly constrained, however, by the orders of magnitude between the smallest and largest units of measure likely to be encountered in a system. If, for instance, ounce and ton are both reasonable measurements for a specific column in a database (which will hardly ever be the case,) it isn't a reasonable expectation that ounce values should have many significant decimal places.

Measurement Ranges

It will be necessary to identify any measurement classes that might be expected to have extremely wide ranges across your enterprise. A common example given earlier is Distance vs. Length; although they are both linear measurements, it was deemed appropriate to segregate them into separate measurement classes.[327]

---

326 A more complete listing is provided in "Appendix C – Weights & Measures – Data" beginning on page 415.

327 See descriptions of the "Distance" and "Length" measurement classes in the table "Measurement Classes in Scope" beginning on page. 210

Multiple Factor Measures

Aside from speed, usually given as miles-per-hour or kilometers-per-hour, no examples of multiple-factor measurements have been considered. Examples of such units include the Measurement Class "Pressure", which is usually given in the United States as "pounds per square inch" and "gas mileage", usually given as "miles per gallon." Although the conversion to alternative combination measurements (e.g. "kilograms per square centimeter" or "kilometers per liter") should be mathematically straightforward, the likely uses of such multiple measures may present additional considerations, particularly in older applications where there are assumed ratios between the two measurements[328] buried in the code. In transportation, for example, where pressures of certain substances in a tanker truck may vary depending on altitude above sea level, alternative or additional approaches to conversion may be required. These are considered out of scope for this discussion.

Conversion between Measurement Classes

The whole concept of the scheme described here is that conversions between two different measurement classes make no sense. Nothing is absolute, however, and this rule needs to be validated in light of your particular business requirements. A good example of an exception to this rule is that many cooks consider that 0.0211 teaspoons of water (clearly a Volume Class measurement) is equal to 0.002 lbs (clearly a Weight Class measurement). Such oddities have not been considered enough of a business issue to discuss here, although similar techniques would apply should this be necessary.[329]

Abbreviations and Symbols

In the conversion factors given as examples so far, several "correct" abbreviations for units of measure that use superscripts (e.g. cm^2, ft^3, etc.) are shown. In

---

328 Recall "Playing with Trucks – Part 1," in which Trux-M-Us had such an inflexible system that comparing miles-per-gallon with kilometers-per-liter became a severe headache.

329 Hint: The weight of a certain volume of something can certainly be predicted, although weights would obviously be different for the same volume of different materials.

the sample data structures and calculations, however, these are shown as "cm2" and "ft3" respectively.

It would obviously be desirable to show these units of measure correctly on display screens, and certainly on any printed output, but storing them as the primary unit-of-measure values in the database would make the construction of queries, particularly from a command line, very tedious. This same issue would apply to any units of measure that use a particular symbol, such as the reading "47°F" for forty-seven degrees Fahrenheit.

No attempt has been made to address this issue here, but a resolution or strategy for handling it will be required as part of any implementation design. Several such abbreviations are included in the table "Conversion Factors" that begins on page 415, and a column (perhaps **UOM_Symbol**) could easily be added to the **Weight_Measure** table shown in the section "Relational Constraints for UOM and Adding Standardized Values" on page 290, but a specific strategy for handling this will be largely dependent on which programming languages, libraries and RDBMS products and the like are available to you, since handling of such characters varies widely among available products.

Transfer of Data to Other Systems

Since systems could be set up in different locales with different sets of root measurement units and different precisions, internal measurements should not be communicated across systems if the original values and units of measure can be transmitted. The original value/unit-of-measurement pair should be transferred and converted to internal units by each receiving system before being stored in the database unless there are good reasons to do otherwise.

Application Considerations and Caveats

Assuming that a system is implemented using the proposed scheme described earlier, it will be necessary to consider some user interface ramifications.

▶   It seems reasonable that a drop down list of some sort will be provided for the selection of a particular unit-of-measure; this would be based on a fixed (hard-coded) measurement class, since that will remain constant for any attribute regardless of the unit-of-measure selected.

▶ It further seems reasonable that a default unit-of-measure will be presented to the user based on locale or some user-specific preference settings.

Neither of these assumptions, by the way, has been considered in the database diagrams provided earlier to illustrate the approach to conversion, since they were not required for that purpose.

Given these assumptions, however, some scenarios come to mind that need to be handled. For example:

▶ If the default unit-of-measure is set to inches, and a user is given a measurement of 400cm to enter, it is possible that the user could overlook changing the unit-of-measure setting on input. A good application design should attempt to preclude this, of course, but given the nature of human activity, this may be difficult.

▶ Upon discovering the error, the user could change the unit-of-measure to centimeters. System options could be:

▼ Allow that change to stand on the assumption that the user intended it (in this case, the correct response).

▼ Recalculate the value of 400 inches (not what the user intended, but what was actually entered) and display a value of 1015.9999 centimeters (probably an annoying response, but valid).

▼ Prompt the user for the appropriate action to take, displaying both results as a choice.

▼ Evaluate the entered value/unit-of-measure combination against a set of "reasonable" values for the particular value being entered. This may not be possible in all circumstances, but should be considered where possible as an added "safety measure," regardless of which approach is chosen.

The actual difficulty, of course, is that the system has no way of knowing whether a user intended to correct an erroneous selection of unit-of-measure or actually meant to change the measurement itself.

From a user interface perspective, it may be desirable to allow input and display of measurements in a mixed form, such as 6' 3", rather than a single value, such as 75", or a decimal value, such as 6.25'. This is not considered in detail in this document, but the following points should be considered:

► It seems reasonable that mixed measurement units would never be comprised of mixed measurement classes, i.e. "6' 7.62mm" (part English and part Metric) should never be permitted and only one selection of class for any mixed measurement pair should be permitted.

► Storage of mixed UOM data would always be in single units of measure, and thus would be required to support fractional units in all cases. In other words, if a user entered 6' 6", only a single value and unit-of-measure would be stored, and this should in all cases be the smallest unit (the math involved in converting 6.5' back to 6' 6" is more expensive than converting 80" back to 6' 6").

The issues above need to be addressed in any design based on the approaches outlined in this book.

Useful References

There are many benefits to generalization of software and data structures in Business; similarly there is a wealth of categorized, standardized, and well organized data available for use in schemes such as the one presented in this and the previous three chapters that has been agreed upon by national and international standards bodies specifically for the purpose of aiding commerce. It is well worth the effort to incorporate these into your own data schemas instead of (as too many Americans do) "reinventing the wheel" and addressing problems that many others have already solved. To that end, the following list will provide a few resources that relate to the subject of Weights and Measures. Many more can easily be found.

▼ United States National Institute of Standards (NIST): NIST Handbook, Appendix C; http://ts.nist.gov/WeightsAndMeasures/Publications/appxc.cfm

- ▼ United States Code Title 15 (Commerce and Trade), Chapter Six (Weights and Measures and Standard Time); http://www4.law.cornell.edu/uscode/15/ch6.html
- ▼ College of Chemistry at the University of California, Berkeley. http://chemistry.berkeley.edu/links/weights/equivalences.htm...
- ▼ English Weights and Measures: http://home.clara.net/brianp/
- ▼ The American Heritage® Dictionary of the English Language, Third Edition copyright © 1992 by Houghton Mifflin Company.
- ▼ The Logic of Modern Physics, 1927, by Percy Williams Bridgman (1882-1961) publ. MacMillan (New York) Edition, 1927. Some information can be found at: http://www.marxists.org/reference/subject/philosophy/works/us/bridgman.htm
- ▼ American Society for Testing and Materials[330] (ASTM): See http://www.techstreet.com/info/astm.tmpl for a listing of their standards publications.

A Final Thought:

"A good solution applied with vigor now is better than a perfect solution applied ten minutes later."[331]

---

330 This particular organization is included for its ironic value. One of the standards promulgated by this body is the range of measurements incorporated in each "size" of clothing (Standard BS3666:1982, issued 30 APR 1982, "Specification for size designation of woman's wear"). According to Jim Lovejoy of SizeUSA, a 2003 survey by industry group [TC]², "vanity sizing" (i.e. ignoring the ASTM standard and putting smaller size numbers on garments than the standard calls for) is more common than standard sizing in woman's clothing. "According to standard size measurements, [the] average 155 pound woman should be wearing a size 16, but thanks to vanity sizing, she's probably buying a 10 or 12," says Lovejoy. See "Skinny is the New Fat" on page 55 of the October 30, 2006 Newsweek.

331 General George S. Patton, major tactician of the European Theater during World War II.

"Skill is fine, and genius is splendid, but the right contacts are more valuable than either."
Sir Arthur Conan Doyle (1859-1930)

Like the four Weights and Measures chapters, this one crosses the imaginary line into a discussion of design techniques, but only far enough to outline and explain a logical, but non-typical, approach to handling Party-based contact attributes.

18

18 - CONTACT MECHANISMS

Introduction

Throughout many of the previous chapters, the **Party** entity/superclass, although of paramount importance to a well-designed Business Database, hasn't been shown with any attributes but the primary key that is inherited by all the Party subclasses (e.g. people) participating in the transactions of the business.

This chapter introduces Contact Mechanisms, which are the most common attributes of the **Party** entity set in most Business Databases.

As used in this chapter, the term "Contact Mechanisms" refers to any means we have for active or passive communications between Parties in connection with the business they are conducting. If the concept of **Party** isn't clear at this point, it may help to review "An I/T Department Must Have Parties," beginning on page 2, once more. Examples of contact mechanisms include telephone numbers

> Attributes versus Columns
>
> There are any number of well-meaning Relational Database design texts stating that any table having nothing but a primary key column can be safely eliminated from the design.
>
> This is nonsense of the first order, possibly originating from the equally silly belief that "Entities become Tables, and Attributes become Columns" in a database.
>
> The reality is that many Attributes become Relationships rather than Columns, and the Party Entity set is the most common example of the use of such relationship attributes.

of various types, mailing addresses, and so forth. The following list discusses several examples of these.[332]

▶ **Address**, as used here, is a grouping of data written or printed on any item as directions for delivery to some Party or some Party's specified location. An Address of this type generally falls into one of two broad classes:

  ▼ **Virtual Address**, defined as a description of a location to which certain items may be sent for immediate **or eventual** delivery to a Party (typically a person or organization), whether the Party generally resides or can be found at that address or not. A Post Office Box is an example of a Virtual Address, as are e-mail "addresses," social media "handles" and other such entities.

  ▼ **Physical Address**, a subset of Virtual Address defined as describing a physical location to which deliveries may be made for a particular Party (typically an organization or person), and/or at which the Party may typically be located or reached. A home address is an example of a Physical Address.

Whether the distinction between Virtual and Physical Addresses is (or may become) important to a particular Business needs to be determined deliberately to avoid introducing any assumptions into the Company's I/T systems which might become difficult to compensate for at a later stage of the company's evolution. The distinction isn't often made at the level of data definitions, since most businesses rely on humans to make such judgments as they process orders for shipping for example. Increasing use of "self-serve" ordering, however, particularly from foreign countries, should cause such distinctions to at least be considered when designing or evaluating a system.

▶ **Device Contact Number**, a grouping of data (usually numeric characters) entered in sequence, and used to establish electronic communications between two or more Parties, their locations, or their electronic devices. The most common example of such an element would be a **Telephone Number**. In normal use, such numbers might need to be combined with addi-

---

332 At the risk of being repetitious, this is not intended primarily as a design tutorial, but rather to provide enough "straw man" examples and information to expose readers to some of the issues that must be considered when designing database schemas that will be appropriate for logical and extensible support of Business activities.

tional numeric characters to indicate certain exception processing, such as specific routing instructions (e.g. to connect to a "foreign" telephone system), billing information, etc., but those are independent attributes.

▼ **to a Location**: examples would include:

… any telephone numbers for an Office or Corporation, a Machine (e.g. fax, modem etc.), a Residence (potentially associated with multiple persons).

… telephone numbers for Alarm systems (1-way, not 2-way), whether land-line or cellular.

… telephone numbers used to connect to other devices (1-way as well as 2-way), whether land-line or cellular. Examples would be wireless Hot Spots (fixed or location independent), household cellular devices linking various wired handset instruments in a household to the telephone infrastructure, etc.

… IP Addresses or MAC Addresses used to route any data communications to a specific device, particularly where the device is associated with some Party.

▼ **to a Person**: examples include telephone numbers for Cellular Phones that are Party-specific, but location independent (typically for an individual person).

► **Broadcast**

▼ **One Way**

Television and Radio channels (always by a Party – usually by a Company).

URLs (Web pages, Podcasts, Blogs & such; done by any subclass of Party).

Media advertising of various other types, e.g. billboards, and other signage, which occur in far too many forms and locations to consider listing.

▼ **Two Way**

Interactive Web Pages, e.g. customer service sites, and the like

The preceding is, of course, not a complete listing of contact mechanisms, nor is it likely to perfectly match the needs of any specific business, and it is the analysis team's responsibility to identify as many potential contact mechanisms as possible while evaluating a database design for some particular business. And, of course, the purpose of such contact mechanisms as well as the technologies used for these mechanisms need to be considered in light of a particular company's needs. Further, the above list doesn't consider the content of messages to such contacts at all, which might range from ad hoc voice or text communications to formal publications, all of which may be relevant to a specific company.

Some Issues of Concern

In far too many business databases, contact mechanisms are handled inadequately, inconsistently, and in a manner guaranteed to promote redundancy in both data structures and application code.

Remember, Redundancy in an operational business database is never good.

To illustrate this claim of inadequacy by a simple example, consider a **single element** of a **single contact mechanism**: the postal code portion of a mailing address. In a typical database, an address group is included in multiple tables, and sadly, often more than once in a single table.[333] Examples might include:

▼ A Vendor Table (probably at least one instance, and possibly more)[334]

▼ A Customer Table (probably at least one instance, and possibly more)

▼ An Employee Table (probably at least one instance)

▼ An Order Table[335] (at least one instance)

▼ An Order Line Item Table (often at least one instance)

▼ Tables related to Service Organizations (e.g. Banking, Janitorial and such)

---

333 The infamous First Normal Form violation which, as stated earlier, is simply a symptom of a more serious problem. See the discussion of this in "Particularly Egregious Beliefs: Normal Forms" on page 31, "Unintended Business Rules enforced by CWX's Customer Table" on page 52, and various other locations.

334 See, for instance, the CWX Vendor Table on page 53.

335 And, as pointed out earlier, this sort of "Address" is not actually the same as the others in this list and is therefore not usually redundant. Reread "Recognizing Purpose in Naming – Beyond Synonyms" on page 75 for a discussion of why this is so.

Scope of this Chapter

We will generally limit this chapter to the handling of mailing addresses, but the principles and approaches used to support other contact mechanisms such as telephone numbers are much the same. To gauge the importance of Contact Mechanisms to your particular business, and the potential for data inconsistency, the following exercises are strongly recommended:

Homework Assignment

Do some Triage on the particular database(s) for which you have responsibility.

► How many examples or instances of Address structures are present in your database schema? (Hint: Sort your database catalog by column name[336])

► How many unique versions of Address structures are there in your schema? Consider any differences in the data types and sizes used, and so forth.

► How many elements in your Address schemas are constrained[337] in some fashion? Or, since we are mostly concerned in this example (mailing addresses) with postal codes, how many (or what percentage) of the postal code elements in your database are constrained?

  ▼ Of these, how many are constrained by value, i.e. from a domain table of valid postal code values?

  ▼ Of these, how many are constrained, albeit to a somewhat lesser degree) by pattern, i.e. a defined format (such as "nnnnn" or an equivalent regular expression)?

  ▼ How many of these are constrained only by external applications, and to what extent? And how many duplications of such code exist in your systems?

  ▼ How many of your postal code elements are restrained only by length?

---

336 In Oracle, a query similar to "SELECT column_name, table_name FROM all_tab_columns WHERE owner = '*Whatever*' ORDER BY column_name, table_name ; " should help. Of course, if your company's column naming isn't consistent, you will need to be inventive.

337 Review the chapter "Handling Constraints" to recall the wide variety of methods and locations used when applying constraints.

► How many of the Address structures in your schema can easily handle at least one foreign address? (And, no, free-form text fields don't qualify! For example, while "60606" represents a section of Chicago, Illinois in the United States, "N6A-4L6" represents a section of London, Ontario in Canada.)

► How many of the Address structures in your schema can easily handle foreign addresses *while still retaining some level of integrity constraints?*

► Identifying which addresses in your database are physical addresses (i.e. ones that you can visit), and which are logical (e.g. postal boxes at a central location) can be important for companies that utilize non-governmental carriers for delivery, most of whom will not deliver to such boxes. Is such a distinction relevant to your Business, and can you easily segregate the types?

► Finally, how many independent segments of application code handle input and editing of each of the address instances you have identified?

From a corporate perspective, of course, the situation you have quantified above is compounded quite significantly if there are multiple databases containing corporate business data. Then consider that, in this exercise, you have reviewed only the handling of postal codes! Managers, take note, and ask questions!

Given that one primary responsibility of I/T is the maintenance and protection of the company's corporate data assets, it is fairly clear what the answers to the above questions *should be*, but likely that the answers may be embarrassing.

Extra Credit Homework Assignment

Ask yourself the same or equivalent questions about each type of contact mechanism that is stored in any of your database tables, particularly those whose structures and rules vary according to geopolitical considerations. In addition to the considerable variation in postal code formats already mentioned, the familiar "3+3+4" telephone number format (area code, exchange, and terminal or instrument number), for instance, is only valid for participants in the North American Numbering Plan Administration (known as NANPA).

Review the data in the columns identified above for hints to fundamental relational database design defects. In a white paper on data quality for instance, one author[338] presented examples of how inconsistently formatted data can contribute to unintentional introduction of redundancy into a database (and how, of course, the product he was promoting could assist in locating and correcting these obvious design deficiencies).

The author's example is shown to the right. The first two entries are clearly the same telephone number, and the last two less obviously so, but if your system can't easily recognize that, you clearly have data quality problems.

Telephone
301-754-6350
(301) 754-6350
301.753.6350
1-866-BIZRULE
866 249-7853

Furthermore, if you have been paying attention, you will have realized that the author's example, although not at all unusual in many business databases, is not a relational table, since it includes two pieces of information in a single data element (the data and the formatting).[339] Database (and application) designs that permit such unstructured entries should simply be unacceptable to contemporary businesses. Printing and displaying data such as this in any format desired is a trivial exercise, and an example of one mechanism for doing that will be shown later in the chapter.

Approaching a Solution

Based on the number of occurrences of such contact structures in a typical database, the amount of redundancy is usually overwhelming, and it can be (and often is) argued that going beyond primitive mechanisms in one location to protect the data when there are other parallel paths into the database from unprotected sources is a waste of time, effort and money. While true, it represents a design failure, and the effects on the integrity of business data are the same.

---

338 Loshin [1]; see page 383 for information.

339 In the early days of personal modems, inconsistent storage of telephone number data forced manufacturers to build in filters that removed the extraneous formatting characters. Use caution when determining what constitutes arbitrary formatting, however. The decimal point separators used in an IP Address, for example, are part of the actual data value, and not merely an aid for human interpretation as the parentheses around an area code are.

In most cases, therefore, triage will quickly expose the fact that only minimal effort was put into handling of contact mechanisms, particularly in cases where they are incorporated as scattered attributes in many disparate tables.

This situation can be corrected, however. As hinted in "A Corporate Merger – Part 1," logical analysis tells us that, since most Contact Mechanisms are common to all subclasses of **Party**, they should therefore be implemented as Attributes of **Party**. Because Contact Mechanisms are quite clearly independent entities, and do not serve to describe or qualify any of the Parties, each class should be modeled as a single entity with an appropriate relationship[340] to **Party**.

Obviously, there will be several key business advantages in relocating all such references as entities that are accessed using the primary key for Party (which, if your design is logically correct, will be identical to that of any Party subclass).

▶ Data Redundancy will be significantly reduced.

▶ Data Consistency will be significantly improved.

▶ With similar contact mechanisms are isolated in one location, devoting more effort to improving constraints for telephone numbers, postal codes, and the like can be justified. Such enhancements also allow constraints to be applied in the future based on the rules of differing geopolitical entities – permitting new business opportunities to be accommodated more easily.

Common Database Support for a Solution

In order to handle most types of Contact Mechanisms that will be used in Business transactions, a number of domains will need to be specified to support a generalized and extensible solution. Many of these domains, in turn, will vary by Country. Regardless of whether your Company is contemplating doing business with Parties in other countries, a **Country** entity set should be specified to contain such information even if it is only populated initially with data related to the United States. In this manner, extending the Business systems to support such activity in other countries will be made much more straightforward if and when

---

340 And, as we shall see, these can be direct or indirect relationships depending on the circumstances of your business and how rigorously you feel the need to enforce integrity.

that time comes. We'll cover some basic supporting domains before introducing the Country entity and progressing to more detailed descriptions of approaches for handling specific contact mechanisms.

Currency – A Sample Supporting Domain Table

If there is any expectation that your Business will ever deal with anything but United States Currency, a reference table should be available that contains, as a minimum, a relevant selection of common reference data as

CURRENCY		Sample Data	
ID_ISO_A3	pk, c3	USD	GBP
Name_English	c	U.S. Dollar	Pound Sterling
Post_Decimal_Digits	int	2	2
Symbol	c	$	£

Figure 18-1

specified by the International Standards Organization. In the case of Currency, the relevant specification is ISO 4217. A wealth of information is available on this specification, so it will not be discussed at any length in this book.

No attempt should be made to use this reference table as a repository of monetary exchange rates, however, since these are far too volatile for such a design.

Language – A Sample Supporting Domain Table

Even for companies that do business internationally, it isn't often necessary that the system needs a reference to languages, but for the sake of the examples that follow, we will assume that such data is utilized.

LANGUAGE		Sample Data	
ID_ISO_A3	pk, c3	ENG	THA
ID_ISO_A2	ak, c2	EN	TH
Name_English	c	English	Thai
Name_French	c	anglaise	thaï
Name_Native	c	English	ä·Â
. . . et cetera			

Figure 18-2

The international standard for language definitions is ISO 639-2, a three-character code. The optional two-character code (ISO 639-1) is used less often and, in fact, two-character codes for several languages are not defined. Since however – inexplicably – these two-character codes are specified for use in several XML "standards," it may be advisable to include them.

You'll note that there are columns for both Name_English and Name_French which might initially appear (now that you're more sensitive to these issues) as the same sort of normal form violation as having **Home_Phone** and **Work_Phone** in a single table. The difference is that, in many International Standards, there is a requirement that descriptions in these two specific languages be provided. Whether storing both is of any benefit to your organization needs to be determined, of course. Since the amount of data is small, and the effort required to remove it is often non-trivial, it is included in the following examples.

Country – A Sample Domain Table

The International Standard for Country Codes is ISO 3166 and, like most ISO standards, information and the standardized elements required to meet that standard are readily available, and so will not be provided here.

An example of one possible general purpose table definition follows. As shown here, it contains various elements referencing several different ISO standards as well as a sampling of other attributes which may or may not be of interest to any specific business; these are simply intended to illustrate the types of data that might be stored in such a table.

COUNTRY		Description of Attribute
ID_ISO_A3	pk, c3	ISO 3166-n three character Country code – arbitrarily set as Primary Key
ID_ISO_A2	ak, c2	ISO 3166-n two character Country code – alternate key
ID_ISO_Numeric	ak, c3	ISO 3166-n three character numeric Country code – alternate key
Name_Native		Name of the Country in the language and character set of that Country
Name_English	unique, c	Name of the Country in English (same data as above in a U.S. system)
Name_French	unique, c	Name of the Country in French
Name_Alternate	c	Obsolete but still recognized Country Name (e.g. "Burma" vice "Myanmar")
Admin_Level_1_Label	c	Top Level Government Admin Entity; for example "State" in the U.S.
Admin_Level_1_Standard	c	Standard from which codes in the level 1 entity are derived (e.g. "FIPS 5.2")
Currency	fk	ISO 4217 3 character currency code; foreign key to Currency table.
Currency_ISO_A3_Alternate	fk	Optional ISO code for a secondary currency recognized by this Country.
Language_ISO_A3	fk	ISO 639-2 three character code for the official language of this Country.
Language_ISO_A3_Alternate	fk	ISO 639-2 three character code for a secondary official language
National_ID_Label	c25	In the United States, for instance, this would be "Social Security Number."
National_ID_Data_Mask	c25	Data format of this Country's National ID Number; e.g. "nnn-nn-nnnn"
Postal_Code_Label	c	Term used for the Postal Code in this Country; e.g. "Zip Code" in the U.S.
Postal_Code_Data_Mask	c	Data format of Postal Code in this Country; e.g. "nnnnnnnnn" in the U.S.[341]

COUNTRY		Description of Attribute
Postal_Code_Display_Mask	c	Display format of Postal Code in this Country; e.g. "nnnnn-nnnn" in the U.S.
Postal_Level_1_Label	c	Top Level Postal Admin Entity; for example "State" in the U.S.
Telephone_Country_Code	nc	Code used to dial into this Country's telephone system.
Telephone_Data_Mask	c	Data format of phone number in this area; e.g. "nnnnnnnnnn" in N. America
Telephone_Display_Mask	c	Default display format of phone number in this area; e.g. "(nnn) nnn-nnnn"

Note that the choice of ID_ISO_A3 as the primary key is arbitrary. Depending on the business being evaluated, it is certainly possible that not all these data elements will be required. Conversely, additional columns may be used to store (for example) tax code as well as other financial and legal references. Comments on some sample entries are discussed below:

Country: Various "Name" Attributes

Examples include Name_Native, Name_English, and so forth. Many are either explained by the descriptions given in the figure above or are self-explanatory.

Country: Various "Label" Attributes

In our U.S.-centric systems, we store data elements that, while common to most countries, are known by names that are unique to our country – such as "Social Security Number" and "Zip Code."[342] Even in other English-speaking countries, these may likely be

> ### Naming, Yet Again
>
> By now, you've noticed quite a number of columns labeled xxxx_ISO_A3 or similar.
>
> It might seem tempting to call the Country table ISO_3166, or to at least name its primary key ID_ISO_3166_A3. Similarly we might be tempted to call the Currency Table ISO_4217.
>
> This wouldn't be in keeping with fundamental principles of database design, however, for two key reasons: 1) Because they are obscure names to most people and 2) because they are subject to change in the future should new standards be agreed upon. Don't do this!

unfamiliar terms. The Country table provides a common location to store the appropriate localized terms. These can easily be accessed for dynamic, country-sensitive application screen display labels as well as reports generated from the database.

---

341 Note that these are quite simplified representations of "masks." A discussion of different approaches for handling these will be presented later in this chapter.

342 Think about it. Translate "Zip" into Greek, for instance. Many U.S. Residents are unaware that ZIP is an acronym, and even fewer know that it means "Zone Improvement Program."

A few "label" columns, however, such as Admin _Level_1_Label[343] (in an actual implementation there might be several such numbered but otherwise identically named columns) and Postal_Level_1_Label require further explanation. In an extensible system capable of smoothly handling business information for multiple countries, it is no longer appropriate to assume that the highest level geopolitical entity (i.e. Administrative_Level_1) is called "State." In Canada, for instance, the corresponding level is called "Province." If, rather than using the term "State" throughout our data and application portfolios (e.g. on screens, in reports, and so forth), we make the label we use dependent on the country with which we are currently dealing, the system will, at first blush, seem more complex, but support for any number of other countries can be added quite smoothly.

For the U.S., the values for Admin_Level_1_Label and Postal_Level_1_Label will be the same, since both are "State." But remember that "Recognizing Purpose in Naming – Beyond Synonyms" on page 75 pointed out that identical attribute **values** do not imply that the attributes themselves are the same – and here they aren't. Consider the values that Admin_Level_2_Label and Postal_Level_2_Label (if these are used) will take. For most States in the U.S., the second level entity is known as "County,"[344] whereas the Postal Service doesn't consider "County" at all, considering "City" to be its second level element of interest.

In this and the previous section, we've distinguished between the use of the _Name and _Label suffixes, but this is simply for convenience. What they are called, or whether they are given different nomenclatures at all, depends on your particular company's needs. What is important to extensibility is that a database design use appropriate (commonly understood) generic terms such as Postal_Code or similar (for example) for its attributes, and obtain the country-specific term (e.g. "Zip Code" for the United States) from the Country table.

---

343 Such names as Admin_Level_1 and so forth may appear to be classic normal form violations like the Phone_1, Phone_2 examples so often given, but they're not. I'll leave it for you to figure out what the difference is.

344 This is a simplification, of course, since Louisiana (to use one example) calls its second administrative level "Parish." A scheme that can easily handle such differences is outlined in more detail later in this chapter.

Country: Data Validation Masks

We can use the Data Mask `'^([0-9]{5})([0-9]{4}|)$'` to validate U.S. Zip Codes (see page 192), but that just won't do for Canadian Postal Codes, which need a validation pattern of `'^([A-Z][0-9][A-Z])([0-9][A-Z][0-9])$'`.[345]

For both the United States and Canada, however, the validation mask for telephone numbers would be `'^([0-9]{0,3})([0-9]{3})([0-9]{4})$'`, since each country conforms to the North American Numbering Plan Administration.

Using Oracle's regular expression syntax as an example, and assuming the format masks given above for U.S. and Canadian postal codes, we can validate any proposed input with code similar to the following:

```
SELECT InputPostalCode INTO ValidatedPostCode FROM …
  WHERE REGEXP_LIKE(InputPostalCode, SelectedValidationMask, 'i');
```

In the appendix, a sample Validate_Postal_Code function is shown that is used in a trigger that is fired before any insert or update. See page 410.

Country: Data Display Masks

In the "Extra Credit Homework Assignment" on page 316, we attempted to show the reasons for eliminating formatting from data columns and applying formatting only as required. Telephone numbers can be formatted with the **Country** table's **Telephone_Display_Mask** (e.g. `'(\1) \2-\3'`), but applications have the flexibility to use another display mask (e.g. `'\1.\2.\3'`) if a different "look" needs to be achieved. Sample outputs (using Oracle's **REGEXP_REPLACE** function) of these two masks using the non-formatted number 1234567890 are:

```
SELECT REGEXP_REPLACE ('1234567890',ValidationMask,FormatMask)FROM …
```

The first mask (`'(\1) \2-\3'`) displays the output "(123) 456-7890," while the second (`'\1.\2.\3'`) gives "123.456.7890."

A significant objective of implementing both Data Validation Masks and Data Display Masks, of course, is the ability to share these across the database itself

---

345 All regular expression samples are as implemented by Oracle's ill-named RDBMS product.

and various applications,[346] since this gives us a desirable approach to achieving enterprise consistency. Since Regular Expressions are "standardized" by POSIX, this might appear to be quite straightforward to accomplish, but the self-preservation strategies we've become accustomed to from our suppliers result in small but significant differences in their implementations. It is sometimes a better strategy, therefore, to simply "roll your own" routines that can be shared.[347]

Country: Various Hierarchy Attributes

The **Country** table provides us with the root of some hierarchies to be modeled for each country. In the earlier example, the column **Admin_Level_1_Label**, as well as the similar **Postal_Level_1_Label** clearly imply that some other levels are contemplated. As shown to the right, the United States, for instance, has an administrative hierarchy consisting of

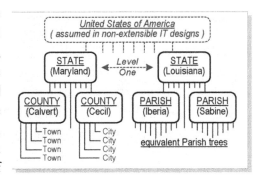

sixty[348] States at the first (top) level; each of these States is then subdivided administratively into a various number of Counties, and so forth.

While the specific hierarchies in this figure may not always be of interest to any particular business, similar examples abound in the "real world," so an examination of some approaches to the logical management of such hierarchies seems both appropriate and beneficial.

Of course, even in this limited example, the hierarchies are anything but "clean" or obvious. In geopolitical entities, any term such as "State," by the way, must be interpreted as "State or State equivalent"[349] since it could just as easily refer to

---

346 See "Sharing Pattern-based Constraints – Possibly Acceptable" on page 192.

347 This isn't as odd a recommendation as it might seem. Regular Expressions are far more powerful than what is typically required by the uses described here. A fairly simple subset that meets the common needs of your system isn't all that difficult to cobble together.

348 Fifty States and ten "State-equivalents," such as the District of Columbia, Puerto Rico, etc.

349 ...and, in many of the national and international standards created for defining such entities,

an independent city (such as Washington, D.C.) that isn't associated with any particular State. It could also be an equivalent level Territory or Possession, such as Puerto Rico.

It can be seen that the names given to the various second-level are also inconsistent. The second-level administrative entity for most States is "County," but for some States such as Louisiana as we've seen, it is the county-equivalent "Parish."

When not handled on a system-wide basis, such inconsistencies are often cited as reasons for avoiding any attempt at domain control, but the problem surrenders easily to a logical data model that will be illustrated below. The additional and very significant benefit is that the approaches shown permit

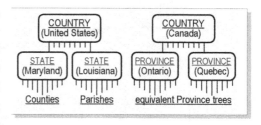

fairly easy accommodation of any number of additional countries by simply inserting the appropriate data as suggested in the figure to the above right.

This book will deal only with Administrative and Postal hierarchies, and will do so in what is **deliberately** an inconsistent manner – intended to demonstrate that there is a variety of modeling solutions; as always, analysts and designers must choose the methods that are most appropriate for any specific business.

Earlier in this chapter, various examples of the type of data that might be retained for a Country table were listed. For a second level entity, such as State in the United States or Province in Canada, examples might include:

► Patterns for State-issued Driver's Licenses, to be used for validation of customer-supplied data that may be relevant for credit checks. For most second-level administrative entities – whether in the United States or elsewhere – such numbers follow a very specific formatting.[350]

---

the term "or equivalent" appears quite commonly.

350 Most U.S. and many foreign drivers' license numbers contain more information than is generally recognized, including last and first names, year and often date of birth, as well as gender. This is why some highway patrolmen seem like they're psychic in their ability to immediately recognize that something is fishy with the license they've been handed.

> ► Applicable Time Zones, as well as use of Daylight Savings Time, are determined for the most part by State or state-equivalent. The caveat "for the most part," of course, indicates that a logical (and data-driven[351]) mechanism for handling exceptions will be necessary, but we'll defer that until a discussion of the next level in the administrative hierarchy.

For now, we'll jump directly to construction, and use some simplified entity-relationship diagrams to explain how hierarchies are implemented in practice.

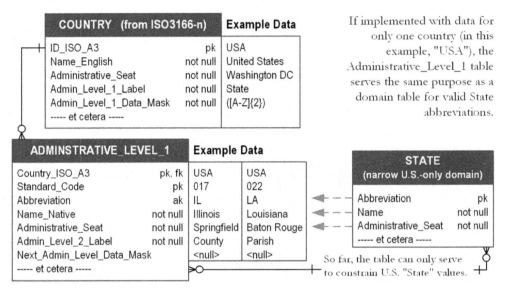

COUNTRY (from ISO3166-n)		Example Data
ID_ISO_A3	pk	USA
Name_English	not null	United States
Administrative_Seat	not null	Washington DC
Admin_Level_1_Label	not null	State
Admin_Level_1_Data_Mask	not null	([A-Z]{2})
----- et cetera -----		

If implemented with data for only one country (in this example, "USA"), the Administrative_Level_1 table serves the same purpose as a domain table for valid State abbreviations.

ADMINSTRATIVE_LEVEL_1		Example Data	
Country_ISO_A3	pk, fk	USA	USA
Standard_Code	pk	017	022
Abbreviation	ak	IL	LA
Name_Native	not null	Illinois	Louisiana
Administrative_Seat	not null	Springfield	Baton Rouge
Admin_Level_2_Label	not null	County	Parish
Next_Admin_Level_Data_Mask		<null>	<null>
----- et cetera -----			

STATE (narrow U.S.-only domain)	
Abbreviation	pk
Name	not null
Administrative_Seat	not null
----- et cetera -----	

So far, the table can only serve to constrain U.S. "State" values.

A prime objective of logical design in this case is to replace a typical **State** table (shown on the lower right of the diagram above) with a more flexible and extensible structure. As explained earlier, this is accomplished by explicitly recognizing that States are associated with and specific to the United States. It can be seen that although the data in the more general **Administrative_Level_1** table is identical to that of the original State table, its primary key has been extended to include the country attribute. Indeed, if the new table contains only values re-

---

351 Because, as demonstrated in "Playing with Trucks – Part 1," we should avoid having procedural code that is intended to determine data definitions. A mechanism to support "Using Default Values and Exception Handling" will be presented on page 328.

lated to the United States, existing queries against the database might well continue to function identically except for the change in the table name.

As was done with the Country table, it is important to give careful consideration to utilizing standardized keys wherever possible to populate any geopolitical data stores. The Administrative_Level_1 table above shows examples of the familiar two-character Federal Information Processing Standard Codes for States (e.g. "IL" and "LA") but in most circumstances, there are multiple "standards" to choose from. In addition to the unique two character abbreviations, the relevant FIPS 5-2 standard, for example, also specifies two-digit numeric codes.

Although not illustrated here, it is often a good practice to record the standards used as primary keys. In the Country table above, for instance, we might have added a column for Admin_Level_1_Standard which, for the USA entry, would have the value FIPS 5-2. Where such tables are utilized, it is often useful to list any alternate keys specified by the standard. For this example, the Standard_Code could be augmented by an Alternate_Standard_Code column.[352]

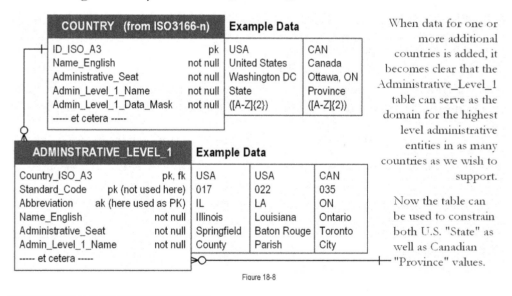

When data for one or more additional countries is added, it becomes clear that the Administrative_Level_1 table can serve as the domain for the highest level administrative entities in as many countries as we wish to support.

Now the table can be used to constrain both U.S. "State" as well as Canadian "Province" values.

Figure 18-8

---

352 Null values would be permitted for this additional column, of course, since it may not be meaningful for every country's top-level entities. If the particular DBMS permitted, the column would also be constrained as Unique to permit its use as an alternate key.

The United States Federal Information Processing Standard (FIPS) specifies codes for several geopolitical or administrative layers. In addition to the FIPS 5-2 standard for States (and State equivalents) mentioned above, the FIPS 6-4 standard uniquely identifies Counties and County equivalents with a three digit number. Because the County codes are unique within a given State, the 2-digit FIPS State code is usually prepended to form a complete FIPS County code.

FIPS Codes for the various geopolitical hierarchies in the United States are readily available. Equivalent domains for other countries are available from a variety of sources. Obviously most Countries have their own specifications, but several United States government entities such as the State Department and Central Intelligence Agency make their own identification data readily available. In addition, agencies of the United Nations (particularly the International Standards Organization, whose identifiers we used as Country codes), publish a variety of identifiers. As with most implementation issues, the choices of which identifiers to use as primary keys must be made to support the known and expected needs of your particular business.[353] Except in extremely rare instances, your business will not be served well by inventing your own codes or keys.

In the illustration on the following page, we show how a few more administrative levels can be handled in a similar fashion. While this scheme can, of course, be extended, it would require some very specific business needs to justify the effort needed to carry it even to the Level_3 shown in the next diagram.

Using Default Values and Exception Handling

We mentioned when discussing "various hierarchy attributes" earlier in this chapter that time zones in the United States are determined "for the most part" by State or State-equivalent.

Illinois, for instance, is in the Central Time Zone while its neighbor Indiana is in the Eastern Time Zone. For obvious reasons, however, Indiana Counties such as Lake, Porter, and others that are part of the greater Chicago metropolitan area follow the Illinois time zone rather than that of their home state.

---

353 Alternate Codes can also be stored and identified as alternate keys as well.

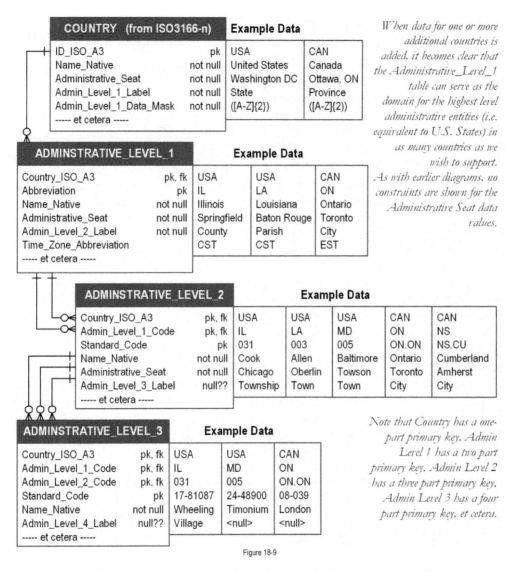

When data for one or more additional countries is added, it becomes clear that the Administrative_Level_1 table can serve as the domain for the highest level administrative entities (i.e. equivalent to U.S. States) in as many countries as we wish to support. As with earlier diagrams, no constraints are shown for the Administrative Seat data values.

Note that Country has a one-part primary key, Admin Level 1 has a two part primary key, Admin Level 2 has a three part primary key, Admin Level 3 has a four part primary key, et cetera.

Figure 18-9

One way of handling "exceptions" such as this is to place a **Time_Zone** attribute[354] in both first and second level entities (State and County).

354 Whether this is stored as a single attribute with an offset from Universal Coordinated Time (known as Greenwich Mean Time in the past, e.g. "-6" for Illinois' Central Time Zone and

In the higher level (in this case level 1 – States or State-equivalents) table, the **Time_Zone** column is specified as NOT NULL. The lower level (in this case level 2 – equivalent to Counties or County-equivalents) is permitted to be null.

ADMIN_LEVEL_1		Sample Data	
Country_Code	pk, fk	USA	USA
Abbreviation	pk	**IL**	**IN**
Time_Zone_Abb	**not null**	CST	EST

Figure 18-10

In this example, the value in what is the "State" table is considered the default, and any NOT NULL value in the "County" table is considered as an exception. A query to determine the time zones for Counties in Indiana would then be:

ADMIN_LEVEL_2		Sample Data		
Country_Code	pk, fk	USA	USA	USA
Abbreviation	pk, fk	IL	IN	IN
Name	pk	**Cook**	**Grant**	**Porter**
Time_Zone_Abb	**nullable**	<null>	<null>	CST

Figure 18=11

```
SELECT t1.Abbreviation
     , NVL(t2.Time_Zone_Abbrev,t1.Time_Zone_Abbrev) [355]
  FROM Admin_Level_1 t1, Admin_Level_2 t2
 WHERE t1.Country_Code = t2.Country_Code
   AND t2.Country_Code = 'USA'
   AND t1.Abbreviation = t2.Abbreviation
   AND t2.Abbreviation = 'IN'
 ORDER BY t1.Abbreviation, t2.Name ;
```

The result is that the time zone for Porter County, although it is in Indiana and specified as "EST" by the Admin_Level_1 table, will be "overridden" by the **not null** value "CST" in the Admin_Level_2 table. Although this technique can be viewed as somewhat procedural, it is data-driven – meaning its behavior can be updated very quickly. It is far faster than procedural code executed outside the database and, because it is centrally located, it promotes consistent system behavior – removing one more thing for each application to handle independently.

"-5" for Indiana's), or as the abbreviation CST, is not relevant here. Of course, if it is desirable to store multiple attributes such as the two mentioned, a "Time Zone" domain table should be used as a constraint. Fair Warning: "Time_Zone" and some variants are reserved words in many RDBMS products, so choose your naming carefully!

355 The Oracle-specific NVL function, can be read as an IF statement: IF the Time_Zone_Abbreviation in the Admin_Level_2 table is not null, return it; otherwise return the value (the default value) of the Time_Zone_Abbreviation in the Admin_Level_1 table. Similar functions in other RDBMS products include ISNULL, IFNULL, and COALESCE.

One Possible Implementation of Address Management

An important example of a contact mechanism is the address. The Entity-Relationship Diagram below provides a sample method of address handling based on the previous discussions. An address life cycle description and a simplified schema, albeit with less support for integrity, is provided later.

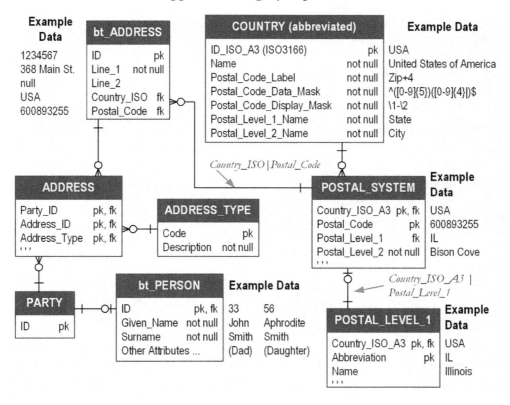

Key Tables in this sample Address Schema

The bt_Address table contains actual address data, and would typically use an auto-incrementing system key, available in most modern RDBMS products. The Address table serves as a cross-reference listing of Parties, Addresses, and Address Types. Key supporting tables include Country, described earlier, as well as tables needed to define the Postal Systems of any supported Countries.

The Postal_System table contains the domain of postal codes for each country supported by the database. The Postal_Code_Data_Mask, obtained from the Country table above is, in this example, used to validate the 600893255 entry; the Postal_Code_Display_Mask, also from the Country table, is used to format the Postal Code as "60089-3255."

POSTAL_SYSTEM		Sample Data
Country_Code	pk, fk	USA
Postal_Code	pk	600893255
Postal_Level_1	fk	IL
Postal_Level_2	fk	Bison Cove
Postal_Level_3		<null>
Postal_Level_4		<null>

Figure 18-13

It should be pointed out that, for many countries, the Postal_Level_1 domain will be identical to the Administrative_Level_1 domain – in this example, the abbreviation "IL" is used for both. These are treated as separate domains, however, since there is no guarantee that they will remain identical, and they are not identical in all countries. Note also that, unlike the approach taken with Administrative Levels, the Postal Level hierarchy has been collapsed, with all the levels of the hierarchy contained as attributes of a single entity. Whether and how much to collapse such hierarchies, and under what circumstances, will be dependent on the needs of a particular business.

Unlike typical address structures in non-relational tables, bt_Address contains no columns equivalent to "City," "State," or "Zip Code." Rather, this data is obtained by using a combination of Country_ISO and Postal_Code as a foreign key to the Postal_System table to obtain the values for Postal_Level_1 ("IL") and Postal_Level_2 ("Bison Cove"). In combination with Country_ISO_A3, Postal_System.Postal_Level_1 has been constrained in turn by the corresponding values in the Postal_Level_1 table. As mentioned earlier, if the only data contained in the Postal_Level_1 table is for United States values, the table is equivalent to a domain of State or State-equivalent values.

The objective of the design is that an address data line (e.g. bt_Address.Line_1) such as "368 Main St." exists only once. For many, this would appear to be extremely difficult to guarantee, since such values are often entered with no pretense at consistency. It would seem on the surface that someone entering the non-abbreviated string "368 Main Street" would immediately cause difficulties by introducing a duplicate (albeit not-exactly-matching) address. Although techniques for determining if a matching address already exists in the database are beyond the scope of this discussion, the following general guidelines will point the way:

► On entry of data, as much standardization should be applied as possible. This includes:

  ▼ Force a hierarchical order of lines in whichever direction is convenient for a particular country. For example, Country, Postal Code, Street Number, Type and Direction, Apartment or Office Number, specific mail stop, or the reverse.

  ▼ Use standardized abbreviations for street types and directionality according to whatever postal guidelines are applicable for a specific country. For example, the US Postal Service prefers "APT" for "Apartment," "BLVD" for "Boulevard," etc.[356]

► On matching, eliminate matches by proceeding from the most general portions of the address structure to the specific.

  ▼ For instance, if the countries don't match, there is no need to check for more specific matches.

  ▼ If postal codes don't match, there is no need to continue. When this and other address elements are matched, consider partial matches. For example, "62435-8442" should be considered a potential match for the simpler value "62435."

Address Life Cycle – Using the Proposed Schema

Assume that we have a Customer named John Smith who, along with his wife Venus and their daughter Aphrodite, lives at 368 Main Street. The Address is present in the bt_Address[357] table, and there is a connection between John and this Address recorded in the three-way Address intersection table. This is illus-

---

356 See the USPS web site https://www.usps.com/send/official-abbreviations.htm; other countries have similar tables of abbreviations available as web sites or printed documentation. Complete instructions for standardized address formatting for the United States is provided in USPS Publication 28, available in print or as a downloadable pdf.

357 As with the examples in "Proper Subsets as Views" beginning on page 132, the "bt" stands for "Base Table." Your data structures should follow some convention similar to this in order to promote some understanding of what the structures represent.

trated in the previous Entity Relationship Diagram. Although sample data is not shown on this diagram, there would for this example be rows containing the values "33, 1234567, HA" and "56, 1234567, HA", indicating that both John Smith and his daughter Aphrodite are living at 368 Main Street.

Let us further assume that John notifies our business that he is retiring and will be moving to a smaller home at 244 Main Street. Furthermore, he and Venus are soon to become "empty-nesters," since Aphrodite, their last of their three children remaining at home, has announced that she is to be married shortly. Aphrodite, who is also one of our customers, and her fiance Agamemnon McCarthy, are planning to purchase a home of their own.

Both Addresses typically exist before, during, and after John and his family move !!

244

368

Main Street

When using a typical application-centric and non-relational table such as that illustrated to the right[358], we're quite used to describing the action we need to perform as "change John's address from '368 Main Street' to '244 Main Street'." This, unfortunately, is yet another example of how the colloquial use of English leads us astray.

CUSTOMER
ID
Name
Street_1
City
State
Zip_Code

In point of fact (i.e. "in the real world"), since the Address is actually itself an independent entity – whether we are comfortable treating it as such[359] or not – we need to recognize that the address isn't what is

---

358 Hopefully by now you are quite chagrined at ever having considered such a table design.

359 … and traditionally, I/T has never been particularly comfortable with logic …

changing at all. In all but the most unusual circumstances, '368 Main Street' will remain in existence without any changes after John and Venus move.[360]

What actually happens is that we are now simply associating John with a different Address, and we need to reflect this association in our database – recognizing, of course, that we may need to add the new Address to the bt_Address table if it is not already there.

What we refer to as "changing an address," then, is not solely a declarative action, since it is dependent on both BUSINESS RULES and DATA RULES. As with the CREATE and DELETE actions described in "Routine Usage of Views" on page 137, what we call an "address change" requires a procedural component rather than a data definition component.

> Real Address Changes
>
> Notwithstanding these discussions, street addresses may in fact actually change. In 1887, for example, after many years of chaotic growth, and recognizing the need to rationalize arbitrary addresses in order to make city services (e.g. police and fire) more responsive, the City of Baltimore undertook a comprehensive renumbering of all buildings. What had previously been 60 Etting Street, for example, became 1228 Etting Street. In 1887, however, their databases consisted of cards that were renumbered and resorted by hand – reportedly with no IT involvement!.

Whether the Address '368 Main Street' is actually removed from the database as part of what we colloquially refer to as "John's address change" is quite dependent on a number of factors, and includes both DATA RULES and BUSINESS RULES:

► **Data Rule**: of course, if there is some other Party-to-Address connection that refers to the '368 Main Street' residence, removal of the Address from the bt_Address table will be prohibited by the database constraints, as it should be. If, for example, we attempt to delete "368 Main St." from the bt_Address table in conjunction with our customer John Smith's "move," this will fail because another entry in the Address table (that of John's daughter Aphrodite) remains.

► **Business Rule**: whether to remove an unreferenced Address from bt_Address is obviously a Business decision that depends on a variety of factors: if the service provided to John was in some way related to the fact that he lived in a home, and the marketing department wishes to pursue and offer similar services to whomever the new resident is (e.g. by sending promo-

---

360 Whether we as a business care that it remains in existence or not doesn't alter this fact.

tional material to "occupant"), it might be appropriate to retain the data. Depending on the type of service, your particular company might wish to add other data to the **bt_Address** table indicating that your service was previously installed,[361] so special promotions might be offered to new residents.

BUSINESS RULES, of course, must be implemented procedurally, although certainly in a common location such as a stored procedure in the database.

After further discussion of everyone's needs, it was decided that Venus's daughter Aphrodite and her husband-to-be Agamemnon McCarthy would purchase her parents' home. "Adding a new address" for Agamemnon (ID #88), of course, is simply a matter of making an entry into the Address table (or replacing an existing entry) with the values "88, 1234567, HA."

If your business will never require the level of detail shown (are you sure?), however, the simpler alternative shown below may suffice:

A Simplified Implementation of Address Management

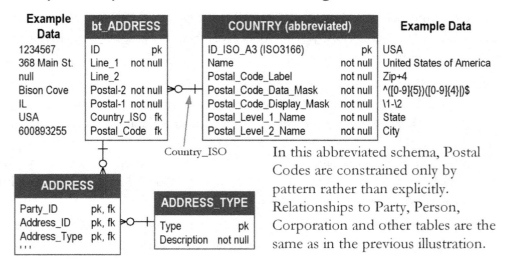

In this abbreviated schema, Postal Codes are constrained only by pattern rather than explicitly. Relationships to Party, Person, Corporation and other tables are the same as in the previous illustration.

---

361 If your company provides some location-based service, such as wired cable television, alarm monitoring, internet service and the like. Of course, details of all such services, which by definition are specific to your company, would be kept in another location entirely.

The main objective of creating contact mechanism structures such as those for addresses described above is, of course, to remove redundancies from the database and centralize the handling of identical Things and Attributes.

Party Relationships

In "Application Changes" on page 130, we introduced a common logical Class structure showing **Employee** as a subclass of **Person**, which in turn was a subclass of **Party**. In the example implementation of this structure (see "Deja Vu" on page 61), we further saw that **Employee.ID** was a foreign key to **Person.ID**, and **Person.ID** was in turn a foreign key to **Party.ID**. Thus, we are able to have a single mechanism for handling addresses and other types of contact mechanisms by simply referring to the **Party** table's relationships with the relevant contact table.

As with the use of Base Table/View scheme recommended in "A Corporate Merger – Part 2," here we find that the Address table (the triple intersection as shown on page 331) proves to be quite easy to use, but only for one of the big-four CRUD[362] operations – that of "Read." As with the use of Views, though, it turns out that the missing CREATE, UPDATE, and DELETE operations are all based on BUSINESS RULES – not DATA RULES[363] - and must be implemented accordingly.

Address Semantics – Pseudo Synonyms

As discussed ad nauseam,[364] great care must be taken to distinguish among those terms that are often used imprecisely in business operations. One such example is the sometimes fuzzy distinction between "Address" and "Location."[365] Colloquialisms, as we have seen, have no place in database design, and any competent Triage must identify such situations.

---

362 CRUD: Create, Read, Update, and Delete.

363 This very important distinction was first introduced in "Data Structures as Unintentional Business Rules" on page 44.

364 Beginning with, for example, "Naming our Things" on page 73.

365 Whether or not this particular distinction is relevant to your own business isn't the point; in any business of any character, it is likely that you may encounter similar named (often colloquially) locations.

An Address might identify a named Location, but it might not. A Location might have one or more Addresses but, even if it is associated with an Address, the Address might not fully specify the Location. "Location" is, of course, only one example, but illustrates the necessity of careful name selection as well as emphasizing the importance during Triage of attempting to state – as a sanity check – any possible relationships and distinctions between similar terms that you encounter. We'll use Location to elaborate.

Using the block map below, for instance, we can observe several things:

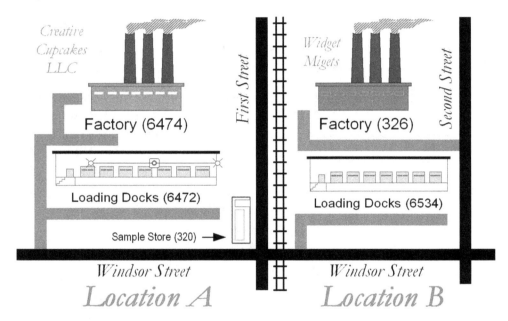

Location A is one of the manufacturing facilities belonging to Creative Cupcakes, LLC. The address of this Site (another common term for such an entity) is 6474 Windsor Street. Their manufactured products are stored in a collocated distribution warehouse with loading docks whose address is 6472 Windsor Street. Creative Cupcakes also has a retail outlet (their "Sample Store") at this Location whose mailing address is 320 First Street. Since the neighborhood in which the factory was built was called "Slippery Beach," this facility was informally known by the Creative Cupcakes as their "Slippery Beach Plant."

Location B, belonging to Widget Midgets, is set up similarly – consisting of both a factory and a distribution center. In this example, however, the respective addresses at which the facilities receive their mail are on different streets – the factory's being `326 Second Street`, and that of the warehouse being `6534 Windsor Street`. Over time, the employees at Widget Midget's corporate headquarters back in Canada began referring to this Location as "Cholesterol Junction" rather than "Slippery Beach" – perhaps because most workers there were known to spend an inordinate amount of time sampling the cupcakes next door.

It would be out of scope here to discuss how such situations are best handled in a database, but creating a series of Propositions can show the way:

Propositions (True)[366]	Commentary
T A Location Identifier (nickname) can be associated with zero, one, or many Addresses **(TRUE)** In this example, Location A is associated with 3 Addresses, and Location B with 2 Addresses.	Yes, zero is possible. Consider that a potential drilling "Location" in the middle of a desert – one that that has no associated Address – might be identified only by GPS coordinates. Take care, however, to distinguish between a "Location" as the term is being used here and a location with continuously variable GPS coordinates, for which the type of table we are discussing is not at all suitable.
T A Location can be associated with zero, one, or many GPS coordinates. **(TRUE)** Neither Location has any associated GPS coordinates.	A Navy ship's "current location" at sea, for example, may only be stated in continuously changing GPS coordinates.[367] Of course, there may still be an address to which mail for individual sailors can be sent, but this Address would not be associated with a Location of the type described here.
T A Location can only be associated with one Organization. **(TRUE)**	Of course, this doesn't imply that many Organizations might not use an identical Identifier for one of their own Locations, since an Identifier is often an arbitrary term based on geography. Whether or not the Proposition above is True depends to a large extent on the circumstances, and thus falls into the gray area between DATA RULE and BUSINESS RULE. The determination should acknowledge the needs of your Organization.

---

366 Recall once again that any Propositions used for database design must be True!

367 These would be stored as time-location pairs in some subsidiary table. This table may or may not be part of the Business Database, but its handling is not in the scope of this book.

Propositions (True)	Commentary

T An Organization (as a subclass of Party) can be associated with zero, one, or many Locations. **(TRUE)**

For clarity in the drawing, the ERD below shows this as a "zero or many to one" relationship.

Of course, one should think hard before dealing with a Corporation that has no Address, but it does happen.

Defining this potential association as being with an Organization rather than with a Party (as is done in the example below) is enforcing a rule that other subclasses of Party, such as Person, may not have Locations. Such a decision depends on whether this Proposition is viewed as a DATA RULE or a BUSINESS RULE in your Organization.

In most business systems, a "Home Address" is not usually given any additional meaning as a "Location," but if your particular business is real estate, then this choice may probably deserve some serious analysis.

The following figure illustrates a possible simplified entity-relationship diagram based on the Propositions as given:

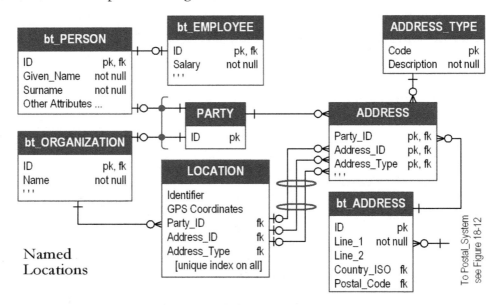

We've seen that Propositions with an "is a" Predicate generally ended up as tables representing subsets/classes of other entities – An Employee is a Person.

being an earlier example. Here, we can see that Propositions formed from "can be associated with" Predicates become optional relationships.

In most implementations, each row in a table like **Location** should be unique. But because such a table often requires NULLs in the optional attribute values that, if they existed, would need to be constrained by foreign keys (such as the composite **Party_ID**, **Address_ID** and **Address_Type** shown), creation of a composite primary key on the full row isn't (and shouldn't be) allowed.

We therefore do the next best thing and create a unique index, which is generally permissible and logically acceptable, since the Location relationship can't be considered an ESSENTIAL ATTRIBUTE of any defined entity.

Also, note that an Address can't be assigned to a Location unless it already exists in the **Address** intersection (and therefore in the **bt_Address** table.)

The additional foreign key between **Location** and **bt_Organization** restricts the use of Named Locations to Organizations; otherwise, any Party could be associated with a named location. As mentioned in the descriptions of the Propositions above, such a choice falls into a gray area between a DATA RULE and a BUSINESS RULE.

Those familiar with SQL will recognize, of course, that defining Locations as optional in this manner will require the use of Outer Joins if a company's named Locations are to be listed along with each associated Address.

The Exclusive Arc symbol[368] is described in Barker [1], page 4-3. Although commonly required in business situations, many data modeling software packages don't support it, and most RDBMS products don't implement it declaratively.

---

368 The arc crossing the relationships between Party-to-Person and Party-to-Organization, and indicating that only one or the other is permissible for any given Party_ID..

Using Propositions in Triage and Design

Database tables are usually implementations of some Proposition.[369]

A corollary to this is that, if a group of normalized True Propositions has been identified, a logical relational database implementation is possible. Of course, because we should never build assumptions or transient "rules" into our database **structures**, the critical distinction between BUSINESS RULES and DATA RULES must always be kept in mind when forming the Propositions.

If such semantic distinctions aren't identified prior to settling on database structures for your business, it is almost guaranteed that the resulting design will lead to system constipation in the not-too-distant future.

The example scripts in "Appendix B – Pseudo-Code Examples" incorporate both Addresses and Locations in a limited manner. Other contact mechanisms such as telephone numbers can handled in a similar fashion, but any further discussions would be out of scope here. Because the handling of Addresses is the most complex of these, however, an understanding of how Addresses are handled will lead quickly to logically defensible solutions for handling other contact mechanisms.

Implementing Contact Mechanism Structures

Reactions of programmers and data management groups to the introduction of reality-based data models are at first skeptical – if not negative. When implemented on even a small scale, however, the benefits of consolidating Contact Management become apparent quickly, as programmers turn their skills toward better and more consistent interfaces rather than data management issues.

Management of Contact data, as well as that of Weights and Measures, is typically responsible for a large percentage of the redundancy that can be found during Triage of most databases and, as with the techniques described in the

---

369 And, as pointed out earlier, stating the Proposition represented by each table during Triage is often quite enlightening – if not painfully humorous – and often identifies serious logical design flaws. If a table seems to represent multiple Propositions, this should certainly be considered a red flag.

various chapters devoted to Weights and Measures, implementation of these or similar structures for the management of contact data will provide opportunities to begin the implementation of common constraints and domains across your company's various systems, and thus contribute to a reduction in data redundancy and eventual consolidation.

One could start, for example, by simply adding the appropriate (and domain constrained) country code to each existing address structure (identified during the homework exercise on page 315). Processes could then be run against each instance to verify the validity of the existing data – then either correct the data, or add it to the domains, etc.

Even for businesses dealing only with the United States, consolidation of contact mechanisms will go a long way toward improving data integrity and consistency, and will permit developers to address whatever inadequate or inconsistent mechanisms exist for entering and editing such data.

For those businesses desiring to seamlessly transition to handling multinational ordering and fulfillment, the flexibility and extensibility of this approach is almost mandatory.

Additional References

In addition to the various ISO standards referenced in this chapter, the following web sites may prove useful for standardized codes relating to entities within the United States:

- The U.S. Geological Survey's "US Geographic Names Information System" website at geonames.usgs.gov/pls/gnispublic, which contains census codes, class codes, General Services Administration (GSA) codes, and Office of Personnel Management (OPM) Codes.

- Federal Information Processing (FIPS) codes can be looked up at http://www.census.gov/geo/reference/ansi.html.

Both these taxpayer-funded sites permit bulk downloading of reference data.

► In most business databases, handling of contact mechanisms – addresses, telephone numbers and the like – is incredibly redundant and inefficient.

► In most businesses, handling of contact mechanisms is done in far more applications and database locations (often multiple times in the same table or the same application), than most people realize, even when they consciously think about such things.

► As a result, there is a correspondingly wide variety of methods for handling contact mechanisms, and a great deal of variance in the capabilities of the methods used.

► In spite of this variety of methods, it is almost always the case that none of these is flexible enough to suit a modern business database.

► In spite of the variety of methods for modeling data structures intended to store contact mechanisms, it is typically the case that the level of data integrity constraints is minimal at best, assuming constraints exist at all.

► Logical analysis will show that contact mechanisms are always Party attributes. Treating them as such presents a real opportunity to enhance data integrity, and expand the flexibility and functionality that can be achieved in software, since the effort to introduce all these capabilities is shared across the enterprise.

► Storing both content and formatting in a single attribute not only violates relational principles, but significantly reduces future business flexibility.

"The programming language fraternity still does not appear to realize that support for the dynamic sharing of data is an absolute requirement." – Dr. Ted Codd, father of the Relational Model [370]

This chapter should be of particular interest to business managers, who can and should understand this issue, and whose businesses can potentially benefit from acting on such understanding.

19 - THE SINGLE OPERATIONAL DATABASE

Throughout this book, I've outlined a variety of reasons for taking the view that professionally responsible data management for Business[371] operations is best accomplished with a single Relational[372] Database instance. Regardless of any steps taken to reduce redundancy within – or improve the integrity of – each independent corporate data store, or to mitigate the effects of inconsistent constraints, the continued existence of multiple schemas – with their overlapping entities and attributes – tends to marginalize the benefits of such localized improvements from a corporate data management perspective.

While discussions about supporting a business with a single operational database are often assumed to be "technical," this really hasn't been the case for more than a decade, so this penultimate chapter is aimed even more at Business

---

370 Codd [3]. See the 1969-1970 entry in the section "Business Joins the Modern Computer Era" that begins on page 102 for more information on Dr. Codd.

371 At the risk of being repetitive, the reader is reminded that the term "business," as I am using it here, is defined at length in "Definition of "Business" beginning on page 1. There are certainly valid (albeit flimsy, and easily countered) arguments that can be made against this view, but please reread chapter 1 before considering how valid they really are.

372 At the risk of being even more repetitive, this does not simply mean the use of a Relational Database Management System (RDBMS) *product*, but an actual Relational Database *design*.

Managers than at developers. Continuing to treat this issue as a technical one sidelines the interests of business stakeholders unnecessarily and unfairly.

It should be emphasized however that the target of achieving a "single business database containing no redundancies" is not intended to preclude the use of any behind-the-scenes technological wizardry such as partitioning, distributed systems and the like; even some types of indexes after all are implemented as physical copies of key data and are therefore "redundant data." "Single business database" simply means that any user or application should be presented with what appears to be and responds as if it were a single physical database.[373]

To provide a framework for discussion, this chapter will provide a short summary of the benefits of a consolidated business database, outline both technical and non-technical objections and, as earlier "Freedom of the Press" chapters have done, present and comment on relevant quotations from several publications.

The Benefits of a Single Corporate Database

The arguments made throughout this book[374] for the benefits of triage and redesign of individual database schemas are fundamentally derived from the idea that the integrity of corporate data stores is the primary responsibility of any information technology group – including those responsible for creating application software as well as those who define a company's data structures.

 Freedom of the Press
"If a family of integrated applications all rely on the same database, then you can be sure that they are always consistent all of the time [sic]"..........................*Fowler [1]*

Martin Fowler, who certainly can be considered a representative of the software development segment of I/T, is fairly explicit in this quote about the benefits of the single database to a business. Nonetheless, he generally opposes it.

---

373 There is a longer discussion of redundancy – what it is and what it isn't – in Chapter 15 of Date [2].

374 See, for example, the chapters titled "A Corporate Merger – Part 1 and Part 2," and the chapters "Playing with Trucks – Part 1 and Part 2.

The comments of Len Silverston and his colleagues in this quoted excerpt, rather than explicitly supporting the use of a single data store, simply allude to the ill effects of not utilizing one, and point out that these are significantly magnified if multiple databases exist. The constipating effects on a business that are described in "Data Structures as Unintentional Business Rules" (see page 44), for example, are magnified exponentially when duplicated across multiple data stores – particularly when there are conflicts across an almost random collection of inconsistent and often unrecognized business rules.

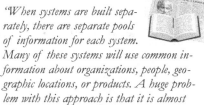

Freedom of the Press

"When systems are built separately, there are separate pools of information for each system. Many of these systems will use common information about organizations, people, geographic locations, or products. A huge problem with this approach is that it is almost impossible to maintain accurate up-to-date information since the same type of information is stored redundantly across many systems."
Silverston [1]

Implicit Acceptance of Multiple Corporate Databases

Unfortunately, the use of application-centric database schemas is the status quo, leading many to assume that use of a single database for business operations isn't widely accepted.[375] This is somewhat misleading, however. The truth is that many practitioners simply never consider the matter. The many limitations of early electronic processing and storage technology described in "Recent History of Data Management" (see page 97) didn't allow for any such consideration. Although those early limitations have largely disappeared, use of application-centric databases remains the pervasive practice – ironic, considering our profession's view of itself as imaginative and forward-thinking, rather than stubbornly resistant to change.

The quote on the right is suggested by some commentators as indicating that database theoretician Chris Date implicitly accepts the use of multiple databases in a single business environment. Although the "great explainer" of

Freedom of the Press

"...database design can be an extremely complex task (at least in a 'large database' environment; the design of 'small' databases is – usually – comparatively straightforward)."
. .Date [1] - "Database Systems," Ch 11.1

---

375 Perhaps unfair – what is certain is that this view has not been widely acted upon, and most businesses have a wide variety of data stores supporting (or impeding) their operations.

Dr. Codd's work at times disagreed with him, it seems to me that this remark – particularly in its full context – is simply an example of overlooking the subject rather than taking a position for or against use of a single database.

Freedom of the Press

"... using the same database ... forces out problems in semantic dissonance. Rather than leaving these problems to fester until they are difficult to solve with transforms, you are forced to confront them and deal with them before the software goes live and you collect large amounts of incompatible data."...................Fowler [1]

The prevalence of products that purport to consolidate the data from multiple databases can also be viewed as a more subtle form of acceptance that multiple corporate databases are, if not a necessity, at least an inevitability. But these consolidation products are seldom capable of recognizing, much less accounting for the often subtle differences in the meaning[376] of entity and attribute names across the corporation. We'll revisit this subject in "Solutions in Sheep's Clothing," beginning on page 363.

Objections to a Single Database – The Gamut

While Dr. Codd bemoaned the lack of "dynamic sharing of data" (see this chapter's heading), he didn't hazard any guesses as to why this might be so.

The most commonly encountered objections to using a single database for support of day-to-day business operations are therefore discussed here. These fall generally into two categories: *Technical* (mostly misguided), and *Sociopolitical* (more insidious). Some objections, of course, straddle both camps, while some that appear to be technical are merely rationalizations for sociopolitical objections. We'll discuss these in no particular order.

Disparate Data Models – Perceived Technical Impediment

"The data models of our company's departments are completely different from one another."

Proper triage will often show that, although true in many corporations, this is typically because one or more (and often all) of these data models is incorrect – defined earlier as not reflecting objective reality!

---

376 What Fowler refers to as "Semantic Dissonances" in the sidebar.

This perceived technical impediment is presented from a developer's standpoint[377] – again by Martin Fowler. In this case, I consider Mr. Fowler's conclusions to be flawed in several respects, since they are based on a flawed premise.

Freedom of the Press

"One of the biggest difficulties with Shared Database is coming up with a suitable design for the shared database. Coming up with a unified schema that can meet the needs of multiple applications is a very difficult exercise, often resulting in a schema that application programmers find difficult to work with."...Fowler [1]

Designing a database schema to meet the needs of an application, or even multiple applications, is not appropriate if a development group is to fulfill its fundamental responsibility for data integrity while still accommodating future change and growth. To accommodate change, which is inevitable in business, a database schema must model the data *as it is*, and not as the data may be currently utilized by a given process. In other words, a suitable design – one that is robust, logical and easily extensible – should always be based on the taxonomies and characteristics of the Things being represented in the database. As discussed in "The Avowed Mission of I/T Departments" (page 5), data management, and all that term implies, is a fundamental responsibility of our profession, and not one that is subsidiary to the automation of business processes.

Likewise, programmer convenience is **not** a valid design criterion for a database schema. While true that a simple application-specific schema permits the use of inexperienced or less competent applications programmers, who "find it difficult to work with" a realistic data model, the long term costs to the enterprise of making this a key design consideration are too significant to ignore.

As Fowler points out in this quote, data models with superficially similar schemas may also suffer from what he earlier called semantic dissonance: chapter 7 discussed how "Customer" may refer to different subsets of **Customer**. Similarly, other generic names often obscure the fact that the data being represented by similarly named entities may in fact be different data and vice-versa.

Freedom of the Press

"A geological database may define an oil well as a single drilled hole that may or may not produce oil. A production database may define a well as multiple holes covered by a single piece of equipment. These cases of semantic dissonance are much harder to deal with than inconsistent data formats."
...................................Fowler [1]; page 47

---

377 It needs to be stressed that Mr. Fowler isn't taking a position here, but simply outlining what he views as valid arguments for and against a "Shared Database." Read the original!

Of course, if one or more of the data models being compared is incomplete, it may just appear that they are different or incompatible, which is not necessarily a significant issue, although Triage should identify such situations.

Not all database designs are under the company's control, however. A special case where differing data models are in use within a single organization results from the use of packaged software, but that will be discussed separately.[378]

Disparate DBMS Products – Technical & Sociopolitical Impediment

 "Our company's data stores are built on a variety of database management systems, ranging from Oracle on Linux to SQL Server on Windows."

The existence of multiple different database platforms – differing Operating Systems, different Database Management Systems and, often, different versions of each – is definitely an issue in some mid-size and larger corporations, particularly those assembled through mergers and acquisitions.

As with many database consolidation considerations, not all the issues are as technical as the proponents of each RDBMS or Operating System – vendors as well as internal technical staff – might be attempting to portray them. What are, in fact, valid technical considerations need to be balanced against the continuing operational costs of having multiple data stores; these costs in turn must be balanced against the anticipated costs of migration to a single corporate database.

► Financial Considerations

▼ The costs for maintenance of multiple licenses and support contracts for both OS and DBMS software – occasionally even multiple versions of each – need to be balanced against any potential savings from consolidation.

▼ The current and projected costs for maintenance of multiple hardware devices, including database servers as well as storage capabilities, need to be balanced against any potential savings from consolidation.

▼ Nonetheless, it is inescapable that, in many circumstances, the costs of migration can be significant, and generalization about the overall benefits isn't possible due to the number of variables.

---

378 See "Integration with Packaged Software" on page 360.

► Technical Considerations

  ▼ Certain product selections can lead to Vendor Lock-in (a few DBMS products are limited to certain operating systems).

  ▼ The internal procedural languages in RDBMS products are usually different and incompatible – see comments under "Sharing Process Based Constraints – A Better Approach" on page 194.

► Sociopolitical Considerations

  ▼ Database consolidation when disparate operating systems or RDBMS products are different can lead to the need for extensive retraining of personnel.

  ▼ Database consolidation when disparate operating systems or RDBMS products are different can lead to the possible loss of personnel that are very familiar with your business, but who don't wish to change their product focus.

  ▼ Database consolidation when disparate operating systems or RDBMS products are involved can lead to a fear of job loss (all database administrators, for instance, perform essentially the same tasks, but these are often handled quite differently in Microsoft products than they are in Oracle's).

Potential Size of Unified Database – Perceived Technical Impediment

"The resulting database would be way too large to maintain – backups, for example, would become more intrusive on business operations."

You need to first ask if the time, expense, and effort to maintain the consolidated database would be less or more than those of maintaining all the individual databases. There are the costs of entering and maintaining redundant data, the impacts of conflicting or out-of-date information, the expenses of separate licenses, etc. It's actually hard to make the case that the costs would be higher with a single database.

Sheer size has faded from general I/T consciousness as a "Gee Whiz" factor. While a 30 terabyte database may have been something wondrous and deserving of media attention ten years ago,[379] multi-terabyte hard drives for personal com-

---

379 Winter Group data as reported in Information Week, November 17, 2003, on page 36. Oracle and IBM reported similar maximum sizes from their contemporary client surveys.

puters are now available at big-box retailers like Costco or Walmart for less than many families' weekly grocery bills. Size itself is no longer an issue.

Likewise, the operational impacts of data backups have been addressed. Over the past decade, modern RDBMS products have introduced a variety of methods to support live continuous backups, and a number of alternatives are provided by independent vendors.

Performance of Unified Database – Perceived Technical Impediment

 "A larger shared database would need to support more users and applications, and would likely therefore perform more slowly."

This perception is closely related to the previous one and is certainly valid, particularly in cases with underpowered database server hardware or inadequate network bandwidth. In the quote below, Fowler again provides a concise summary of the concerns.

Although increased contention is certainly a possibility, use of the word "frequently" is disturbing because it is a relative term with no stated point of reference. Frequent deadlocks almost certainly indicate some problem beyond the use of shared data. During Triage, a good architect needs to question

Freedom of the Press

"Multiple applications using a shared database to frequently read and modify the same data can turn the database into a performance bottleneck and can cause deadlocks as each application locks others out of the data."
....*Fowler [1]*

why multiple applications regularly lock the same data. Several common possibilities need to be explored during Triage before the problem is simply dismissed as a natural and inevitable outcome of sharing data:

► Poor granularity of the data structures themselves, which force excess and unneeded data into applications, thus locking more data than required.

► Poor granularity in the processes by which data is locked. For example, applications that regularly query more data than is necessary:

▼ Use of application code rather than declarative SQL to isolate the desired data – gathering data in bulk and then isolating the required data within the application.

▼ The use of "SELECT * FROM" queries by poorly written applications.

- ▼ The use of "SELECT FOR UPDATE" queries when simply reading data. The most common excuse for this seems to be "just in case."

- ▼ The use of RDBMS products that lack sufficiently granular locking options.

- ▼ The use of automatic code generators for database access and update can often be helpful, but thorough examination of the generated SQL statements under different circumstances needs to be accomplished. Surprises are common.

► Batch data update processes running during normal "live" operations.

- ▼ Batch processes may use higher priority than necessary.

- ▼ Batch processes may lock excessive quantities of data.

- ▼ Batch processes implemented with infrequent COMMIT statements.

► Finally, poor operational (non-I/T) processes themselves may contribute. Lack of well-thought-out customer service support policies can result in multiple departments attempting to modify the identical customer records simultaneously, which is a common cause for this.

This is analogous to having three doctors prescribe the same medication through two different pharmacies – benevolence and good customer service intentions[380] aside, process control (feeding requests through a single responsible funnel) is necessary for good data management.

Skilled DBAs can generally identify and address all such concerns.

It is also important to recognize that modern RDBMS products provide far more support for contention management than any "bolted on" or hand-crafted means. Leftover solutions of this type from earlier systems may often cause more harm than good when paired with contemporary products. Good Triage requires measurements.

Freedom of the Press

"If you do get simultaneous updates to a single piece of data from different sources, then you have transaction management systems that handle that about as gracefully as it can ever be managed. Since the time between updates is so small, any errors are much easier to find and fix."....................Fowler [1]

Finally, hiding problems is never an appropriate architectural approach and, unfortunately, even those with good intentions may unwittingly hide problems if they are unaware of their existence.

---

380 There are unconfirmed rumors that a few examples of such attitudes still exist.

Complexity of Unified Database – Perceived Technical Impediment

"With a large database intended for general use, we'll need to spend an excessive amount of time writing complicated SQL statements."

Any response to this begins with the comments regarding programmer convenience under "Disparate Data Models – Perceived Technical Impediment" above. Such objections also reflect the need for precision in language – specifically the clear distinction between the words "complex" and "complicated."

Any complexity is simply a reflection of reality; if the reality is understood, then the requisite SQL statements, however involved, can be constructed. If the queries required are "complicated," it seems fair to assume that perhaps the person constructing them is unfamiliar with either the reality or the technology, or both. Either circumstance should suggest at least a need for training.

Single Point of Failure – Perceived Technical Impediment

"The use of a single database instance presents a single point of failure, thus increasing risk."

This is probably a somewhat legitimate concern, but I would view this in comparison to the increased probability of failure when multiple applications are built in a manner that is made unnecessarily complicated because of poor database design. In many cases, and depending on the particular independent system that fails, failure of one instance can have the same effect on a company's operations. It is also necessary to consider Hardware and DBMS issues separately when evaluating such "single point of failure" concerns.

Security Considerations – Perceived Technical Impediment

"The use of a single database instance presents too many security issues, thus increasing our risk."

Actually, security is less complex and much easier to implement and control when there are fewer databases and access mechanisms to be concerned with. The level and granularity of data security that is available from most RDBMS products (assuming decent design and implementation by the company that purchased them) are sufficient for the needs of most corporations, and are fairly mature and well understood. Most also support fairly sophisticated Identity Management as well.

The environmental consistency that comes with a single data store brings a number of benefits by allowing for more sophisticated management that can be costly and time consuming with multiple data stores, including:

▼ Easier Auditing, with more confidence in the results.

▼ Time-of-Day access.

▼ Machine-specific or user-specific access controls.

▼ Use of roles to simplify controls.

▼ Reduction in the number of passwords required by users, thus reducing user effort (single sign-on notwithstanding) as well as enhancing security.

There is a legitimate view that compartmentalization of data (the "need to know" viewpoint) increases security, but this has little to do with the number of physical data stores and, in any case, can much more easily be controlled, even if by a judicious use of views, to isolate access in a sufficiently granular fashion.

The use of Views can also address situations where knowledge of the mere existence of certain data – even without access to specifics – can itself be a security risk. This is mostly of concern to politicians and spies, however, so isn't appropriate for this discussion. Also see "Rationalization – Security" on page 359.

Habit or Inertia – Sociopolitical Impediment

"My department's systems probably aren't perfect, but they're nothing to be ashamed of. As they say, if it ain't broke, don't fix it."

While simple fear of change can be a factor, particularly in those who have had to suffer through all the transitions of the past several decades of "innovation," other factors are often responsible for (or at least contribute to) a desire to retain the "status quo."

One reason, often expressed privately by developers, is based on an intimate knowledge of the existing system's fragility. This can be loosely expressed as "If I touch it, I'm afraid it might break." Be sensitive to this during Triage.

There are two primary subclasses in the Habit or Inertia class: Ignorance and Myopia, each of which merits a few comments.

Ignorance of History – Sociopolitical Impediment

"If consolidation is a good idea, why hasn't it become the norm?"

Designers and developers are often unaware that traditional technical constraints have disappeared. Long-standing traditions of this sort are simply accepted without much thought.

Myopia – Sociopolitical Impediment

"I'm paid to optimize my own group's operations." Compromise doesn't help and may even hinder me.

Some managers and developers, mistakenly considering themselves "owners" rather than "stewards" of their respective databases, have a single-minded focus on their own niches, and are unwilling or unmotivated to expend the time necessary to play well with others. This is, of course, understandable for various reasons, including lack of awareness of the needs of other business units, the reward systems and budgetary processes in most enterprises (see below), etc.

Inappropriate Budgetary Processes – Sociopolitical Impediment

"Coordinating an effort of this magnitude with other departments has too great an impact on my group's budget."

Overall data architecture is primarily a corporate objective and this is often perceived as conflicting with the needs and objectives of individual departments. Moreover, budget processes tend to exacerbate this conflict. Capital is typically requested by and allocated to individual departments, and there are seldom provisions in place for providing cross-departmental allocations and, perhaps more importantly, handling the management and responsibility for these allocations.

Need for Speed & Lack of Recognition – Sociopolitical Impediments

"We're expected to be *Agile*, and to deliver results quickly."

Department, project, and technical managers, database designers and application programmers are often judged primarily by speed of delivery, followed by a variety of other short-term factors.

Fowler, in the quote to the right, once again provides a succinct summary of the misguided emphasis on speed. Concern for implementation delays is of course fairly universal, but thorough Triage will show that, in many cases, the root cause of many development delays can be found in the compromises to database integrity or structural definitions made during earlier projects.

Freedom of the Press

"And if the technical difficulties of designing a unified schema aren't enough, there are also severe political difficulties. If a critical application is likely to suffer delays in order to work with a unified schema, then often there is irresistible pressure to separate." ....*Fowler [1]*

The putative advantages of Agile Development[381] (which are enhanced, by the way, when reality-based data structures are in place), while sometimes apparent in application design, have no place in database design. Applications, being implementations of arbitrary and often changing requirements and processes, can benefit from rapid turnaround. Data structures, being reflections of reality, never do; procedural requirements have no bearing on a database schema – only on which portions of it need to be implemented at any given time.

"As a developer, I get no recognition for working on longer-term goals; in fact, I often pay a significant penalty."

It is very difficult to quantify the benefits of design efforts aimed at the longer-term, and any such benefits (enabling future projects to proceed more efficiently and cost-effectively) are seldom directly or solely attributable to any single programmer or project. For these reasons, there are no rewards for those who aim for long-term strategic benefits. Since there are often delays (however slight) in project delivery when long-term benefits are considered, the project team may actually be penalized for actually delivering long-term benefits.

Similarly, there is a lack of recognition of the long-term negative impacts of narrowly focused design efforts – certainly resulting in significant unnecessary

---

381 A technique in which an application developer avoids formal processes and "throws something out" to see if it's satisfactory to an application's users, then continues by modifying the result until the complaints die down. Not the way you'd want an aircraft or even your house designed, but quite popular among the cowboy crowd. It's a great technique for trying out paint colors and wallpaper, arranging furniture and such things, but the location of your home's bathrooms and plumbing really needs to be settled before construction begins.

expense for most corporations, but since these effects are also not directly or solely attributable to any single developer or project, there are no penalties for continuing these habits.

Magnitude of Task – Sociopolitical Impediment

Magnitude of Task
"βρεκεκέξ, κωάξ κωάξ"
"The Frogs" by Aristophanes – 405 bce Tony winner. New Chorus: "This sounds like an impossible task that will leave us with no time for our 'day jobs'."

Anyone having a passing familiarity with the application and report portfolios of most companies can't help being intimidated by the size of the task. American business still has a firmly entrenched base of decades old software and data structures.

At best, this objection represents a corporate double standard. From a management perspective, should it be discovered that the organization and integrity of physical corporate assets in, for instance, a parts or distribution warehouse was inept enough to cause loss and damage, objections by the existing staff to the effort involved in reworking its structure and operating policies would not carry a lot of weight. The tactics and financial considerations in approaching mismanagement of data assets are essentially identical, and should be pursued just as aggressively.

A project intended to address database consolidation can often engender a sense of futility among many employees.[382] Because most designers and developers have no control over the corporate data architecture, data structures, or data element definitions, particularly in purchased software, it can often seem pointless to begin such a Sisyphean task.

Loss of Control – Sociopolitical Impediment

"If all the company's data is thrown together, I'll lose control of my department's Data."

To some Database Administrators, and even many programmers and managers, sharing access to data stores (or worse, allowing updates to "their" data)

---

382 ... which can only be mitigated successfully by demonstrating a detailed understanding of the problem, a realistic plan for addressing it, and a clearly stated intent to address it.

represents a loss of control. There are several factors that come into play here – some benign or well-intentioned, but some representing a corporate malignancy.

Sometimes Control is a department function, but it is always a Corporate Management (not I/T management) function, and even where it is a department function or responsibility, it is a delegated one.

In order of the effort to overcome them, at least four rationalizations for this class of objections include:

Rationalization – Data Contamination

"Our Data will become contaminated. Others don't have the same level of data validation that our group imposes."

Fear of data contamination from "foreign" applications is legitimate and the folks making these arguments can usually provide many examples – but in most cases, Triage will show that these derive from poor database and/or application design, usually in the form of constraints that should have been implemented at the database level but are currently implemented only with external code. Conversely, one or more departmental databases may implement "department-only" BUSINESS RULES in their Database. See "Handling Constraints."

This is an easy objection to overcome, and ongoing Triage and correction within individual groups should be a priority if eventual consolidation is a goal.

Rationalization – Security

"I'm concerned for the Security of any data I expose to those who don't understand it."

This is similar to the idea that "others can't be trusted with our data" discussed above, and is also encountered as a rationalization for often vague feelings of losing control.

Rationalization – Conflicting Data Definitions

"Some traditional terms used within our department may be affected if certain data element names are altered."

This is not quite the same as the "Disparate Data Models" objection described earlier. Some departments, particularly ones that have been acquired, may use terminology that, while logically incorrect, is ingrained in their operations. Concerned managers can see this as potentially leading to user confusion if certain element names are changed. (remember semantic dissonance?)

Departmental managers and developers have little interest in engaging in inter-departmental squabbling in order to achieve a "corporate" goal, since the "loser" will need to modify what is sometimes a surprising number of applications and reports for each naming correction or data structure change that may be required. This is often presented as a "fairness" issue.

Rationalization – Loss of Power & Authority

"My power and authority as a department manager will be threatened."

If "Knowledge is Power"[383] then a certain class of department head (the class known informally as "Empire Builders") will always oppose database consolidation. The loss of personal or at least departmental control of key data also represents a loss of power or perceived authority for some managers. This is the most insidious factor and, while not commonly encountered, has a far more significant business impact than most other sociopolitical factors.

Integration with Packaged Software

Thus far, this discussion of creating a single business database has proceeded as if all the many disparate data stores to be combined were under the control of the organization. In the case of purchased software, however, this is clearly not the case.

While it is tempting to believe that the major packaged software applications utilize well-designed database schemas that meet all the criteria discussed so far, this is not at all the case, and there are several significant characteristics of these systems that can impede if not prevent any meaningful integration.

---

383 A cliché, of course, but an idea expressed at least as far back as the Book of Proverbs (24:5) in the Judao-Christian Old Testament: "... knowledge increases ... strength."

Martin Fowler's comment in the sidebar points out just one of these. What he doesn't say is that these **changes** are typically not simply extensions to a schema – which wouldn't necessarily be cause for concern – but often involve significant refactoring[384] of table layouts and structures.

Freedom of the Press

"Adding to the problem, software vendors usually reserve the right to change the schema with every new release of the software."

....*Fowler [1]*

Experience suggests that these vendors are encumbered with the archaic view that data stores exist as storage for applications.[385]

Constantly changing database schemas also suggest that either these schemas didn't reflect reality in the first place, or that no distinctions were made between enforcement of BUSINESS RULES and DATA RULES.

The Cynics Corner

Ἀντισθὲνης (Antisthenes), might have suggested that the Vendors of such Applications are simply attempting to maintain a proprietary control that is clearly not in their customers' best interests.

In a defense of this sort of architecture, one vendor explained that its application had to be viewed as a total system. The question of how or where constraints were enforced[386] was moot, they continued, since direct access to **their** database was severely limited, and extensive APIs[387] were provided for situations where external applications needed to access or update the data. Such a view, they argued, also minimizes the need to modify any of the company's reports or other applications when the underlying data structures change, since great care was taken to avoid changing the APIs themselves. Draw your own conclusions.

---

384 "Refactoring" is an I/T euphemism for fixing or simply improving things that weren't done correctly in the first place. In a continually changing application, this is sometimes inevitable due to time pressures; in a database design, it generally indicates sloppy analysis and design.

385 See "The Avowed Mission of I/T Departments" on page 5 for commentary on this heresy.

386 See the chapter "Handling Constraints," beginning on page 169, that explains the importance of locating constraints within a corporate information system.

387 For management personnel who have survived this far, this acronym means "Application Program Interfaces." Essentially, programs or reports not provided as part of the vendor's software package would read or update **their** (think about who "their" refers to) data by making a request to the vendor's package rather than accessing the database directly.

If the company on/for which Triage is being performed uses nothing but such a packaged software product to run their business, such arguments are not of much consequence. For most other businesses – who typically have a significant portfolio of external reports and applications – evaluation of such packages requires far more than comparing the vendor's list of features against your needs.

Without making any pretensions of offering comprehensive guidelines for such "buy or build" decisions (there are many good sources already available that few people pay any attention to, so why bother?), I feel compelled to point out that the issues raised in this book have a direct, but often unrecognized bearing on these decisions, so the following comments are offered.

▶ When evaluating packaged application software, particularly if there is any concern about the long term costs or the difficulties that might be encountered with implementation, it is imperative that the vendor's overall data model and its provisions for customization or integration with other sources be carefully evaluated.

    ▼ This evaluation should be carried out as if it were a Triage of your own database. Regardless of the vendor's terminology it is, after all, **your data**, and therefore **your database**.

    ▼ A vendor's unwillingness to share significant parts of their data model[388] should be a serious cause for alarm.

    Although this might seem on the surface to ignore the vendors' need (and right) to protect their proprietary designs – and they will certainly argue that point – we are talking about definitions and means of organizing data that belongs to your company, not to the automation of processes (i.e. their software, which is where any proprietary advantage is presumably gained).

    If you were purchasing a storage mechanism for any other commodity of value to your business, it would certainly not be considered unreasonable to have the vendor explain clearly how their containers and organization provided the protection necessary to assure the integrity and availability of your product!

---

388 "Significant parts" means, of course, virtually everything but incidental parameters that control their software's behavior.

Too often the response from an application software vendor who declines to share these details is analogous to a warehouse manager or landlord saying "We'll store your critical inventory, but you have no say or control over the conditions in which it is stored; furthermore, you may only access this inventory on our terms." I suspect your C-Level management would not be amused.

The continuing horror stories of packaged software installations gone wrong make it difficult not to wonder if there is some cause-effect relationship between these stories and the data models of the packages involved. Not that columns named `Flex_Field_1` and `Flex_Field_2` don't suggest fully normalized, logical, reality-based and extensible relational designs, of course![389]

For certain applications, of course, use of packaged software is clearly appropriate and, if there is little value in integration of the package with other systems, may present no architectural issues. But poor underlying data models in certain packaged software are often responsible for many of the horror stories alluded to above, and will eventually have an adverse impact on the business.

Solutions in Sheep's Clothing

Although implicit support for having a single operational business database exists, and was discussed earlier in this chapter, the business benefits of such an architecture seem to be explicitly recognized by certain segments of the industry that offer "alternative solutions." Sometimes, however, what appear to be reasonable solutions simply tend to obscure the real problem while adding yet another layer of complexity and cost to the corporation's infrastructure.

Any good enterprise architect must be very wary of these; we'll briefly discuss two such approaches, each of which recalls the moral of "The Emperor's New Clothes"[390] in its own way.

---

389 This sort of data model, even when touted as a means of extensibility, is particularly reprehensible when it comes from any company that aspires to a leadership position in the Relational (or even RDBMS) world. The reader probably doesn't need to be reminded that smooth or easy integration of your vendor's systems with your company's or others' systems likely doesn't top the list of your vendor's commercial interests.

390 Hans Christian Andersen; first published by C. A. Reitzel in Copenhagen on 7 April 1837.

Data Aggregation Products

A decade ago, in a survey[391] of Chief Financial Officers by IBM Business Consulting Services, only 21% claimed to have ready access to integrated, company-wide information. This percentage hasn't changed significantly since.

To see one explicit acknowledgment of the benefits of a shared corporate data store, simply browse the marketing materials for any data aggregation product based on this need while ignoring the specific solution the vendor is touting!

Industry pundits (and the business folks who feed them), have been brain-washed into believing that having a "consolidated view of corporate data" is somehow equivalent to having a single database, and vendors have responded to the marketing advantages resulting from this perception (which it seems they have encouraged). Each of the major RDBMS vendors now has one or more data aggregation (aka consolidation or federation) products. Additionally, third party vendors now offer such products, although in some cases they are aiming somewhere between transactional and analytical systems and thus not hitting either target squarely.

 Freedom of the Press
"In large organizations, it is not uncommon to see information about customers, employees, or-ganizations, products, and locations stored in dozens of separate systems. How is it possible to know which source of information is most current or accurate."...............*Silverston [1]*

Silverston poses an important question that can be asked about such products in the quote given here. Very little post-installation analysis is required to see that many cross-schema Data Aggregation products could compete on an equal footing with any Las Vegas magic act in their use of misdirection.[392] It hardly needs to be pointed out, however, that the continued availability of such products clearly acknowledges that there must be some legitimate business benefits to having what at least appears to be a consolidated data store.

---

391 Reported in Information Week, December 1, 2003, on page 18. Numerous other published surveys in subsequent years continue to show similar results.

392 Which of any conflicting elements is correct? Are the elements actually semantically identi-cal? Does the product take a vote across systems? Does the product use the entry with the most recent time-stamp? Any of these can be proven to be unreliable. The key to accurate data is to remove the possibility of duplicates and invalid data in the first place.

But, in the end, and regardless of how accurate they are, these products simply collect and present data from disparate sources – really only useful from a data analysis standpoint – and the use of any such products to coordinate integrity constraints across the corporation has never been convincingly demonstrated. Additionally, any attempt to use them in such a manner places an enormous burden on system resources. Whether or not they are expensive relative to their worth depends, of course, on a company's management reporting needs.

Database Synchronization Products

Another class of products goes a step further, installing what amounts to monitors on each separate database instance and then utilizing messaging to keep each instance "synchronized" with the others. While this is conceptually identical to the processes major RDBMS products use to keep their internal copies of data synchronized, one key difference is that these latter processes operate on a controlled instance of a single logical database, and are therefore far less intrusive.

The timing of data synchronization between internal elements of a single database instance is, from a logical standpoint, not an issue. What matters is that a program or user accessing the database will never see any conflict between these elements.

Attempts to provide integration across multiple database instances, however, can result in measurable periods of time where these can present conflicting results – problematic enough with simple queries, but quite interesting[393] in the case of attempted updates.

To the extent that two-phase commit mechanisms – keeping in mind that, depending on your circumstance, may even need to be cross platform – are able to ensure consistency, they do so at a cost in response time and potential locks.

---

393 … as in the traditional Chinese curse "May you live in interesting times!"

Entity Types for Data Structures

Another particularly insidious "solution" to having disparate data structure definitions is the addition in the SQL-3 standard for an "entity type." Chris Date, in *An Introduction to Database Systems,*[394] outlines the many theoretical flaws with this, but my main objection is much simpler – by supporting (and therefore promoting) the idea of a "type" for a single entity, such a declarative language construct is effectively promoting or at least accepting multiple instances of a "type" – utterly contrary to the goals of responsible data management. While creating all Customer tables with identical structures is probably better than having disparate definitions, this tends to foster rather than preclude data silos. This approach appears to mimic the idea of a "user-defined data type" in programming languages; it possibly might be a good or at least useful idea in application code, but a bad one when defining actual data structures. The objectives are simply not the same. If this were a good idea, corporate data models would have had stunning success rates by now, and anyone who has attempted to create one of these realizes there are more fundamental issues to grapple with.

Moving toward a Single Business Database

In "Business and Current Data Management Practices" (see page 11), it was suggested that what most business managers want is to have all their data in a single, internally consistent, easily accessible, secure and reliable database! However desirable that may be, the idea of undertaking any effort to achieve this goal is quite intimidating. A transition to such a state will certainly entail a large and ongoing effort – one demanding a long-term management view, strong planning, interdepartmental coordination and incremental execution – and can make even the initiation of such a project, much less the likelihood that it will continue to eventual success, initially seem highly improbable.

For these reasons it often happens that a few departments, recognizing significant business or technical benefits within their own domain, will proceed with triage and modification of their own systems – a fallback measure that neatly

---

394 Date [1]; see page 382 for information.

avoids the numerous political, social and budgetary impediments associated with an enterprise-wide project.

Such an insular approach presents some clear dangers, however. The redesign of individual systems may undoubtedly represent localized improvements – but will simply result in better designed systems that still contain redundant and inconsistent data when viewed from a corporate management perspective. Of particular concern is that, without taking such a corporate perspective from the outset, naming conflicts and semantic differences across the business will remain undetected and unresolved.

Although the immediate likelihood of consolidation may seem minimal, management intention for such an eventual outcome must be stated unequivocally in order to avoid the dangers discussed above – and good (i.e. corporate-centric) habits for handling the triage and redesign of business data stores must be established early on.

Thus, management should forcefully guide any departmental efforts toward becoming **inter-**departmental efforts as early as possible. It is almost certain, for instance, that most if not all the existing systems share common flaws such as inadequate and inflexible handling of Weights & Measures and Contact Mechanisms, and these areas are suitable for initial projects that cross departmental boundaries and serve as non-threatening venues for cooperation.[395]

A collaborative project can begin, for instance, with a corporate mandate that all systems (databases, applications, reports, and so on) be updated to support flexible Weights & Measures. A further mandate should be that all systems utilize the same (or at least identical) database support structures.

Depending on the variety of DBMS products and programming languages in use, this may initially result in identical structures and data in several disparate systems, and a variety of both calculation and user-interface implementations in multiple different languages, but this will nonetheless constitute progress on several fronts:

---

395 Now you can stop wondering why these particular subjects have been given a special focus in this book

- The first and foremost benefit is, of course, the collaboration across departments, and the potential for not only the sharing of knowledge, but possibly the sharing of code and scripts will become evident. These interactions will pay off with the more complex and politically sensitive efforts to come as further steps toward consolidation are contemplated.

- Almost as important to the company will be the potential for expanding business opportunities arising from the increased data handling flexibility.

- The first steps toward resolving naming discrepancies across instances can be negotiated – these would include the elements to which additional Weights & Measures attributes are added, but need not be limited to those. See the chapter "Grammar, Sets, and (Predicate) Logic – Part 1," particularly the section "Naming our Things" that begins on page 73.

- For a project such as the introduction of additional Weights & Measures attributes and calculations, testing across whatever applications and schemas are present, however disparate they may be, will likely be more comprehensive and will serve to establish or enhance the independence of various testing groups within the corporation.

As development on individual systems proceeds, veterans of such semi-independent but clearly collaborative activities can be tasked with extending their triage efforts to identifying the corporation's semantic dissonances – without any immediate commitment to resolve them – but with a mandate to identify and document the scope of such issues. This again should be an interdepartmental effort.

- Examine the available documentation of every data element in every database schema in use. This may include internal database comments on tables, columns, and other elements, as well as Entity-Relationship Diagrams and any extant build scripts.

- Examine the implicit documentation of every data element accessed by existing application software and reports. Pay particular attention to data elements that require application processing to determine their meaning.

► Identify naming problems – see the chapter "Grammar, Sets, and (Predicate) Logic – Part 1," particularly the section "Naming our Things" that begins on page 73. Further identify naming inconsistencies and conflicts across systems.

► Identify discrepancies in constraint definitions (ranges, domains, specifications, etc.) across similar data elements. All forms of Constraints must be examined, including those in applications as well as database definitions.

A concurrent effort by selected technical and financial representatives should begin to document the impact of maintaining multiple systems within the corporation.

► Identify all associated hardware, Operating System, DBMS, and software licenses and support contract costs, expiration dates, and the like. Consider the anticipated end-of-life projections.

► Attempt an initial balance between the current costs for maintenance of multiple hardware devices, including database servers as well as storage capabilities, and any potential savings from consolidation.

The foregoing activities will likely identify certain systems as more troublesome[396] than most, and two of these should be selected for an initial attempt at consolidation.[397] While it is normally desirable to avoid dramatic changes to more than one system at a time in any one development effort, it is only by dealing with two systems at once that insular thinking and design can be mitigated. Selection of which systems to begin with should likely be based on the findings of the above efforts – specifically the level of pain related to the management of the code in these systems, as well as the potential business benefits to be achieved. Whether the use of identical DBMS products and programming languages is a factor in the choice of the first systems to be consolidated will depend a great deal on factors beyond the scope of this discussion, many of

---

396 For any of a variety of reasons ranging from significantly higher maintenance costs, failure rates, constipation (defined in earlier chapters as being particularly difficult to extend), or simply technical obsolescence (hardware, programming language and so forth).

397 … in a closed test environment of course.

which will involve significant management decisions if the process is to be successful.

Although the steps for approaching each instance are much the same as those described in "The Migration Process" beginning on page 292, as well as in the "Homework Assignment" on page 315, it goes without saying that a global view be considered and enforced from the outset. Development in a vacuum is obviously not a good tactic if the ultimate aim is further consolidation; knowledgeable representatives of those groups who are not part of the first consolidation effort should be included in analysis and design sessions to detect and contain any efforts to stray from reality-based models into those of convenience.

Experience suggests that the initial consolidation efforts will likely result in a system that, although seemingly more complex, is noticeably simpler to maintain and extend than either original.

► Data Management is a fundamental responsibility of any I/T department; viewing it as "support" for applications, particularly when such a view impacts the design of a database, is guaranteed to create difficulties for any business that chooses to grow or even maintain a market position.

► Many factors suggest the need for a consolidated operational database:

▼ Eventual reduction in operating costs.

▼ Better and more consistent data management.

▼ Higher quality of data constraints.

▼ Improved audit capabilities, both for normal business management as well to accommodate local, national, and foreign government regulations.

▼ More straightforward support for internationalization and much simpler methods of localization.

▼ All the benefits of migrating individual database schemas are magnified as each step to overall consolidation takes place. A particularly important benefit is easier localization of applications.

► Barring significant operational reasons for doing otherwise, support for the day-to-day operations of most businesses by utilizing a single operational database is the most appropriate means of fulfilling our corporate responsibility for handling data management.

"database design is not my favorite subject" [398]
"we need more science in this field." [399]
- C.J. Date

"The reasonable man adapts himself to the world; the unreasonable one persists in trying to adapt the world to himself. Therefore all progress depends on the unreasonable man."
- George Bernard Shaw

20

20 - DENOUEMENT

The primary function of any Information Technology group is managing data. All their other responsibilities, including application programming, provision of computers and networks, and so forth, while critically important in their own right, serve primarily to support data management. Although discussed more thoroughly in chapter 1, this conclusion follows from a rather simple observation concerning the impact of data loss relative to other types of loss, and is buttressed by the various names Businesses have given over the years to what we now refer to as Information Technology.

► Databases are ends in themselves; treating them as "persistence mechanisms" for applications is irresponsible and eventually leads to business difficulties, ironically even when attempting to extend the applications those "persistence mechanisms" were originally intended to support.

► There are significant and fundamental differences between managing Data and Process. Although I/T is tasked with applying automation to both, it needs to be understood that while data definitions are based on physical reality, business processes reflect what are inherently transient rules.

---

398 Date [2]; one can only imagine how much he would have written on the subject if it were.
399 Ibid; just a few lines later.

▶ While there are certainly those who could be termed Computer Scientists,[400] current businesses don't seem to enjoy I/T support that could in any way justify the use of the term "Science." Our industry provides itself with ever improving and innovative ways of solving the wrong problems while ignoring the fundamentals – as Chris Date's quote in the introduction to this chapter states, "we need more science in this field."

Throughout this book, I've outlined a variety of reasons for taking the view that most, if not all, transactional business databases (as defined in Chapter 1), should be implemented as Relational Databases. Not simply as databases built using an RDBMS product – most of which in my experience aren't really relational at all – but actual relational designs based on Predicate Logic. I believe that anything less is professionally irresponsible.

▶ Business databases without a Party entity set are likely not designed with any logical structure, and are unlikely to serve a business well, or to easily support business expansion. See chapter 1.

Beware, however, of invalid corollaries; the previous statement does not in itself suggest that those schemas with a Party entity set have a logical structure; Party is a necessary entity for a logically defensible design, but it is not by itself sufficient.

▶ Inconsistent data – incorrect data – inaccessible data – missing data: the data problems that have plagued Businesses since the heyday of the punched card are all amenable to improvements through good database design. Techniques for logically correct organization of facts (data) have been known for centuries, but they seem to be widely ignored. See chapter 2.

▶ While there are advantages to purchasing a commercial RDBMS product, the return on investment for these products can often be reduced substantially when their relational capabilities aren't utilized. See chapter 3.

---

400 As examples, one thinks of those who, over the years, developed the steadily improving algorithms for laying out the traces on integrated circuits, or implemented probabilistic encryption techniques – both subjects randomly chosen from a single recent issue of CASM.

► Although RDBMS products are quite capable of supporting logically correct organization of data, many, if not most are not utilized in a logical manner. Furthermore, a substantial percentage of things written about relational database design is ill-advised at best. See chapter 3.

► Good relational models of fundamental business entities often bear a surprising (to some folks) resemblance to good object models. See chapter 4.

► Data *structures* (including foreign key constraints, triggers, etc.) should never be used to enforce BUSINESS RULES, only to enforce DATA RULES. BUSINESS RULES may certainly be placed in a database as data or stored procedures and, in many cases, there are clear benefits to doing so, but BUSINESS RULES are by definition arbitrary and subject to change. See chapter 4.

► Commonly used database designs impose far too many unrecognized and unintentional business constraints. See chapter 4.

► Commonly used database designs impose far too few data integrity constraints. See chapters 4 and 11.

► An understanding of Grammar and Logic is far more important to creating good database designs than is generally acknowledged. See chapter 5.

► Aristotle has many important things to say about database design. The distinctions he makes between Essential and Accidental attributes, for instance, help to solve many common design quandaries in a logical manner, specifically providing (in this case) a basis for logically resolving NULL issues. See chapter 5.

► The introduction of the modern computer era came with the promise of significant benefits to business operations – both in the automation of business processes and the management of data. See chapter 6.

Automation of business processes began to produce results almost immediately, and continued to improve over time, leading to adoption by even the smallest of businesses. Limited capacity for data storage, however, not only delayed any improvements in data management for decades, but actually exacerbated the misguided view that Data was meant to serve Applications.

- Many traditional and commonly accepted I/T beliefs and practices are rooted in early technological limitations that no longer exist. See chapter 6 and others.

- Common wisdom suggests that there is an inherent mismatch between the object and relational worlds. This is baloney, a conclusion based mostly on unsuccessful attempts to integrate illogically designed database structures with poorly conceived object models. See chapter 9.

- The distinction between BUSINESS RULES and DATA RULES, particularly during the design process, is more significant to a logically correct and extensible database design than is generally realized. See chapter 11.

- Data constraints must be built into the database definitions, without regard for impacts on speed. If the resulting tradeoff between data integrity and response time (often incorrectly characterized as "performance") seems unacceptable, write better software, buy new hardware or both! See chapter 11.

- Data structures should never conflict with reality, although the data model does not need to fully reflect reality. See chapter 12 and elsewhere.

- Recording incomplete data for certain types of data elements results in the enforcement of unwarranted and often unrecognized assumptions; such imprecision further impedes many business opportunities. A common example of this is the handling of Weights & Measures in many typical business database tables. See chapters 12 and 13.

  Extended support for Weights & Measures must be handled carefully, however, or many difficulties can be exacerbated. See chapters 16 and 17.

- The discovery during Triage of multiple associated columns that form an entity in and of themselves within another entity is a sure sign of a poor and illogical design. A typical example of this is the presence of several address attributes contained within a Customer or Employee entity. See chapter 18.

  Traditional techniques (for example Normal Form categorization) can only expose such problems some of the time and, in any case, too late in the development process to prevent the early stages of application constipation from forming.

- Handling of Contact Mechanisms such as addresses, telephone numbers, and the like is a significant cause of inconsistency and redundancy in many business database designs. Additionally, the prevalence of multiple unique (but functionally equivalent) blocks of code to support maintenance of this data contributes not only to wasteful effort on the part of programmers, but this dilution of coding effort results in less than optimal software. See chapter 18.

  Although, if asked, most database designers will acknowledge that placing two different pieces of data in the same attribute/column is not desirable, many of them do this habitually without even recognizing it. A typical example of this malpractice is permitting a combination of data and formatting in the same element, such as when parentheses or dashes are stored with telephone numbers; such practices reduce the chances of achieving data integrity and minimizing data redundancy substantially. Stifling!

- Finally, I've further argued in chapter 19 that, rather than having multiple Relational Databases – even if these were all well-designed – most businesses would be far better served with a single Relational Database.

  Most objections to consolidation of a company's business databases are more related to politics or simple inertia, although the difficulties in achieving consolidation are very real and very significant. As well as the expected planning and effort, successful consolidation of corporate operational data stores requires both management and technical expertise.

The Rant Ends

In footnote 278 (see page 249), I said that I was retired and no longer care. The retired part is true, but the not caring part seems questionable given the number of pages thrown into this book. I attribute that, however, to some subconscious attempt to avoid the embarrassment of having been associated with this field for several years, and possibly to make some recompense.

Further information about publications (informal or otherwise) mentioned in this book.

A

APPENDIX A – BIBLIOGRAPHY

This quasi-bibliography is a listing of published material mentioned in the book, and categorizes the material with Roger Ebert-style "thumbs" ratings that are explained below. It may or may not come as a surprise that, although the authors listed are generally considered "experts" in their fields, there are many instances where they are not in agreement on every given subject. Chris Date, for instance, has a reputation as Ted Codd's most prominent evangelist, but doesn't always agree with him; Joe Celko and Chris Date seem to have differing views on several issues, and so forth. All are worth studying, however, even if only to force you to think through the issues and take sides.

Recommended Material (suitable for Learning)

 Material that is useful for learning various aspects of database design is indicated with a thumbs-up icon in the left column.

Recommended Material (suitable for Learning, but with Caveats)

 Material that is generally useful for learning various aspects of database design, but which contains some examples or conclusions that I disagree with (sometimes strongly), is indicated with a hold-on-for-a-second icon in the left column.

Not Recommended Material (suitable only for Laughing or Crying)

 Material that is useful for laughing and/or crying is indicated with a thumbs-down icon in the left column. There are, in my view, so many flaws in the material presented that it is useless as a source for database design information.

Bibliography with Ratings

 Aristotle [1]

Aristotle; "Organon" (Tools of Logic). 350 bce; of special interest to data organizers is the Introduction and Categories (Κατηγορίαι) section, which is a valuable guide to approaching the design of a database. Κατηγορίαι, usually almost transliterated to the word Categories, also meant **Predicates** in common Greek usage at the time.

Other sections of Organon which are referenced in this book are "Prior Analytics" (Αναλυτικων Προτερων) and "Posterior Analytics" (Αναλυτικων Υξτερων). The section "On Interpretation" (Περι Επμηνειας) has not been referenced, since I have used Lewis Carroll's text[401] on the same subject matter for variety.

All these works are easily located on the internet, and most libraries will have them in some form, but the translations vary considerably in readability, since only Aristotle's rather inelegant and terse teaching notes have survived. The standard translation is by Ella Mary Edghill M.A. (1881-after 1938) Although, since it was first published in 1928, sounds somewhat archaic to contemporary readers. Other English translations available include those of G. R. G. Mure and A. J. Jenkinson.

For those lucky enough? to have studied ancient Greek during their younger years, the Harvard University Press published the side-by-side (English and Greek) Loeb Classical Library translations of much of Aristotle's works in the United States. Of particular interest are "On Interpretation" (translated by Harold P. Cook), "Prior Analytics," and "Posterior Analytics" (both translated by Hugh Tredennick). These are also readily available for purchase or download on the internet.

 Barker [1]

Richard Barker; "CASE*Method – Entity Relationship Modelling"[402]; Addison-Wesley Publishing Company; Copyright © 1990 Oracle Corporation UK Limited; ISBN 0-201-41696-4

---

401 See Carroll [1] below.

402 Sic; this is the British spelling of "Modeling."

Bridgman [1]

Percy Williams Bridgman (1882-1961); "The Logic of Modern Physics"; The Macmillan Company, 1927. Most recently released by the Amo Press in 1980.

Carroll [1]

Lewis Carroll; "Symbolic Logic" (1896). This is currently available in "Mathematical Recreations of Lewis Carroll" which contains both "Symbolic Logic" (1896) and his "Game of Logic" (1887) in one volume: Dover paperback ISBN: 0-486-20492-8.

Although Carroll's *Symbolic Logic* doesn't make the distinction between Sets and Classes which is critically important for database design, nor between Essential and Accidental Attributes, equally important for database design, his writing is very straightforward and entertaining. It is therefore, in my humble opinion, essential reading for those who wish to explore the byways of Logic while being entertained.

More formal discussions of these subjects are provided by Aristotle and Russell.

Celko [1]

Joe Celko; "Data and Databases – Concepts in Practice"; Morgan-Kaufmann Publishers; Copyright © 1999 Morgan-Kaufmann; ISBN 1-55860-432-4

Any of this author's publications is well-worth reading for any database professional.

Codd [1]

Edgar Frank (Ted) Codd; "A Relational Model of Data for Large Shared Data Banks" (1970); CACM 13(6): pp 377-387 CACM is the commonly used acronym for the newsletter "Communications of the Association of Computing Machinery." This article introduced the concept of "Relational Database" to the world.

Codd [2]

Edgar Frank (Ted) Codd; Two part article published in ComputerWorld 1985; "Is Your DBMS Really Relational? " (14 October) and "Does Your DBMS Run By the Rules?" 21 October). Codd's famous twelve rules (all 13 of them!) are also available from several web sites, some of which include additional commentary and discussion. Example URLs include: www.utexas.edu/cc/database/datamodeling/index.html and www.informatik.uni-trier.de/~ley/db/journals/cacm/Codd70.html

Codd [3]

Edgar Frank (Ted) Codd; Interview published in ComputerWorld October 14, 1985.

Date [1]

Christopher J. (Chris) Date: "An Introduction to Database Systems" (currently in its eighth edition); Copyright © 2003, by Addison-Wesley Publishing Company; ISBN 0-321-19 784-4. This is widely acknowledged as the "bible" for Relational Database theory.

 Date [2]

Christopher J. (C.J.) Date: "Database Design and Relational Theory", subtitled "Normal Forms and All that Jazz"; Copyright © 2012, by Addison-Wesley Publishing Company; ISBN: 978-1-4493-2801-6; ISBN 10: 1-4493-2801-6.

The author's stated intent with this book (albeit in my words) is to familiarize database designers with a better understanding of relational theory and how it can improve design practices. I'm not convinced he succeeds, and have reservations about some of the content but, as with all of Date's writings, every practitioner should attempt to become familiar with this work.

 Date [3]

Christopher J. (C.J.) Date: "What not How – The Business Rules Approach to Application Development"; Copyright © 2000, by Addison-Wesley Publishing Company; ISBN: 0-201-70850-7. Some detailed comments on this book appear on page 79.

 Dodgson

Reverend Charles Lutwidge Dodgson; more commonly known by his pseudonym Lewis Carroll; see Carroll [1] above.

 Euclid [1]

Euclid: "The Elements" (Στοιχεῖα); circa 300 bce; this is one of a very select group of books in continuous publication since it was first released, and is a great example of the use of step-by-step logic to reach its conclusions.

 Fowler [1]

Martin Fowler; "Shared Database" section of the book "Enterprise Integration Patterns."; see Hohpe [1].

Extracts relevant to this book are in the Shared Database section, provided by contributor Martin Fowler, well-known OO author[403]. This section appears on pages 47 to 49 of the book. If the book is not immediately available to you, see http://www.enterpriseintegrationpatterns.com/SharedDataBaseIntegration.html.

---

403 See http://martinfowler.com/books.html#eip for a list of his books, the most well-known of which is UML Distilled.

Hay [1]

David C. Hay; "Data Model Patterns – Conventions of Thought"; Copyright © 1997 by David C. Hay; Dorset House; ISBN: 0-932633-29-3.

Hohpe [1]

Gregor Hohpe and Bobby Woolf (with contributors); "Enterprise Integration Patterns"; Copyright © 2004 by Pearson Education, Inc.; Addison Wesley; ISBN 0321200683.

Of particular interest is Chapter 2, covering Integration Styles by contributor Martin Fowler (see Fowler [1] above).

Josuttis [1]

Nicolai Josuttis; "Object-Oriented Programming in C++"; Copyright © 2001 by Nicolai Josuttis; John Wiley & Sons; ISBN-10: 0470843993; ISBN-13: 978-0470843994.

Loshin [1]

David Loshin; "The Data Quality Business Case: Projecting Return on Investment," a White Paper published 20 June 2006 by Informatica Corporation as Pub J50954 6731

Kimball [1]

Ralph Kimball and Margie Ross; "Fables and Facts," a classic (in my view) article in the October 16, 2004 issue of Intelligent Enterprise magazine.

Kimball [2]

Ralph Kimball; "The Data Warehouse Toolkit," John Wiley & Sons, 1996). This is, of course, applicable only to what I earlier refer to as "read-only" databases involving a relatively low number of transactions having relatively high volumes of data.

Knuth [1]

Donald Knuth; "The Art of Computer Programming", Volumes 1-4A; it is also quite enlightening to read an interview he gave on 25 April 2008 (see URL http://www.informit.com/articles/article.aspx?p=1193856). He pronounces his name "Kanuthe," by the way, not as one syllable with a silent "k" (as in "knife").

Mann [1]

Anthony T. Mann; "Microsoft® SQL Server™ 2000 for Dummies®"; Copyright © 2001 IDG Books Worldwide, Inc.; ISBN: 0-7645-0775-3. This book has been republished for several subsequent versions of Microsoft's RDBMS product, albeit with different authors. The "thumbs-down" rating refers solely to the book's suitability for database design information – something that is incidental to the book's subject.

Mead [1]

Carver Mead; Interview in Technology Review, September 2004. Mead was an early pioneer in computer science, and was a contributor to Moore's Law.

Mellor

Stephen Mellor; see Schlaer [1] below.

Moeller [1]

Jonathan Moeller; "The Ubuntu Beginner's Guide – Fourth Edition"; e-Book publication available from several sources, 2012

Rumbaugh [1]

James Rumbaugh, M. Blaha, W. Premerlani, F. and W. Lorensen; "Object-Oriented Modeling and Design"; Prentice-Hall, 1991

Russell [1]

Bertrand Russell; "Introduction to Mathematical Philosophy"; Second Edition; The MacMillan Company; April 1920. This book is the author's introduction to some of what is contained in "Principia Mathematica," first published with his coauthor Alfred Whitehead in several volumes in 1910, 1911, and 1913.

Among subjects of interest to database designers, he introduces the connections and transference between Philosophy and Mathematics (Lord Russell was preeminent in both fields), and covers the concepts of Logic and Classes from a modern perspective.

Savant [1]

Marilyn vos Savant; "The Power of Logical Thinking"; Copyright © 1996 by Marilyn vos Savant; St. Martin's Press; ISBN 0-312-13985-3.

Schlaer [1]

Sally Schlaer and Stephen Mellor, "Object-Oriented Systems Analysis: Modeling the World in Data"; Prentice-Hall, 1988. This is the original "OO Classic."

Silverston [1]

Len Silverston, W. H. Inmon, Kent Graziano; "The Data Model Resource Book"; Copyright © 1997 by John Wiley & Sons, Inc.; ISBN: 0471-15364-8. This book has some very good cookbook-type examples, although it doesn't always explain why they are correct, or how to best utilize them in support of applications.

Simsion [1]

Simsion, Graeme; "Data Modeling Essentials – Analysis, Design and Innovation"; Copyright © 1994 by International Thomson Computer Press; ISBN: 1-850-32877-3. There is much good information in this book and, although it is well-written and easy to understand, there is – unfortunately – enough misleading information in this book that it is difficult to recommend without reservations.

 ### Waymire [1]

Richard Waymire and Rick Sawtell; Sams "Teach Yourself Microsoft SQL Server 7.0 in 21 Days"; Copyright © 1999 Sams Publishing; ISBN 0-672-31290-5.

 ### Welling [1]

Luke Welling and Laura Thomson; PHP and MySQL Web Development second edition; Developer's Library/Sams; Copyright © 2003 Sams Publishing; ISBN 0-672-32525-X. This book, although containing some unexpected (for this class of book) discussions of such things as update anomalies, also contains some horrendous errors in logic, and thus cannot be recommended for use in the design of business databases.

APPENDIX B – PSEUDO-CODE EXAMPLES

Although the example SQL statements and SQL*Plus scripts in this book run unaltered in most versions of Oracle, they are not meant as examples of good coding practice[404], but rather as pseudo-code to illustrate one or more points made in the accompanying text. This appendix is provided to allow easier experimentation with the concepts discussed in the chapters referenced. These scripts can easily be extended and used with substantially larger data sets in order to permit benchmarking.

It is important to note that no transaction control is illustrated in these code segments, but is required in practice as described in the referenced chapters. Much more complete scripts, including significant sample data, are available for download.

---

404 These are fairly complete as far as functionality, but not suitable for production use for the many reasons outlined in the relevant chapters. Additionally it should be noted that there are not even any COMMIT statements. For those not using Oracle, the formatting is hopefully consistent enough that a judicious use of GREP or a similar facility should suffice to prepare these for experimentation purposes with another RDBMS.

Chapter 8 - A Corporate Merger – Part 2

Table and View Creation for Chapter 8 Examples

```
CREATE TABLE PARTY
 ( ID            NUMBER (2)     NOT NULL
 , CONSTRAINT PK_ID PRIMARY KEY ( ID )
 );


CREATE TABLE bt_PERSON
 ( ID            NUMBER(2)      NOT NULL
 , Given_Name  VARCHAR2(12)     NOT NULL
 , Surname     VARCHAR2(12)     NOT NULL
 , Soundex     CHAR(4)          NOT NULL
 , CONSTRAINT PK_pID PRIMARY KEY ( ID )
 , CONSTRAINT FK_ID FOREIGN KEY ( ID )
            REFERENCES PARTY ( ID )
 );


CREATE TABLE bt_ORGANIZATION
 ( ID            NUMBER(2)      NOT NULL
 , Name        VARCHAR2(35)     NOT NULL
 , CONSTRAINT PK_oID PRIMARY KEY ( ID )
 , CONSTRAINT FK_oID FOREIGN KEY ( ID )
            REFERENCES PARTY ( ID )
 );


CREATE TABLE bt_CUSTOMER
 ( ID            NUMBER(2)      NOT NULL
 , Account_No   VARCHAR (5)     NOT NULL
 , Credit_Limit NUMBER (9,2)    NOT NULL
 , CONSTRAINT PK_cID PRIMARY KEY ( ID )
 , CONSTRAINT FK_cID FOREIGN KEY ( ID )
            REFERENCES PARTY ( ID )
 );



CREATE TABLE bt_EMPLOYEE
 ( ID            NUMBER(2)      NOT NULL
 , Salary       NUMBER (7,2)    NOT NULL
 , Grade_Level  NUMBER (1)      NOT NULL
 , CONSTRAINT PK_eID PRIMARY KEY ( ID )
 , CONSTRAINT FK_eID FOREIGN KEY ( ID )
          REFERENCES bt_PERSON ( ID )
 )
 ;
```

```
CREATE OR REPLACE VIEW Customer_Person AS
  SELECT p.ID
         , Given_Name
         , Surname
         , Account_No
         , Credit_Limit
    FROM bt_PERSON p
         , bt_CUSTOMER c
   WHERE p.ID = c.ID
   WITH CHECK OPTION
   ;




CREATE OR REPLACE VIEW
Customer_Organization AS
  SELECT o.ID
         , Name
         , Account_No
         , Credit_Limit
    FROM bt_ORGANIZATION o
         , bt_CUSTOMER c
   WHERE o.ID = c.ID
   WITH CHECK OPTION
   ;




CREATE OR REPLACE VIEW Employee AS
  SELECT p.ID
         , Given_Name
         , Surname
         , e.Salary
         , e.Grade_Level
    FROM bt_PERSON p
         , bt_EMPLOYEE e
   WHERE e.id = p.ID
   WITH CHECK OPTION
   ;
```

```
INSERT INTO PARTY (ID) VALUES (33);
INSERT INTO bt_PERSON (ID, Given_Name,    Surname,      Soundex)
              VALUES (33, 'John',      'Smith',     Soundex('Smith') ) ;
INSERT INTO PARTY (ID) VALUES (35);
INSERT INTO bt_PERSON (ID, Given_Name,    Surname,      Soundex)
              VALUES (35, 'Rebecca',   'Apple',     Soundex('Apple') ) ;
INSERT INTO PARTY (ID) VALUES (37);
INSERT INTO bt_PERSON (ID, Given_Name,    Surname,      Soundex)
              VALUES (37, 'Steve',     'Banana',    Soundex('Banana') ) ;
INSERT INTO PARTY (ID) VALUES (39);
INSERT INTO bt_PERSON (ID, Given_Name,    Surname,      Soundex)
              VALUES (39, 'Theresa',   'Caramel',   Soundex('Caramel') ) ;
INSERT INTO PARTY (ID) VALUES (41);
INSERT INTO bt_PERSON (ID, Given_Name,    Surname,      Soundex)
              VALUES (41, 'Victor',    'Donut',     Soundex('Donut') ) ;
INSERT INTO PARTY (ID) VALUES (43);
INSERT INTO bt_PERSON (ID, Given_Name,    Surname,      Soundex)
              VALUES (43, 'Adam',      'Eclair',    Soundex('Eclair') ) ;
INSERT INTO PARTY (ID) VALUES (45);
INSERT INTO bt_PERSON (ID, Given_Name,    Surname,      Soundex)
              VALUES (45, 'Beth',      'Frosty',    Soundex('Frosty') ) ;
INSERT INTO PARTY (ID) VALUES (47);
INSERT INTO bt_PERSON (ID, Given_Name,    Surname,      Soundex)
              VALUES (47, 'Denise',    'Gelato',    Soundex('Gelato') ) ;
INSERT INTO PARTY (ID) VALUES (49);
INSERT INTO bt_PERSON (ID, Given_Name,    Surname,      Soundex)
              VALUES (49, 'Frank',     'Hamburger', Soundex('Hamburger') ) ;


-- Sample Organizations
INSERT INTO PARTY (ID) VALUES (53);
INSERT INTO bt_ORGANIZATION (ID, Name)
                  VALUES (53, 'Wonderful Widgets Corporation') ;
INSERT INTO PARTY (ID) VALUES (55);
INSERT INTO bt_ORGANIZATION (ID, Name)
                  VALUES (55, 'Corporate Widgets Experts') ;
INSERT INTO PARTY (ID) VALUES (57);
INSERT INTO bt_ORGANIZATION (ID, Name)
                  VALUES (57, 'Phenomenal Widget Masters') ;
INSERT INTO PARTY (ID) VALUES (59);
INSERT INTO bt_ORGANIZATION (ID, Name)
                  VALUES (59, 'Widgets for All, Inc.') ;
INSERT INTO PARTY (ID) VALUES (61);
INSERT INTO bt_ORGANIZATION (ID, Name)
                  VALUES (61, 'The Widget Factory') ;
INSERT INTO PARTY (ID) VALUES (64);
INSERT INTO bt_ORGANIZATION (ID, Name)
                  VALUES (64, 'Mary Smith, Inc.') ;
INSERT INTO PARTY (ID) VALUES (65);
```

```
INSERT INTO bt_ORGANIZATION (ID, Name)
                 VALUES (65, 'Potential Widgets') ;
INSERT INTO PARTY (ID) VALUES (67);
INSERT INTO bt_ORGANIZATION (ID, Name)
                 VALUES (67, 'Creative Cupcakes, LLC') ;
INSERT INTO PARTY (ID) VALUES (71);
INSERT INTO bt_ORGANIZATION (ID, Name)
                 VALUES (71, 'XYZ Consulting Corp') ;


-- Sample Employees (already exist as Persons)
-- Employee-specific data for Rebecca Apple (35)
INSERT INTO bt_EMPLOYEE (ID, Salary,   Grade_Level)
             VALUES (35, 23456.98, 1);
-- Employee-specific data for Steve Banana (37)
INSERT INTO bt_EMPLOYEE (ID, Salary,   Grade_Level)
             VALUES (37, 34567.96, 2);
-- Employee-specific data for Theresa Caramel (39)
INSERT INTO bt_EMPLOYEE (ID, Salary,   Grade_Level)
             VALUES (39, 45678.94, 3);
-- Employee-specific data for Victor Donut (41)
INSERT INTO bt_EMPLOYEE (ID, Salary,   Grade_Level)
             VALUES (41, 56780.92, 3);


-- Sample Customers that are Persons
-- Customer-specific data for Steve Banana
INSERT INTO bt_CUSTOMER (ID, Account_No, Credit_Limit)
             VALUES (37, 'IL421',   1000.00) ;
-- Customer-specific data for Theresa Caramel
INSERT INTO bt_CUSTOMER (ID, Account_No, Credit_Limit)
             VALUES (39, 'TX715',   1000.00) ;
-- Customer-specific data for Adam Eclair
INSERT INTO bt_CUSTOMER (ID, Account_No, Credit_Limit)
             VALUES (43, 'MO158',   1000.00) ;
-- Customer-specific data for Beth Frosty
INSERT INTO bt_CUSTOMER (ID, Account_No, Credit_Limit)
             VALUES (45, 'FL622',   1000.00) ;
-- Customer-specific data for Denise Gelato
INSERT INTO bt_CUSTOMER (ID, Account_No, Credit_Limit)
             VALUES (47, 'CT841',   1000.00) ;
-- Customer-specific data for Frank Hamburger
INSERT INTO bt_CUSTOMER (ID, Account_No, Credit_Limit)
             VALUES (49, 'MD359',   1000.00) ;


-- Sample Customers that are Organizations
-- Customer-specific data for Wonderful Widgets Corporation
INSERT INTO bt_CUSTOMER (ID, Account_No, Credit_Limit)
             VALUES (53, 'CA833',   120000.00) ;
-- Customer-specific data for Corporate Widgets Experts
INSERT INTO bt_CUSTOMER (ID, Account_No, Credit_Limit)
             VALUES (55, 'MS587',   120000.00) ;
```

```
-- Customer-specific data for Phenomenal Widget Masters
INSERT INTO bt_CUSTOMER (ID, Account_No, Credit_Limit)
             VALUES (57, 'DE923',    120000.00) ;
-- Customer-specific data for Widgets for All, Inc.
INSERT INTO bt_CUSTOMER (ID, Account_No, Credit_Limit)
             VALUES (59, 'WA385',    140000.00) ;
-- Customer-specific data for The Widget Factory
INSERT INTO bt_CUSTOMER (ID, Account_No, Credit_Limit)
             VALUES (61, 'TX774',    120000.00) ;
-- Customer-specific data for Potential Widgets
INSERT INTO bt_CUSTOMER (ID, Account_No, Credit_Limit)
             VALUES (65, 'RPG23',    165000.00) ;
```

Updating Merger Sample Data

```
-- Change Last Name of Victor Donut (id 41) to "Newname" in Employee VIEW
-- SurName is originally from bt_PERSON
-- Changes should appear in bt_Person, Employee
   UPDATE EMPLOYEE SET Surname = 'Newname' WHERE ID = 41 ;


-- Give Employee Rebecca Apple (id 35) a five percent raise in Employee VIEW
-- Salary is originally from bt_EMPLOYEE
-- Changes should appear in bt_Employee and Employee
   UPDATE EMPLOYEE SET Salary = (Salary * 1.05) WHERE ID = 35 ;


-- Change Last Name of Theresa Caramel (id 39) to "Butterscotch" in Employee VIEW
-- SurName is originally from bt_PERSON
-- Changes should appear in bt_Person and Employee
   UPDATE EMPLOYEE SET Surname = 'Butterscotch' WHERE ID = 39 ;


-- Raise credit limit for Theresa Caramel from 1000 to 2500 in Customer_Person VIEW
-- Credit_Limit is originally from bt_Customer
-- Changes should appear in bt_Customer and Customer_Person
   UPDATE CUSTOMER_PERSON SET Credit_Limit = 2500 WHERE ID = 39 ;


-- Change Given Name of Beth Frosty to Bethany in Customer_Person VIEW
-- Given_Name is originally from bt_Person
-- Changes should appear in bt_Person TABLE and Customer_Person VIEW
   UPDATE CUSTOMER_PERSON SET Given_Name = 'Bethany' WHERE ID = 45 ;


-- Change surname of Rebecca Apple to Eclair - should affect both bt_Person and Employee
-- This should FAIL because Rebecca Apple is not a Customer.
-- Surname is originally from bt_Person
   UPDATE CUSTOMER_PERSON SET Surname = 'Eclair' WHERE ID = 35 ;


-- Change surname of Denise Gelato to Eclair - should affect both bt_Person and Employee
-- Surname is originally from bt_Person
   UPDATE CUSTOMER_PERSON SET Surname = 'Eclair' WHERE ID = 47 ;
```

```
-- Raise credit limit of Wonderful Widgets to 123456 in Customer_Organization VIEW
-- Credit_Limit is originally from bt_Customer
   UPDATE CUSTOMER_ORGANIZATION SET Credit_Limit = 123456 WHERE ID = 53 ;


-- Rename The Widget Factory to "Midget Widgets" in Customer_Organization VIEW
-- Name is originally from bt_Organization
-- Changes should appear in bt_Employee, bt_Person, and Customer_Person
   UPDATE CUSTOMER_ORGANIZATION SET Name = 'Midget Widgets' WHERE ID = 61 ;


-- Change first name of Steve Banana to Stephen
-- First_Name is originally from bt_Person
-- Changes should appear in bt_Employee, Person, and Customer_Person
   UPDATE EMPLOYEE SET Given_Name = 'Stephen' WHERE ID = 37 ;
```

Chapter 11 - Handling Constraints

Table and View Creation for Chapter 11 Examples

```
CREATE TABLE Country
   (ID     CHAR     (3) NOT NULL,
    Name   VARCHAR (100) NOT NULL,
    CONSTRAINT PK_country_ID PRIMARY KEY ( ID )
   );


-- Based on the 3 character ISO 3166 Code
INSERT INTO Country (ID, Name) VALUES ('CAN', 'Canada');
INSERT INTO Country (ID, Name) VALUES ('USA', 'United States of America');


CREATE TABLE Postal_Code
   (Country_ID  CHAR     (3) NOT NULL,
    Postal_Code VARCHAR (20) NOT NULL,
    CONSTRAINT PK_postal_ID PRIMARY KEY ( Country_ID, Postal_Code ),
    CONSTRAINT FK_postal_ID FOREIGN KEY ( Country_ID )
              REFERENCES Country ( ID )
   );


-- Some examples
INSERT INTO Postal_Code (Country_ID, Postal_Code) VALUES ('USA', '60601');
INSERT INTO Postal_Code (Country_ID, Postal_Code) VALUES ('CAN', 'N6A4L6');

COMMIT WORK;

CREATE TABLE ConditionalFK
   (Name         VARCHAR (25) NOT NULL,
    Address      VARCHAR (25) NOT NULL,
    Country_ID   CHAR     (3) NOT NULL,
    Postal_Code VARCHAR (20) NOT NULL,
    CONSTRAINT FK_Conditional FOREIGN KEY ( Country_ID, Postal_Code )
              REFERENCES Postal_Code ( Country_ID, Postal_Code )
```

```
    );

-- These should succeed
INSERT INTO ConditionalFK (Name, Address, Country_ID, Postal_Code)
        VALUES ('Jack Kennedy', '123 Main Street', 'USA', '60601');
INSERT INTO ConditionalFK (Name, Address, Country_ID, Postal_Code)
        VALUES ('Pierre Trudeau', '456 Main Street', 'CAN', 'N6A4L6');

-- These should fail
INSERT INTO ConditionalFK (Name, Address, Country_ID, Postal_Code)
        VALUES ('Lyndon Johnson', '789 Other Road', 'USA', '71295');
INSERT INTO ConditionalFK (Name, Address, Country_ID, Postal_Code)
        VALUES ('John Kerry', '875 Left Boulevard', 'CAN', 'B4A5K8');

-- These temporary tables need to be dropped to avoid later conflicts.
DROP TABLE ConditionalFK;
DROP TABLE Postal_Code;
DROP TABLE Country;
```

Chapters 12 & 13 - Weights & Measures Parts 1 & 2

Table and View Creation for Chapter 12 Examples

```
CREATE TABLE Weight_Measure_Class
  ( UOM_Class              VARCHAR2(15)  NOT NULL
  , Description            VARCHAR2(100)
  , CONSTRAINT PK_WEIGHT_MEASURE_CLASS PRIMARY KEY ( UOM_Class )
  );

-- Many more samples are included in the electronic version of these scripts

INSERT INTO Weight_Measure_Class (UOM_Class, Description)
    VALUES ('Linear',
            'Length of a straight one-dimensional line between two points.');
INSERT INTO Weight_Measure_Class (UOM_Class, Description)
    VALUES ('Temperature',
            'A measure of the degree of heat (molecular motion) within or'
        || ' around an object.');
INSERT INTO Weight_Measure_Class (UOM_Class, Description)
    VALUES ('Weight',
            'The mathematical product of a solid object''s mass and'
        || ' gravity');

CREATE TABLE Weight_Measure
  ( UOM_Class              VARCHAR2(15)                NOT NULL
  , Unit_of_Measure        VARCHAR2(10)                NOT NULL
  , Name                   VARCHAR2(25)
  , Root_Unit_of_Measure   VARCHAR2(10)                NOT NULL
  , Multiplier             NUMBER(20, 12)              NOT NULL
```

```
          , Offset                      NUMBER(10, 0)      DEFAULT 0 NOT NULL
          , CONSTRAINT PK_WEIGHT_MEASURE  PRIMARY KEY
                                          (UOM_Class, Unit_of_Measure)
          , CONSTRAINT FK1_WEIGHT_MEASURE FOREIGN KEY (UOM_Class)
                                          REFERENCES WEIGHT_MEASURE_CLASS (UOM_Class)
          , CONSTRAINT FK2_WEIGHT_MEASURE FOREIGN KEY
                                          (UOM_Class, Root_Unit_of_Measure)
                                          REFERENCES WEIGHT_MEASURE
                                          (UOM_Class, Unit_of_Measure)   );
-- Note that additional constraints should be implemented in production:
-- 1. Only one Unit_of_Measure per UOM_Class can have a Multiplier value of 1
--    and an Offset of 0.
--    This implies that only one row for each UOM_Class can have a
--    Unit_of_Measure that is the same as the Root_Unit_of_Measure.
-- 2. A conversion pair (e.g. kg-lb) should never exist in 2 directions
--    (e.g. if kg-lb exists, lb-kg must not exist)
-- The sample Trigger below will illustrate enforcement of both these constraints.

CREATE OR REPLACE TRIGGER biu_Weight_Measure
  BEFORE INSERT OR UPDATE
  ON Weight_Measure
  FOR EACH ROW
  DECLARE
    TempValue  INTEGER;
  BEGIN
    -- Ensure there is no other row for the specified UOM_Class that has
    -- a Multiplier of 1 and an Offset of 0.
    SELECT COUNT(*)
      INTO TempValue
      FROM Weight_Measure
     WHERE UOM_Class = :new.UOM_Class
       AND 1         = :new.Multiplier
       AND 0         = :new.Offset
      ;
    IF TempValue > 0 THEN
        RAISE_APPLICATION_ERROR ( -20001, 'Only one row per Class may have Multiplier=1
and Offset=0.' );
    END IF;
    -- Ensure that, for any Unit_of_Measure | Root_Unit_of_Measure pair,
    -- there is no existing Root_Unit_of_Measure | Unit_of_Measure pair
    -- with the same values.
    SELECT COUNT(*)
      INTO TempValue
      FROM Weight_Measure
     WHERE Root_Unit_of_Measure = :new.Unit_of_Measure
       AND Unit_of_Measure      = :new.Root_Unit_of_Measure
      ;
    IF TempValue > 0 THEN
        RAISE_APPLICATION_ERROR ( -20002, 'Symmetrical conversion factors are not
permitted.' );
```

```
        END IF;
END;
/
-- More samples are included in the electronic version of these scripts
INSERT INTO Weight_Measure
  (UOM_Class, Name, Unit_of_Measure, Root_Unit_of_Measure, Multiplier, Offset)
    VALUES ('Linear',         'Inch',                  'in',    'in',
        1,                    0)    ;
INSERT INTO Weight_Measure
  (UOM_Class, Name, Unit_of_Measure, Root_Unit_of_Measure, Multiplier, Offset)
    VALUES('Weight',          'Pound',                 'lb',    'lb',
        1,                    0)    ;
-- Note that this table is not intended to be symmetrical (i.e. if there is a
-- degrees celsius to degrees fahrenheit conversion factor row, there should
-- *not* be a degrees fahrenheit to degrees celsius row. The reasons for this
-- are spelled out in the book referenced above.)

-- ***** Linear *********************************************************
INSERT INTO Weight_Measure
  (UOM_Class, Name, Unit_of_Measure, Root_Unit_of_Measure, Multiplier, Offset)
    VALUES('Linear',          'Centimeter',            'cm',    'in',
        2.53999999,           0)    ;
INSERT INTO Weight_Measure
  (UOM_Class, Name, Unit_of_Measure, Root_Unit_of_Measure, Multiplier, Offset)
    VALUES('Linear',          'Decimeter',             'dm',    'in',
        0.25399999,           0)    ;
INSERT INTO Weight_Measure
  (UOM_Class, Name, Unit_of_Measure, Root_Unit_of_Measure, Multiplier, Offset)
    VALUES('Linear',          'Foot',                  'ft',    'in',
        0.0833333333333,      0)    ;
INSERT INTO Weight_Measure
  (UOM_Class, Name, Unit_of_Measure, Root_Unit_of_Measure, Multiplier, Offset)
    VALUES('Linear',          'Meter',                 'm',     'in',
        0.025399999,          0)    ;
INSERT INTO Weight_Measure
  (UOM_Class, Name, Unit_of_Measure, Root_Unit_of_Measure, Multiplier, Offset)
    VALUES ('Linear',         'Micron',                'mic',   'in',
        25399.9999,              0)    ;
INSERT INTO Weight_Measure
  (UOM_Class, Name, Unit_of_Measure, Root_Unit_of_Measure, Multiplier, Offset)
    VALUES('Linear',          'Millimeter',            'mm',    'in',
        25.399999,            0)    ;
INSERT INTO Weight_Measure
  (UOM_Class, Name, Unit_of_Measure, Root_Unit_of_Measure, Multiplier, Offset)
    VALUES('Linear',          'Yard',                  'yd',    'in',
        0.0277777777777,      0)    ;

-- ***** Weight *********************************************************
INSERT INTO Weight_Measure
  (UOM_Class, Name, Unit_of_Measure, Root_Unit_of_Measure, Multiplier, Offset)
```

```
                      VALUES('Weight',         'Gram',                      'g',    'lb',
              454.54545454,          0)   ;
INSERT INTO Weight_Measure
  (UOM_Class, Name, Unit_of_Measure, Root_Unit_of_Measure, Multiplier, Offset)
      VALUES('Weight',         'Kilogram',                  'kg',   'lb',
              0.454545454,          0)   ;
INSERT INTO WEIGHT_MEASURE
  (UOM_Class, Name, Unit_of_Measure, Root_Unit_of_Measure, Multiplier, Offset)
      VALUES('Weight',         'Ounce',                     'oz',   'lb',
              16,                   0)      ;
INSERT INTO Weight_Measure
  (UOM_Class, Name, Unit_of_Measure, Root_Unit_of_Measure, Multiplier, Offset)
      VALUES('Weight',         'Ton',                       'ton',  'lb',
              0.0005,               0)   ;
```

Bare Bones UOM_Convert Function in PL/SQL

```
CREATE OR REPLACE
FUNCTION UOM_CONVERT(FromUOM              Weight_Measure.Unit_Of_Measure%TYPE,
                     ToUOM                Weight_Measure.Unit_Of_Measure%TYPE,
                     FromMeasurementValue NUMBER,
                     MeasurementClass     Weight_Measure.UOM_Class%TYPE)
RETURN NUMBER
IS
-- Use uppercase on units of measure to be sure....
    -- This function will convert the value in one unit of measure to the value
    -- in another unit of measure.
    -- See chapter the book referenced in the header for an explanation of the
    -- approach used. Briefly, this approach is to use a single factor for
    -- conversions in either direction in order to avoid cumulative errors: we
    -- multiply to convert from a root to a non-root measure and divide to
    -- convert from a non-root to a root measure.

    -- Variable Declarations
    Root                 NUMBER;          -- 1 if FromUOM is a Root
    OutMeasurementValue  NUMBER;          -- Return value
    plOffset             Weight_Measure.Offset%TYPE;
    plMultiplier         Weight_Measure.Multiplier%TYPE;
    -- Variable Declarations required for non-root to non-root conversions
    TempMeasurementValue NUMBER;              -- Intermediate FromMeasurementValue
    RootAlt              NUMBER;          -- 1 if ToUOM   is a Root
    RootUOM              Weight_Measure.Root_Unit_of_Measure%TYPE;

BEGIN
  SELECT Multiplier
    INTO Root
    FROM Weight_Measure wm
   WHERE wm.UOM_Class       = MeasurementClass
     AND wm.Unit_of_Measure = FromUOM       ;
```

```
-- Determine if the "From" Unit of Measure is a Root Unit or not. This
-- determines whether we need to do the conversion by multiplying the
-- factors or dividing them. We always use the same factor and then multiply
-- or divide depending on the direction to avoid any possibility of cumula-
-- tive conversion errors.
IF Root = 1
THEN
    -- FromUOM *IS* a root unit of measure
    SELECT Multiplier, Offset
      INTO plMultiplier, plOffset
      FROM Weight_Measure wm
     WHERE wm.UOM_Class        = MeasurementClass
       AND wm.Unit_of_Measure       = ToUOM
       AND wm.Root_Unit_of_Measure = FromUOM     ;
    OutMeasurementValue := (FromMeasurementValue - plOffset) * plMultiplier;
ELSE
    -- FromUOM is *NOT* a root unit of measure
    IF FromUOM = ToUOM
    THEN
        -- FromUOM and ToUOM *ARE* the same value
        -- When converting FROM a root unit of measurement, trapping of like
        -- inputs is not required, since the formula has the necessary
        -- information. In this case, however, because the conversion is non-
        -- symmetrical, no value will be returned unless we explicitly set it.
        -- Under controlled circumstances, there doesn't seem to be any reason
        -- why this function would be deliberately called with like units of
        -- measurement types, but it may be possible if the routine is used
        -- within batch programs, so it's covered.
        OutMeasurementValue := FromMeasurementValue;
    ELSE
-- FromUOM and ToUOM are *NOT* the same value
-- Since this is not a general purpose conversion routine (see comments above
-- on why non-symmetrical conversion is used), this function only supports
-- direct conversion between root and non-root values in the same system of
-- measures. Non supported conversions are trapped implicitly by the absence
-- of any row entries containing the two UOMs, and handled by the exception
-- clause below.
        TempMeasurementValue := FromMeasurementValue;
        -- Assume that ToUOM is the RootUOM until we find out otherwise.
        RootUOM := ToUom;
-- TO MAKE THE ROUTINE SYMMETRICAL INCLUDE THE SECTION BELOW =========================:
        -- We make this a general purpose conversion routine by first checking
        -- to see if the ToUOM is the root unit of measure. If it isn't (and
        -- we have already determined that FromUOM isn't either), we first
        -- need to convert the ToUOM into the Root Unit, so that the remainder
        -- of this ELSE clause won't generate a WHEN NO_DATA_FOUND condition.
        SELECT Multiplier
          INTO RootAlt
          FROM Weight_Measure wm
         WHERE wm.UOM_Class        = MeasurementClass
```

```
                 AND wm.Unit_of_Measure = ToUOM              ;
           IF RootAlt <> 1
           THEN
              -- ToUOM is *NOT* a root unit of measure
              -- FromUOM is *NOT* a root unit of measure
              -- Convert the FromMeasurementValue to the Root measurement value
              -- for this Class
              SELECT Multiplier, Offset, Root_Unit_of_Measure
                INTO plMultiplier, plOffset, RootUOM
                FROM Weight_Measure wm
               WHERE wm.UOM_Class       = MeasurementClass
                 AND wm.Unit_of_Measure = ToUOM              ;
              TempMeasurementValue := (FromMeasurementValue - plOffset) * plMultiplier;
           END IF;
-- TO MAKE THE ROUTINE SYMMETRICAL INCLUDE THE SECTION ABOVE ========================;
           -- Now do the conversion to the (possibly other) non-root UOM
           SELECT Multiplier, Offset
             INTO plMultiplier, plOffset
             FROM Weight_Measure wm
            WHERE wm.UOM_Class       = MeasurementClass
              AND wm.Unit_of_Measure    = FromUOM
              AND wm.Root_Unit_of_Measure = RootUOM             ;
           OutMeasurementValue := (TempMeasurementValue / plMultiplier) + plOffset;
        END IF;
     END IF;

RETURN OutMeasurementValue;

EXCEPTION
  -- DBMS_OUTPUT used only for testing; replace this section for actual use.
  WHEN NO_DATA_FOUND
  THEN
     DBMS_OUTPUT.PUT_LINE('Conversion from "' || FromUOM || '" to "' || ToUOM
                    || '" is not supported');
     RETURN NULL;

  WHEN OTHERS
  THEN
     -- Obviously this needs to be expanded somewhat....
     DBMS_OUTPUT.PUT_LINE('Something surprising occurred ...');
     RETURN NULL;
END;
/
```

Bare Bones WM_SYS_VAL Function in PL/SQL

```
-- This is a very abbreviated conversion function used solely in Triggers to
-- set the *_SYS column values to the internal standard value in the system
-- Unit of Measure.
CREATE OR REPLACE
```

```
FUNCTION WM_SYS_VAL(FromMeasurementValue NUMBER,
                    FromUOM             Weight_Measure.Unit_Of_Measure%TYPE,
                    MeasurementClass    Weight_Measure.UOM_Class%TYPE)
RETURN NUMBER
IS

    -- Variable Declarations
    RootMeasurementValue  NUMBER;                         -- Return value
    plOffset              Weight_Measure.Offset%TYPE;
    plMultiplier          Weight_Measure.Multiplier%TYPE;

BEGIN
-- Find the Root Unit of Measure for the Class whose Value is being converted
    SELECT Multiplier, Offset
      INTO plMultiplier, plOffset
      FROM Weight_Measure wm
     WHERE wm.Unit_of_Measure = FromUOM
       AND wm.UOM_Class        = MeasurementClass  ;

  IF plMultiplier = 1
  THEN
    -- FromUOM *IS* a root unit of measure; pass input value to output.
    RootMeasurementValue := FromMeasurementValue;
  ELSE
    -- FromUOM is *NOT* a root unit of measure; convert the input value and
    -- pass it to the output.
    RootMeasurementValue := (FromMeasurementValue / plMultiplier) + plOffset;
  END IF;

RETURN RootMeasurementValue;

EXCEPTION
    -- DBMS_OUTPUT used only for testing; replace this section for actual use.
    WHEN NO_DATA_FOUND
    THEN
      DBMS_OUTPUT.PUT_LINE('Conversion of "' || FromUOM || '" value failed. "');
      RETURN NULL;

    WHEN OTHERS
    THEN
      -- Obviously this needs to be expanded somewhat....
      DBMS_OUTPUT.PUT_LINE('Something surprising occurred ...');
      RETURN NULL;
END;
/
```

Chapter 14 - Grammar, Sets, and Predicate Logic – Part 2

```
-- Sample Persons
INSERT INTO PARTY (ID) VALUES (21);
```

```
INSERT INTO bt_PERSON (ID, Given_Name,    Surname,      Soundex)
             VALUES (21, 'John',      'Doe',        Soundex('Doe') ) ;
-- Employee-specific data for John Smith (21)
INSERT INTO bt_EMPLOYEE (ID, Salary,    Grade_Level)
             VALUES (21, 56789.12, 2);
INSERT INTO PARTY (ID) VALUES (32);
INSERT INTO bt_PERSON (ID, Given_Name,    Surname,      Soundex)
             VALUES (32, 'Mary',      'Smith',      Soundex('Smith') ) ;
-- Bill Jones is an Employee of XYZ Consulting Corporation (Party ID 71)
INSERT INTO PARTY (ID) VALUES (76);
INSERT INTO bt_PERSON (ID, Given_Name,    Surname,      Soundex)
             VALUES (76, 'Bill',      'Jones',      Soundex('Jones') ) ;

CREATE TABLE Project_Role
 ( ID          NUMBER(2)       NOT NULL
 , Role_Name  VARCHAR2 (25)    NOT NULL
 , CONSTRAINT PK_pRole PRIMARY KEY ( ID ) ) ;

INSERT INTO Project_Role VALUES (46, 'C++ Programmer') ;

CREATE TABLE Project
 ( ID          NUMBER(2)      NOT NULL
 , DESCRIPTION   VARCHAR2(40)  NOT NULL
 , CONSTRAINT PK_prj PRIMARY KEY ( ID ) ) ;

INSERT INTO Project (ID, Description)
         VALUES (93, 'Rewrite Antikythera Mechanism in C++');

CREATE TABLE Project_Staffing
 ( Project_ID   NUMBER(2)       NOT NULL
 , Person_ID    NUMBER(2)       NOT NULL
 , Role_ID      NUMBER(2)       NOT NULL
 , CONSTRAINT PK_pkPrjStf PRIMARY KEY ( Project_ID, Person_ID, Role_ID )
 , CONSTRAINT FK_prProject FOREIGN KEY ( Project_ID )
                 REFERENCES PROJECT      ( ID )
 , CONSTRAINT FK_prPerson FOREIGN KEY ( Person_ID )
                 REFERENCES BT_PERSON    ( ID )
 , CONSTRAINT FK_prRole FOREIGN KEY ( Role_ID )
                 REFERENCES PROJECT_ROLE ( ID ) ) ;

-- John Doe as a C++ Programmer on the Antikythera Mechanism Project
INSERT INTO Project_Staffing (Project_ID, Person_ID, Role_ID)
         VALUES (93, 21, 46);
-- Mary Smith as a C++ Programmer on the Antikythera Mechanism Project
INSERT INTO Project_Staffing (Project_ID, Person_ID, Role_ID)
         VALUES (93, 32, 46);
-- Bill Jones as a C++ Programmer on the Antikythera Mechanism Project
INSERT INTO Project_Staffing (Project_ID, Person_ID, Role_ID)
         VALUES (93, 76, 46);
```

WM_Widget Demonstration Table

```
-- First build and populate the sample table as a baseline
CREATE TABLE Widget
   (ID          NUMBER          NOT NULL,
    Length      NUMBER          NOT NULL
                CONSTRAINT chk_Length_Range CHECK (Length BETWEEN 0 AND 100),
    Weight      NUMBER          NOT NULL
                CONSTRAINT chk_Weight_Range CHECK (Weight BETWEEN 0 AND 20),
    Color       VARCHAR2(10)    NOT NULL,
    CONSTRAINT PK_WIDGET PRIMARY KEY (ID)    );

INSERT INTO Widget (ID, Length, Weight, Color) VALUES (32,  32.4, 10,    'Green');
INSERT INTO Widget (ID, Length, Weight, Color) VALUES (37,  17.0, 14,    'Red');
INSERT INTO Widget (ID, Length, Weight, Color) VALUES (46,  28.6, 8.875, 'Green');
INSERT INTO Widget (ID, Length, Weight, Color) VALUES (59,  22.8, 8.6,   'Blue');

-- Display the original structure and data as a reference
SELECT TO_CHAR(ID, 999) "ID",
       TO_CHAR(a.Length,    999.999),
       TO_CHAR(a.Weight,    999.999),
       Color
  FROM Widget a
 ORDER BY ID;

-- *** THE SYSTEM MUST BE CLOSED OFF TO USER ACTIVITY AT THIS POINT ***
-- This is where the modifications described in the chapter "Weights &
-- Measures - Part 3" (see page 271) are demonstrated.
-- Remove the value-range constraints on Length and Weight, since these
-- will be dependent on the Unit-of-Measure being used. The constraints
-- will be replaced by identical ones (assuming the old UOM has become
-- the SYS UOM) on the Length_SYS and Weight_SYS columns.

ALTER TABLE Widget  DROP CONSTRAINT chk_Length_Range;

ALTER TABLE Widget  DROP CONSTRAINT chk_Weight_Range;

COMMIT;

-- Demonstrate that constraints have been removed; roll back transaction at
-- this point to remove this undesired insert.
INSERT INTO Widget (ID, Length, Weight, Color) VALUES (61, 101.9, 7.4,   'Purple');

ROLLBACK;

-- Alter the Widget Table to add the new data elements
ALTER TABLE Widget
```

```
         ADD (Length_Class  VARCHAR2(15) DEFAULT 'Linear',
              Length_UOM     VARCHAR2(10) DEFAULT 'in',
              Length_SYS     NUMBER
                 CONSTRAINT chk_Length_Range CHECK (Length_SYS BETWEEN 0 AND 100),
              Weight_Class  VARCHAR2(15) DEFAULT 'Weight',
              Weight_UOM     VARCHAR2(10) DEFAULT 'lb',
              Weight_SYS     NUMBER
                 CONSTRAINT chk_Weight_Range CHECK (Weight_SYS BETWEEN 0 AND 20)     );

-- Display the altered structure and data as a reference
SELECT TO_CHAR(ID, 999) "ID"
     , TO_CHAR(a.Length,     999.999) || ' ' || a.Length_UOM "Length"
     , TO_CHAR(a.Length_SYS, 999.999) || ' '
                                      || b.Root_Unit_of_Measure "Length (SYS)"
     , TO_CHAR(a.Weight,     999.999) || ' ' || a.Weight_UOM "Weight"
     , TO_CHAR(a.Weight_SYS, 999.999) || ' '
                                      || c.Root_Unit_of_Measure "Weight (SYS)"
     , Color
  FROM Widget a, Weight_Measure b, Weight_Measure c
 WHERE a.Length_Class = b.UOM_CLASS
   AND a.Length_UOM   = b.UNIT_OF_MEASURE
   AND a.Weight_Class = c.UOM_CLASS
   AND a.Weight_UOM   = c.UNIT_OF_MEASURE
 ORDER BY ID;

-- Copy the existing Widget base values to the new system columns
UPDATE WIDGET SET
       Length_SYS = Length,
       Weight_SYS = Weight;

-- Display the altered structure and data as a reference (rerun above query)
-- Now Alter the Widget Table to add the new foreign key constraints
ALTER TABLE Widget
  ADD (CONSTRAINT Widget_FK1 FOREIGN KEY (Length_Class, Length_UOM)
       REFERENCES WEIGHT_MEASURE (UOM_Class, Unit_of_Measure));
ALTER TABLE Widget
  ADD (CONSTRAINT Widget_FK2 FOREIGN KEY (Weight_Class, Weight_UOM)
       REFERENCES WEIGHT_MEASURE (UOM_Class, Unit_of_Measure));

-- Now Alter the Widget Table to add NOT NULL constraints
ALTER TABLE Widget
  MODIFY (Length_Class  NOT NULL,
          Length_UOM    NOT NULL,
          Length_SYS    NOT NULL,
          Weight_Class  NOT NULL,
          Weight_UOM    NOT NULL,
          Weight_SYS    NOT NULL);
```

```
-- Now Alter the Widget Table to add an insert/update trigger
CREATE OR REPLACE TRIGGER Widget_Measure_BIU
BEFORE INSERT OR UPDATE
    ON WIDGET
   FOR EACH ROW
BEGIN
    :new.Weight_SYS :=
                 WM_SYS_VAL(:new.Weight, :new.Weight_UOM, :new.Weight_Class);
    :new.Length_SYS :=
                 WM_SYS_VAL(:new.Length, :new.Length_UOM, :new.Length_Class);
END;
/


/* **** THE SYSTEM CAN BE RE-OPENED TO USER ACTIVITY AT THIS POINT **** */

-- Now set values to desired UOMs as shown in Chapter 16's sample data
UPDATE Widget
   SET Length     = 2.7,
       Length_UOM = 'ft',
       Weight     = 160,
       Weight_UOM = 'oz'
 WHERE ID         = 32;
UPDATE Widget
   SET Weight     = 142,
       Weight_UOM = 'oz'
 WHERE ID         = 46;
UPDATE Widget
   SET Length     = 1.9,
       Length_UOM = 'ft'
 WHERE ID         = 59;
-- Display the altered structure and data as a reference (rerun earlier query)

-- Now demonstrate how data changes are handled
UPDATE Widget
   SET Length     = 5.7,
       Length_UOM = 'ft'
 WHERE ID         = 37;

-- Display the altered data (rerun earlier query)
-- Note that when the Length of Widget 37 was changed, the System value
-- was updated transparently.
```

Table for Weights & Measures Test Cases

```
CREATE TABLE WM_Test_Case
   ( UOM_Class              VARCHAR2(15)          NOT NULL
   , Input_UOM              VARCHAR2(10)          NOT NULL
   , Input_Value            NUMBER
```

```
, Output_UOM             VARCHAR2(10)                  NOT NULL
, Desired_Value          NUMBER
, CONSTRAINT FK1_WM_TEST FOREIGN KEY (UOM_Class, Input_UOM)
                      REFERENCES WEIGHT_MEASURE (UOM_Class, Unit_of_Measure)
, CONSTRAINT FK2_WM_TEST FOREIGN KEY (UOM_Class, Output_UOM)
                      REFERENCES WEIGHT_MEASURE (UOM_Class, Unit_of_Measure)   );
```

Sample Data for Weights & Measures Test Cases

```
INSERT INTO WM_Test_Case
          ( UOM_Class, Input_Value, Input_UOM, Desired_Value, Output_UOM )
   VALUES ( 'Linear'     ,     7       , 'ft',      84.0000000, 'in'   );
INSERT INTO WM_Test_Case
          ( UOM_Class, Input_Value, Input_UOM, Desired_Value, Output_UOM )
   VALUES ( 'Linear'     ,     3       , 'ft',       .9144000, 'm'    );
INSERT INTO WM_Test_Case
          ( UOM_Class, Input_Value, Input_UOM, Desired_Value, Output_UOM )
   VALUES ( 'Weight'     ,  1000      , 'g',        2.2000000, 'lb'   );
INSERT INTO WM_Test_Case
          ( UOM_Class, Input_Value, Input_UOM, Desired_Value, Output_UOM )
   VALUES ( 'Weight'     ,    36      , 'g',        1.2672000, 'oz'   );
```

Sample SQL Query for Weights & Measures Test Run

```
DEFINE Precision = 3;
-- "Precision" is used below and must obviously be set for your own needs.
SELECT '(' || UOM_Class || ')'                            "Class"
     , Input_Value                                        "Input Value"
     , Input_UOM                                          "UOM"
     , Desired_Value                                      "Desired Value"
     , Output_UOM                                         "UOM"
     , UOM_CONVERT(Input_UOM, Output_UOM, Input_Value, UOM_Class)  "Output Value"
     , DECODE( ROUND(Desired_Value, &Precision)
         - ROUND(UOM_CONVERT(Input_UOM, Output_UOM, Input_Value, UOM_Class) , &Precision ),
             0, ' Pass', ' Fail ***')                     "RESULT"
  FROM WM_Test_Case;
```

Chapter 18 - Contact Mechanisms

Table Creation and Population for Chapter 18 Examples

```
CREATE TABLE Currency
  ( ID_ISO_A3           CHAR(3)        NOT NULL PRIMARY KEY
  , Name_English        VARCHAR2(50)   NOT NULL
  , Post_Decimal_Digits NUMBER         NOT NULL
  , Symbol              VARCHAR2(3)    NOT NULL );

INSERT INTO Currency
          (ID_ISO_A3, Name_English,                Post_Decimal_Digits, Symbol)
   VALUES ('USD',    'United States Dollar'      ,         2,          '$')   ;
     -- The United States actually has three codes assigned: USD, USS (same
```

```
          -- day), and USN (next day); see UN/CEFACT recommendation 9, paragraphs
          -- 8-9 ECE/TRADE/203, 1996. This is of concern in Financial databases.
INSERT INTO Currency
          (ID_ISO_A3, Name_English,                       Post_Decimal_Digits, Symbol)
     VALUES ('USS',   'United States Dollar - Same Day',        2,             '$')   ;
INSERT INTO Currency
          (ID_ISO_A3, Name_English,                       Post_Decimal_Digits, Symbol)
     VALUES ('USN',   'United States Dollar - Next Day',        2,             '$')   ;
INSERT INTO Currency
          (ID_ISO_A3, Name_English,                       Post_Decimal_Digits, Symbol)
     VALUES ('GBP',   'Pound Sterling',                         2,             '£')   ;
          -- Great Britain also uses GBX for Penny Sterling in certain trading
          -- applications. This is of concern in Financial databases.
INSERT INTO Currency
          (ID_ISO_A3, Name_English,                       Post_Decimal_Digits, Symbol)
     VALUES ('GBX',   'Penny Sterling',                         2,             'p')   ;
INSERT INTO Currency
          (ID_ISO_A3, Name_English,                       Post_Decimal_Digits, Symbol)
     VALUES ('CAD',   'Canadian Dollar',                        2,             '$')   ;
INSERT INTO Currency
          (ID_ISO_A3, Name_English,                       Post_Decimal_Digits, Symbol)
     VALUES ('MXN',   'Mexican Peso',                           2,             'P')   ;

CREATE TABLE Language
  ( ID_ISO_A3    CHAR(3)         NOT NULL  PRIMARY KEY
  , ID_ISO_A2         CHAR(2)         NOT NULL  UNIQUE
  , Name_Native       VARCHAR2(20)    NOT NULL
  , Name_English      VARCHAR2(20)    NOT NULL
  , Name_French       VARCHAR2(20)    NOT NULL  );


INSERT INTO Language
          (ID_ISO_A3, ID_ISO_A2, Name_Native,  Name_English, Name_French)
     VALUES ('ENG',   'EN',      'English',    'English',    'Anglaise')   ;
INSERT INTO Language
          (ID_ISO_A3, ID_ISO_A2, Name_Native,  Name_English, Name_French)
     VALUES ('FRE',   'FR',      'Français',   'French',     'Français')   ;
INSERT INTO Language
          (ID_ISO_A3, ID_ISO_A2, Name_Native,  Name_English, Name_French)
     VALUES ('ESM',   'SM',      'Espanol',    'Spanish',    'Espagnol')   ;

CREATE TABLE Time_Zone
  ( Time_Zone_Abbreviation VARCHAR2(4)      NOT NULL
  , Time_Zone_Designator   VARCHAR2(30)     NOT NULL
  , UTC_Offset             NUMBER(2,0)      NOT NULL
  , CONSTRAINT PK1_TimeZone_1 PRIMARY KEY (Time_Zone_Abbreviation)  );

INSERT INTO Time_Zone
          ( Time_Zone_Abbreviation, Time_Zone_Designator, UTC_Offset)
     VALUES ('MST', 'Mountain Standard Time',          -7)    ;
```

```
INSERT INTO Time_Zone
        ( Time_Zone_Abbreviation, Time_Zone_Designator, UTC_Offset)
    VALUES ('CST',  'Central Standard Time',          -6)    ;
INSERT INTO Time_Zone
        ( Time_Zone_Abbreviation, Time_Zone_Designator, UTC_Offset)
    VALUES ('CDT',  'Central Daylight Savings Time',  -5)    ;
INSERT INTO Time_Zone
        ( Time_Zone_Abbreviation, Time_Zone_Designator, UTC_Offset)
    VALUES ('EST',  'Eastern Standard Time',          -5)    ;
INSERT INTO Time_Zone
        ( Time_Zone_Abbreviation, Time_Zone_Designator, UTC_Offset)
    VALUES ('EDT',  'Eastern Daylight Savings Time',  -4)    ;
INSERT INTO Time_Zone
        ( Time_Zone_Abbreviation, Time_Zone_Designator, UTC_Offset)
    VALUES ('AST',  'Atlantic Standard Time Zone',    -4)    ;

CREATE TABLE Country
  ( ID_ISO_A3                CHAR(3)       NOT NULL  PRIMARY KEY
  , ID_ISO_A2                CHAR(2)       NOT NULL  UNIQUE
  , ID_ISO_Numeric           VARCHAR2(3)   NOT NULL  UNIQUE
  , Name_Native              VARCHAR2(80)  NOT NULL  UNIQUE
  , Name_English             VARCHAR2(80)  NOT NULL  UNIQUE
  , Name_French              VARCHAR2(80)  NOT NULL  UNIQUE
  , Administrative_Seat      VARCHAR2(80)  NOT NULL
  , Admin_Level_1_Label      VARCHAR2(80)  NOT NULL
  , Admin_Level_1_Data_Mask  VARCHAR2(50)  NOT NULL
  , Admin_Level_1_Standard   VARCHAR2(50)
  , Currency_ISO_A3          CHAR(3)       NOT NULL
  , Language_ISO_A3          CHAR(3)       NOT NULL
  , National_ID_Label        VARCHAR2(25)
  , National_ID_Data_Mask    VARCHAR2(50)
  , Postal_Code_Label        VARCHAR2(20)  NOT NULL
  , Postal_Code_Data_Mask    VARCHAR2(50)  NOT NULL
  , Postal_Code_Display_Mask VARCHAR2(50)  NOT NULL
  , Postal_Level_1_Label     VARCHAR2(30)  NOT NULL
  , Postal_Level_2_Label     VARCHAR2(30)  NOT NULL
  , Telephone_Country_Code   VARCHAR2(6)
  , Telephone_Data_Mask      VARCHAR2(50)  NOT NULL
  , Telephone_Display_Mask   VARCHAR2(25)  NOT NULL
  , CONSTRAINT FK1_Country FOREIGN KEY (Currency_ISO_A3)
            REFERENCES Currency (ID_ISO_A3)
  , CONSTRAINT FK2_Country FOREIGN KEY (Language_ISO_A3)
            REFERENCES Language (ID_ISO_A3)  );

INSERT INTO Country
        ( ID_ISO_A3, ID_ISO_A2, ID_ISO_Numeric, Name_Native
        , Name_English, Name_French, Administrative_Seat
        , Admin_Level_1_Label, Admin_Level_1_Data_Mask
        , Currency_ISO_A3, Language_ISO_A3
        , National_ID_Label, National_ID_Data_Mask
```

```
        , Postal_Code_Label, Postal_Code_Data_Mask, Postal_Code_Display_Mask
        , Postal_Level_1_Label, Postal_Level_2_Label
        , Telephone_Country_Code
        , Telephone_Data_Mask, Telephone_Display_Mask)
    VALUES ('USA', 'US', '840', 'United States of America'
        , 'United States of America', 'États-Unis', 'Washington, D.C.'
        , 'State', '([A-Z]{2})'
        , 'USD', 'ENG'
        , 'Social Security Number', '^[0-9]{3}-[0-9]{2}-[0-9]{4}$'
        , 'Zip+4', '^([0-9]{5})([0-9]{4}|)$', '\1-\2'
        , 'State', 'City'
        , '011', '^([0-9]{3})([0-9]{3})([0-9]{4})$', '(\1) \2-\3')    ;

UPDATE Country SET Admin_Level_1_Standard = 'FIPS 5.2'
    WHERE ID_ISO_A3 = 'USA'   ;

-- Now add Canada, Great Britain, and Mexico to the Country table ...
INSERT INTO Country
        ( ID_ISO_A3, ID_ISO_A2, ID_ISO_Numeric, Name_Native
        , Name_English, Name_French, Administrative_Seat
        , Admin_Level_1_Label, Admin_Level_1_Data_Mask
        , Currency_ISO_A3, Language_ISO_A3
        , National_ID_Label, National_ID_Data_Mask
        , Postal_Code_Label, Postal_Code_Data_Mask, Postal_Code_Display_Mask
        , Postal_Level_1_Label, Postal_Level_2_Label
        , Telephone_Country_Code
        , Telephone_Data_Mask, Telephone_Display_Mask)
    VALUES ('CAN', 'CA', '124', 'Commonwealth of Canada'
        , 'Canada', 'Canada', 'Ottawa, Ontario'
        , 'Province', '([A-Z]{2})'
        , 'CAD', 'ENG'
        , 'Social Insurance Number', '^[0-9]{3}-[0-9]{3}-[0-9]{3}$'
        , 'Postal Code', '^([A-Z][0-9][A-Z])([0-9][A-Z][0-9])$', '\1-\2'
        , 'Province', 'Town'
        , '011', '^[0-9]{5}[0-9]{4}$', '\1.\2.\3')    ;
INSERT INTO Country
        ( ID_ISO_A3, ID_ISO_A2, ID_ISO_Numeric, Name_Native
        , Name_English, Name_French, Administrative_Seat
        , Admin_Level_1_Label, Admin_Level_1_Data_Mask
        , Currency_ISO_A3, Language_ISO_A3
        , National_ID_Label, National_ID_Data_Mask
        , Postal_Code_Label, Postal_Code_Data_Mask, Postal_Code_Display_Mask
        , Postal_Level_1_Label, Postal_Level_2_Label
        , Telephone_Country_Code
        , Telephone_Data_Mask, Telephone_Display_Mask)
    VALUES ('GBR', 'BG', '826', 'Commonwealth of Great Britain'
        , 'United Kingdom', 'Royaume-Uni', 'London'
        , 'Province', '([A-Z]{2})'
        , 'GBP', 'ENG'
        , 'National ID', '^([FAKE][0-9][0-9][0-9][0-9][0-9])'
```

```
             , 'Post Code', '^([A-Z]{1,2}[0-9]{2})( )([0-9]{1}[A-Z]{2})$', '\1\2\3'
             , 'Province', 'Town'
             , '44', '^([0-1]{0,1})([0-9]{4})([0-9]{6})$', '(\1) \2 \3')      ;
INSERT INTO Country
          ( ID_ISO_A3, ID_ISO_A2, ID_ISO_Numeric, Name_Native
          , Name_English, Name_French, Administrative_Seat
          , Admin_Level_1_Label, Admin_Level_1_Data_Mask
          , Currency_ISO_A3, Language_ISO_A3
          , National_ID_Label, National_ID_Data_Mask
          , Postal_Code_Label, Postal_Code_Data_Mask, Postal_Code_Display_Mask
          , Postal_Level_1_Label, Postal_Level_2_Label
          , Telephone_Country_Code
          , Telephone_Data_Mask, Telephone_Display_Mask)
     VALUES ('MEX', 'MX', '484', 'Estados Unidos Mexicanos'
          , 'Mexico', 'Mexico', 'Mexico City'
          , 'State', '([A-Z]{2})'
          , 'MXN', 'ESM'
          , 'Credencial de Elector', '^[0-9]{3}-[0-9]{2}-[0-9]{4}$'
          , 'Postal Code', '^([0-9]{5})([0-9]{4}|)$', '\1-\2'
          , 'State', 'City'
          , '052', '^([0-9]{3})([0-9]{3})([0-9]{4})$', '(\1) \2-\3')      ;

-- Equivalent in the U.S. to a table listing States or State-equivalents
CREATE TABLE Admin_Level_1
  ( Country_ISO_A3          CHAR(3)      NOT NULL
  , Abbreviation            VARCHAR2(10) NOT NULL
  , Standard_Code           VARCHAR2(4)  NOT NULL
  , Name_Native             VARCHAR2(80) NOT NULL
  , Administrative_Seat     VARCHAR2(80)
  , Admin_Level_2_Label     VARCHAR2(80)
  , Admin_Level_2_Data_Mask VARCHAR2(50)
  , Time_Zone_Abbrev        VARCHAR2(4)  NOT NULL
  , CONSTRAINT PK1_Admin_1 PRIMARY KEY (Country_ISO_A3, Abbreviation)
  , CONSTRAINT FK1_Admin_1 FOREIGN KEY (Country_ISO_A3)
             REFERENCES Country (ID_ISO_A3)
  , CONSTRAINT FK2_Time_Zone FOREIGN KEY (Time_Zone_Abbrev)
             REFERENCES Time_Zone (Time_Zone_Abbreviation)  );

-- Equivalent in the U.S. to a table listing Counties or County-equivalents
CREATE TABLE Admin_Level_2
  ( Country_ISO_A3          CHAR(3)       NOT NULL
  , Admin_Level_1_Code      VARCHAR2(10)  NOT NULL
  , Standard_Code           VARCHAR2(10)  NOT NULL
  , Name_Native             VARCHAR2(80)
  , Administrative_Seat     VARCHAR2(80)
  , Admin_Level_3_Label     VARCHAR2(10)
  , Time_Zone_Abbrev        VARCHAR2(4)
  , CONSTRAINT PK1_Admin_2 PRIMARY KEY (Country_ISO_A3, Admin_Level_1_Code,
                                        Standard_Code)
  , CONSTRAINT FK1_Admin_2 FOREIGN KEY (Country_ISO_A3, Admin_Level_1_Code)
```

```sql
                REFERENCES Admin_Level_1 (Country_ISO_A3, Abbreviation)  );

-- Equivalent in the U.S. to a table listing Towns, Cities or City-equivalents
CREATE TABLE Admin_Level_3
  ( Country_ISO_A3        CHAR(3)       NOT NULL
  , Admin_Level_1_Code    VARCHAR2(10)  NOT NULL
  , Admin_Level_2_Code    VARCHAR2(10)  NOT NULL
  , Standard_Code         VARCHAR2(10)  NOT NULL
  , Name_Native           VARCHAR2(80)
  , Administrative_Seat   VARCHAR2(80)
  , Admin_Level_4_Label   VARCHAR2(10)
  , CONSTRAINT PK1_Admin_3 PRIMARY KEY (Country_ISO_A3, Admin_Level_1_Code,
                                  Admin_Level_2_Code, Standard_Code)
  , CONSTRAINT FK1_Admin_3 FOREIGN KEY (Country_ISO_A3, Admin_Level_1_Code,
                                  Admin_Level_2_Code)
            REFERENCES Admin_Level_2 (Country_ISO_A3, Admin_Level_1_Code,
                                  Standard_Code)  );

ALTER TABLE bt_Person
      ADD Country_ISO_A3 CHAR    (3) ;
ALTER TABLE bt_Person
      ADD National_ID    VARCHAR2(16)  UNIQUE ;
-- Add a UNIQUE constraint for the Country-SSAN combination ...
ALTER TABLE bt_Person
      ADD CONSTRAINT unq_Country_ID UNIQUE (Country_ISO_A3, National_ID) ;
```

Populate Admin_Level Tables

```sql
INSERT INTO Admin_Level_1
        ( Country_ISO_A3, Abbreviation, Standard_Code, Name_Native
        , Administrative_Seat, Admin_Level_2_Label, Time_Zone_Abbrev )
   VALUES ('USA', 'IL', '017', 'Illinois'        , 'Springfield',    'County', 'CST');
INSERT INTO Admin_Level_1
        ( Country_ISO_A3, Abbreviation, Standard_Code, Name_Native
        , Administrative_Seat, Admin_Level_2_Label, Time_Zone_Abbrev )
   VALUES ('USA', 'LA', '022', 'Louisiana '
        , 'Baton Rouge',    'Parish', 'CST')            ;
INSERT INTO Admin_Level_1
        ( Country_ISO_A3, Abbreviation, Standard_Code, Name_Native
        , Administrative_Seat, Admin_Level_2_Label, Time_Zone_Abbrev )
   VALUES ('USA', 'MD', '024', 'Maryland '
        , 'Annapolis',      'County', 'EST')            ;
INSERT INTO Admin_Level_1
      ( Country_ISO_A3, Abbreviation, Standard_Code, Name_Native
      , Administrative_Seat, Admin_Level_2_Label, Time_Zone_Abbrev )
 VALUES ('CAN', 'NS', '12', 'Nova Scotia',            'Halifax',      'County', 'AST');
INSERT INTO Admin_Level_1
        ( Country_ISO_A3, Abbreviation, Standard_Code, Name_Native
        , Administrative_Seat, Admin_Level_2_Label, Time_Zone_Abbrev )
 VALUES ('CAN', 'ON', '35', 'Ontario',                'Toronto',      'County', 'EST');
```

```
INSERT INTO Admin_Level_2
   (Country_ISO_A3, Admin_Level_1_Code, Standard_Code, Name_Native, Admin_Level_3_Label)
    VALUES ('USA', 'IL', '031', 'Cook',        'Township')     ;
UPDATE Admin_Level_2 SET Administrative_Seat = 'Chicago'
   WHERE Admin_Level_1_Code = 'IL' AND Standard_Code = '031' ;
INSERT INTO Admin_Level_2
        (Country_ISO_A3, Admin_Level_1_Code, Standard_Code, Name_Native
        , Admin_Level_3_Label, Administrative_Seat)
 VALUES ('USA', 'MD', '005', 'Baltimore',         'Township', 'Towson')      ;
```

Create Postal Reference and Address Tables

```
CREATE TABLE Postal_System
   ( Country_ISO_A3     CHAR(3)      NOT NULL
   , Postal_Code        VARCHAR(14) NOT NULL
   , Postal_Level_1     VARCHAR(40) NOT NULL
   , Postal_Level_2     VARCHAR(40)
   , Postal_Level_3     VARCHAR(40)
   , Postal_Level_4     VARCHAR(40)
   , CONSTRAINT PK_Postal_System PRIMARY KEY  (Country_ISO_A3, Postal_Code)
   , CONSTRAINT FK1_Postal_System FOREIGN KEY (Country_ISO_A3)
                       REFERENCES Country (ID_ISO_A3)    );
```

Bare Bones Validate_Post_Code Function and Trigger

```
CREATE OR REPLACE
FUNCTION VALIDATE_POST_CODE(InputText      Postal_System.Postal_Code%TYPE,
                         InputCountry  Country.ID_ISO_A3%TYPE)
RETURN VARCHAR
IS
   -- Variable Declarations
   FormatMask          Country.Postal_Code_Data_Mask%TYPE;
   ValidatedPostCode   Postal_System.Postal_Code%TYPE;        -- Return value

BEGIN
-- Find the Postal Code Data Mask for the Country this entry refers to...
   SELECT Postal_Code_Data_Mask
     INTO FormatMask
     FROM Country
    WHERE ID_ISO_A3 = InputCountry    ;

   SELECT InputText
     INTO ValidatedPostCode
     FROM dual
    WHERE REGEXP_LIKE(InputText, FormatMask, 'i');

RETURN ValidatedPostCode;

EXCEPTION
```

```
      -- DBMS_OUTPUT used only for testing; replace this section for actual use.
      WHEN NO_DATA_FOUND
      THEN
         DBMS_OUTPUT.PUT_LINE('Validation of "' || InputText || '" seemed to fail. "');
         RETURN NULL;

      WHEN OTHERS
      THEN
         -- Obviously this needs to be expanded somewhat....
         DBMS_OUTPUT.PUT_LINE('Something surprising occurred ...');
         RETURN NULL;

END;
/

CREATE OR REPLACE TRIGGER Postal_System_BIU
BEFORE INSERT OR UPDATE
    ON Postal_System
    FOR EACH ROW
BEGIN
    :new.Postal_Code :=
        VALIDATE_POST_CODE(:new.Postal_Code, :new.Country_ISO_A3);
END;
/
CREATE TABLE bt_Address
    ( ID              NUMBER        NOT NULL  PRIMARY KEY
    , Line_1          VARCHAR2(50)  NOT NULL
    , Line_2          VARCHAR2(50)
    , Country_ISO_A3  CHAR(3)       DEFAULT 'USA' NOT NULL
    , Postal_Code     VARCHAR(20)   NOT NULL
    , CONSTRAINT FK1_btAddress FOREIGN KEY (Country_ISO_A3, Postal_Code)
                REFERENCES Postal_System (Country_ISO_A3, Postal_Code)   );
```

Populate Postal System and Address Tables

```
INSERT INTO Postal_System
          (Country_ISO_A3, Postal_Code
          , Postal_Level_1, Postal_Level_2
          , Postal_Level_3, Postal_Level_4)
    VALUES ('USA','600893255'
          , 'IL', 'Bison Cove'
          , NULL, NULL)     ;
INSERT INTO Postal_System
          (Country_ISO_A3, Postal_Code
          , Postal_Level_1, Postal_Level_2
          , Postal_Level_3, Postal_Level_4)
    VALUES ('CAN','N6A4L6'
          , 'ON', 'London'
          , NULL, NULL)     ;
INSERT INTO Postal_System
```

```
                (Country_ISO_A3, Postal_Code
               , Postal_Level_1, Postal_Level_2
               , Postal_Level_3, Postal_Level_4)
        VALUES ('GBR','SE99 0BB'
              , 'London', 'London-West'
              , NULL, NULL)      ;

CREATE TABLE Address_Type
   ( Code          CHAR(3)      NOT NULL  PRIMARY KEY
   , Description   VARCHAR2(50) NOT NULL );

INSERT INTO Address_Type (Code, Description)
                VALUES ('HA', 'Home Address');
INSERT INTO Address_Type (Code, Description)
                VALUES ('MF', 'Manufacturing Facility');
INSERT INTO Address_Type (Code, Description)
                VALUES ('RT', 'Retail Outlet');

CREATE TABLE Address
   ( Party_ID      NUMBER (2)   NOT NULL
   , Address_ID    NUMBER       NOT NULL
   , Address_Type  CHAR(3)      NOT NULL
     -- Including the Type_Code may or may not be desirable: it depends!!
     -- Obviously this PK also precludes having more than one "Home Address"
   , CONSTRAINT PK_ptAddress PRIMARY KEY  (Party_ID, Address_ID, Address_Type)
   , CONSTRAINT FK1_ptAddress FOREIGN KEY (Party_ID)
                REFERENCES Party      (ID)
   , CONSTRAINT FK2_ptAddress FOREIGN KEY (Address_ID)
                REFERENCES bt_Address    (ID)
   , CONSTRAINT FK3_ptAddress FOREIGN KEY (Address_Type)
                REFERENCES Address_Type (Code)    );
```

Address Life Cycle Examples

```
INSERT INTO PARTY (ID) VALUES (56);
INSERT INTO bt_PERSON (ID, Given_Name,   Surname,     Soundex)
                VALUES (56, 'Aphrodite', 'Smith',     Soundex('Smith') ) ;
-- Current home of John Smith, his wife Venus, and their daughter Aphrodite
INSERT INTO bt_Address
        ( ID, Line_1, Line_2, Country_ISO_A3, Postal_Code)
  VALUES ( 1234567, '368 Main Street', NULL, 'USA', '600893255');
-- Now we associate John Smith with his Home Address in Illinois
INSERT INTO Address (Party_ID, Address_ID, Address_Type)
            VALUES (33, 1234567, 'HA');
-- Now we associate Aphrodite Smith (John's daughter) with her Home Address in Illinois
INSERT INTO Address (Party_ID, Address_ID, Address_Type)
            VALUES (56, 1234567, 'HA');


-- When the John Smith and his wife move down the street:
INSERT INTO bt_Address
```

```
            ( ID, Line_1, Line_2, Country_ISO_A3, Postal_Code)
VALUES ( 1235533, '244 Main Street', NULL, 'USA', '600893255');
-- Associate the new address with John and his wife.
UPDATE Address SET Address_ID = 1235533
 WHERE Party_ID    = 33
   AND Address_ID   = 1234567
   AND Address_Type = 'HA'    ;
-- Aphrodite remains at the old address which she and her new husband purchased.
INSERT INTO PARTY (ID) VALUES (88);
INSERT INTO bt_PERSON (ID, Given_Name,   Surname,    Soundex)
                VALUES (88, 'Agamemnon', 'McCarthy',  Soundex('McCarthy') ) ;
-- Now we associate Agamemnon McCarthy (Aphrodite's husband) with the address.
INSERT INTO Address (Party_ID, Address_ID, Address_Type)
                VALUES (88, 1234567, 'HA');
```

Addresses and Locations

```
CREATE TABLE Location
    ( Identifier       VARCHAR2(25) NOT NULL
    , Party_ID         NUMBER(2)    NOT NULL
    , Address_ID       NUMBER            -- can be NULL!!
    , Address_Type     CHAR(3)           -- can be NULL!!
    , GPS_Coordinate   VARCHAR2(10)      -- can be NULL!!
    , CONSTRAINT FK_locID FOREIGN KEY ( Party_ID, Address_ID, Address_Type )
                REFERENCES Address ( Party_ID, Address_ID, Address_Type )
    , CONSTRAINT FK_orgID FOREIGN KEY ( Party_ID )
                REFERENCES bt_Organization ( ID )   );
CREATE UNIQUE INDEX LocIndex ON Location ( Identifier, Party_ID, Address_ID,
                                           Address_Type, GPS_Coordinate ) ;


-- Factory & Loading Dock Addresses for Creative Cupcakes, LLC
INSERT INTO bt_Address
        ( ID, Line_1, Line_2, Country_ISO_A3, Postal_Code)
VALUES ( 1234578, '6474 Windsor Street', NULL, 'GBR', 'SE99 0BB');
INSERT INTO Address (Party_ID, Address_ID, Address_Type)
            VALUES (67, 1234578, 'MF');
INSERT INTO Location (Identifier, Party_ID, Address_ID, Address_Type)
            VALUES ('Old Town', 67, 1234578, 'MF');
INSERT INTO bt_Address
        ( ID, Line_1, Line_2, Country_ISO_A3, Postal_Code)
VALUES ( 1234579, '6472 Windsor Street', NULL, 'GBR', 'SE99 0BB');
INSERT INTO Address (Party_ID, Address_ID, Address_Type)
            VALUES (67, 1234579, 'MF');
INSERT INTO Location (Identifier, Party_ID, Address_ID, Address_Type)
            VALUES ('Old Town', 67, 1234579, 'MF');
INSERT INTO bt_Address
        ( ID, Line_1, Line_2, Country_ISO_A3, Postal_Code)
VALUES ( 1234580, '320 First Street', NULL, 'GBR', 'SE99 0BB');
INSERT INTO Address (Party_ID, Address_ID, Address_Type)
            VALUES (67, 1234580, 'RT');
```

```
INSERT INTO Location (Identifier, Party_ID, Address_ID, Address_Type)
            VALUES ('Old Town', 67, 1234580, 'RT');

-- Factory & Loading Dock Addresses for Midget Widgets
INSERT INTO bt_Address
       ( ID, Line_1, Line_2, Country_ISO_A3, Postal_Code)
VALUES ( 1234583, '6534 Windsor Street', NULL, 'GBR', 'SE99 0BB');
INSERT INTO Address (Party_ID, Address_ID, Address_Type)
            VALUES (61, 1234583, 'MF');
INSERT INTO Location (Identifier, Party_ID, Address_ID, Address_Type)
            VALUES ('Old Town', 61, 1234583, 'MF');
INSERT INTO bt_Address
       ( ID, Line_1, Line_2, Country_ISO_A3, Postal_Code)
VALUES ( 1234585, '326 Second Street', NULL, 'GBR', 'SE99 0BB');
INSERT INTO Address (Party_ID, Address_ID, Address_Type)
            VALUES (61, 1234585, 'MF');
INSERT INTO Location (Identifier, Party_ID, Address_ID, Address_Type)
            VALUES ('Old Town', 61, 1234585, 'MF');
-- Change Location Name after employees become addicted to the Cupcakes ...
UPDATE Location
   SET Identifier = 'Cholesterol Junction'
 WHERE Party_ID      = 61
   AND Address_ID   = 1234583
   AND Address_Type = 'MF'
   ;
UPDATE Location
   SET Identifier = 'Cholesterol Junction'
 WHERE Party_ID      = 61
   AND Address_ID   = 1234585
   AND Address_Type = 'MF'
   ;
```

APPENDIX C – WEIGHTS & MEASURES – DATA

Conversion Factors

Sample conversion factors were given in the section "Sample Conversion Calculations" on page 227; the table in this appendix provides a more extensive list of the possible contents of the Weights and Measures entity set described above. Actual values required in any given implementation will depend on the level of precision required, and the particular unit-of-measure chosen as the enterprise standard reference.

For each Measurement Class, there must be one and only one unit-of-measure with a multiplier of 1 and an offset of 0; this defines the root unit-of-measure for a particular Measurement Class. Because of the requirement to prevent cumulative changes in value with multiple conversions (e.g. converting from grams to pounds and then back to grams), the table is non-symmetrical. It must be stressed, therefore, that this is not intended or designed to be a general purpose bi-directional conversion factor table: it is intended to provide only factors used to convert from non-root units of measure into root units. This means that if there is a kg-to-lb conversion factor listed, there must not be a corresponding lb-to-kg conversion listed. All the "to" values are root units of measure. A "from" unit-of-measure with a multiplier factor of 1 is a root unit-of-measure, and there must be only one row for each Measurement Class/"from" unit-of-measure pair (the enforcement of this will be design dependent, but is intended to be at the database level).

For a description of the various Measurement Classes referenced in this table, see "Measurement Classes in Scope" beginning on page 210. For the mathematical formulas to use the data in this table, see "Converting from a root UOM to a non-root UOM:" on page 228 and "Converting from a non-root UOM to a root UOM:" on page 229.

Measurement Class	Unit of Measure	To Convert ... from UOM	to UOM	Multiplier	Offset
Angular	Degrees (stated as decimal number)	deg	deg	1	0
Angular	Radians (stated as decimal number)	rad	deg	0.0174533	0
Apothecary	Dram(s) 3 scruples in 1 dram	dr	gr	0.0166667	0
Apothecary	Grain(s) Approximately .09 square meters.	gr	gr	1	0
Apothecary	Ounce(s) 8 drams in 1 ounce	oz	gr	0.0020833	0
Apothecary	Pound(s) 12 ounces in 1 pound	lb	gr	0.0001736	0
Apothecary	Scruple(s) 20 grains in 1 scruple	scr	gr	0.05	0
Area	Hectare (Square Hectometer)	ha / hm²	ft²		0
Area	Square Centimeter(s) Approximately 0.16 square inches.	cm² or cm2	ft² or ft2	929.0304	0
Area	Square Foot (Feet) Approximately 0.09 square meters.	ft² or ft2	ft² or ft2	1	0
Area	Square Inch(es)	in²	ft²	144	0
Area	Square Kilometer(s)	km²	ft²		0
Area	Square Meter(s) (Centare) Approximately 11 square feet or 1.2 square yards.	m²	ft²	0.092903	0

Measurement Class	Unit of Measure	To Convert ...		Multiplier	Offset
		from UOM	to UOM		
Consumption	Kilometers per Liter	kpl	mpg	0.425132	0
Consumption	Miles per Gallon	mpg	mpg	1	0
Distance	(Air) Mile(s) A unit of distance in air travel, equal to one international nautical mile (6,076.115 feet or 1852 meters).	am	mi	0.8689762	0
Distance	Kilometer(s) One thousand meters (qv) or approximately .62 statute miles.	km	mi	1.6093	0
Distance	Mile(s) Statute Mile(s) Land Mile(s) A unit of length equal to 5,280 feet or 1,760 yards (1,609 meters), used in the United States and other English-speaking countries.	mi	mi	1	0
Distance	Nautical Mile(s) Sea Mile(s) A unit of length used in sea and air navigation, based on the length of one minute of arc of a great circle, especially an international and U.S. unit equal to 1,852 meters (about 6,076 feet).	nm	mi	0.8689762	0
Dry Volume	Cubic Foot (Feet) 1,728 cubic inches	ft^3	ft^3	1	0
Dry Volume	Cubic Meter(s) Approximately 35 cubic feet or 1.3 cubic yards	m^3	ft^3	0.0283168	0
Dry Volume	Cubic Yard(s)	yd^3	ft^3	0.0370370	0
Dry Volume	Gallon(s), Dry, Imperial Approximately 277.27 cubic inches	galI	ft^3	6.2321924	0
Dry Volume	Gallon(s), Dry, U.S. 231 cubic inches	gal	ft^3	7.4805194	0

Measurement Class	Unit of Measure	from UOM	to UOM	Multiplier	Offset
Frequency	Hertz	hz	khz		0
Frequency	Kilohertz	khz	khz	1	0
Frequency	Megahertz	mhz	khz		0
Frequency	Gigahertz	ghz	khz		0
Linear	Foot (Feet) A unit of length in the U.S. Customary and British Imperial systems equal to 12 inches (0.3048 meter).	ft	in	0.08333333	0
Linear	Inch(es) A unit of length in the U.S. Customary and British Imperial systems, equal to 1/12 of a foot (2.54 centimeters or 25.4 millimeters).	in	in	1	0
Linear	Meter(s) The international standard unit of length, approximately equivalent to 39.37 inches or 3.3 feet. It was redefined in 1983 as the distance traveled by light in a vacuum in 1/299,792,458 of a second.	m	in	0.02539999	0
Linear	Millimeter(s) One one-hundreth of a meter (qv) or approximately .0394 inches.	mm	in	2.5399999	0
Linear	Yard(s) A fundamental unit of length in both the U.S. Customary System and the British Imperial System, equal to 3 feet, or 36 inches (0.9144 meter).	yd	in	0.0277777	0
Liquid Volume	Barrel(s) of Petroleum and Petroleum-based products	bbl	gal	0.0238095	0
Liquid Volume	Barrel(s) of Spirits (e.g. Wine, Whiskey, etc.– generally obsolete)	bbl-sp	gal	0.025	0
Liquid Volume	Barrel(s) of Beer	bbl-b	gal	0.032258	0

| Measurement Class | Unit of Measure | To Convert ... | | | |
		from UOM	to UOM	Multiplier	Offset
Liquid Volume	Gallon(s), Liquid, Imperial A unit of volume in the British Imperial System, used in liquid **and dry** measure, equal to 4 quarts (4.546 liters).	gal(I)	gal	Currently Unknown	0
Liquid <u>Volume</u>	Gallon(s), Liquid, U.S. A unit of volume in the U.S. Customary System, used in liquid measure, equal to 4 quarts (3.785 liters).	gal	gal	1	0
Liquid Volume	Liter(s) A metric unit of volume equal to approximately 1.056 liquid quarts, 0.908 dry quart, or 0.264 gallon.	l or lit	gal	3.7854118	0
Liquid Volume	Milliliter(s)	ml or mlit	gal	3785.4118	0
Liquid Volume	Ounce(s)	oz	gal	128	0
Liquid Volume	Quart(s)	qt	gal	4	0
Speed	Kilometers per Hour	kph	mph	1.609344	0
Speed	Knots (Nautical Miles per Hour) Approximately 1.85 Kilometers per Hour or 1.15 Statute Miles per Hour.	Knots	mph	0.8689762	0
<u>Speed</u>	Miles per Hour (statute)	mph	mph	1	0
Temperature	Degrees Celsius A degree is a unit division of a temperature scale and has no inherent value without reference to that scale. The Celsius scale registers the freezing point of water at normal atmospheric pressure at 0°. The Celsius scale registers the boiling point of water at normal58 atmospheric pressure at 100°.	degC or °C	°F	1.8	32
<u>Temperature</u>	Degrees Fahrenheit A degree is a unit division of a temperature scale and has no inherent value	°F or degF	°F	1	0

Measurement Class	Unit of Measure	To Convert ...			
		from UOM	to UOM	Multiplier	Offset
	without reference to that scale. The Fahrenheit scale registers the freezing point of water at normal atmospheric pressure at 32°. The Fahrenheit scale registers the boiling point of water at normal atmospheric pressure at 212°.				
Troy	Grain(s)	grt	grt	1	0
Troy	Ounce(s) (Troy) There are 20 pennyweights to an ounce (troy)	ozt	grt	0.0020833	0
Troy	Pennyweight There are 24 grains (troy) to a pennyweight	pwt	grt	0.0416666	0
Troy	Pound(s) (Troy)	lbt	grt	0.0001736	0
Weight	Kilogram(s) Approximately 2.2 pounds	Kg	lb	2.204623	0
Weight	Long Ton(s) A unit of weight equal to 2,240 pounds (1.016 metric tons or 1,016.05 kilograms).	ton (long)	lb	Currently Unknown	0
Weight	Ounce(s)	oz	lb	16	0
Weight	Pound(s) A unit of weight equal to 16 ounces (453.592 grams).	lb	lb	1	0
Weight	Ton(s) ("net" or "short" ton) A unit of weight equal to 2,000 pounds (0.907 metric ton or 907.18 kilograms).	Ton	lb	0.0005	0

Remember, however, that this data will be quite different if different units of measure are selected as references/roots for a specific system, or if the system requires differences in the level of precision.

Look for 'Business Database Design' – due for publication in 2015.

Business Database Design – Class Notes from the Lyceum
ISBN: 978-0692329481

Visit www.AntikytheraPubs.com for details of this upcoming book,
or to download some free database design notes.

www.ingramcontent.com/pod-product-compliance
Lightning Source LLC
Chambersburg PA
CBHW082108070326
40689CB00052B/3821